INFORMATION FORAGING THEORY

Information Foraging Theory
Adaptive Interaction with Information

Peter Pirolli

2009

OXFORD
UNIVERSITY PRESS

Oxford University Press, Inc., publishes works that further
Oxford University's objective of excellence
in research, scholarship, and education.

Oxford   New York
Auckland   Cape Town   Dar es Salaam   Hong Kong   Karachi
Kuala Lumpur   Madrid   Melbourne   Mexico City   Nairobi
New Delhi   Shanghai   Taipei   Toronto

With offices in
Argentina   Austria   Brazil   Chile   Czech Republic   France   Greece
Guatemala   Hungary   Italy   Japan   Poland   Portugal   Singapore
South Korea   Switzerland   Thailand   Turkey   Ukraine   Vietnam

Published by Oxford University Press, Inc.
198 Madison Avenue, New York, New York 10016

www.oup.com

First issued as an Oxford University Press paperback, 2009

Oxford is a registered trademark of Oxford University Press

Library of Congress Cataloging-in-Publication Data
Pirolli, Peter.
Information foraging theory : adaptive interaction with information / Peter Pirolli.
   p. cm. — (Oxford series in human-technology interaction)
ISBN 978-0-19-538779-7
1. Information behavior.   2. Human-computer interaction.   I. Title.   II. Series.
ZA3075.P57 2007
025.5'24—dc22   2006021795

Preface

To understand the evolution of things, one must understand something about their history as well as the environmental forces that had shaping influences upon them. Information Foraging Theory evolved through a series of fortuitous historical accidents, as well as a number of enduring shaping forces. A critical event was my move to the Palo Alto Research Center (PARC). Soon after I came to PARC at the beginning of 1992, I became involved in trying to develop studies and models around a set of projects that were collectively called intelligent information access. This included the novel information visualization systems investigated in the User Interface Research Area (see, e.g., Card et al., 1999) as well as the new techniques for browsing and searching being created in the Quantitative Content Area (e.g., Rao et al., 1995). As part of this effort, a group of us (including Stu Card, Dan Russell, Mark Stefik, and John van Gigch from California State University—Sacramento) were running some quick-and-dirty studies of people such as business intelligence analysts and MBA students. Our studies of people doing information-intensive work started to give me some sense of the range of phenomena that we would need to address. Our study participants clearly were faced with massive volumes of information, often under deadline conditions, and making complex search decisions based on assessments that were enveloped in a great deal of uncertainty.

These information-intensive tasks seemed to be different than the human-computer interaction tasks that were being addressed by cognitive engineering models in the early 1990s, or the science, math, and programming tasks addressed by intelligent tutoring systems of that same period. Such cognitive models addressed tasks that tended to occur in task environments that (although large and complex) were well defined by a circumscribed domain of possible goals, elements of domain knowledge (e.g., about Lisp programming, algebra, word processing), and potential actions (e.g., in a formal language, or in a user interface). In contrast, the behavior of people seeking information appeared to be largely shaped by the structure or architecture of the content—the *information environment*—and only minimally shaped by the user's knowledge of user interface. In addition, the structure of the information environment was fundamentally probabilistic. Consequently, behavior was also dominated by choices made in the face of uncertainty and the continual evaluation of the expected costs and benefits of various actions in the information environment, in contrast to the near-certain costs and benefits of actions taken in traditional cognitive modeling domains of the time.

It was clear that it was going to be a challenge to develop theories for information-intensive tasks. Mulling about this issue, I was drawn to work in two areas in which I had done some reading. The first was the work in the late 1980s of John R. Anderson (e.g., Anderson, 1990), who was putting forth the argument that to understand mechanisms of the mind, one must first try to figure out the environmental problems that it solves. John developed the method of rational analysis and applied this approach to memory, categorization, and other areas of cognition with considerable success. I wondered if the approach could be applied to the analysis of the information environment and how it shapes information seeking behavior.[1] The second area of interest was behavioral ecology (e.g., Smith, 1987), which suggested that very diverse strategies adopted by people could be systematically predicted from optimization analysis that focused first on scrutiny of the environment. This particular interest of mine originated as an undergraduate at Trent University, where physiological psychology included coverage of ethology (the precursor to behavioral ecology) and anthropology included what is known as cultural materialism (the precursor to current evolutionary-ecological approaches to anthropology). Working through the literature in these areas, I was led to optimal foraging theory, and particularly to the book by Stephens and Krebs (1986) that is the source of the conventional models discussed in chapter 2. I quite literally had an "ah-ha" experience in the middle of a late-night conversation with Jacqui LeBlanc in which I laid out the basic analogies between information foraging and optimal foraging theory.

In July 1992, I wrote a working paper titled "Notes on Adaptive Sense Making in Information Ecologies," which discussed the possible application of conventional foraging models and the core mathematics of Stephens and Krebs to idealized information foraging tasks. The working paper got two kinds of reactions. The first was one of disbelief in the analogy, for a variety of relatively good reasons (e.g., humans are not rational, information is not food). The second was that the ideas were "audacious" (to quote Jock Mackinlay). Fortunately, Stu Card (my manager and colleague in the User Interface Research Area) pushed me to pursue this approach, and he has been my main sounding board for the development of the theory over the years. By the fall of 1993, I had enough material to present a seminar at the University of California—Berkeley called "Sense Making in Complex Information Ecologies."

In the decade that followed, the fruitfulness of Information Foraging Theory was apparent from the way that it could be used to bring messy data into crystal clear focus. The first time this happened was in application to the Scatter/Gather study presented in chapter 6. Simple analyses of the logs of users interacting with the system seemed to indicate that users where behaving in a nonsystematic way in their allocation of time or in their choices of interface actions. The application of optimal foraging models resulted in another of those "ah-ha" experiences in which suddenly the data plots all fell neatly on lines predicted by theory. Like catching a perfect wave in surfing, the feeling one gets from that moment when one gains power over a small portion of the universe is hard to recount without the skill of poetry (which I do not have), and it is the reward that keeps you coming back.

Acknowledgments

In writing this book, I was fortunate to have input from a great panel of reviewers: Marc Mangel, Julie Heiser, John R. Anderson, and Jakob Nielsen. Jacqui LeBlanc read the earliest versions of the manuscript. Each provided a unique perspective from their respective fields. I am particularly grateful to Marc, who made many suggestions about the math and about connections to a richer history of work in "traditional" foraging theory. I have also been fortunate to work with Alex Kirlik, an editor who provided much-needed collegial advice throughout this project.

PARC has been an especially fertile and supportive environment and I must especially thank my managers Stu Card, Kris Halvorsen, and Mark Stefik for their continued interest in this work. I also have been the beneficiary of funding support from the most enlightened government funding agencies. I must thank the Office of Naval Research for continued funding over many years and intellectual support from three great program managers, Helen Gigley, Astrid Schmidt-Nielsen, and Susan Chipman. The Advanced Development Research Activity has provided substantial funding support and sustained passion and interest from Lucy Nowell and Heather McMonagle. The Spencer Foundation provided discretionary funding as part of my National Academy of Education Fellowship that was used to support my dilettante ventures into behavioral ecology and evolutionary-ecological anthropology.

Many people have collaborated and contributed to this project over the years. Stu Card helped me shape many of the ideas by asking the right questions. Bernardo Huberman provided a wealth of innovative ideas from a physicist's perspective, most notably about ultradiffusion, random graph processes, and cooperative computational processes. Jim Pitkow was the force that got many of us interested in analyzing the emergent dynamical properties of large aggregates of content, users, and topology on the Web. Special thanks go to Dan Russell, who got all of us interested in sense making in the first place. Pamela E. Sandstrom independently discovered the idea of Information Foraging Theory in her work on scholarly communication (chapter 8), and she has graciously shared her insights and results over the years. Lada Adamic provided me with unpublished data used to calculate the correlation between inlinks and outlinks in chapter 3. Ed Chi took up the notion of information scent and cashed the idea into real usability analysis systems, and more recently has taken on the idea of social information foraging as the backbone for new information access techniques. Wai-Tat Fu helped move Information Foraging Theory into the realm of the Web with his leadership on the SNIF-ACT project. Ayman Farahat, Christiaan Royer, and Raluca Budiu helped developed a hardened system for generating spreading activation networks from online collections to replace the ad hoc code I initially started with. Hinrich Schuetze is credited with providing me with the first statistics from a large document corpus that were used to demonstrate that spreading activation nets could be used to predict information scent. Sara Kiesler provided useful recommendations on the literature on the relation of cooperative processes and innovation. Julie Morrison, Rob Reeder, Pam Schraedley, Mija Van Der Wege, and Vikram Jiswal contributed enormously to the efforts to study Web users. Marti Hearst provided data that proved to be crucial to the analysis of Scatter/Gather and collaborated with me on the Scatter/Gather studies along with Patti Schank and Chris Diehl. I also thank Jan Pedersen for inviting me to work on Scatter/Gather in the first place. Jakob Nielsen has been my guide in understanding how information foraging theory relates to concrete Web usability issues. Over the years, Jared Spool has developed the notion of information scent as a conceptual tool for practitioners, and he has always been generous in sharing the specific guidelines that have been developed as a result (many of these are presented in chapter 9).

Finally, I thank Jacqui LeBlanc for being there when the lightning first struck and for her support during the first chapter drafts written during an idyllic stretch of time on the porch of the Dolphin Inn in Cayucos after morning surf sessions. A more loving and lovely muse I could not ask for.

Note

1. As a graduate student working with Anderson, I have notes and working papers from 1982 in which Anderson was already beginning to suggest that function with respect to the environment would be a crucial to developing and evaluating theories of cognition.

References

Anderson, J. R. (1990). *The adaptive character of thought*. Hillsdale, NJ: Lawrence Erlbaum Associates.

Card, S. K., Mackinlay, J. D., & Schneiderman, B. (1999). *Information visualization: Using vision to think*. San Francisco: Morgan-Kaufman.

Rao, R., Pedersen, J. O., Hearst, M. A., Mackinlay, J. D., Card, S. K., Masinter, L., et al. (1995). Rich interaction in the digital library. *Communications of the ACM*, 38(4), 29–39.

Smith, E. A. (1987). Optimization theory in anthropology: Applications and critiques. In J. Dupré (Ed.), *The latest on the best* (pp. 201–249). Cambridge, MA: MIT Press.

Stephens, D. W., & Krebs, J. R. (1986). *Foraging theory*. Princeton, NJ: Princeton University Press.

Contents

INFORMATION FORAGING THEORY

1

Information Foraging Theory

Framework and Method

Knowledge is power.
  —*Sir Francis Bacon,*
    Meditationes Sacræ.
    De Hæresibus (1597)

Modern mankind forages in a world awash in information, of our own creation, that can be transformed into knowledge that shapes and powers our engagement with nature. This information environment has coevolved with the epistemic drives and strategies that are the essence of our adaptive toolkit. The result of this coevolution is a staggering volume of content that can be transmitted at the speed of light. This wealth of information provides resources for adapting to the problems posed by our increasingly complex world. However, this information environment poses its own complex problems that require adaptive strategies for information foraging. This book is about *Information Foraging Theory*, which aims to explain and predict how people will best shape themselves for their information environments and how information environments can best be shaped for people.

Information Foraging Theory is driven by three maxims attributable in spirit, if not direct quotation, to Allen Newell's (1990) program of Unified Theories of Cognition:[1]

1. *Good science responds to real phenomena or real problems.* Human psychology has evolved as an adaptation to the real world. Information foraging theory is concerned with understanding representative problems posed by the real-world information environment and adaptive cognitive solutions to those problems.
2. *Good science makes a difference.* Information Foraging Theory is intended to provide the basis for application to the design and evaluation of new technologies for human interaction with information, such as better ways to forage for information on the World Wide Web.
3. *Good science is in the details.* The aim is to produce working formal models for the analysis and prediction of observable behavior.

Like much of Newell's work, the superficial elegance and simplicity of these maxims unfurls into complex sets of entailments. In this book I argue that the best approach to studying real information foraging problems is to adopt *methodological adaptationism*, which directs our scientific attention to the ultimate forces driving adaptation and to the proximate psychological mechanisms that are marshaled to produce adaptive solutions. Thus, the methodology of Information Foraging Theory is more akin to the methodology of biology than that of physics, in contrast with the historical bulk of experimental psychology. To some extent, this choice of methodology is a consequence of the success with which Information Foraging Theory has been able to draw upon metaphors, models, and techniques from optimal foraging theory in biology (Stephens & Krebs, 1986). The concern with application (Newell & Card, 1985) drives the theory to be relevant to technological design and evaluation, which requires that models be truly predictive a priori (even if approximately so) rather than a "good fit" explanation of the data a posteriori, as is the case with many current psychological models. Being concerned with the details drives the theory to marshal a variety of concepts, tools, and techniques that allow us to build quantitative, predictive models that span many levels of interrelated phenomena and interrelated levels of explanation. This includes the techniques of task analysis through state-space and problem-space representations, rational analysis and optimization analysis of adaptive solutions, and production system models of the cognitive systems that implement those adaptive solutions.

Audience

The intent of this book is to provide a comprehensive presentation of Information Foraging Theory, the details of empirical investigations of its predictions, and applications of the theory to the engineering and design of user interfaces. This book aims primarily at an interdisciplinary audience with backgrounds and interests in the basic and applied science aspects of cognitive science, computer science, and the information and library sciences. The theory and methodology have been developed by drawing upon work on the rational analysis of cognition, computational cognitive modeling, behavioral ecology, and microeconomics. The crucible of empirical research that has shaped Information Foraging Theory has been application problems in human-information interaction, which is emerging as a new branch in the field traditionally known as human-computer interaction. Although the emphasis of this book is on theory and research, the insights and results are intended to be relevant to the practitioner interested in a deeper understanding of information-seeking behavior and guidance on new designs. Chapter 9 is devoted entirely to practical applications of the theory.

By its nature, Information Foraging Theory involves the use of technical material such as mathematical models and computational models that may not be familiar to a broad audience. Generally, the technical aspects of the theory and models are presented along with succinct discussion of the key concepts, insights, and principles that emerge from the technical parts, along with illustrative examples, metaphors, and graphical methods for understanding the key points. The aim of this presentation is to provide intuitive understanding along with technical precision and insight.

Frameworks, Theories, and Models

Like other programs of research in the behavioral and cognitive sciences, Information Foraging Theory can be discussed in terms of the underlying framework, the theory itself, and the models that specify predictions in specific situations. *Frameworks* are the general pools of concepts, assumptions, claims, heuristics, and so forth, that are drawn from to develop theories, as well the methods for using them to understand and predict the world. Often, frameworks will overlap. For instance, information processing psychology is a broad framework that assumes that theories about human behavior can be constructed out of information processing concepts, such as processes that transduce physical sensations into sensory information, elements storing various kinds of information, and computational processes operating over those elements. A related framework, connectionism, shares these assumptions but makes additional ones about the nature of information processing being neuronlike. Although bold claims may be made by frameworks, these are typically not testable in and of themselves. For instance, whether the mind is mostly a general purpose learning machine or mostly a collection of exquisitely evolved computational modules are not testable claims in and of themselves.

Theories can be constructed within frameworks by providing additional assumptions that allow one to make predictions that can be falsified. Typically, this is achieved by specifying a *model* for a specific situation or class of situations that makes precise predictions that can be fit to observation and measurement. For instance, a model of information seeking on the Web (SNIF-ACT) is presented in chapter 5 that predicts the observed choice of Web links in given tasks. It includes theoretical specifications of the information processing model of the user, as well as assumptions about the conditions under which it applies (e.g., English-speaking adults seeking information about unfamiliar topics). The bulk of this book is about Information Foraging Theory and specific models. The aim of this introductory chapter is to provide an outline of the underlying framework and methodology in which Information Foraging Theory is embedded. However, before presenting such abstractions, a simple example is offered in order to illustrate the basic elements and approach of Information Foraging Theory.

Illustration

The basic approach of Information Foraging Theory can be illustrated with a simple example that I hope is familiar to many, involving the task of finding a good, reasonably priced hotel using the World Wide Web (Pemberton, 2003). A typical hotel Web site (see figure 1.1) will allow a user to search for available hotels in some specified location (e.g., "Paris") and then allows the user to sort the results by the hotel star rating (an indicator of quality) or by price (but not both). The user must then click-select each result to read it, because often the price, location, and features summaries are inaccurate. Lamenting the often poor quality of such hotel Web sites, Pemberton (2003) suggested that improved "usability is about *optimizing the time* you take to achieve your purpose, how well you achieve it, and the satisfaction in doing it. . . . How fast can you find the perfect hotel?" This notion of usability is at the core of Information Foraging Theory.

For illustration, consider the somewhat simplified and idealized task of finding a low-priced, two-star hotel in Paris.[2] This example shows (in much simplified form) the key steps to developing a model of information foraging: (a) a rational analysis of the task and information environment that draws on optimal foraging theory from biology and (b) a production system model of the cognitive structure of task.

Rational Analysis of the Task and Information Environment

Figure 1.2 presents an analysis of results of search for two-star Paris hotels that I conducted on a popular hotel Web site. The Paris hotel descriptions and prices were returned as a vertical list presented over several Web pages. I sorted the list by star rating and went to the page that began to list two-star hotels. In figure 1.2, the x-axis indicates the order of two-star hotel listings in the search result list when sorted by star rating, beginning at the first two-star hotel through the last two-star hotel, and the y-axis indicates price. Prices fluctuate as one proceeds down the list of Paris hotels. As noted above, this particular hotel Web site, like many others, does not allow the user to sort by both quality (star rating) and price—one must choose one or the other sorting. Assume a rational (and perhaps somewhat boring) hotel shopper who was concerned only with being frugal and sleeping in a two-star hotel. If that shopper methodically scanned the two-star hotel listings, keeping track of only the lowest priced hotel found so far, the lowest price encountered would decrease as plotted in figure 1.3. That is, the shopper would at first find a relatively rapid decrease in lowest price, followed by fewer improvements as the scan progressed. Figure 1.4 shows the savings attained (compared with the very first hotel price found on the list) by continuing to scan down the list. Figure 1.4 is a typical *diminishing returns* curve in which additional benefits (returns) diminish as one invests more resources (in this case, scan time).

A diminishing returns curve such as figure 1.4 implies that the expected value of continuing to scan diminishes with each additional listing scanned. If the list of search results were very long—as is often the case with the results produced by Web search engines—there is usually a point at which the information forager faces the decision of whether it is worth the effort of continuing to search for a better result than anything encountered so far. In the particular example plotted in figure 1.2, there were no additional savings for the last 18 items scanned. Figure 1.3 includes a plot of the expected minimum price encountered as a function of scanning a search result list, and figure 1.4 includes a plot of the expected savings as a function of scanning. These expectations were computed assuming that observed hotel prices in figure 1.2 come from a standard

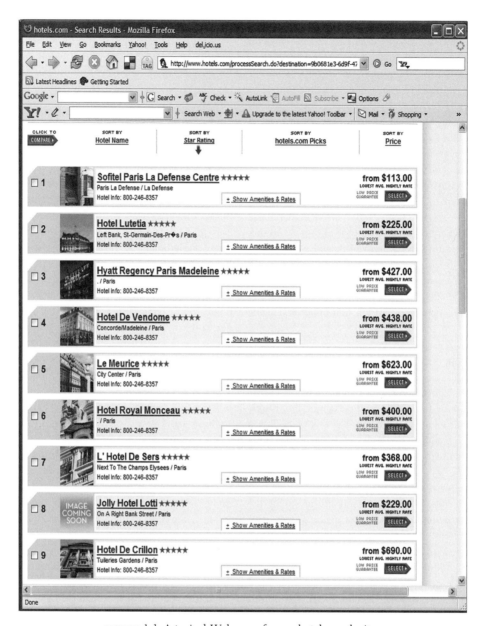

FIGURE 1.1 A typical Web page from a hotel search site.

distribution of commodity prices (see the appendix for details). Assuming that our hypothetical rational hotel shopper valued time (time is money), the question would be whether the savings expected to be gained by additional scanning of hotel results was worth the time expected to be expended.

In contrast to this simple illustration, typical information problems solved on the Web are more complicated (Morrison, Pirolli, & Card, 2001), and the assessments of the utility of encountered items in information foraging depend on more subtle cues than just prices. However, the basic problem of judging whether continued foraging will be useful or a waste of valuable time is surely familiar to Web users. It turns out that this problem is very similar to one class of problems dealt with in optimal foraging theory.

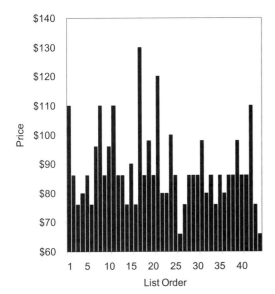

FIGURE 1.2 Prices of two-star Paris hotels in the order encountered in the results of a search of a hotel Web site.

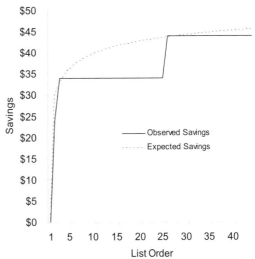

FIGURE 1.4 Diminishing returns of savings as a function of list order. The observed savings is the difference between the observed minimum price found so far and the first price encountered ($110), presented in figure 1.3. The expected savings is the difference between the expected minimum price and first price encountered.

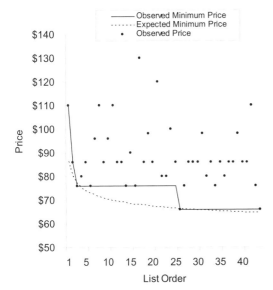

FIGURE 1.3 The minimum two-star Paris hotel price as a function of order of encounter. The observed prices are the same as those in figure 1.2. The observed minimum is the least expensive hotel price found so far in a process that proceeds through the prices in the order listed. The expected minimum is a prediction based on the assumption that prices are being sequentially and randomly sampled from a fixed distribution of prices (see the appendix for details).

An Optimal Foraging Analogy

Many animals forage in patchy environments, with food arranged into clumps. For instance, a bird that feeds on berries in bushes will spend part of its time searching for the next bush and part of its time berry picking after having found a bush. Often, as an animal forages in a patch, it becomes harder to find food items. In other words, foraging within a food patch often exhibits a diminishing returns curve similar to the one in figure 1.5. Such diminishing returns may occur, for instance, because prey actively avoid the forager as they become aware of the threat of predation. Diminishing returns may also occur because the forager has a strategy of picking off the more highly profitable items first (e.g., bigger berries for the hypothetical bird) from a patch with finite resources. Like the hypothetical Web shopper discussed above, the problem for a food forager facing diminishing returns in a patch is whether to continue investing efforts in getting more out of the patch, or to go look for another patch.

Figure 1.5 is a graphical version of a simple *conventional patch model* (Stephens & Krebs, 1986) based on *Charnov's Marginal Value Theorem* (Charnov,

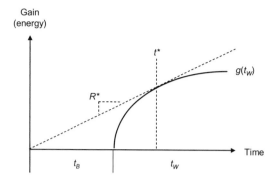

FIGURE 1.5 Charnov's Marginal Value Theorem states that the rate-maximizing time to spend in patch, t^* occurs when the slope of the within-patch gain function g is equal to the average rate of gain, which is the slope of the tangent line R^*.

1976). The model depicted in figure 1.5 assumes that an animal foraging for food encounters only one kind of food patch at random that is never reencountered. When searching for the next food patch, it takes an average of t_B amount of time to find the next patch (between-patch time). Once a patch is encountered, foraging within the patch returns some amount of energy (e.g., as measured by calories) that increases as a function, g, of the time, t_W, spent foraging within the patch. Figure 1.5 shows a diminishing returns function, g, for within-patch foraging. The problem for the forager is how much time, t_W, to spend within each patch before leaving to find the next patch.

The conventional patch model assumes that the animal forager optimizes the overall rate of gain, R, that characterizes the amount of energy gained per unit time of foraging:

$$R = \frac{g(t_W)}{t_B + t_W},\qquad(1.1)$$

or the amount of energy (calories) gained from an average patch divided by the time spent traveling from one patch to the next (t_B) plus the time spent foraging within a patch (t_W). The optimal amount of time, t^*, to spend in a patch is the one that yields the maximum rate of gain, R^*,

$$R^* = \frac{g(t^*)}{t_B + t^*}.\qquad(1.2)$$

Charnov's Marginal Value Theorem (Charnov, 1976) is a mathematical solution to this problem of determining t^*. It basically says that a forager should leave a patch when the rate of gain within the patch [as measured by the slope of $g(t_W)$ or more specifically the derivative $g'(t_W)$] drops below the rate of gain that could be achieved by traveling to, and foraging in, a new patch. That is, the optimal forager obeys the rule,

if $g'(t_W) \geq R^*$, then continue foraging in the patch; otherwise,
when $g'(t_W) < R^*$, then start looking for a new patch.

Charnov's Marginal Value Theorem can be illustrated graphically in figure 1.5 for this simple problem (one kind of patch, randomly distributed in the world). First, note that the gain function g begins to climb only after t_B, which captures the fact that it takes t_B time to go from the last patch to a new patch. If we draw a line beginning at the origin to any point on the gain function, g, then the slope of that line will be the overall rate of gain R, as specified in equation 1.1. Figure 1.5 shows such a line drawn from the origin to a point just tangent to the function g. The slope of this line is the optimal rate of gain R^* as computed in equation 1.2. This can be verified graphically by imagining other lines drawn from the origin to points on the function g. None of those lines will have a steeper slope than the line plotted in figure 1.5. The point at which the line is tangent to g will be the point at which the rate of gain, $g'(t_W)$ within the patch is equal to R^*. This point also determines t^*, the optimum time to spend within the average patch.

Production System Models

The rational analyses in Information Foraging Theory, which often draw from optimal foraging theory, are used to inform the development of production system models. These rational analyses make minimal assumptions about the capabilities of foragers. Herbert Simon (1955) argued that organisms are not optimal, rational agents having perfect information and unlimited computational resources. Rather, organisms exhibit *bounded rationality*. That is, agents are rational and adaptive, within the constraints of the environment and the psychological machinery available to them biologically. Production system models provide a way of specifying the mechanistic structures and processes that implement bounded rationality. On the one hand, production systems have been used in psychology as a particular kind of computer simulation formalism for specifying the information processing that theorists believe people are performing. On the other hand, production systems have evolved into something more than just a class of computer simulation languages: They have become theories about the basic information processing architecture of cognition that is implemented in human brains (Anderson, 1983; Anderson & Lebiere, 1998; Newell, 1990).

In general, as used in psychology,[3] production systems are composed of a set of *production rules* that specify the dynamics of information processing performed by cognition (*how* we think). Production rules operate over memories (or databases) that contain symbolic structures that represent aspects of the external environment and internal thought (*what* we think about). The system operates in a cyclical fashion in which production rules are selected based on the contents of the data memories and then executed. The execution of a production rule typically results in some change to the memories.

The production system models presented in this book are extensions of ACT theory (Anderson et al., 2004; Anderson & Lebiere, 1998). ACT (Adaptive Control of Thought) theory assumes that there are two kinds of knowledge, *declarative* and *procedural* (Ryle, 1949). Declarative knowledge is the kind of knowledge that a person can attend to, reflect upon, and usually articulate in some way (e.g., by declaring it verbally or by gesture). Declarative knowledge includes the kinds of factual knowledge that users can verbalize, such as "The 'open' item on the 'file' menu will open a file." Procedural knowledge is the know-how we display in our behavior, without conscious awareness. For instance, knowledge of how to ride a bike and knowledge of how to point a mouse to a menu item are examples of procedural knowledge. Procedural knowledge specifies how declarative knowledge is transformed into active behavior.

ACT-R (the most recent of the ACT theories) has a memory for each kind of knowledge (i.e., a *declarative memory* and a *procedural memory*) plus a special *goal memory*. At any point in time, there may be a number of goals in goal memory, but the system behavior is focused to achieve just one goal at a time.

Complex arrangements of goals and subgoals (e.g., for developing and executing plans to find and use information) can be implemented by manipulating goals in goal memory.

Production rules (or *productions*) are used to represent procedural knowledge in ACT-R. That is, they specify how to apply cognitive skill (know-how) and how to retrieve and use declarative knowledge. Table 1.1 presents an example of a production system for the task of finding a low-cost hotel using a Web site. The example in table 1.1 is not intended to be a psychologically plausible model, but rather it illustrates key aspects of production system models and how they are used in this book. The productions in table 1.1 are English glosses of productions written in ACT-R 5.0, which is discussed in greater detail below.[4] Each production rule is of the form

IF ⟨condition⟩, THEN ⟨actions⟩.

The condition of a rule specifies a pattern. When the contents of declarative working memory match the pattern, the rule may be selected for application. The actions of the rule specify additions and deletions of content in declarative working memory, as well as motor commands. These actions are executed if the rule is selected to apply. In ACT-R, each production rule has conditions that specify which goal information must be matched and which declarative memory must be retrieved. Each production rule has actions that specify behavioral actions and possibly the setting of subgoals. Typically, ACT-R goal memory is operated on as what is known in computer science as a push-down stack: a kind of memory in which the last item stored will be the first item retrieved. Hence, storing a new goal is referred to as "pushing a goal on the stack," and retrieval is referred to as "popping a goal from the stack."

The production rules in table 1.1 assume that declarative memory contains knowledge encoded from the external world about the location and content of links on a Web page. The productions also assume that an initial goal is set to find a hotel price, and the productions accomplish the task by "scanning" through the links keeping track of the lowest price found so far. This involves setting a subgoal to judge the minimum of the current best price and the price just attended when each link is scanned. Table 1.2 presents a trace of the productions in table 1.1

TABLE 1.1 A production system for the task of finding a low hotel price.

P1: Start
IF the goal is to find a hotel
  & there is a page of Web results
  & no link location has been processed
THEN modify the goal to specify that the first location is to be processed

P2: First-link
IF the goal is to find a hotel
  & a link location is specified
  & no best price has been noted yet
  & the link at the location indicates a price
  & the link is followed by a link at a new location
THEN note that the best price is the price from the link at that location
  & modify the goal to specify the new location of the next link

P3: Next-link
IF the goal is to find a hotel
  & a link location is specified
  & there is a current best price
  & the link at the location indicates a new price
  & the link is followed by a link at a new location
THEN create a subgoal to find the minimum of the current price and the new price
  & push the subgoal on the goal stack
  & modify the current goal to specify the new location of the next link
  & note the resulting new minimum price as the best price

P4: Minimum-price-stays-the-same
IF the goal is to find the minimum of the current price and the new price
  & there is a current best price
  & there is a new price
  & the current best price is less than or equal to the new price
THEN note that the current best price is the minimum
  & pop the subgoal

P5: New-minimum-price
IF the goal is to find the minimum of the current price and the new price
  & there is a current best price
  & there is a new price
  & the current best price is greater than the new price
THEN note that the new price is the minimum
  & pop the subgoal

P6: Go-do-something-else (Done)
IF the goal is to find a hotel
  & there is a current best price
THEN stop

operating to scan the list of hotel prices depicted in figure 1.1 and graphed in figure 1.2.

Production "P1: Start" in table 1.1 applies at cycle 0 in table 1.2 when the goal is to find a hotel price. Production "P2: First-link" applies at cycle 1 to scan the first link location and set the initial minimum hotel price. Then, production "P3: Next-link" applies repeatedly to scan subsequent links (cycles 2–53). For each link scanned, P3 sets a subgoal—by creating a new goal and making it the focus in goal memory—to compare the currently scanned price to the current minimum price. This subgoal evokes either production "P4: Minimum-price-stays-the-same" or "P5: New-minimum-price." When either P4 or P5 applies, it pops the subgoal to determine the minimum, and control passes back to the top-level goal of finding a hotel price.

Note in table 1.2 that the trace ends at cycle 52 with the execution of production "P6: Done" after

TABLE 1.2 Trace of the production system specified in table 1.1.

Cycle 0: Start
    Cycle 1: first-link Location: 1 Link-Price: 110 Current-Best: 110
    Cycle 2: next-link Location: 2 Link-Price: 86 Current-Best: 110
        Cycle 3: new-minimum-price
    Cycle 4: next-link Location: 3 Link-Price: 76 Current-Best: 86
        Cycle 5: new-minimum-price
    Cycle 6: next-link Location: 4 Link-Price: 80 Current-Best: 76
        Cycle 7: minimum-price-stays-same
    Cycle 8: next-link Location: 5 Link-Price: 86 Current-Best: 76
        Cycle 9: minimum-price-stays-same
    Cycle 10: next-link Location: 6 Link-Price: 76 Current-Best: 76
        Cycle 11: minimum-price-stays-same
    Cycle 12: next-link Location: 7 Link-Price: 96 Current-Best: 76
        Cycle 13: minimum-price-stays-same
    Cycle 14: next-link Location: 8 Link-Price: 110 Current-Best: 76
        Cycle 15: minimum-price-stays-same
    Cycle 16: next-link Location: 9 Link-Price: 86 Current-Best: 76
        Cycle 17: minimum-price-stays-same
    Cycle 18: next-link Location: 10 Link-Price: 96 Current-Best: 76
        Cycle 19: minimum-price-stays-same
    Cycle 20: next-link Location: 11 Link-Price: 110 Current-Best: 76
        Cycle 21: minimum-price-stays-same
    Cycle 22: next-link Location: 12 Link-Price: 86 Current-Best: 76
        Cycle 23: minimum-price-stays-same
    Cycle 24: next-link Location: 13 Link-Price: 86 Current-Best: 76
        Cycle 25: minimum-price-stays-same
    Cycle 26: next-link Location: 14 Link-Price: 76 Current-Best: 76
        Cycle 27: minimum-price-stays-same
    Cycle 28: next-link Location: 15 Link-Price: 90 Current-Best: 76
        Cycle 29: minimum-price-stays-same
    Cycle 30: next-link Location: 16 Link-Price: 76 Current-Best: 76
        Cycle 31: minimum-price-stays-same
    Cycle 32: next-link Location: 17 Link-Price: 130 Current-Best: 76
        Cycle 33: minimum-price-stays-same
    Cycle 34: next-link Location: 18 Link-Price: 86 Current-Best: 76
        Cycle 35: minimum-price-stays-same
    Cycle 36: next-link Location: 19 Link-Price: 98 Current-Best: 76
        Cycle 37: minimum-price-stays-same
    Cycle 38: next-link Location: 20 Link-Price: 86 Current-Best: 76
        Cycle 39: minimum-price-stays-same
    Cycle 40: next-link Location: 21 Link-Price: 120 Current-Best: 76
        Cycle 41: minimum-price-stays-same
    Cycle 42: next-link Location: 22 Link-Price: 80 Current-Best: 76
        Cycle 43: minimum-price-stays-same
    Cycle 44: next-link Location: 23 Link-Price: 80 Current-Best: 76
        Cycle 45: minimum-price-stays-same
    Cycle 46: next-link Location: 24 Link-Price: 100 Current-Best: 76
        Cycle 47: minimum-price-stays-same
    Cycle 48: next-link Location: 25 Link-Price: 86 Current-Best: 76
        Cycle 49: minimum-price-stays-same
    Cycle 50: next-link Location: 26 Link-Price: 66 Current-Best: 76
        Cycle 51: new-minimum-price
    Cycle 52: DONE!!! Best price is: 66
Total Time: 782.30005 sec

---

scanning the link at location 26 in the list of results. The list actually contains 44 links in the result list (figure 1.2). The production system stops at link location 26 because of the way it implements elements of the rational analysis described above. Productions "P3: Next-link" and "P6: Done" match very similar patterns in declarative memory. In fact, on every cycle that P3 or P6 fires in the trace, the other production also matches. In production system terminology, P3 and P6 form a *conflict set* when on a particular cycle they both match the current pattern in the goal stack and declarative memory. In such cases, the *utility* of each production in the conflict set is evaluated and used to perform *conflict resolution* to determine which production to execute.

Production "P6: Done" is associated with a utility that corresponds to R discussed above: the overall rate of gain. I simply assumed that this corresponds to how the production system values its time. For the trace in table 1.2, I assumed that the production system valued its time at $R = \$10$/hour.

Production "P3: Next-link" is associated with a utility that corresponds to $g'(t)$ discussed above: the rate of savings that would be achieved by looking at the next link: expected savings from scanning next link/time to scan link (in hours). The appendix discusses how expected savings is computed assuming the distribution of hotel prices evident in figure 1.2. From self-observation, I noted that it took 30 sec (30/3600 hour) to scan a link on the Web site depicted in figure 1.1. The competition between productions P3 and P6 implements the key idea of Charnov's Marginal Value Theorem: As long as the rate of savings expected for production "P3: Next-link" is greater than the overall rate of gain, R, associated with "P6: Done," then the system continues to scan links; otherwise, it quits.

Summary

I have presented this simple concrete example to sketch out the overall framework and approach of Information Foraging Theory before beginning more abstract discussion of framework and method. At this preliminary stage, it was necessary to gloss over unrealistic assumptions about Web use and the technical details of the analysis and model. However, it is important to point out two realistic aspects of the example. First, as will become clear in chapter 3, the Web does have a patchy structure (e.g., Web sites and

search results), and diminishing returns within those information patches is common. For instance, figure 1.6 is based on data from a study of medical information seeking (Bhavnani, 2005).[5] Bhavnani, Jacob, Nardine, and Peck (2003) asked melanoma experts to identify melanoma risk facts that they identified as important for a melanoma patient to understand. Figure 1.6a shows the distribution of melanoma risk facts across Web pages. Very few pages contain all 14 expert-identified melanoma risk concepts, but many contain one of the melanoma risk facts. Figure 1.6b is an estimate of the number of melanoma risk facts that a user would encounter as a function of visits to melanoma-related pages (Bhavnani et al., 2003). Note that it is a diminishing returns curve

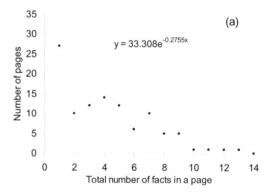

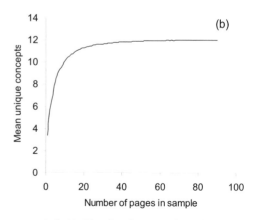

FIGURE 1.6 (a) The distribution of number of key concepts about melanoma risk across Web pages, and (b) the cumulative number of key concepts encountered as a function of size of sample of pages (Bhavnani, 2005; Bhavnani et al., 2003).

and that the user is expected to require 25 page visits to find all expert-identified melanoma risk facts.

In the remaining sections of this chapter, I provide an overview of broader framework and method. The remainder of this book is about the empirical and theoretical details.

Man the Informavore

All men by nature desire knowledge. —*Aristotle*, Metaphysics

The human propensity to gather and use information to adapt to everyday problems in the world is a core piece of human psychology that has been largely ignored in cognitive studies. George A. Miller (1983), however, recognized the centrality of this human propensity to our cognitive natures and argued that mankind might fruitfully be viewed as a kind of *informavore*: a species that hungers for information in order to gather it and store it as a means for adapting to the world. Picking up on this idea, Dennett (1991) traced out a plausible evolutionary history in which he suggested that our ancestors might have developed vigilance behaviors that required surveying and assessing the current state of the environment, much like the prairie dogs who pop up on two feet to perform their situation appraisals or the harbor seals that break the surface in the middle of a beach break to check out whether the surfers are friends, foe, or prey. Adaptive pressures to gain more useful, actionable knowledge from the environment could lead to the marshaling of available cognitive and behavioral machinery, resulting in organisms, such as primates, that have active curiosity about the world and themselves. Humans, of course, are extreme in their reliance on information, with language and culture, and now modern technology, providing media for transmission within and across generations. Humans are the *Informavores rex* of the current era.

George Miller's notion of humans as informavores suggests that our genes have bestowed upon us an evolving behavioral repertoire that now includes the technological aspects of our culture associated with finding, saving, and communicating information. It is common in evolutionary discussions to distinguish between *genotype* and *phenotype* (Johanssen, 1911). The genotype is the blueprint for an individual. What gets passed from one generation to the next (if it survives and reproduces) are the genotypic blueprints. Phe-notypes are the outward manifestation of the genotype. Typically, people think of this as the bodily structure and behavior of the individual organism. However, Dawkins (1989) introduced the notion of *extended phenotype* to clarify the observation that the genotype has extended effects on the world at large that go beyond the actual body and behavior of the individual. Not only do beavers have tails, but they use them to make dams. Not only do spiders have legs, but they use them to make webs. Humans have not only brains but also external technology for storing information, and information foraging strategies that can be invoked to call forth the right knowledge, at the right time, to take useful action. It remains an open question as to why humans have evolved such information collection strategies—a question that I raise again at the end of this book.

The Adaptive Pressure of the Wealth of Information

Thanks to science and technology, access to factual knowledge of all kinds is rising exponentially while dropping in unit cost....We are drowning in information, while starving for wisdom. —*E. O. Wilson*, Consilience

Information Foraging Theory emerges from a serious consideration of Miller's notion of informavores. A serious consideration of the concept leads to questions regarding the adaptive forces that drive human interaction with information. Simon (1971) articulated the basic design problem facing us: "What information consumes is rather obvious: it consumes the attention of its recipients. Hence a wealth of information creates a poverty of attention, and a need to allocate that attention efficiently among the overabundance of information sources that might consume it" (pp. 40–41).

According to statistics compiled by the University of California–Berkeley School of Information Science (Lyman & Varian, 2003), almost 800 megabytes of recorded information are produced per person per year, averaged over the estimated 6.3 billion people in the world. This is the equivalent of about 30 linear feet of books. In an information-rich world, the real design problem to be solved is not so much how to collect and distribute more information but rather how to increase the rate at which persons can find and attend to information that is truly of value to them.

The Principle of the Extremization of Information Utility as a Function of Interaction Cost

An investment in knowledge always pays the best interest.—Benjamin Franklin

In modern society, people interact with information through technology that more or less helps them find and use the right knowledge at the right time. In evolutionary terms, one can argue that increasing the rate of gain of valuable information increases fitness. As Sir Francis Bacon observed, "knowledge is power." Power (control over the world to achieve one's goals) can be improved by better knowledge, or lower costs of access and application of knowledge. In evolutionary terms, an agent's fitness is improved to the extent that it can predict and control the environment in order to solve the problems it faces in everyday life. In psychological terms, increasing the rate at which people can find, make sense of, and use valuable information improves the human capacity to behave intelligently. We should expect adaptive systems to evolve toward states that maximize gains of valuable information per unit cost (Resnikoff, 1989, p. 97). A useful way of thinking about such adaptation is to say that

> Human-information interaction systems will tend to maximize the value of external knowledge gained relative to the cost of interaction.

Schematically, we may characterize this maximization tendency[6] as

$$\max \left[\frac{\text{Expected value of knowledge gained}}{\text{Cost of interaction}} \right]. \quad (1.3)$$

Cognitive systems engaged in information foraging will exhibit such adaptive tendencies, and they will prefer technologies that tend to maximize the value (or utility) of knowledge gained per unit cost of interaction. For instance, sensory systems appear to evolve in ways that deliver more bits of information for the amount of calories expended. Similarly, offices, with their seeming chaotic mess of piles of papers, books, and files, appear to become organized in ways that optimize access costs of frequently needed information (Case, 1991; Malone, 1983; Soper, 1976). Resnikoff (1989, pp. 112–117) presented a mathematical analysis suggesting that physical library cata-

log card systems would become arranged in ways that minimized manual search time. Information Foraging Theory assumes that people prefer information-seeking strategies that yield more useful information per unit cost. People tend to arrange their environments (physical or virtual) to optimize this rate of gain. People prefer, and consequently select, technology designs that improve returns on information foraging.

The Exaptation of Food Foraging Mechanisms

Natural selection favored organisms—including our human ancestors—that had better mechanisms for extracting energy from the environment and translating that energy into reproductive success. Organisms with better food-foraging strategies (for their particular environment) were favored by natural selection. Our ancestors evolved perceptual and cognitive mechanisms and strategies that were very well adapted to the task of exploring the environment and finding and gathering food. Information Foraging Theory assumes that modern-day information foragers use perceptual and cognitive mechanisms that carry over from the evolution of food-foraging adaptations.

If information foraging is like food foraging, then models of optimal foraging developed in the study of animal behavior (Stephens & Krebs, 1986) and anthropology (Winterhalder & Smith, 1992) should be relevant. Figure 1.5 presents the conventional patch model and Charnov's Marginal Value Theorem as a possible analog for information foraging at a Web site. A typical optimal foraging model characterizes an agent's interaction with the environment as an optimal solution to the tradeoff of costs of finding, choosing, and handling food against the energetic benefit gained from that food. These models would look very familiar to an engineer because they are basically an attempt to understand the design of an agent's behavior by assuming that it is well engineered (adapted) for the problems posed by the environment. Information foraging models include optimality analyses of different information-seeking strategies and technologies as a way of understanding the design rationale for user strategies and interaction technologies.

Optimal foraging theorists assume that energy, originating predominantly from the sun, seeps through the food chain to be deposited in various plants and animals that are distributed variably through the environment. Food foragers may have different mechanisms and strategies available to them for navigating through the environment. Their potential sources of food may have different prevalences in different habitats and may have different profitabilities in terms of how many calories can be extracted when foraged. The optimal forager is one who has the strategies, mechanisms, diets, and so forth, that maximize the calories gained per unit of effort expended.[7] Similarly, Information Foraging Theory assumes that information comes to be stored in various prevalences in different kinds of repositories, in various forms and media. The information forager has different means available for navigating and searching the information environment, and different information sources have different profitabilities in terms of the interaction cost required to gain useful information. As suggested by equation 1.3, the optimal information forager is one who maximizes the value of knowledge gained per unit cost of interaction.

Application to Human-Information Interaction

The legacy of the Enlightenment is the belief that entirely on our own we can know, and in knowing, understand, and in understanding, choose wisely. — E. O. Wilson, Consilience

Human-information interaction (HII) is a nascent field that is concerned with how people interact with, and process, outwardly accessible information in service of their goals.[8] It adopts an information-centric approach rather than the computer-centric approach of the field of human-computer interaction (HCI) (Lucas, 2000). This shift to an information-centric focus is a natural evolution for the field of HCI because of the increasing *pervasiveness* of information services, the increasing *transparency* of user interfaces, the *convergence* of information delivery technologies, and the trend toward *ubiquitous computing*.

Access to the Internet is pervasive in the developed world through land lines, satellite, cable, and mobile devices. The field of HCI, over the past two decades and more, has led to the development of computers and computer applications that are transparent to users performing their tasks. In parallel, the business world around consumer media technologies shows excitement over the convergence of television, cell phones, personal computers, PDAs (personal digital assistants), cars, set-tops, and other consumer electronics devices, as well as the convergence among the

means for transporting information, such as the Internet, radio, satellite, and cable. Research on ubiquitous computing looks forward to a world in which computational devices are basically everywhere in our homes, mobile devices, cars, and so on, and these devices can be marshaled to perform arbitrary tasks for users. The net effect of these trends is to make computers invisible, just as electricity and electric motors are invisible in homes today (Lucas, 2000). As computers become invisible, and information becomes ample and pervasive, we expect to see a shift in studies from HCI to HII. Rather than focus on the structure of devices and application programs, the focus of HII research must center on content and interactive media.

Information Foraging Theory arose during the 1990s, coinciding with an explosion in the amount of information that became available to the average computer user and with the development of new technologies for accessing and interacting with information. The late 1980s witnessed several strands of HCI research that were devoted to ameliorating problems of exploring and finding electronically stored information. It had become apparent that users could no longer remember the names of all their electronic files, and it was even more difficult for them to guess the names of files stored by others (Furnas, Landauer, Gomez, & Dumais, 1987). One can see proposals in the mid- to late 1980s HCI literature for methods to enhance users' ability to search and explore external memory. Jones (1986) proposed the Memory Extender (ME), which used a model of human associative memory (Anderson, 1983) to automatically retrieve files represented by sets of keywords that were similar to the sets of keywords representing the users' working context. Latent Semantic Analysis (LSA; Dumais, Furnas, Landauer, Deerwester, & Harshman, 1988) was developed to mimic human ability to detect deeper semantic associations among words, such as "dog" and "cat," to similarly enhance information retrieval. Interestingly, the work on ME and LSA was contrasted with work in the "traditional" field of information retrieval in computer science, which had a relatively long history of developing automated systems for storing and retrieving text documents. The CHI '88 conference where LSA was introduced also hosted a panel bemoaning the fact that automated information retrieval systems had not progressed to the stage where anyone but dedicated experts could operate them (Borgman, Belkin, Croft, Lesk, & Landauer, 1988). Such systems, however, were the direct ancestors of modern search engines found on the World Wide Web.

Hypermedia also became a hot topic during the late 1980s, with Apple's introduction of HyperCard in 1987, the first ACM Conference on Hypertext in 1987, and a paper session at the CHI '88 conference. The very idea of hypertext can be traced back to Vannevar Bush's *Atlantic Monthly* article, "As We May Think," published in 1945. Worried about scholars becoming overwhelmed by the amount of information being published, Bush proposed a mechanized private file system, called the Memex, that would augment the memory of the individual user. It was explicitly intended to mimic human associative memory. Bush's article influenced the development of Douglas Engelbart's NLS (oNLine System), which was introduced to the world in a tour-de-force demonstration at the 1968 Fall Joint Computer Conference. The demonstration of NLS—a system explicitly designed to "augment human intellect" (Engelbart, 1962)—also introduced the world to the power of networking, the mouse, and point-and-click interaction. Hypertext and hypermedia research arose during the late 1980s because personal computing power, networking, and user interfaces had evolved to the point where the visions of Bush and Engelbart could finally be realized for the average computer user.

The confluence of increased computing power, storage, networking and information access, and hypermedia research in the late 1980s set the stage for the widespread deployment of hypermedia in the form of the World Wide Web. In 1989, Tim Berners-Lee (1989) proposed a solution to the problems that were being faced by the CERN community in dealing with distributed collections of documents, which were stored on many types of platforms, in many types of formats. This proposal led directly to the development of HTML, HTTP, and, in 1990, the release of the World Wide Web. Berners-Lee's vision was not only to provide users with more effective access to information but also to initiate an evolving web of information that reflected and enhanced the community and its activities.

The emergence of the Web in the 1990s provided new challenges and opportunities for HCI. The increased wealth of accessible content, and the use of the Web as a place to do business, exacerbated the need to improve the user experience on the Web.

The usability literature that has evolved surrounding the Web user experience is incredibly rich with design principles and maxims (Nielsen, 2000; Spool, Scanlon, Schroeder, Snyder, & DeAngelo, 1999), the most important of which is to test designs with users. Much of this literature is based on a mix of empirical findings and expert ("guru") opinion. A good deal of it is conflicting. The development of theory in this area can greatly accelerate progress and meet the demands of changes in the way we interact with the Web. Greater theoretical understanding and the ability to predict the effects of alternative designs could bring greater coherence to the usability literature and provide more rapid evolution of better designs. In practical terms, a designer armed with such theory could explore and explain the effects of different design decisions on Web designs before the heavy investment of resources for implementation and testing. This exploration of design space is also more efficient because the choices among different design alternatives are better informed: Rather than randomly generating and testing design alternatives, the designer is in a position to know which avenues are better to explore and which are better to ignore. Unfortunately, cognitive engineering models that have been developed to deal with the analysis of expert performance on well-defined tasks involving application programs (Pirolli, 1999) have little applicability to understanding foraging through content-rich hypermedia, and consequently new theories are needed.

Methodological Adaptationism

Adaptationist reasoning is not optional; it is the heart and soul of evolutionary biology.—D. C. Dennett, Darwin's Dangerous Idea

The concept of informavores, and concern with the application domain of HII, leads us to reconsider the dominance of strictly mechanistic analyses of HCI. Miller, in his 1983 article about "informavores," commented on the incompleteness of the mechanistic approach by using the following analogy:

> Insofar as a limb is a lever, the theory of levers describes its behavior—but a theory of levers does not answer every question that might be asked about the structure and function of the limbs of animals. Insofar as the mind is used to process information, the theory of information processing describes its behavior—but a theory of information processing does not answer every question that might be asked about the structure and function of the minds of human beings. (p. 112)

Information processing (mechanistic) analyses of HCI—by themselves—give only partial explanations. They provide mechanistic explanations of the "levers" of the mind. In reaction to this inadequacy, Information Foraging Theory has been guided by the heuristics and explanatory framework of *methodological adaptationism*, and the specific version of it developed by Anderson (1990) called *rational analysis* (see also Oaksford & Chater, 1998). The illustration above concerning hotel prices on the Web involved a very simple rational analysis. Methodological adaptationism presumes that it is a good heuristic for scientists to assume that evolving, behaving systems are rational, or well designed, for fulfilling certain functions in certain environments. There is an assumption of *ecological rationality* regarding the behavior of the system being observed (Bechtel, 1985; Dennett, 1983, 1988, 1995; Gigerenzer, 2000). The adaptationist approach involves a kind of reverse engineering in which the analyst asks (a) *what* environmental problem is solved, (b) *why* is a given system a good solution to the problem, and (c) *how* is that solution realized (approximated) by mechanism.

Versions of methodological adaptationism have shaped research programs in behavioral ecology (e.g., Mayr, 1983; Stephens & Krebs, 1986; Tinbergen, 1963), anthropology (e.g., Winterhalder & Smith, 1992), and neuroscience (e.g., Glimcher, 2003). The approach gained currency in cognitive science during the 1980s as a reaction to ad hoc models of how people performed complex cognitive or perceptual tasks. At that time, models of cognition and perception were generally mechanistic, detailing perceptual and cognitive structures and the processes that transformed them. The Model Human Processor (MHP) and GOMS (Goals, Operators, Methods, and Selection rules; Card, Moran, & Newell, 1983) are cognitive engineering examples in the field of HCI that derive from this approach. The MHP specifies a basic set of information storage and processing machinery, much like a specification of the basic computer architecture for a personal computer. GOMS specifies basic task performance processes, much like a mechanical program that "runs" on the MHP.

Around the same time that GOMS and MHP were introduced into HCI, there emerged a concern among cognitive scientists that mechanistic information processing models, by themselves, were not enough to understand the human mind (Anderson, 1990; Marr, 1982). A major worry was that mechanistic models of cognition had been developed in an ad hoc way and provided an incomplete explanation of human behavior. It had become common practice to cobble together a program that simulated human performance on some task and then claim that the program was in fact a theory of the task (Marr, 1982, p. 28). Anderson (1990) lamented that cognitive modelers "pull out of an infinite grab bag of mechanisms bizarre creations whose only justification is that they predict the phenomena in a class of experiments.... We almost never ask the question of *why* these mechanisms compute the way they do" (p. 7, emphasis added).

Figuring out a mechanistic account of human behavior—for instance, with MHP analysis—is no small feat. However, as the Miller quote above suggests, such accounts do not explain everything. The mind is not just any old arbitrary, cobbled-together machine; rather, it is a fantastically complex machine that has been designed by evolution to be well tailored to the demands of surviving and reproducing in the environment. The adaptationist approach recognizes that one can better understand a machine by understanding its *function*. By this I mean both that (a) adaptationist accounts make more sense and (b) the search for better understanding proceeds at a faster pace.

Levels of Explanation

The analysis of people interacting with information involves interrelated layers of explanation. This is because scientific models in this area assume that human activity is (a) purposeful and adaptive, which requires a kind of rational analysis, (b) based on knowledge, (c) computed by information processing mechanisms, which are (d) realized by physical, biological, processes. Table 1.3 presents a summary of the relevant framework that has emerged in the behavioral sciences (see, e.g., Anderson, 1990; Cosmides, Tooby, & Barow, 1992; Gigerenzer, 2000; Winterhalder & Smith, 1992a).

Rational analysis, in the case of Information Foraging Theory, focuses on the task environment that is the aim of performance, the information environment that structures access to valuable knowledge, and the adaptive fit of the HII system to the demands of these environments. Rational analysis assumes that the structure of behavior can be understood in terms of its adaptive fit to the structure and constraints of the environment. The analysis of

TABLE 1.3 Levels of explanation.

Level	Question	Stance	Analysis Elements	Examples
Rational	What environmental problem is solved? Why is this solution a good one?	Design	• States, resources, state dynamics • Constraints, affordances • Feasible strategies • Optimization criteria	• Optimal foraging theory • Information Foraging Theory
Knowledge	What does the system know?	Intentional	• Environment • Goals, preferences • Knowledge • Perception, action	• Knowledge-level analysis
Cognitive	How does the system do it?	Information processing	• Cognitive states • Cognitive processes	• ACT-R • Soar
Biological	How does the system physically do it?	Biophysical	• Neural processes	• Neural models

searching for hotel prices on Web involved a rational analysis of the expected savings to be gained from information search and an analysis of the rational choice to make when faced with decisions of whether to continue search or to give up. When performing a rational analysis the theorist may be said to take a *design stance* (Dennett, 1995) that focuses on an analysis of the functionality of the system with respect to its ostensive purpose. At this level, the analyst acts most purely as an engineer concerned with why users' behavior is rational given the task context in which it occurs, and it is assumed that users are optimizing their performance in achieving their goals.

Knowledge-level analysis concerns the knowledge content involved in achieving goals. Knowledge-level analysis involves descriptions of a system in intentional terms with the assumption that behavior is the product of purposes, preferences, and knowledge. The knowledge level has been important in artificial intelligence since its introduction by Newell (1982). A knowledge-level analysis of the task of searching for hotel prices on the Web was a prerequisite to the specification of the production rules and chunks involved in the cognitive simulation. Dennett (1988) defined an observer who describes a system using an intentional vocabulary (e.g., "know," "believe," "think") as one taking an *intentional stance*. Typically, a task analysis focuses mainly on an analysis of users' knowledge, preferences, perceptions, and actions, with respect to the goal and environment. At

this level of analysis, it is assumed that users deploy their knowledge to achieve their goals, and the focus is on identifying what knowledge is involved.

Modern cognitive psychology assumes that the knowledge level can be given a scientific account (i.e., be made predictable) by explaining it in terms of mechanistic information processing (Newell, 1990). This is the *cognitive level* of explanation. This level of analysis focuses on the properties of the information processing machinery that evolution has dealt to humans to perceive, think, remember, learn, and act in what we would call purposeful and knowledgeable ways. This is the level of most traditional theorizing in cognitive psychology and HCI—the level at which computational models may, in principle, be developed to simulate human cognition. GOMS (Card et al., 1983), described above, is an example of an analysis method aimed at cognitive-level analysis. Cognitive architectures such as ACT-R (Anderson et al., 2004) or Soar (Newell, 1990) and the simulations developed in those architectures are developed at the cognitive level. The production system specified in table 1.1 was a simple example of a cognitive-level analysis.

Accounts at the cognitive level are assumed to be instantiated at the *biological level* by the physical machinery of the brain and body. The biological level of explanation specifies the proximal physical mechanisms underlying behavior. For instance, Anderson et al. (2004) have recently presented results suggesting the mapping of the ACT-R architecture onto neural structure and functioning.

Phenomena at Different Time Scales of Behavioral Analysis

Many of our goals can drive our behavior for days, months, and even years. These longer term goals are typically realized by task structures composed of many shorter term goals. Card et al. (1983) suggested that there is a base level of tasks, called the *unit task level*, that controls immediate behavior. Unit tasks empirically take about 10 seconds. To an approximation, unit tasks are where "the rational rubber meets the mechanistic road." To an approximation, the structure of behavior above the unit task level largely reflects a rational structuring of the task within the constraints of the environment, whereas the structure within and below the unit task level reflects cognitive and biological mechanisms. Phenomena occur at multiple grain sizes of time, and effects propagate in both upward and downward directions: Rational/ecological structuring goes downward from longer time scales of phenomena, and environment and proximal mechanism constraints go upward. A significant claim of the framework adopted by Information Foraging Theory from Newell (1990) and Anderson (2002) is that the phenomena of human cognition can be decomposed and modeled at many different time scales.

Newell (Newell, 1990; Newell & Card, 1985) argued that human behavior arises from a hierarchically organized system in which the basic time scale of operation of each system level increases by a factor of 10 as one moves up the hierarchy (table 1.4). The phenomena at each band in table 1.4 are largely dominated by different kinds of factors. Behavioral analysis at the *biological band* (approximately milliseconds to tens of milliseconds) is dominated by biochemical, biophysical, and especially neural processes, such as the time it takes for a neuron to fire. The *psychological band* of activity (approximately hundreds of milliseconds to tens of seconds) has been the main preoccupation of cognitive psychology (Anderson, 1983, 1993; Newell, 1990). At this time scale, it is assumed that elementary cognitive mechanisms play a major part in shaping behavior. The typical unit of analysis is a single response function, involving a perceptual input stage, a cognitive stage,

TABLE 1.4 Time scale on which human action occurs.

Scale (seconds)	Time Unit	Band
10^7	Months	Social
10^6	Weeks	
10^5	Days	
10^4	Hours	Rational
10^3	10 minutes	
10^2	Minutes	
10^1	10 seconds	Cognitive
10^0	1 second	
10^{-1}	100 milliseconds	
10^{-2}	1 millisecond	Biological

Different bands are quite different phenomenological worlds.

Adapted from Newell (1990, p. 122).

and a stage of action output—for instance, finding a word in the menu of a text editor and moving a mouse to select the menu item. The mechanisms involved at this level of analysis include elementary information processing functions such as memory storage and retrieval, recognition, categorization, comparison of one information element to another, and choosing among alternative actions.

As the time scale of activity increases, "there will be a shift towards characterizing a system ... without regard to the way in which the internal processing accomplishes the linking of action to goals" (Newell, 1990, p. 150). This is the *rational band* of phenomena (minutes to days). The typical unit of analysis at this level is the *task*, which is defined, in part, by a *goal*. It is assumed that an intelligent agent will have *preferences* for *actions* that it *perceives* to be applicable in its *environment* and that it *knows* will move the current situation toward the goal. So, on the one hand, goals, knowledge, perceptions, actions, and preferences shape behavior. On the other hand, the structure, constraints, and resources of the environment in which the task takes place—called the *task environment* (Newell & Simon, 1972)—will also greatly shape behavior. Explanations at the rational band assume that behavior is governed by rational principles and that it is largely shaped by the structure and constraints of the task environment, although it is also realized that people are not infinitely and perfectly rational (Simon, 1955). The rationale for behavior at this level is its adaptive fit to its task environment.

Task Environments and Information Environments

To understand information foraging requires analysis of the environment in addition to analysis of the forager. The importance of the analysis of the environment to psychology was a more general point made by Brunswik (1952) and Simon (1981). It is useful to think of two interrelated environments in which an information forager operates: the *task environment* and the *information environment*. The classical definition of the task environment is that it "refers to an environment coupled with a goal, problem or task—the one for which the motivation of the subject is assumed. It is the task that defines a point of view about the environment, and that, in fact allows an environment to be delimited" (Newell & Simon, 1972, p. 55). The task environment is the scientist's analysis of those aspects of the physical, social, virtual, and cognitive environments that drive human behavior.

The information environment is a tributary of knowledge that permits people to more adaptively engage their task environments. Most of the tasks that we identify as significant problems in our everyday life require that we get more knowledge—become better informed—before taking action. What we know, or do not know, affects how well we function in the important task environments that we face in life. External content provides the means for expanding and improving our abilities. The information environment, in turn, structures our interactions with this content. Our particular analytic viewpoint on the information environment will be determined by the information needs that arise from the embedding task environment. From the standpoint of a psychological analysis, the information environment is delimited and defined in relation to the task environment.

Problem Spaces

A large class of tasks may be understood as variations on problem solving. Indeed, Newell (1990) essentially argued that all of cognition could be understand by taking this stance. Newell and Simon (1972) characterized problem solving formally as a process of *search* through a *problem space*. A problem space consists of an initial situation called the *start state* and some desired situation called the *goal state*. Other situations that may occur while solving the problem are *intermediate states*. Problem-solving *operators* (e.g., actions performed by the problem solver) transform problem states. For instance, the problem faced by a toddler seeking to eat cookies from a cupboard may have an initial state that consists of the child standing on the floor and a chair some distance away, and the child may apply problem-solving operators such as moving the chair, climbing on the chair, and opening the cupboard to transform the initial state toward the goal state. The various states that can be achieved are referred to as a problem space (or sometimes a *state space*). Often, any given problem state is a situation that affords many possible actions (operators). In such cases, each state branches to many possible subsequent states, with each branch in each path corresponding to the application of an operator. The problem is to find some path through the maze of possible states. Finding this path is a process of search through a problem space.

Ill-Structured Problems and Knowledge Search

Well-structured problems, such as puzzles and games, have well-defined initial states, goal states, operators, and other problem constraints, which contrasts with the ill-structured problems. Ill-structured problems, such as choosing a medical treatment or buying a house, typically require additional knowledge from external sources in order to better understand the starting state, to better define a goal, or to specify the actions that are afforded at any given state (Simon, 1973). People typically need to perform *knowledge search* in order to solve their ill-structured problems (e.g., to define aspects of a problem space that permit effective or efficient problem space search). The information environment is a potential source of valuable knowledge that can improve our ability to achieve our goals, especially when they involve ill-structured tasks. More generally, knowledge shapes human functionality, and consequently external access to large volumes of widely variegated knowledge may improve our range of adaptation because we can solve more problems, or solve problems using better approaches.

Knowledge-Level Systems

Knowledge, if it does not determine action, is dead to us.—*Plotinus*

Externally available content provides us with knowledge valuable to the achievement of our goals. Given the central role of external knowledge to Information Foraging Theory, it is useful to review Newell's (1982) influential framework for the study of knowledge systems. This provides a way of characterizing adaptation in terms of knowledge content. This framework, which arises from the cognitive sciences, assumes that knowledge shapes the functionality of our cognitive abilities and that intelligent behavior depends on finding and using the right knowledge at the right time. This framework was largely articulated by Allen Newell (1982, 1990, 1993) and Daniel Dennett (1988, 1991). Traditionally (e.g., Dennett, 1988; Newell, 1990), the information processing system under consideration for analysis is an unaided person or computer program working in some task environment. However, we can extend the approach to understand a system that consists of a person tightly coupled with technological support and access to a teeming world of information.

Over the course of 20 years, Newell (Moore & Newell, 1973; Newell, 1982, 1990; Newell et al., 1992) developed a set of ideas about understanding how physical systems could be scientifically characterized as knowledge systems. A parallel set of ideas was developed by Dennett (1988) in his discussion of intentional systems.[9] The notions developed by Newell and Dennett derive from the philosophical contributions of Brentano (1874/1973). The knowledge level was developed by Newell (1982) as a way to address questions about the nature of knowledge and the nature of scientifically ascribing knowledge to an agent.

In the frame of reference developed by Newell and Dennett, scientific observers ascribe knowledge to behaving systems. A key assumption is that knowledge-level systems can be specified completely by reference to their interaction with the external world, without reference to the mechanical means by which the interactions take place. A knowledge-level system consists of an *agent* behaving in an *environment*. The agent consists of a set of *actions*, a set of *perceptual devices*, a *goal* (of the agent), and a body of *knowledge*. The operation of such systems is governed by the *principle of rationality*: If the agent knows that one of its actions will lead to a situation preferred according to its goal, then it will *intend* the action, which will then be taken if it is possible. As Newell (1982) stated, *knowledge* is "whatever can be ascribed to an agent, such that its behavior can be computed according to the principle of rationality" (p. 105). In essence, the basic observations at the knowledge level are statements of the form:

In situation S, agent A behaves as if it has knowledge K.

Value and Structure of Knowledge

New knowledge is the most valuable commodity on earth. The more truth we have to work with, the richer we become.—*Kurt Vonnegut*, Breakfast of Champions

Our ability to solve ill-structured problems such buying a house, finding a job, or throwing a Super Bowl party is, in large part, a reflection of the particular external knowledge used to structure and solve the problem. Consequently, the value of external content may often ultimately be measured in the improvements to the outcomes of an embedding task. The value of knowledge gained may be measured in terms of what additional value it attains for the agent. Of course, a lot of external content provides no new knowledge (e.g., perhaps it is "old news" to us), or information that does not contribute to our goals.

In simple well-structured problems, the value of knowledge gained from information foraging can be generally expressed as a difference between two strategies: one that rationally uses knowledge acquired by foraging from external information sources to choose among outcomes, and another that does not use such information.[10] For instance, suppose a man who has a budget wants to purchase a product on the Web and knows of a price comparison Web site (e.g., as in the hotel illustration above). If blindly purchasing a product costs a certain expected amount X, but after visiting the price comparison Web site the man will be able to find a less expensive product Y, then the net value of that knowledge will be $X - Y - C$, where C is some measure of the cost of gaining the knowledge. If the analysis in the hotel price illustration above were correct, then the expected price of a hotel (without knowledge) would have been about $86 (see the appendix), but after looking at a Web site, the price would have been $66, and the time cost would be approximately $13 \text{min}/60 \text{min} \times \$10/\text{hr} = \$2$, so the value of the Web site knowledge would be $86 - $66 - $2 = 18. In simple cases such as these, one may imagine that a person could completely construct a decision model in which all possible decision outcomes are specified, as well as the relationships among information sources, potential results from those sources, and the relation of information results gathered to decisions and the utility of those decisions. Indeed, artificial intelligence systems (e.g., Grass &

Zilberstein, 2000) have been developed to use this approach to tackle problems such as purchasing a digital camera, purchasing a removable media device, or choosing a restaurant. Real-world problems, however, typically require a more complicated analysis of the value of knowledge.

Knowledge and Intelligence

Knowledge is of two kinds: we know a subject ourselves, or we know where we can find information upon it.
—*Samuel Johnson*

Physically instantiated cognitive systems are limited in their ability to behave as rational knowledge-level systems. Newell (1990) proposed that "intelligence is the ability to bring to bear all the knowledge that one has in service of one's goals" (p. 90).[11] This corresponds to our everyday notion that we can behave more intelligently by being better informed. In the idealized view of the knowledge level, everything in a body of knowledge (including all possible entailments) is instantly accessible. However, people, or any physical system, can only approximate such perfect intelligent use of knowledge because the ability to bring forth the right knowledge at the right time is physically limited. The laws of physics limit the amount of information that can be stored or processed in a circumscribed portion of space and time. Within those limits, however, intelligence increases with the ability to bring to bear the right knowledge at the right time.

Dennett (1991, pp. 222–223) notes that this conception of knowledge and intelligent reasoning goes back to Plato (*Theaetetus*, 197–198a, Cornford translation). Plato saw knowledge as something that one could possess like a man who keeps captured wild birds in an aviary. There is a sense in which the man has the birds, but a sense in which he has none of them until he can control each bird by calling forth the bird at will. Plato saw intelligent reasoning as not only having the birds but also having the control to bring forth the right bird at the right time.

Newell's discussions focused on unaided intelligent systems (people or computer programs) and the knowledge that they had available in their local memories. But there is a sense in which the world around us provides a vast external memory teeming with knowledge that can be brought forth to remedy a lack on the part of the individual. We can extend Newell's notion of intelligence and argue that intelligence is improved by enhancement of our ability to bring forth the right knowledge at the right time from the external world. Of course, the world (both physical and virtual) shapes the manner in which we can access and transform knowledge-bearing content and thus shapes the degree to which we reason and behave intelligently. The task of acquiring knowledge from external sources is itself a task that can be performed more or less intelligently.

Consider the illustration above in which a hypothetical user searches for hotel prices on the Web. From a knowledge-level perspective, the user has knowledge of how to navigate the Web, operate the Web site search engine, and perform price comparisons. The illustration assumed that the user applies this knowledge flawlessly, but the structure of the Web environment determines the rate at which new knowledge (of hotel prices) is gained. A different design could improve the rate at which the user accomplishes the task. For instance, if the Web site sorted hotels by both quality (star rating) and price, the user could accomplish the task much faster. Although the user's navigation and calculation knowledge has not changed, it is being applied more efficiently because of a change in the information environment. In other words, a change in the information environment has made the user more intelligent.

Rational Analysis

Anderson's rational analysis approach is a specific version of methodological adaptationism applied to the development of cognitive theory. It was inspired by Marr's (1982) influential approach to computer vision, in which Marr argued that visual processing algorithms (and other intelligent information processes) are "likely understood more readily by understanding the nature of the problem being solved than by examining the mechanism (and the hardware) in which it is solved" (p. 92).[12] The term "rational analysis" was inspired by rational choice theory in economics, in which people are assumed to be rational decision makers who optimize their behavioral choices in order to maximize their goals (utility). In rational analysis, however, it is not the person who is the agent of rational choice, but rather it is the selective forces of the environment that choose better biological and behavioral designs.

Anderson has used rational analysis to study the human cognitive architecture by assuming that natural information processing mechanisms involved in such functions as memory (Anderson & Milson, 1989; Anderson & Schooler, 1991) and categorization (Anderson, 1991) were well designed by evolutionary forces to meet the problems posed by the environment. The key assumption behind rational analysis could be stated as

> *Principle of rationality*: The cognitive system optimizes the adaptation of the behavior of the organism.

As developed by Anderson (1990), rational analysis requires a focus on understanding the structure and dynamics of the environment. This understanding provides a rationale for the design of information processing mechanisms. Anderson proposed the following recipe for rational analysis:

1. Precisely specify the goals of the agent.
2. Develop a formal model of the environment to which the agent is adapted.
3. Make minimal assumptions about the computational costs.
4. Derive the optimal behavior of the agent considering items 1–3.
5. Test the optimality predictions against data.
6. Iterate.

Note, generally, the emphasized focus on optimal behavior under given goals and environmental constraints and the minimal assumptions about the computational structure that might produce such behavior.

Probabilistically Textured Environments

Interaction with the information environment differs in a fundamental way from well-defined task environments that have been the dominant paradigms in HCI, such as expert text editing (Card et al., 1983) or telephone assistance (Gray et al., 1993). In contrast to such tasks—in all but the most trivial cases—the information forager must deal with a *probabilistically textured* information environment (Brunswik, 1952). In contrast to application programs such as text editors and spreadsheets, in which actions have fairly determinate outcomes,[13] foraging through a large volume of information involves uncertainties—for a variety of reasons—about the location, quality, relevance, veracity, and so on, of the information sought and the effects of foraging actions. The ecological rationality

of information foraging behavior must be analyzed through the theoretical lens and tools appropriate to *decision making under uncertainty*. The determinate formalisms and determinate cognitive mechanisms that are characteristic of the HCI paradigm are inadequate for the job of theorizing about information foraging in probabilistically textured environments. Models developed in Information Foraging Theory draw upon probabilistic models, and especially Bayesian approaches, and they bear similarity to economic models of decision making (rational choice) under uncertainty and engineering models.

Role of Optimization Analysis

Optimization models[14] are a powerful tool for studying the design features of organisms and artifacts. Consequently, optimization models are often found in the toolbox of the methodological adaptationist (e.g., as found in Anderson's rational analyses). Optimization models are mathematical models borrowed from engineering and economics. They are used to model a rational decision process faced with a problem and constraints. In engineering, they are used as a tool for quantifying the quality of design alternatives with respect to some problem specification. In economics, they are used typically to characterize a rational decision maker choosing among courses of action in order to maximize utility (a *rational choice model*), often operating in situations of limited or uncertain knowledge about possible outcomes. Optimization models in general include the following three major components:

- *Decision assumptions* that specify the decision problem to be analyzed, such as the amount of time to spend on an activity, or whether or not to pursue a particular type of information content.
- *Currency assumptions*, which identify how choices are to be evaluated, such as time or money or other resources.
- *Constraint assumptions*, which limit and define the relationships among decision and currency variables. Examples of constraints include the rate at which a person can navigate through an information access interface, or the value of results returned by bibliographic search technology.

All cognitive agents must reason about the world with limited time, knowledge, and computational power. Consequently, the use of optimization models cannot be taken as a hypothesis that human behavior is omnisciently rational, with perfect information and infinite computational resources. Indeed, unbounded optimization models are likely to fail in predicting any complex behavior. Anderson's (1990) rational analysis approach is based on optimization under constraints. The basic idea is that the constraints of the environment place important shaping limits on the optimization that is possible.

Optimization models, such as rational choice models from economics, allow us to define the behavioral problems that are posed by the environment, and they allow us to determine how well humans (or animals or other cognitive agents) perform on those problems. This does not mean that one assumes that the cognitive agent is performing the same calculations as the optimization models. It is possible that simple mechanisms and heuristics may achieve optimal or near optimal performance once the limits of the environment are taken into account (Todd & Gigerenzer, 2000). This is the essence of *bounded rationality* and the notion that real cognitive agents make choices based on *satisficing* (Simon, 1955).

Generally, "One does not treat the optimization principle as a formula to be applied blindly to any arbitrarily selected attribute of an organism. It is normally brought in as a way of expanding our understanding from an often considerable base of knowledge" (Williams, 1992, p. 62). As eloquently stated by the evolutionary theorist G. C. Williams (1992),

> Organisms are never optimally designed. Designs of organs, developmental programs, etc. are legacies from the past and natural selection can affect them in only two ways. It can adjust the numbers of mutually exclusive designs until they reach frequency-dependent equilibria, often with only one design that excludes alternatives. It can also optimize a design's parameters so as to maximize the fitness attainable with that design under current conditions. This is what is usually meant by optimization in biology. An analogy might be the common wooden-handled, steel-bladed tool design. With different parameter values it could be a knife, a screw driver, or many other kids of tool—*many*, but not *all*. The fixed-blade constraint would rule out turning it into a drill with meshing gears. The wood-and-steel constraint would rule it out as a hand lens. (p. 56, emphasis original)

Activities can be analyzed according to the value of the resource currency returned and costs incurred. Generally, one considers two types of costs: (1) *re-*

source costs and (2) *opportunity costs* (Hames, 1992). Resource costs are the expenditures of calories, money, and so forth, that are incurred by the chosen activity. Opportunity costs are the benefits that could be gained by engaging in other activities but are forfeited by engaging in the chosen activity. For instance, junk mail incurs a resource cost in terms of the amount of money (not to mention trees) involved in delivering the junk, but it also incurs an opportunity cost for the recipients who read the junk because they have forgone gains that could have been made by engaging in other activities.

Production System Theories of Cognition

Production systems have had a successful history in psychology (Anderson et al., 2004; Neches, Langley, & Klahr, 1987) since their introduction into the field by Newell (1973a). The ACT family of production system theories has the longest history of these kinds of cognitive architectures. The seminal version of the ACT theory was presented in Anderson (1976), shortly after Newell's (1973b) challenge to the field of cognitive psychology to build unified theories of cognition, and it has undergone several major revisions since then (Anderson, 1976, 1983, 1990, 1993; Anderson et al., 2004; Anderson & Lebiere, 1998). Until recently, it has been primarily a theory of higher cognition and learning, without the kind of emphasis on perceptual-motor processing found in EPIC (Kieras & Meyer, 1997) or MHP (Card et al., 1983). The success of ACT as a cognitive theory has been historically in the study of memory (Anderson & Milson, 1989; Anderson & Pirolli, 1984), language (Anderson, 1976), problem solving (Anderson, 1993), and categorization (Anderson, 1991). As a learning theory, ACT has been successful (Anderson, 1993) in modeling the acquisition of complex cognitive skills for tasks such as computer programming, geometry, and algebra and in understanding transfer of learning across tasks (Singley & Anderson, 1989). ACT has been strongly tested (Anderson, Boyle, Corbett, & Lewis, 1990) by application in the development of computer tutors, and less so in the area of HCI. The production system models presented in this book are extensions of the ACT theory.

Figure 1.7 presents the basic cognitive architecture used in this book. It couples the basic ACT-R architecture to a module that computes *information scent* (a kind of utility metric), which for convenience I will call the ACT-Scent[15] architecture. This book

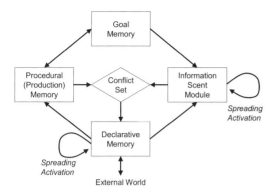

FIGURE 1.7 The ACT-Scent cognitive architecture. Information perceived from the external world is encoded into chunks in declarative memory. Goals and subgoals controlling the flow of cognitive behavior are stored in goal memory. The system matches production rules in production memory against goals and activated information in declarative memory, and those that match form a conflict set. The matched rule instantiations in the conflict set are evaluated by utility computations performed in the information scent module. Based on the utility evaluation, a single production rule instantiation is executed, updates are made to goal memory and declarative memory, if necessary, and the cycle begins again. ACT-Scent uses a process called spreading activation to retrieve information (in declarative memory) and to evaluate productions (in the information scent module).

presents specific models of Web foraging (SNIF-ACT 1.0 and SNIF-ACT 2.0) and Scatter/Gather (Cutting, Karger, Pedersen, & Tukey, 1992) browsing (ACT-IF) that were developed within the ACT-Scent architecture. The architecture includes a declarative memory containing chunks, a procedural memory containing production rules, and a goal stack containing the hierarchy of intentions driving behavior. The information scent module is a new addition to ACT that is used to compute the utility of actions based on an analysis of the relationship of content cues from the user interface to the user's goals. The theory behind this module is described in detail in chapter 4.

Summary

Humans are informavores. We adapt to the world by seeking and using information. As a result, we create a glut of information. This causes a poverty of attention and a greater need to allocate that attention

effectively and efficiently. Information Foraging Theory is being developed to understand and improve human-information interaction. It borrows from optimal foraging theory, but it assumes that humans optimize the gain of information per unit time cost. The following chapters deal with various applications of the framework, method, and theory. This includes analyses of information foraging on the Web, in document browsers, and in social networks. In addition, I discuss design and engineering applications of the theory that illustrate its practical utility.

APPENDIX

The analysis presented in this section is provided for those readers with a background that includes exposure to basic probability theory and who are interested in the mathematics involved in calculating the expected value of searching for better hotel prices in the illustration.

The observed frequency distribution of Paris two-star hotel prices presented in figure 1.2 is presented in figure 1.A.1. Also shown in figure 1.A.1 is a best-fit lognormal distribution, which is typically found for commodity prices and would probably be characteristic of many of the things that one could buy on the Web. The estimate was performed by starting with the maximum likelihood estimates, which can be biased for small samples, and then adjusting the parameters slightly to obtain best linear fits on a Q–Q plot.

A variable X (e.g., prices) is lognormal distributed if the natural log of X, $\ln(X)$, is normal distributed. The probability density function of the lognormal distribution is

$$f(x) = \frac{1}{x\sigma\sqrt{2\pi}}\, e^{-\left(\ln(x)-\mu\right)^2/2\sigma^2}, \qquad (1.A.1)$$

where μ is the mean of $\ln(X)$ and σ is the standard deviation of $\ln(X)$. For the prices in figure 1.A.1, $\mu = 4.45$ and $\sigma = 0.13$. The cumulative distribution function, $F(x)$, for the lognormal is typically computed numerically using the cumulative distribution function Φ for the normal distribution,

$$F(x) = \Phi\left(\frac{\ln(x)-\mu}{\sigma}\right). \qquad (1.A.2)$$

The expected value of a lognormal distributed variable X is

$$E(X) = e^{\mu + \sigma^2/2}, \qquad (1.A.3)$$

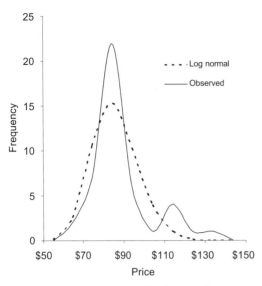

FIGURE 1.A.1 The observed distribution of Paris two-star hotel prices is approximately lognormal, which is typical of commodity prices.

and the variance is

$$\text{var}(X) = (e^{\sigma^2} - 1)e^{2\mu + \sigma^2}. \qquad (1.A.4)$$

The distribution in figure 1.A.1 has an expected value of \$86.35 and a variance of \$127.09.

The expected minimum price in figure 1.3 and expected savings in figure 1.4 were computed from the probability density function of minimum values. Assume that prices are sampled n times from a random variable, such as X characterized above. The minimum value of that sample of size n can be characterized as another random variable Y_n,

$$Y_n = \min\{X_i, X_2, \ldots, X_n\}, \qquad (1.A.5)$$

where the X_i are independent random draws from the random variable X. From the basic definitions of probability, the cumulative density function for the minimum of a random sample of size n, Y_n, is defined as the probability that a randomly sampled value (minimum prices in this case) will be less than some value y,

$$G_n(y) = \Pr(Y_n \leq y), \qquad (1.A.6)$$

which is equivalent to the probability that the minimum Y_n is not greater than y,

$$G_n(y) = 1 - \Pr(Y_n > y). \qquad (1.A.7)$$

The probability, $\Pr(Y_n > y)$, that the minimum value of a sample is greater than some value y would be the

same as the probability that every sampled value from the random variable X was greater than y, so

$$\Pr(Y_n > y) = \Pr(X_1 > y) \cdot \Pr(X_2 > y) \cdots$$
$$\Pr(X_n > y) \qquad (1.A.8)$$
$$= \Pr(X > y)^n.$$

Since the meaning of the cumulative density function for X is

$$F(x) = \Pr(X \leq x), \qquad (1.A.9)$$

one can define

$$\Pr(X > y) = 1 - F(y). \qquad (1.A.10)$$

Now, one can substitute equation 1.A.10 into 1.A.8 into 1.A.7 to get

$$\begin{aligned} G_n(y) &= \Pr(Y_n \leq y) \\ &= 1 - \Pr(Y_n > y) \\ &= 1 - \Pr(X > y)^n \\ &= 1 - [1 - F(y)]^n \end{aligned} \qquad (1.A.11)$$

The probability density function is defined as the derivative of the cumulative density function. So, taking the derivative of equation 1.A.11, the probability density function of the random variable Y_n representing the minimum of a sample of size n drawn from variable X will be

$$g_n(y) = n[1 - F(y)]^{n-1} f(y), \qquad (1.A.12)$$

where the probability density function $f(x)$ and cumulative density function $F(x)$ are for the sampled random variable X. The expected minimum prices and expected savings in figures 1.3 and 1.4 were computed using equation 1.A.5 assuming the probability density function and cumulative distribution function in equations 1.A.1 and 1.A.2, with the parameters $\mu = 4.45$ and $\sigma = 0.13$ estimated in fitting the lognormal in figure 1.A.1.

The utility of production "P3: Next-link" in table 1.1 was computed by determining the expected savings that would be attained by randomly sampling the lognormal distribution of prices in figure 1.A.1 while having a minimum price m already in hand. This expected savings can be computed by integrating over all savings achieved by prices less than m and greater than 0, weighted by the probability of getting those lower prices. So the expected savings to be achieved by a randomly sampled price x given that one has a current minimum price m in hand is

$$S(m) = \int_0^m (m - x) f(x) dx. \qquad (1.A.13)$$

Given the lognormal distribution of prices in figure 1.A.1, if the lowest price found so far were $100, then the expected savings of taking looking at the next price would be

$$S(\$100) = \$14.43.$$

Some other example expected savings would be

$$S(\$90) = \$6.62$$
$$S(\$80) = \$1.86$$
$$S(\$70) = \$0.23$$

Notes

1. http://www-2.cs.cmu.edu/~hzhang/Newell.Good Science.

2. This example is inspired by a microeconomic analysis of the value of information in consumer purchasing by Stigler (1961).

3. For early uses of production systems in psychology, see Newell (1973a) and Newell and Simon (1972). For overviews and history of their use in psychology, see Anderson (1993), and Klahr, Langley, and Neches (1987).

4. For those familiar with ACT-R 5.0, the productions run without the perceptual-motor modules or the subsymbolic computations.

5. Data provided courtesy of Suresh Bhavnani.

6. I purposely use the phrase "maximization tendency" because of the assumption that this is an ongoing process limited by physical and biological bounds on instantaneously achieving omniscient optimality. It is a bounded rationality process.

7. The implicit assumption is that energy translates into fitness.

8. As far as I can tell, the term "human-information interaction" first appeared in the public literature in the title of Gershon (1995).

9. To clarify terminology, what I am calling "knowledge" corresponds to Newell's (e.g., 1982, 1990) use of the term. This, in turn, corresponds to Dennett's use of "belief," which is consistent with common philosophical usage.

10. This definition is based on Pearl (1988, pp. 313–314).

11. Newell's technical definition was that "[a] system is *intelligent* to the degree that it approximates a knowledge-level system" (Newell, 1990). Knowledge-level systems are discussed below.

12. See Glimcher (2003) for how Marr's work inspired a parallel rational analysis approach to understanding neuroscience.

13. Barring bugs, of course.

14. Following natural selection theorist G. C. Williams (1992), I prefer the term "optimization model" over "optimality model" to acknowledge a focus on corrective processes rather than optimal end states.

15. Pronounced "accent."

References

Anderson, J. R. (1976). *Language, memory, and thought.* Hillsdale, NJ: Lawrence Erlbaum Associates.

Anderson, J. R. (1983). *The architecture of cognition.* Cambridge, MA: Harvard University Press.

Anderson, J. R. (1990). *The adaptive character of thought.* Hillsdale, NJ: Lawrence Erlbaum Associates.

Anderson, J. R. (1991). The adaptive nature of human categorization. *Psychological Review, 98,* 409–429.

Anderson, J. R. (1993). *Rules of the mind.* Hillsdale, NJ: Lawrence Erlbaum Associates.

Anderson, J. R. (2002). Spanning seven orders of magnitude: A challenge for cognitive modeling. *Cognitive Science, 26*(1), 85–112.

Anderson, J. R., Bothell, D., Byrne, M. D., Douglass, S., Lebiere, C., & Qin, Y. (2004). An integrated theory of mind. *Psychological Review, 11*(4), 1036–1060.

Anderson, J. R., Boyle, C. F., Corbett, A., & Lewis, M. W. (1990). Cognitive modeling and intelligent tutoring. *Artificial Intelligence, 42,* 7–49.

Anderson, J. R., & Lebiere, C. (1998). *The atomic components of thought.* Mahwah, NJ: Lawrence Erlbaum Associates.

Anderson, J. R., & Milson, R. (1989). Human memory: An adaptive perspective. *Psychological Review, 96,* 703–719.

Anderson, J. R., & Pirolli, P. (1984). Spread of activation. *Journal of Experimental Psychology: Learning, Memory, and Cognition, 10,* 791–798.

Anderson, J. R., & Schooler, L. J. (1991). Reflections of the environment in memory. *Psychological Science, 2,* 396–408.

Bechtel, W. (1985). Realism, instrumentalism, and the intentional stance. *Cognitive Science, 9,* 473–497.

Berners-Lee, T. (1989). *Information management: A proposal.* Geneva, Switzerland: CERN.

Bhavnani, S. K. (2005). Why is it difficult to find comprehensive information? Implications of information scatter for search and design. *Journal of the American Society for Information Science and Technology*, 56(9), 989–1003.

Bhavnani, S. K., Jacob, R. T., Nardine, J., & Peck, F. A. (2003, April). *Exploring the distribution of online healthcare information*. Paper presented at the CHI 2003 Conference on Human Factors in Computing Systems, Fort Lauderdale, FL.

Borgman, C. L., Belkin, N. J., Croft, W. B., Lesk, M. E., & Landauer, T. K. (1988, October). *Retrieval systems for the information seeker: Can the role of intermediary be automated?* Paper presented at the CHI 1988 Conference on Human Factors in Computing Systems, Washington, DC.

Brentano, F. (1973). *Psychology from an empirical standpoint*. New York: Humanities Press. (Original work published 1874)

Brunswik, E. (1952). *The conceptual framework of psychology*. Chicago: University of Chicago Press.

Bush, V. (1945). As we may think. *Atlantic Monthly*, 176, 101–108.

Card, S. K., Moran, T. P., & Newell, A. (1983). *The psychology of human-computer interaction*. Hillsdale, NJ: Lawrence Erlbaum Associates.

Case, D. O. (1991). The collection and use of information by some American historians: A study of motives and methods. *Library Quarterly*, 61, 61–82.

Charnov, E. L. (1976). Optimal foraging: The marginal value theorem. *Theoretical Population Biology*, 9, 129–136.

Cosmides, L., Tooby, J., & Barkow, J. H. (1992). Introduction: Evolutionary psychology and conceptual integration. In J. H. Barkow, L. Cosmides, & J. Tooby (Eds.), *The adapted mind: Evolutionary psychology and the generation of culture* (pp. 3–15). New York: Oxford University Press.

Cutting, D. R., Karger, D. R., Pedersen, J. O., & Tukey, J. W. (1992, June). *Scatter/gather: A cluster-based approach to browsing large document collections*. Paper presented at the 15th annual International ACM Conference on Research and Development in Information Retrieval, New York.

Dawkins, R. (1989). *The extended phenotype*. Oxford: Oxford University Press.

Dennett, D. C. (1983). Intentional systems in cognitive ethology: The "Panglossian Paradigm" revisited. *Behavioral and Brain Sciences*, 6, 343–390.

Dennett, D. C. (1988). *The intentional stance*. Cambridge, MA: Bradford Books, MIT Press.

Dennett, D. C. (1991). *Consciousness explained*. Boston, MA: Little, Brown & Co.

Dennett, D. C. (1995). *Darwin's dangerous idea*. New York: Simon & Schuster.

Dumais, S. T., Furnas, G. W., Landauer, T. K., Deerwester, S., & Harshman, R. (1988, October). *Using latent semantic analysis to improve access to textual information*. Paper presented at the CHI 1988 Conference on Human Factors in Computing Systems, Washington, DC.

Engelbart, D. C. (1962). *Augmenting human intellect: A conceptual framework* (No. AFOSR-3223). Menlo Park, CA: Stanford Research Institute.

Furnas, G. W., Landauer, T. K., Gomez, L. W., & Dumais, S. T. (1987). The vocabulary problem in human-system communication. *Communcations of the ACM*, 30, 964–971.

Gershon, N. (1995, December). Human information interaction. In *Proceedings of the Fourth International World Wide Web Conference*. Retrieved October 29, 2006, from http://www.w3.org/Conferences/WWW4/bofs/hii-bof.html.

Gigerenzer, G. (2000). *Adaptive thinking: Rationality in the real world*. Oxford: Oxford University Press.

Glimcher, P. W. (2003). *Decisions, uncertainty, and the brain: The science of neuroeconomics*. Cambridge, MA: MIT Press.

Grass, J., & Zilberstein, S. (2000). A value-driven system for autonomous information gathering. *Journal of Intelligent Information Systems*, 14, 5–27.

Gray, W. D., John, B. E., & Atwood, M. E. (1993). Project Ernestine: A validation of GOMS for prediction and explanation of real-world task performance. *Human-Computer Interaction*, 8, 237–309.

Hames, R. (1992). Time allocation. In E. A. Smith & B. Winterhalder (Eds.), *Evolutionary ecology and human behavior* (pp. 203–235). New York: de Gruyter.

Johanssen, W. (1911). The genotype conception of heredity. *American Naturalist*, 45, 129–159.

Jones, W. P. (1986, April). *The memory extender personal filing system*. Paper presented at the CHI 1986 Conference Human Factors in Computing System, Boston, MA.

Kieras, D. E., & Meyer, D. E. (1997). An overview of the EPIC architecture for cognition and performance with application to human-computer interaction. *Human-Computer Interaction*, 391–438.

Klahr, D., Langley, P., & Neches, R. (Eds.). (1987). *Production system models of learning and development*. Cambridge, MA: MIT Press.

Lucas, P. (2000, April). *Pervasive information access and the rise of human-information interaction*. Paper presented at the CHI 2000 Human Factors in Computing Systems, The Hague.

Lyman, P., & Varian, H. R. (2003). *How much information*. Retrieved February 2005 from http://www.sims.berkeley.edu/how-much-info-2003.

Malone, T. (1983). How do people organize their desks? Implications for the design of office systems. *ACM Transactions on Office Systems, 1*, 25–32.

Marr, D. (1982). *Vision.* San Francisco: W.H. Freedman.

Mayr, E. (1983). How to carry out the adaptationist program? *American Naturalist, 121*, 324–334.

Miller, G. A. (1983). Informavores. In F. Machlup & U. Mansfield (Eds.), *The study of information: Interdisciplinary messages* (pp. 111–113). New York: Wiley.

Moore, J., & Newell, A. (1973). How can MERLIN understand? In L. Gregg (Ed.), *Knowledge and cognition* (pp. 201–252). Hillsdale, NJ: Lawrence Erlbaum Associates.

Morrison, J. B., Pirolli, P., & Card, S. K. (2001). A taxonomic analysis of what World Wide Web activities significantly impact people's decisions and actions. *CHI 2001, ACM Conference on Human Factors in Computing Systems, CHI Letters, 3*(1), 163–164.

Neches, R., Langley, P., & Klahr, D. (1987). Learning, development, and production systems. In D. Klahr, P. Langley, & R. Neches (Eds.), *Production system models of learning and development* (p. 1). Cambridge, MA: MIT Press.

Newell, A. (1973a). Production systems: Models of control structures. In W. G. Chase (Ed.), *Visual information processing* (pp. 283–308). New York: Academic Press.

Newell, A. (1973b). You can't play 20 questions with nature and win: Projective comments on the paper of this symposium. In W. G. Chase (Ed.), *Visual information processing* (pp. 283–308). New York: Academic Press.

Newell, A. (1982). The knowledge level. *Artificial Intelligence, 18*, 87–127.

Newell, A. (1990). *Unified theories of cognition.* Cambridge, MA: Harvard University Press.

Newell, A. (1993). Reflections on the knowledge level. *Artificial Intelligence, 59*, 31–38.

Newell, A., & Card, S. K. (1985). The prospects for a psychological science in human-computer interactions. *Human-Computer Interaction, 2*, 251–267.

Newell, A., & Simon, H. A. (1972). *Human problem solving.* Englewood Cliffs, NJ: Prentice Hall.

Newell, A., Yost, G., Laird, J. E., Rosenbloom, P. S., & Altmann, E. (1992). Formulating the problem-space computational model. In R. F. Rashid (Ed.), *CMU Computer Science: A 25th anniversary commerative* (pp. 255–293). New York: ACM Press.

Nielsen, J. (2000). *Designing Web usability.* Indianapolis, IN: New Riders.

Oaksford, M., & Chater, N. (Eds.). (1998). *Rational models of cognition.* Oxford: Oxford University Press.

Pearl, J. (1988). *Probabilistic reasoning in intelligent systems: Networks of plausible inference.* Los Altos, CA: Morgan Kaufman.

Pemberton, S. (2003). Hotel heartbreak. *Interactions, 10,* p. 64.

Pirolli, P. (1999). Cognitive engineering models and cognitive architectures in human-computer interaction. In F. T. Durso, R. S. Nickerson, R. W. Schvaneveldt, S. T. Dumais, D. S. Lindsay, & M. T. H. Chi (Eds.), *Handbook of applied cognition* (pp. 441–477). West Sussex, UK: John Wiley & Sons.

Plato (360 B.C.E/1985). *Theaetetus* (F. M. Cornford, Trans.). New York: Prentice-Hall.

Resnikoff, H. L. (1989). *The illusion of reality.* New York: Springer-Verlag.

Ryle, G. (1949). *The concept of mind.* London: Hutchinson.

Simon, H. A. (1955). A behavioral model of rational choice. *Quarterly Journal of Economics, 69,* 99–118.

Simon, H. A. (1971). Designing organizations in an information-rich world. In M. Greenberger (Ed.), *Computers, communications and the public interest* (pp. 37–53). Baltimore, MA: Johns Hopkins University Press.

Simon, H. A. (1973). The structure of ill-structured problems. *Artificial Intelligence, 4,* 181–204.

Simon, H. A. (1981). *The sciences of the artificial* (2nd ed.). Cambridge, MA: MIT Press.

Singley, M. K., & Anderson, J. R. (1989). *Transfer of cognitive skill.* Cambridge, MA: Harvard University Press.

Soper, M. E. (1976). Characteristics and use of personal collections. *Library Quarterly, 46,* 397–415.

Spool, J. M., Scanlon, T., Schroeder, W., Snyder, C., & DeAngelo, T. (1999). *Web site usability.* San Francisco, CA: Morgan Kaufman.

Stephens, D. W., & Krebs, J. R. (1986). *Foraging theory.* Princeton, NJ: Princeton University Press.

Stigler, G. J. (1961). The economics of information. *Journal of Political Economy, 69,* 213–225.

Tinbergen, N. (1963). On the aims and methods of ethology. *Zeitschrift für Tierpsychologie, 20,* 410–463.

Todd, P. M., & Gigerenzer, G. (2000). Simple heuristics that make us smart. *Behavioral and Brain Sciences, 22,* 727–741.

Williams, G. C. (1992). *Natural selection: Domain, levels, and challenges.* New York: Oxford University Press.

Wilson, E. O. (1998). *Consilience.* New York: Knopf.

Winterhalder, B., & Smith, E. A. (1992). Evolutionary ecology and the social sciences. In E. A. Smith & B. Winterhalder (Eds.), *Evolutionary ecology and human behavior* (pp. 3–23). New York: de Gruyter.

2

Elementary Foraging Models

The detailed analyses and models presented in later chapters draw upon various parts of optimal foraging theory as well as other general approaches to rational analysis. This chapter provides a very general overview of the conventional models of optimal foraging (Stephens & Krebs, 1986). These conventional models make unrealistic assumptions about the fine-grained details of cognition—for instance, they assume perfect knowledge of the environment—but at the rational band of analysis (see chapter 1) they provide useful first approximations to information foraging situations. When the details of these models are elaborated by assumptions about the limitations of the cognitive architecture, they have resulted in highly predictive models such as SNIF-ACT (chapter 5) and ACT-IF (chapter 6).

The approach taken in this chapter is to present several basic foraging models and then illustrate the models with idealized examples from food foraging and from information foraging. Like illustrations used in physics that require the assumption of frictionless

surfaces, the examples of food foraging and information foraging are purposely simplified in order to focus the discussion on the rational models. The complexity of the real world will be met head-on in later chapters.

Optimal Foraging Theory

As implied by its name, Information Foraging Theory has drawn heavily upon models and techniques developed in *optimal foraging theory* (Stephens & Krebs, 1986). Optimal foraging theory seeks to explain adaptations of organism structure and behavior to the environmental problems and constraints of foraging for food. Optimal foraging theory originated in attempts to address puzzling findings that arose in ethological studies of food seeking and prey selection among animals (Stephens & Krebs, 1986). For instance, why would a predator eat a particular kind of prey in one environment but ignore the same prey in another environment? It has had an enormous impact in anthropology (Smith & Winterhalder, 1992), where it has been used to explain dietary choice (Kaplan & Hill, 1992), variations in land tenure and food sharing (Smith, 1987), group size (Smith, 1981), habitat choice (Cashdan, 1992), time allocation (Hames, 1992), and many other aspects of hunter-gatherer culture. Independent of the development of Information Foraging Theory, Sandstrom (1994) has suggested that optimal foraging theory may successfully address the complex empirical phenomena that arise in the scientific literatures.

Optimal foraging theory (Stephens & Krebs, 1986) seeks to explain adaptations of organism structure and behavior to the environmental problems and constraints of foraging for food. A key assumption is that animals (including humans) should have well-designed food-seeking strategies because higher rates of energy consumption should generally translate in higher reproductive success.[1] Consider a hypothetical predator, such as a bird of prey. Its fitness will depend on its reproductive success, which in turn will depend on how well it finds food that provides energy. The environment surrounding this bird will have a patchy structure, with different types of habitat (e.g., meadows, woodlots, and ponds) containing different amounts and kinds of prey. For the bird of prey, different types of habitat and prey will yield different amounts of net energy if included in the diet. Furthermore, the different prey types will have different distributions over the environment. For the bird of prey, this means that the different habitats or prey will have different access or navigation costs. Different species of birds of prey might be compared on their ability to extract energy from the environment. Birds are better adapted if they have evolved strategies that better solve the problem of maximizing the amount of energy returned per amount of effort. Conceptually, the optimal forager is one that has the best solution to the problem of maximizing the rate of net energy returned per effort expended, given the constraints of the environment in which it lives.

In their comprehensive survey of the field, Stephens and Krebs (1986) begin with discussion of two conventional models: (a) the *patch model*, which addresses decisions related to searching and exploiting an environment that has a patchy distribution of resources, and (b) the *diet model*, which addresses what kinds of things to eat and what to ignore. I follow their discussion using some simple hypothetical examples. As with many elegant theoretical models, these are certainly wrong in detail, but they provide understanding and insight. It should be noted that there are many other optimal foraging models in the literature that consider many other fascinating decision problems. Stephens and Krebs (1986) provide an excellent introduction to many of these models in behavioral ecology, Winterhalder and Smith (1992b) collect many summary papers in the study of human behavior, Mangel and Clark (1988) present dynamic models of foraging, and Bell (1991) provides an excellent summary of observed food search strategies in the context of optimal foraging theory.

Patch Model

Chapter 1 presents a summary version of Charnov's Marginal Value Theorem (Charnov, 1976), which was developed in optimal foraging theory to deal with predictions of the amount of time an organism would forage in a patch before leaving to search for another. This is the *conventional patch model* in optimal foraging theory. Here, I provide a more detailed account of Charnov's Marginal Value Theorem, and additional mathematical details are presented in the appendix.

Characterizing Foraging in Patches by the Rate of Gain

As discussed in chapter 1, the conventional patch model deals with situations in which organisms face an environment in which food is distributed in a patchy manner. By analogy, information patch models may deal with situations in which the information forager deals with information that is distributed in a patchy manner. For instance, chapters, books, bookshelves, and libraries impose a hierarchical structure on the arrangement of information. Our offices tend to have a patchy structure that evolves from use. For instance, my immediate desk work area may contain a variety of information items that are involved in some current task. Within arms' reach there may be a variety of piles of documents that may contain topically related content (e.g., my pile of papers about foraging theory) or task-related content (e.g., my itinerary and receipts related to a travel expense report). Within the office there are also file cabinets (with a hierarchically organized file system), bookshelves, and books. As discussed in chapter 3, the World Wide Web also exhibits a patchy structure.

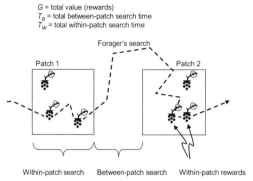

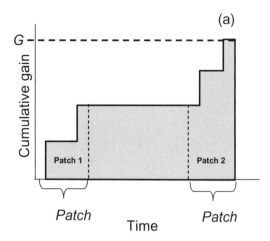

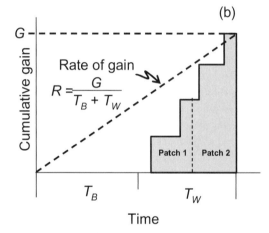

FIGURE 2.1 A hypothetical bird forages in an environment consisting of patches containing berry clusters. The foraging behavior can be characterized in terms of total rewards (G) and time spent between (T_B) and within (T_W) patches.

Figure 2.1 presents the idealized view of a forager assumed in the conventional patch model. It is assumed that a forager, such as a bird, searches through the environment and on occasion encounters a patch of food resources, such as a berry bush containing clusters of berries. The forager must expend some amount of *between-patch* time getting to the next food patch. Once in a patch, the forager engages in *within-patch* foraging and faces the decision of continuing to forage in the patch or leaving to seek a new one. Frequently, as an animal forages within a patch, the amount of food diminishes or depletes. For instance, a bird might deplete the berries on a bush as it eats them. In such cases, there will be a point at which the expected future gains from foraging within a current patch of food diminish to the point that they are less than the expected gains that could be made by leaving the patch and searching for a new one.

To generalize across the two domains of food foraging and information foraging, let us assume that the activity of foraging results in some total gain, G, in some measurable thing of value. In the case of food foraging, this may be the number of calories of energy gained from eating. In the case of information foraging, this might be some other utility that results from achieving a goal. Figure 2.2a is a hypothetical graph of the cumulative gains for the foraging behavior illustrated in figure 2.1. The time expended on the forager's search process proceeds left to right on the abscissa of the graph in figure 2.2a. As depicted in figure 2.1, the hypothetical forager encounters one

FIGURE 2.2 (a) The cumulative gain of rewards for the behavior of the hypothetical forager in figure 2.1, and (b) the average rate of gain R expressed as a ratio of total rewards (G) to the total between-patch time (T_B) and total with-patch time (T_W).

patch, consumes a couple of berry clusters, leaves the patch, searches for a new patch, encounters a second patch, and consumes a couple of more berry clusters. For simplicity, figure 2.2a assumes that the cumulative rewards gained from consuming the berry clusters in figure 2.1 come in discrete chunks. Each time a cluster of berries is consumed, the cumulative gains jump up in figure 2.2a. As time proceeds to the right in figure 2.2a, some gains accumulate in the first patch encountered, no further gains accumulate between patches, and some more gains are added after encountering the second patch.

The patch model assumes that the total foraging time of the hypothetical bird can be divided into two mutually exclusive activities: (a) the total amount of time spent between patches (searching for the next patch), T_B, and (b) exploiting within patches T_W (e.g., handling and consuming the berries).[2] Figure 2.2b is a rearrangement of the plot in figure 2.2a. In figure 2.2b, the right portion of the graph plots the cumulative gains shown in figure 2.2a purely as a function of the within-patch foraging time T_W. Figure 2.2b also graphically illustrates the average rate of gain or rewards, R, which, as will become clear, is the key factor that characterizes the efficiency of the forager. The average rate of gain of value (calories; utility), R, is the ratio of the net value accumulated, G, divided by the total time spent between and with patches:

$$R = \frac{G}{T_B + T_W} \text{ value-units/time cost units.} \quad (2.1)$$

(The appendix lists the definitions of variables used in models throughout this chapter.)

Holling's Disk Equation: Using Averages to Characterize the Rate of Gain

Figure 2.2 (and equation 2.1) characterizes the average rate of gain, R, in terms of total rewards gained and total time taken. This formulation is not particularly useful, but with some additional assumptions, it can be used to develop a way of characterizing the average rate of gain in terms of averages (rather than totals). The assumptions are as follows:

1. The number of patches foraged is linearly related to the amount of time spent in between-patch foraging activities.
2. The average time between patches, when searching, is t_B.
3. The average gain per patch is g.
4. The average time to process each patch is t_W.

On average, as the forager searches for patches, the patches will be encountered at an average rate of

$$\lambda = 1/t_B \text{ patches per unit time.} \quad (2.2)$$

This rate can be used to define the expected total cumulative gain, G, as a linear function of between-patch foraging time,

$$G = \lambda T_B g. \quad (2.3)$$

In equation 2.3, λT_B is the product of the total time spent searching for patches multiplied by the average rate of encountering patches, which produces the expected total number of patches that will be encountered. Since each patch produces an average reward, g, the product $\lambda T_B g$ gives the expected total cumulative gain. Likewise, the expected total amount of within-patch time can be represented as

$$T_W = \lambda T_B t_W. \quad (2.4)$$

Equation 2.4 multiplies the expected number of patches encountered λT_B by the average amount of within-patch foraging time, t_W.

Given the assumptions listed above, equation 2.1 can be rewritten to express the expected average rate of gain,

$$R = \frac{\lambda T_B g}{T_B + \lambda T_B t_W}$$
$$= \frac{\lambda g}{1 + \lambda t_W}. \quad (2.5)$$

This is what is known as *Holling's Disk Equation* (Holling, 1959).[3] In contrast to equation 2.1, which requires knowledge about total times and rewards, Holling's Disk Equation is expressed in terms of averages that could be obtained by sample measurements from an environment. Holling's Disk Equation serves as the basis for deriving several optimal foraging models. Stephens and Charnov (1982) have shown that broadly applicable stochastic assumptions lead asymptotically to equation 2.5 as foraging time grows large.

Additional Characterizations of the Environment: Prevalence and Profitability

Two useful characterizations of the foraging environment can be made using equation 2.5 as context (see figure 2.3). In comparison to some baseline environment containing a patchy distribution of resources (figure 2.3a), another environment may be "richer" because it has a higher *prevalence* of patches (figure 2.3b). In comparison to figure 2.3a, the average time spent between patches is expected to be decrease in figure 2.3b because patches are more prevalent. Another way that the environment can become richer is because the patches themselves yield a higher rate of reward (figure 2.3c). In other words, the patches are more *profitable*.

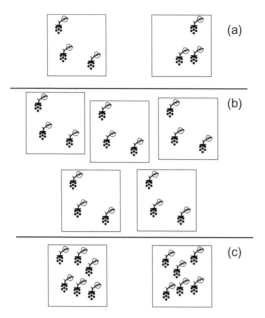

FIGURE 2.3 In comparison to some baseline patchy environment (a), another foraging environment may be richer because patches are more *prevalent* (b) or because the patches themselves are more *profitable* (c).

In Holling's Disk Equation (equation 2.5), the prevalence of patches is captured by λ (the rate of encountering patches). Increased prevalence would mean that the average time between patches, t_B, would decrease, and the rate $\lambda = 1/t_B$ would increase. The profitability, π, of patches can be defined as the a ratio of the net rewards gained from a patch to the time cost of within-patch foraging,

$$\pi = g/t_W.$$

In the context of equation 2.5, increasing the profitability of within-patch activities increases the overall rate of gain, R. Decreasing the between-patch costs, t_B (or equivalently, increasing prevalence λ), increases the overall rate of return, R, toward an asymptote equal to the profitability of patches, $R = \pi$.

Within-Patch Gain Curves

The conventional patch model of optimal foraging theory (Stephens & Krebs, 1986) is an elaboration of equation 2.5. It addresses the optimal allocation of total time to between-patch activities versus within-

patch activities, under certain strong assumptions. Rather than having a fixed average gain per patch and a fixed average within-patch cost, the patch model assumes (a) that there may be different kinds of patches and (b) that the expected gains from a patch can depend on the within-patch foraging time, which is under the control of the forager. The optimization problem is how much time to spend in each kind of patch before leaving to search for another.

The conventional patch model (Stephens & Krebs, 1986) assumes that the environment can be characterized as consisting of P different patch types that can be indexed using $i = 1, 2, \ldots, P$. The conventional patch model assumes that the forager must expend some amount of time going from one patch to the next. Once in a patch, the forager faces the decision of continuing to forage in the patch or leaving to seek a new one. Each type of patch is characterized by

λ_i, the prevalence (or encounter rate) of patches of type i,

t_{Wi}, the patch residence time, which is the amount of time the forager spends within patches of type i, and

$g_i(t_{Wi})$, the gain function for patches of type i that specifies the expected net gain as a function of foraging time spent within type i patches.

As discussed in the appendix, the conventional patch model can be expressed as a variant of Holling's Disk Equation (equation 2.5):

$$R = \frac{\sum_{i=1}^{P} \lambda_i g_i(t_{Wi})}{1 + \sum_{i=1}^{P} \lambda_i t_{Wi}.} \qquad (2.6)$$

The numerator of equation 2.6 sums the expected gains from encountered patches of each type, and the denominator sums the time spent between and within patches.

Figure 2.4 presents a simple kind of gain function. In this example, there is a linear increase in cumulative within-patch gains up to the point at which the patch is depleted. In the information foraging domain, this might occur, for example, for an information forager who collects relevant citations from a finite list of citations returned by a search engine, where the relevant items occur randomly in the list.

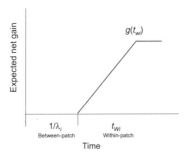

FIGURE 2.4 A gain function, g, characterizing a type of patch that yields rewards as a linear function of within-patch time, up to the point at which the patch is depleted.

As the forager processes the items, the cumulative gain function increases linearly, and when the end of the list is reached, the patch is depleted and the expected cumulative gain function plateaus.

Figure 2.5 illustrates graphically how the average rate of gain, R, will vary with different time allocation policies. Imagine that the forager's environment is composed of just one kind of patch that has the simple linear within-patch gain function that eventually depletes, as illustrated in figure 2.4. Assume that the average time (t_B) spent between patches is $1/\lambda_i$. Imagine that the forager can decide among three possible within-patch time allocation policies, t_1, t_2, and t^*, as illustrated in figure 2.5. To see graphically the average rate of gain R that would be achieved by the different policies, one can plot lines, such as R^*, from the origin and intersecting with the gain function, g_i, at each particular within-patch time policy, such as t_1, t_2, or t^*. The slope of these lines will be the average rate of gain because the slope will correspond to the expected amount of value gained from patches, $g_i(t_{Wi})$, divided by the average time spent in between-patch activities, t_B, and the time spent within patches, t_{Wi}. For cases such as figure 2.5 (linear but finite gains), a line, R^*, tangent to g_i and passing through the origin gives a slope equal to the optimal average rate of gain, and an optimal within-patch time allocation policy of t^*. Policies of staying for shorter periods of time within patches (t_1) or longer (t_2) yield less than optimal average rates of gain. A forger should stay in such linear gain patches until the patches are exhausted (and no longer than that). When the patch is exhausted, the forager should move on the next patch.

Charnov's Marginal Value Theorem

Animals often forage in a patch that will have diminishing returns. The example of the hotel Web site in chapter 1 illustrates diminishing returns in the domain of information foraging. As mentioned in chapter 1, Charnov's (1976) *Marginal Value Theorem* was developed to deal with the analysis of time allocation for patches that yield diminishing returns curves, such as the ones depicted in figure 2.1. The theorem, presented in detail in the appendix, deals with situations in which foraging within a patch has a decelerating expected net gain function, such as those in figure 2.6a. The theorem implies that a forager should remain in a patch as long as the slope of g_i (i.e., the marginal value of g_i) is greater than the average rate of gain R for the environment.

Figure 2.6 shows graphical representations of Charnov's Marginal Value Theorem that appear in many discussions of optimal foraging theory.[4] Figure 2.6a captures the basic relations for the situation in which there is just one kind of patch-gain function. The prevalence of patches in the environment (assuming random distribution) can be captured by either the mean between-patch search time, t_B, or the rate at which patches are encountered is $\lambda = 1/t_B$. To determine the optimal rate of gain, R^*, one draws

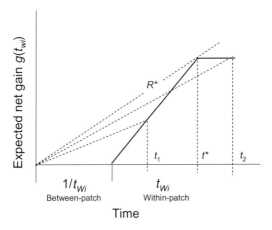

FIGURE 2.5 For the gain function in figure 2.4, a within-patch time allocation policy of t^* yields an optimal rate of gain (which is the slope of the line R^*). Time allocation policies that are less than t^* (e.g., t_1) or more than t^* (e.g., t_2) will yield suboptimal overall rates.

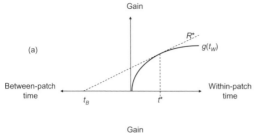

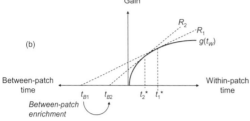

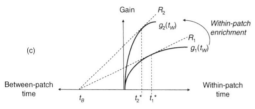

FIGURE 2.6 (a) Charnov's Marginal Value Theorem states that the rate-maximizing time to spend in patch, t^*, occurs when the slope of the within-patch gain function g is equal to the average rate of gain, which is the slope of the tangent line R^*; (b) the average rate of gain increases with decreases in between-patch time costs; and (c) under certain conditions, improvements in the gain function also increase the average rate of gain.

a line tangent to the gain function $g_i(t_W)$ and passing through t_B to the left of the origin. The slope of the tangent will be the optimal rate of gain, R. The point of tangency also provides the optimal allocation to within-patch foraging time, t^*. The point of tangency is the point at which the slope (marginal value) of g_i is equal to the slope of tangent line, which is the average rate of gain R.

To capture figure 2.6 mathematically, for the case in which there is just one kind of patch, let $R(t_W)$ be the overall rate of gain as a function of the time allocation policy, and let g' indicate the marginal value (the derivative or instantaneous slope) of the gain function g. For the case in which there is just

one kind of patch, the patch model in equation 2.6 could be stated as

$$R(t_W) = \frac{\lambda g(t_W)}{1 + \lambda t_W}, \qquad (2.7)$$

Then, Charnov's Marginal Value Theorem says that the optimal time to spend within each patch is that value t^* that satisfies the equation

$$g'(t^*) = R(t^*)$$
$$= \frac{\lambda g(t^*)}{1 + \lambda t^*}. \qquad (2.8)$$

The left side of equation 2.8 is the marginal rate of the expected net within-patch gain function, and the right side is the overall rate of gain. As discussed in more detail in the appendix, for an environment in which there are P types of patches, the overall rate of gain depends on the time allocation policy $\hat{t}_{Wi}$ for each type of patch i. Charnov's Marginal Value Theorem says that the optimal set of $\hat{t}_{Wi}$ value satisfies the condition that the marginal rate of gain for each type of patch is equal to the overall rate of gain,

$$g'_1(\hat{t}_{W1}) = R(\hat{t}_{w1}, \hat{t}_{w2}, \ldots, \hat{t}_{wP})$$
$$g'_2(\hat{t}_{W2}) = R(\hat{t}_{w1}, \hat{t}_{w2}, \ldots, \hat{t}_{wP})$$
$$\vdots \qquad (2.9)$$
$$g'_p(\hat{t}_{WP}) = R(\hat{t}_{w1}, \hat{t}_{w2}, \ldots, \hat{t}_{wp})$$

It should be noted that this more general form of Charnov's Marginal Value Theorem, which deals with multiple kinds of patches, is not neatly captured by the simple one-patch model illustrated in figure 2.6. It is also important to note that the theorem is applied to situations in which the gain function eventually becomes negatively accelerated.

Effects of Between-Patch and Within-Patch Enrichment

The conventional patch models of optimal foraging theory deal with an unmoldable environment. The forager must optimize its selection of feasible strategies to fit the constraints of the environment. The information forager, however, can often mold the environment to fit the available strategies. This process is called *enrichment*.

One kind of environmental enrichment is to reduce the average cost of getting from one information patch to another. That is, the forager can modify the environment so as to minimize the between-patch foraging costs. Office workspaces tend to evolve layouts that seem to minimize the between-patch search cost for needed information. Such enrichment activities create a trade-off problem: Should one invest in reducing between-patch foraging costs, or should one turn to exploiting the patches?

A second kind of environmental enrichment involves making information patches that yield better returns of valuable information. That is, the forager can modify the environment so as to improve within-patch foraging results. For example, one may invest time in constructing and refining keyword queries for a search engine so that it returns lists with higher proportions of potentially relevant document citations. One may also enrich information patches by using filtering processes. For instance, people often filter their readings on a topic by first generating and filtering bibliographic citations and abstracts. Many computer systems for electronic mail, news, and discussion lists now include filters. Such enrichment activities create a trade-off problem: Should one continue to enrich patches to improve future within-patch foraging, or should one turn to exploiting them?

We may use the conventional patch model to reason qualitatively about these enrichment activities. Figure 2.6b illustrates the effects of enrichment activities that reduce between-patch time costs. As between-patch time costs are reduced from t_{B1} to t_{B2}, the overall rate of gain increases from the slope of R_1 to the slope of R_2, and optimal within-patch time decreases from t_1^* to t_2^*. Not only does reducing between-patch costs improve the overall average rate of gain, but also the optimal gain is achieved by spending less time within a patch (when the conditions satisfying Charnov's Marginal Value Theorem hold; see the appendix).

Figure 2.6c illustrates the effects of enrichment activities that improve the returns from a patch. Figure 2.6c shows that as within-patch foraging gains are improved from g_1 to g_2, the optimal average rates of gain improve from the slope of R_1 to R_2 and the optimal within-patch time decreases from t_1^* to t_2^*. Again, within-patch enrichment not only improves the overall rate of gain but also reduces the optimal amount of time needed to spend within patches (when the conditions satisfying Charnov's Marginal Value Theorem hold; see the appendix).

Food Foraging Illustration: Birds and Mealworms

To illustrate concretely the predictions of the conventional patch model, I use data from one of the earliest tests of the model in Cowie (1977). Great tits (*Parus major*) were studied in a large artificial aviary containing artificial trees. The branches of the artificial trees contained sawdust-filled cups containing hidden mealworms. These cups constituted the patches sought out by the birds. Hiding the mealworms in sawdust in the cups produced a diminishing cumulative food-intake curve as in figure 2.6. Travel time was increased experimentally to effect the between-patch enrichment in figure 2.6b. This was done by placing lids on the sawdust-filled cups containing mealworms. Without the lids, the average time to go from one cup to begin feeding in the next cup took about 5 sec, and with the top on the cup the travel time increased to 20 sec. Figure 2.7 shows that—as predicted—the birds had a policy of leaving patches earlier when the interpatch time was shorter (figure 2.7a) than when it was higher (figure 2.7b).

To effect an enrichment of the cumulative gain curves, as in figure 2.6c, Cowie (1977) manipulated the intercatch time of mealworms within the artificial food patches (the cups). As predicted by the model in figure 2.6c, improvements in feeding rates within patches produced shorter within-patch times. Although these empirical studies do find deviations from the conventional patch model, it has been generally successfully studied in a variety of species and environments (Stephens & Krebs, 1986).

Information Foraging Illustration: Search Engines

Chapter 1 presents an illustration involving the search for the lowest two-star hotel price in Paris on a hotel Web site. Imagine an even more idealized case in which there is an information worker whose job is to take information-seeking tasks from a queue that arrives by some electronic means such as e-mail, perform searches on the Web for those tasks, and return as much relevant information as possible overall. Assume that for any given query the search engines return links to documents, and if one were to actually

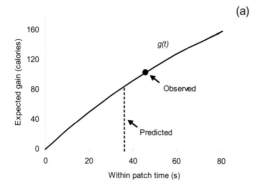

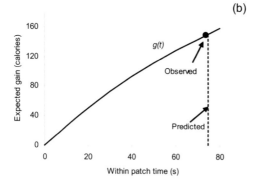

FIGURE 2.7 Increased travel time from (a) $t_B = 4.76$ sec to (b) $t_B = 21.03$ sec increased the observed average patch-leaving time in Great Tits studied in Cowie (1977). The predicted patch-leaving times are indicated by the dashed lines, and are not significantly different from the observed rates.

read each and every document there would be a diminishing returns curve because there is some amount of redundancy among documents and some finite pool of ideas that one is drawing upon. This characterization has been found for medical topics (see figure 1.6) and is likely to be generally true of many domains.

Imagine that the search engines used by the information worker have very little variation in performance. Assume that the worker is very good at examining the search result links and estimating the expected amount of relevant (and previously unencountered) concepts or propositions in each document. Figure 2.8 presents a hypothetical gain curve for the number of relevant concepts or propositions per document as a function of the order in which the documents are returned by the typical search engine used by this hypothetical information worker. The cumulative gain curve, $g_1(t)$, was derived by fitting a

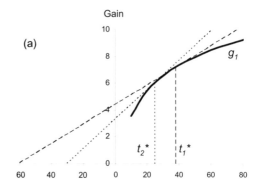

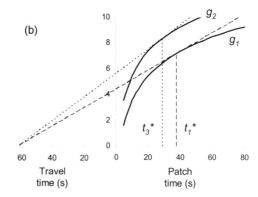

FIGURE 2.8 (a) A reduction in between-patch travel time from 60 s to 30 s reduces the optimal within-patch time allocation from $t_1^* = 38$ s to $t_2^* = 25$ s, and (b) improving the within-patch gain function from g_1 to g_2 reduces the optimal within-patch time allocation from $t_1^* = 38$ s to $t_3^* = 29$ s.

function to the data in Bhavnani et al. (2003) and making the simplifying assumptions that (a) links can be scanned and processed at an average rate of one every 10 seconds (this includes scanning and possibly cutting and pasting the links into a report) and (b) other costs such as scrolling and paging through results can be ignored. The resulting gain function is for the cumulative amount of new information encountered in search results as a function of time,

$$g_1(t) = 2.76 \ln(t) - 2.83 \text{ concepts/sec} \qquad (2.10)$$

Effects of Changes in Travel Time

Figure 2.8 shows the predicted effects on optimal patch residence time of two hypothetical between-patch travel time costs, which would represent the time it takes to acquire a new task, navigate to search engine, formulate and enter a query, and wait for search engine results. In one case the travel time is assumed to be $t_B = 60$ sec, and in the second case it is assumed to be $t_B = 30$ sec. For the case in which travel time is $t_B = 60$, the overall rate of gain R is

$$
\begin{aligned}
R &= \frac{g_1(t_W)}{t_B + t_W} \\
&= \frac{g_1(t_W)}{60 + t_W}.
\end{aligned}
\tag{2.11}
$$

In order to determine the optimal amount of time to spend within information patches, $t_W = t^*$, we need to determine when the slope of $g_1(t_W)$ is equal to R. We can do this by finding the derivative

$$
\begin{aligned}
g_1'(t_W) &= \frac{d}{dt_W} g_1(t_W) \\
&= \frac{d}{dt_W}[2.76 \ln(t_W) - 2.83] \\
&= \frac{2.76}{t_{tW}}
\end{aligned}
\tag{2.12}
$$

and then solving the equality

$$
\begin{aligned}
g'(t^*) &= R \\
\frac{2.76}{t^*} &= \frac{g(t^*)}{60 + t^*} \\
t^* &= 37.50 \text{ sec}.
\end{aligned}
\tag{2.13}
$$

Solving for the case in which the travel time is $t_B = 30$ sec, we find that

$$
\begin{aligned}
\frac{2.76}{t^*} &= \frac{g(t^*)}{30 + t^*} \\
t^* &= 25.06 \text{ sec}.
\end{aligned}
\tag{2.14}
$$

A reduction in travel time of 30 seconds would cause an optimal forager to reduce time in each information patch by nearly 12 seconds. This is shown in figure 2.8.

Effects of Improved Processing of Links

Figure 2.8 shows the predicted effects of an improvement in the rate of processing links from 10 seconds per link to 5 seconds per link. The rate of gain in this case would be

$$
g_2(t_W) = 2.76 \ln(t) - 0.92.
\tag{2.15}
$$

The derivative of the rate of gain remains the same as in equation 2.12. Following the same steps as above, one finds that improving the time to process links would result in the forager reducing the time spent with each patch down to

$$
t^* = 29.22 \text{ sec}.
\tag{2.16}
$$

This reduction in optimal within-patch time allocation is illustrated in figure 2.8.

Summary

The purpose of this illustration is to show the calculations involved in the conventional patch model to make quantitative predictions, as well as to provide a more concrete understanding of the qualitative relationships that it captures. Many simplifying assumptions are made, but later chapters fill in some of the details. Chapters 3–5 present more detailed rational analyses and productions system models of Web use. It should be noted, however, that there is some evidence that changes in travel time on the Web have an effect on patch residence time (Baldi, Frasconi, & Smyth, 2003), as qualitatively predicted by the conventional patch model. In chapter 9, I discuss Web usability advice that centers on this relationship.

Diet Model

Imagine a hypothetical situation in which a bird of prey, such as a red-tailed hawk (*Buteo jamaicensis*), forages in a habitat that contains a variety of prey of various sizes, prevalences, and ease of capture, such as mice, ground squirrels, rabbits, and hares. Typically, such a hawk may soar for hours on end, or perch in a high tree, waiting to detect potential prey. The environment poses the following problem for the predator: What kinds of prey should the predator pursue, and what kinds should be ignored? One may think of this in terms of diet breadth: A broad (generalized) diet will include every type of prey encountered, but a narrow (specialized) diet will include only a few types. If a predator is too specialized, it will spend all of its time searching. If the predator is too generalized, then it will pursue too much unprofitable prey.

The conventional diet model (Stephens & Krebs, 1986) addresses these trade-offs. The diet model assumes (strongly) that

- prey are encountered at a constant rate as a function of search time;
- search and handling (which includes pursuit) are mutually exclusive processes;
- the forager has perfect knowledge about the prey and the environment with respect to prevalence, energetic value, and search and handling costs; and
- information about prey is assessed perfectly and used in a decision instantaneously when prey are encountered.

The details and derivation of the conventional diet model are presented in the appendix. The model assumes that prey can be classified by the forager into $i = 1, 2, \ldots, n$ types and that the forager knows information concerning the profitability and prevalence each kind of prey. The average time between finding prey of type i is t_{Bi}. The rate of encountering prey of type i is assumed to be a random (Poisson) process. So prey will be encountered at a rate

$$\lambda_i = 1/t_{Bi}.$$

Each kind of prey, i, is characterized by the average amount of energy, g_i, that could be gained by pursuing, capturing, and consuming the prey. The average time cost, t_{Wi}, of pursuit, capture, and eating is usually referred to as the *handling cost* associated with the prey type. The profitabilities of each type of prey, π_i, are defined as the energetic value of the prey type divided by the handling time cost of pursuit, capture, and consumption of the prey,

$$\pi_i = \frac{g_i}{t_{Wi}}. \quad (2.17)$$

The diet of a forager can be characterized as the set of available prey types that the organism chooses to pursue when encountered. Let D be a set representing the diet of a forager; for example, $D = \{1, 2, 3\}$ represents a diet consisting of prey types 1, 2, and 3. The average rate of gain, R, yielded by such a diet would be given by another variation on Holling's Disk Equation (equation 2.5),

$$R = \frac{\sum_{i \in D} \lambda_i g_i}{1 + \sum_{i \in D} \lambda_i t_{Wi}}. \quad (2.18)$$

Optimal Diet Selection Algorithm

If we assume that the time costs needed to recognize prey are effectively zero, then an optimal diet can be constructed by choosing prey types in an all-or-none manner according to their profitabilities (this is known as the *zero-one rule*; see the appendix). In general (Stephens & Krebs, 1986), the following algorithm can be used to determine the rate-maximizing subset of the n prey types that should be selected:

- Rank the prey types by their profitability, $\pi_i = g_i/t_{Wi}$. To simplify our presentation, we and let the index i be ordered such that $\pi_1 > \pi_2 > \cdots > \pi_n$.
- Add prey types to the diet in order of increasing rank (i.e., decreasing profitability) until the rate of gain for a diet of the top k prey types is greater than profitability of the $k + 1$st prey type,

$$R(k) = \frac{\sum_{i=1}^{k} \lambda_i g_i}{1 + \sum_{i=1}^{k} \lambda_i t_{Wi}} > \frac{g_{k+1}}{t_{Wk+1}}. \quad (2.19)$$

- The left side of the inequality in equation 2.19 concerns the rate of gain obtained by the diet of the k highest profitability prey types, computed according to equation 2.18. The right side of the inequality concerns the profitability of the $k + 1$st prey type.

Conceptually, one may imagine an iterative process that considers successive diets of the prey types. Initially, the diet, D, contains just the most profitable type, $D = \{1\}$; the next diet considered contains the two most profitable types, $D = \{1, 2\}$; and so on. At each stage, the process tests the rate of gain $R(k)$ for the current diet containing $D = \{1, 2, \ldots, k\}$ types against the profitability of the next type π_{k+1}. As long as the gain of the diet is less than the profitability of the next prey type, $R(k) \leq \pi_{k+1}$, then the process should go on to consider the next diet $D = \{1, 2, \ldots, k+1\}$. Otherwise, the iterative process terminates, and one has obtained the optimal diet. Adding the next prey type would decrease the rate of gain for the diet.

To illustrate this graphically, consider figure 2.9, which presents a set of hypothetical prey types having

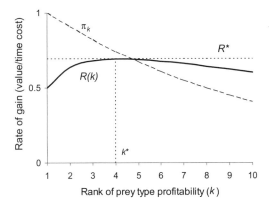

FIGURE 2.9 A hypothetical example of the relationship between profitability (π_k) and rate of gain [$R(k)$] for diets including prey types 1, 2,... k. In this illustration, it is assumed that when the prey types are ranked according to profitability, the profitabilities, π_k, decrease exponentially. The rate of gain, $R(k)$, increases to an optimum R^* as the diet is expanded to include the four highest profitability prey types and decreases if lower ranked types are included.

an exponential distribution of profitabilities indicated by π_k. Assume that these prey types are all encountered at an equal rate of $\lambda_k = 1$. Figure 2.9 also presents $R(k)$ calculated according to equation 2.18, for diets including prey types up to and including each type k. One can see that $R(k)$ increases at first as the diet is expanded up to an optimum diet containing the top four prey types and then decreases as additional items are included in the diet. The optimum, R^*, occurs just prior to the point where $R(k)$ crosses π_k. Increasing the profitability of higher ranked items tends to change the threshold, yielding fewer types of items in the diet. A similar diet-narrowing effect is obtained by increasing the prevalence (λ) of higher ranked prey.

Principles of Diet Selection

The diet selection algorithm suggests the following:

Principle of Lost Opportunity. Intuitively, the information diet model states that a class of items is predicted to be ignored if the profitability, π_i, for those items is less than the expected rate of gain, R, of continuing search for other types of items. This is because the gain obtained by processing items of that low-profitability prey type is less than the lost opportunity to get higher profitability types of items.

Independence of Inclusion from Encounter Rate. An implication of the diet selection algorithm (Stephens & Krebs, 1986) is that the decision to pursue a class of prey is independent of its prevalence. The decision to include lower ranked prey in a diet is solely dependent on their profitability and not on the rate at which they are encountered, λ_i. However, the inclusion of a class of prey is sensitive to changes in the prevalence of more profitable classes of prey. This can be seen by examination of equation 2.19, where λ_i appears on the left side of the inequality but not the right side. Generally, increases in the prevalence of higher profitability prey (or equivalently increases in their encounter rates) make it optimal to be more selective.

Conventional models of optimal foraging theory—the patch model and the diet model—have generally proven to be productive and resilient in addressing food-foraging behaviors studied in the field and the lab (Stephens, 1990). However, these models do not take into account mechanisms that organisms actually use to achieve adaptive foraging strategies. The conventional models also make the strong assumption that the forager has perfect "global" information concerning the environment. Moreover, the models are static rather than dynamic (dependent on changing state or time).

Food Foraging Illustrations

Returning to our hypothetical hawk, imagine that the hawk lives in an environment that hosts two kinds of rabbits (see table 2.1): (1) big rabbits that are scarce, rich in calories, and take a half hour to chase and consume and (2) small rabbits that are plentiful but low in calories, although quickly chased and consumed.[5] Should the hawk pursue just the big rabbits, or should the hawk include both kinds of rabbits in its diet?

From table 2.1, we can calculate the rate of return for the narrow diet that includes only big rabbits:

$$R_{Big} = \frac{g_{Big}\,\lambda_{Big}}{1 + \lambda_{Big}\,t_{Big}} \qquad (2.20)$$

$$= 1.85\,kCal/sec$$

A broad diet that includes both kinds of rabbits turns out to have a lower rate of return:

$$R_{Both} = \frac{g_{Big}\lambda_{Big} + g_{Small}\lambda_{Small}}{1 + \lambda_{Big}t_{Big} + \lambda_{Small}t_{Small}} \qquad (2.21)$$

$$= 1.15\,kCal/sec$$

TABLE 2.1 Hypothetical parameters for a hawk faced with a diet choice problem.

Rabbit Type	Parameters			
	λ	g	t_W	$\pi = g/t_W$
Big	1/3600 sec	10,000 kCal	1800 sec	5.56 kCal/sec
Small	100/3600 sec	100 kCal	120 sec	0.83 kCal/sec

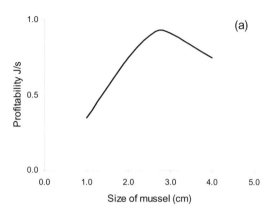

The hawk should spend its time foraging just for big rabbits because they are so profitable (as indicated by g/t_W). Pursuing the small rabbits would incur an opportunity cost that is greater than the gains provided by the small rabbits.

As an exercise, substitute various values for λ_{Small} (the rate of encounter with small rabbits) in equation 2.21, ranging from very low (e.g., $\lambda_{Small} = 1/3600$ sec) to very high (e.g., $\lambda_{Small} = 1/sec$). This will illustrate the principle that inclusion in the diet is independent of the encounter rate. Below I describe as an analogy the junk mail, received by virtually everyone, that has no value whatsoever (i.e., there is always something better to do than read junk mail). No matter how much the rate of delivery of junk increases, it would remain unprofitable to read a single piece of it.

Figure 2.10 presents data that are generally consistent with the predictions of the diet model. Figure 2.10 shows the diet of shore crabs when offered the choice of mussels of different sizes when each type was equally prevalent (Elner & Hughes, 1978). The crabs choose the most profitably sized mussels. Human hunter-gatherers have complex diets that appear to conform to the conventional diet model. For instance, the men of the Aché in Paraguay choose food types that are above the average rate of return for the environment (Kaplan & Hill, 1992).

Information Foraging Examples

The diet model developed in optimal foraging theory is the basis for aspects of information foraging models developed in chapter 6, where it will be used to predict how people select subcollections of documents based on the expected profitability of the subcollections in terms of the rate of extracting relevant documents per unit cost of interaction time. The general analogy is that one may think of an in-

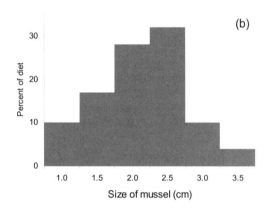

FIGURE 2.10 Shore crabs tend to choose the mussel that has the highest profitability: (a) the profitability curve for mussels as a function of their size is mirrored by (b) the histogram of the size of mussel consumed by shore crabs when presented at equal prevalence in the environment (Elner & Hughes, 1978).

formation forager as an information predator whose aim is to select information prey so as to maximize the rate of gain of information relevant to their task. These information prey might be relevant documents or document collections. Different sources will differ in their access costs or prevalences, and they will differ in profitability. The profitability of an information source may be defined as the value of information gained per unit cost of processing the source. For instance, physical and electronic mail may come from a variety of sources that have different arrival rates and profitabilities. Clearly, low-profitability junk mail should be ignored if it would cost the reader the opportunity of processing more profitable mail. We might also expect the diet of an information forager to broaden or narrow depending on the prevalences and profitabilities of information sources.

The general principles of opportunity cost and independence of inclusion from encounter rate can be illustrated by a hypothetical information foraging example that may resonate with many people who use e-mail. Suppose we observe a woman who runs a small business that she conducts using e-mail. Assume that each e-mail from a prospective customer is an order for the businesswoman's product (let us assume that all other aspects of customer service are handled by others) and that she makes $g_o = \$10$ profit on each order. The businesswoman also receives unsolicited e-mail (junk mail or spam) that occasionally offers some service or product savings of relevance to the woman. Suppose that, on average, 1/100 spam e-mails offers something that saves the woman $10 ($g_s = \$10/100 = \$0.10$), and she receives one spam e-mail a minute (her encounter rate with spam is $\lambda_s = 1/\text{minute}$). Suppose that when she first started her business, the businesswoman received two orders during an 8-hour day (her encounter rate was $\lambda_o = 1/240$ orders per minute), but now it has improved to one order per hour ($\lambda_o = 1/60$ orders per minute). Assume that it takes one minute to read and process an e-mail ($h_0 = h_s = 1$). The analysis in table 2.2 suggests that when the order rate is low ($\lambda_o = 1/240$), the woman should read both orders and spam, but when the rate of the more profitable order e-mails increases (to $\lambda_o = 1/60$), her information diet should narrow to processing just the orders. With the order rate high at $\lambda_o = 1/60$, one should ignore spam re-

gardless of its prevalence (the value of λ_s). In general, as the prevalence of profitable information increases, one should expect a narrowing of the information diet. For the optimal forager who has decided to ignore spam, she should do so regardless of increases in its volume.

Discussion

Optimal foraging theory has been applied with considerable success in the field of behavioral ecology (Stephens, 1990; Stephens & Krebs, 1986) and cultural anthropology (Winterhalder & Smith, 1992a). Historically, the first proposal of an optimal foraging model appeared in MacArthur and Pianka's (1966) model of how the diet of species might change in reaction to invasion by competitor species, which made explicit predictions about how diets would change depending on prey availability. By the 1980s, optimal foraging theory had been used to bring orderly predictions to the study of behavior in hunter-gatherer societies (Smith, 1981, 1987). As noted in chapter 1, optimal foraging theory has arisen from the use of methodological adaptationism. This paradigm, including optimal foraging theory, came under a flurry of attacks precipitated by a paper by Gould and Lewontin (1979), which caused the field to become more rigorous in its methodology and more careful about its philosophy (Mayr, 1983, 1988).[6] While the behavior of real animals and real people often departs from that of the optimal forager, the theory has been very productive in generating useful predictions. Departures from optimality often reveal hidden constraints or other important aspects of the decision problem and environment facing the forager. Once these are revealed, they can feed back into the rational analysis of the forager.

The development of the information foraging models that are presented in the chapters that follow often emerged from considering an elementary optimal foraging theory model and adding detail where necessary. There are certainly differences between food and information, the most notable being that information can be copied, and the same content viewed twice often is not informative the second time around. But it is the nature of metaphors and analogies that they are productive, but not completely equivalent.

TABLE 2.2 Hypothetical rates of return on the e-mail diets of a hypothetical information worker at two different rates of encounter of orders in the e-mail

	Rate of Return ($/min)	
Order Encounter Rate	Orders Only $\dfrac{\lambda_c g_o}{1 + \lambda_o h_o}$	Orders + Spam $\dfrac{\lambda_o g_o + \lambda_s g_s}{1 + \lambda_o h_o + \lambda_s h_s}$
Low ($\lambda_o = 1/240$)	0.041	0.071
High ($\lambda_o = 1/60$)	0.164	0.132

When orders are low, the worker should process both orders and spam. When the orders are high, the worker should ignore spam.

APPENDIX: PATCH RESIDENCE TIME AND DIET MODELS

Patch Residence Time Model

For the patch model, Holling's Disk Equation (equation 2.5) is instantiated (Stephens & Krebs, 1986) as equation 2.6. Assume that patches of type i are encountered with a rate λ_i as a linear function of the total between-patch foraging time, T_B. Now imagine that the forager can decide to set a policy for how much time, t_{Wi}, to spend within each type of patch. The total gain could be represented as

$$G = \sum_{i=1}^{P} \lambda_i T_B g_i(t_{Wi})$$

$$= T_B \sum_{i=1}^{P} \lambda_i g_i(t_{Wi}). \qquad (2.A.1)$$

Likewise, the total amount of time spent within patches could be represented as

TABLE 2.A.1 Notation used in conventional information foraging models.

Notation	Definition
R	Rate of gain of information value per unit time cost
G	Total information value gained
T_B	Total time spent in between-patch foraging
T_W	Total time spent in within-patch foraging
G	Average information value gained per item
g_i	Average information value gained per item of type i
$G(t_W)$	Cumulative value gained in information patches as a function of time t_W
$g_i(t_{Wi})$	Cumulative value gained in information patches of type i as a function of time t_{Wi}
t_B	Average time cost for between-patch foraging
t_W	Average time cost for within-patch foraging
λ	Average rate of encountering information patches
t_{Bi}	Time spent between patches of type i
t_{Wi}	Time spent foraging within patches of type i
λ_i	Average rate of encountering information patches of type i
π_i	Profitability of item type i
pi	Probability of pursuing items of type i (diet decision model)

$$T_W = \sum_{i=1}^{P} \lambda_i T_B t_{Wi}$$

$$= T_B \sum_{i=1}^{P} \lambda_i t_{Wi}. \qquad (2.A.2)$$

The overall average rate of gain will be

$$R = \frac{G}{T_B + T_W}$$

$$= \frac{T_B \sum_{i=1}^{P} \lambda_i g_i(t_{Wi})}{T_B + T_B \sum_{i=1}^{P} \lambda_i t_{Wi}}. \qquad (2.A.3)$$

$$= \frac{\sum_{i=1}^{P} \lambda_i g_i(t_{Wi})}{1 + \sum_{i=1}^{P} \lambda_i t_{Wi}}.$$

Equation 2.A.3 is presented as equation 2.6 in the text as the conventional patch model.

The task is to determine the optimal vector of collection residence times $(t_{W1}, t_{W2}, \ldots, t_{WP})$ for a set of patches, $\rho = \{1, 2, \ldots, i, \ldots P\}$, that maximizes the rate of gain R. To differentiate R in equation 2.A.3 with respect to an arbitrary t_{Wi}, we first get

$$R = \frac{\lambda_i g_i(t_{wi}) + k_i}{c_i + \lambda_i t_{Wi}}, \qquad (2.A.4)$$

where k_i is the sum of all terms in the numerator of equation 2.A.3 not involving t_{Wi},

$$k_i = \sum_{j \in \rho - \{i\}} g_j(t_{Wj}),$$

and c_i is the sum of all terms in the denominator of equation 2.A.3 not involving t_{Wi},

$$c_i = 1 + \sum_{j \in \rho - \{i\}} \lambda_j t_{Wj}.$$

So, for a given t_{Wi}, we get

$$\frac{\partial R}{\partial t_{wi}} = \frac{\lambda_i g_i'(t_{wi})[\lambda_i t_{Wi} + c_i] - \lambda_i[\lambda_i g_i(t_{Wi}) + k_i]}{(\lambda_i t_{Wi} + c_i)^2}. \qquad (2.A.5)$$

R is maximized when $\partial R/\partial t_{Wi} = 0$ (Charnov, 1976), and so

$$g_i'(t_{wi})[\lambda_i t_{wi} + c_i] - [\lambda_i g_i(t_{wi}) + k_i] = 0, \qquad (2.A.6)$$

which becomes

$$g_i'(t_{wi}) = \frac{\lambda_i g_i(t_{wi}) + k_i}{\lambda_i t_{wi} + c_i}, \qquad (2.A.7)$$

so the right-hand side of equation 2.A.4 (average rate of gain) is the same as the right-hand side of equation 2.A.7 (instantaneous rate of gain when the average rate of gain is maximized),

$$g_i'(t_{wi}) = R. \qquad (2.A.8)$$

If we replace R with a function $R(t_{W1}, t_{W2}, \ldots, t_{Wi}, \ldots, t_P)$, the full vector of rate maximizing t_{Wi} values, $(\hat{t}_{w1}, \hat{t}_{w2}, \ldots, \hat{t}_{wp})$, must fulfill the condition specified by

$$\begin{aligned}
g_1'(\hat{t}_{W1}) &= R(\hat{t}_{w1}, \hat{t}_{w2}, \ldots, \hat{t}_{wP}) \\
g_2'(\hat{t}_{W2}) &= R(\hat{t}_{w1}, \hat{t}_{w2}, \ldots, \hat{t}_{wP}) \\
&\vdots \\
g_p'(\hat{t}_{WP}) &= R(\hat{t}_{w1}, \hat{t}_{w2}, \ldots, \hat{t}_{wP})
\end{aligned} \qquad (2.9)$$

This is the formal condition (Charnov, 1976) of Charnov's Marginal Value Theorem: Long-term rate of gain is maximized by choosing patch residence times so that the marginal value (instantaneous rate) of the gain at the time of leaving each patch equals the long-term average rate across all patches.

Diet Model

Following Stephens and Krebs (1986), we assume that the items encountered can be classified into n types. The average rate of gain R can be represented as

$$R = \frac{\sum_{i=1}^{n} p_i \lambda_i g_i}{1 + \sum_{i=1}^{n} p_i \lambda_i t_{wi}}, \qquad (2.A.10)$$

where, for each item type i, λ_i is the encounter rate while searching, t_{Wi} is the expected processing time for each item type, g_i is the expected net currency gain, and p_i is the probability that items of type i should be pursued (the decision variable to be set by the optimization analysis). In the case of food forag-

ing, equation 2.A.10 might be applied under the assumption that the modeled organism partitions the space of the observed feature combinations exhibited by its potential prey into discrete categories, $i = 1$, $2, \ldots n$. One may also think of equation 2.A.10 as being applicable when an organism can predict (recognize) the net gain, processing time, and encounter rate for an encountered prey. To maximize with respect to any given p_i, we differentiate

$$R = \frac{p_i \lambda_i g_i + k_i}{c_i + p_i \lambda_i t_{Wi}}, \qquad (2.A.11)$$

where k_i is the sum of all terms not involving p_i in the numerator of equation 2.A.10 and c_i is the sum of all terms in the denominator not involving p_i, and we assume that the gain, processing time, and encounter rate variables are not dependent on p_i. Differentiating equation 2.A.11 obtains

$$\frac{\partial R}{\partial p_i} = \frac{\lambda_i g_i c_i - \lambda_i t_{Wi} k_i}{(c_i + p_i \lambda_i t_{Wi})^2}. \qquad (2.A.12)$$

Zero-One Rule

Inspection of equation 2.A.12 shows that R is maximized by either $p_i = 1$ or $p_i = 0$ (Stephens & Krebs, 1986). Note that this occurs under the constraint that the time it takes to recognize an item is assumed to be zero. This is known as the *Zero-One Rule*, which simply states that the optimal diet will be one in which items of a given profitability level are chosen in an all-or-none fashion, where profitability, π_i, is defined as

$$\pi_i = \frac{g_i}{t_{Wi}}. \qquad (2.A.13)$$

The decision to set $p_i = 1$ or $p_i = 0$ is reduced to the following rules, which determine the numerator of equation 2.A.12:

Set $p_i = 0$ if $g_i/t_{Wi} < k_i/c_i$ (the profitability for i is less than that for everything else).

Set $p_i = 1$ if $g_i/t_{Wi} < k_i/c_i$ (the profitability for i is greater than that for everything else).

For the n item types, there are n such inequalities. This provides the basis for the diet optimization algorithm presented in the main text.

Notes

1. More strongly stated, the implicit assumption in optimal foraging models is usually that fitness is an increasing linear function of energy, whereas it is more likely that there is a saturating relationship (i.e., at some point, further increases in energy intake have little or no effect on fitness).

2. Note that this assumption does not always apply to real situations. For instance, web-weaving spiders can capture new patches of food (e.g., insects) in their webs while engaged in the activities of consuming a patch of food, and this requires some elaborations to the conventional patch model (McNair, 1983). Pirolli and Card (1998) apply such a model to an information browser that has multithreaded processing.

3. In his seminal work, Holling (1959) developed a model by studying a blindfolded research assistant who was given the task of picking up (foraging for) randomly scattered sandpaper disks—hence the name "disk equation." Holling validated the model later by observing three species of small mammals preying upon sawfly cocoons in controlled experiments.

4. Figure 2.6 also uses the convention in optimal foraging theory in which the average between-patch time is plotted on the horizontal axis starting at the origin and moving to the left, and within-patch time is plotted on the horizontal axis moving to the right. This differs from preceding figures in this book.

5. Wild rabbit has about 500 kCal per pound of meat.

6. This debate is part of a broader one incited by the emergence of sociobiology in the 1970s, which continues to reverberate in the behavioral and social sciences. For a fascinating rendition of this "opera," see Segerstrale (2000).

References

Baldi, P., Frasconi, P., & Smyth, P. (2003). *Modeling the Internet and the Web*. Chichester, UK: Wiley and Sons.

Bell, W. J. (1991). *Searching behavior: The behavioral ecology of finding resources*. London: Chapman & Hall.

Bhavnani, S. K., Jacob, R. T., Nardine, J., & Peck, F. A. (2003). *Exploring the distribution of online healthcare information*. Paper presented at the CHI 2003 Conference on Human Factors in Computing Systems, Fort Lauderdale, FL.

Cashdan, E. (1992). Spatial organization and habitat use. In E. A. Smith & B. Winterhalder (Eds.), *Evolutionary ecology and human behavior* (pp. 237–266). New York: de Gruyer.

Charnov, E. L. (1976). Optimal foraging: The marginal value theorem. *Theoretical Population Biology, 9,* 129–136.

Cowie, R. J. (1977). Optimal foraging in great tits (Parus major). *Nature, 268,* 137–139.

Elner, R. W., & Hughes, R. N. (1978). Energy maximization in the diet of the shore crab, *Carcinus maenas* (L.). *Journal of Animal Ecology, 47,* 103–116.

Gould, S. J., & Lewontin, R. C. (1979). The spandrels of san marcos and the panglossian paradigm: A critique of the adaptationist programme. *Proceedings of the Royal Society of London (B), 205,* 581–598.

Hames, R. (1992). Time allocation. In E. A. Smith & B. Winterhalder (Eds.), *Evolutionary ecology and human behavior* (pp. 203–235). New York: de Gruyter.

Holling, C. S. (1959). Some characteristics of simple types of predation and parasitism. *Canadian Entomology, 91,* 385–398.

Kaplan, H., & Hill, K. (1992). The evolutionary ecology of food acquisition. In E. A. Smith & B. Winterhalder (Eds.), *Evolutionary ecology and human behavior* (pp. 167–201). New York: de Gruyter.

MacArthur, R. H., & Pianka, E. R. (1966). On the optimal use of a patchy environment. *American Naturalist, 100,* 603–609.

Mangel, M., & Clark, C. W. (1988). *Dynamic modeling in behavioral ecology*. Princeton, NJ: Princeton University Press.

Mayr, E. (1983). How to carry out the adaptationist program? *American Naturalist, 121,* 324–334.

Mayr, E. (1988). *Toward a new philosophy of biology*. Cambridge, MA: Harvard University Press.

McNair, J. N. (1983). A class of patch-use strategies. *American Zoologist, 23,* 303–313.

Pirolli, P., & Card, S. K. (1998). Information foraging models of browsers for very large document spaces. In T. Catarci, M. F. Costabile, G. Santucci, & L. Tarantino (Eds.), *Advanced Visual Interfaces Workshop, AVI '98* (pp. 83–93). Aquila, Italy: Association for Computing Machinery.

Sandstrom, P. E. (1994). An optimal foraging approach to information seeking and use. *Library Quarterly, 64,* 414–449.

Segerstrale, U. (2000). *Defenders of the truth: The battle for science in the sociobiology debate and beyond*. Oxford: Oxford University Press.

Smith, E. A. (1981). The application of optimal foraging theory to the analysis of hunter-gatherer group size. In B. Winterhalder & E. A. Smith (Eds.), *Hunter-gatherer foraging strategies* (pp. 36–65). Chicago: University of Chicago.

Smith, E. A. (1987). Optimization theory in anthropology: Applications and critiques. In J. Dupré (Ed.),

The latest on the best (pp. 201–249). Cambridge, MA: MIT Press.

Smith, E. A., & Winterhalder, B. (Eds.). (1992). *Evolutionary ecology and human behavior.* New York: de Gruyter.

Stephens, D. W. (1990). Foraging theory: Up, down, and sideways. *Studies in Avian Biology, 13,* 444–454.

Stephens, D. W., & Charnov, E. L. (1982). Optimal foraging: Some simple stochastic models. *Behavioral Ecology and Sociobiology, 10,* 251–263.

Stephens, D. W., & Krebs, J. R. (1986). *Foraging theory.* Princeton, NJ: Princeton University Press.

Winterhalder, B., & Smith, E. A. (1992a). Evolutionary ecology and the social sciences. In E. A. Smith & B. Winterhalder (Eds.), *Evolutionary ecology and human behavior* (pp. 3–23). New York: de Gruyter.

Winterhalder, B., & Smith, E. A. (Eds.). (1992b). *Evolutionary ecology and human behavior.* New York: de Gruyter.

3

The Ecology of Information Foraging on the World Wide Web

In this chapter, I present some basic analyses of information foraging behavior on the World Wide Web. This analysis has its foundations in Newell and Simon's (1972) methodology for understanding complex human information processing, elaborated with an ecological approach echoing the psychology of Egon Brunswik (1952; Cooksey, 2001). This chapter presents an information processing analysis that focuses simultaneously on understanding the foraging environment posed by the Web and on the human forager whose goal-driven behavior is fashioned by the structure and constraints of that environment. The heart of this analysis deals with laboratory data from participants working on tasks that are representative of those faced by average users in everyday life. The results illustrate how the structure of the Web environment and the goals and heuristics of human information foragers mutually shape foraging behavior.

This chapter is the first of three that deal with information foraging behavior on the Web. The focus of this chapter is on a general analysis of the environment in which the behavior occurs, as well as some general observations about Web foraging behavior. Chapter 4 provides rational analyses of the problems posed by the Web environment, as well as a theory of information scent that concerns how people make navigation decisions. Chapter 5 describes detailed computational cognitive models of users foraging on the Web. This sequence of chapters traces through the rational analysis methodology, in which the theorist asks (a) *what* environmental problem is solved, (b) *why* a given behavioral strategy is a good solution to the problem, and (c) *how* that solution is realized by cognitive mechanisms. The products of this approach include (a) characterizations of the relevant goals and environment, (b) mathematical rational choice models (e.g., optimization models) of idealized behavioral strategies for achieving those goals in that environment, and (c) computational cognitive models.

As noted in chapter 1, we may think of the information foraging environment really as an ecology of two interrelated environments: (a) the task environment that is shaped by the goals of the agent, and (b) the information environment that structures the way the agent can access and process information content into useful knowledge. I begin the discussion with the information environment of the Web and then present the tasks people perform within that environment.

Aspects of the Structure of the Web

Foraging on the Web depends on several key types of virtual locomotion, including navigation through hypermedia links, the use of search engines, the direct typing of URLs (uniform resource locators), and use of browser navigation buttons (e.g., history). Foraging through these structures is shaped by the arrangement of content and navigation cues relevant to users' information needs, so it is worth reviewing some structural properties of the Web before delving into the laboratory study of information foraging on the Web.

Hierarchical Patch Structure of the Web

In keeping with the literature on foraging theory, I refer to groupings of information generically as *information patches*—the idea being that it is easier to navigate and process information that resides within the same patch than to navigate and process information across patches. The term "patch" suggests a locality in which within-patch distances are smaller than between-patch distances. As eloquently presented in Simon's (1962) seminal work on the architecture of complexity, information systems tend to evolve toward hierarchical organizations. In part, this has to do with robustness (failures in a subhierarchy part need not affect the whole), but it also has to do with efficiency. Efficient hierarchically arranged information systems can emerge from decentralized social processes (Resnikoff, 1989). Empirical studies of the Web suggest that it is arranged into hierarchical patches that have evolved through decentralized social evolutionary processes.

The Web is conceptually and structurally arranged into hierarchical patches, although there may be quibbles about exactly how it arranged. The *Web page* constitutes a basic information patch on the Web. Web pages collect together content and a variety of other interactive hypermedia elements such as links, pull-down menus, and search boxes. Web pages often have spatial layouts designed to evoke the perception of different areas related to different kinds of content or interactive activities. For instance, a Web page may have a banner area for advertisements, a site map area for navigation, and several areas each containing content about some topic. *Web sites* typically provide access to Web pages as well as other information technologies (e.g., proprietary databases or consumer services) about some related set of topics or purposes. URLs used to identify and retrieve Web content at a Web site also tend to be structured hierarchically. Large portions of the Web are accessed through *Web portals* that act as central hubs for foraging the Web. These may group links to the Web according to semantic relatedness. Some Web portals, such as Yahoo! or the dmoz Open Directory Project, may contain hundreds of millions of links hierarchically arranged by hundreds of thousands of semantic categories. Web portals such as Google may also use search engine technology to index the Web and dynamically generate links to Web content relevant to a user's query, typically delivered to the user in the form of a Web page. On the Web, lower level information patches, such as Web pages and search result pages, are collected into higher level information patches, such as Web sites and Web portals.

Empirical studies of the link structure of the Web reveal a patchy structure. Web sites tend to have more links to other pages within the same Web site than links to other Web sites. Eiron and McCurley (2003) studied the hierarchical arrangement of the Web in an analysis of 616 million pages from 12.5 million Web sites sampled from a crawl by a computer program of the Web conducted in 2002. Eiron and McCurley divided a sample of 534,894 links into Intradirectory links (as indicated by the URL; see above), Up and Down links (those that go up or down the directory hierarchy), Across links (links within the host Web site that do not belong to the previous categories), and External links that go outside the Web site host. The distribution of links was 41.1% Intradirectory, 11.2% Up, 3.9% Down, 18.7% Across, and 25.0% External (this analysis ignored 0.9% of links that were self-referential). In other words, 75.0% of the links from Web pages go to other Web pages within the same Web site, and 54.8% of the within-site links go to Web pages in the same directory.

Eiron and McCurley (2003) found a strong correlation between the tree distance measured on the directory structure of a Web site (as indicated by the URL structure) and the probability of occurrence of a hyperlink at that distance. In particular, the probability of a hyperlink existing between two Web pages decreases exponentially with their tree distance in the directory structure of a Web site host. Eiron and McCurley suggested that this localization of hyperlinks reflects the social organizations surrounding the authorship process. For instance, the organization of groups within departments, within schools, and within universities might be reflected in a Web site directory structure. Authors will tend to link to pages written by authors they know, and the likelihood of interauthor familiarity will decrease with tree distance in the hierarchy of the social organization, which is often reflected in the Web site directory structure. Regardless of the ultimate evolutionary causes, it is clear that the Web is organized into a hierarchy of patches.

Hubs and Authorities

The link structure of the Web has evolved without any global centralized design. One pattern of interest is the arrangement of connections on the Web, which bears similarity to the structure of scientific literatures. Bibliometrics is the application of quantitative methods in the library sciences to understand the structure and dynamics of information sources and products (Egghe & Rousseau, 1990). One domain of interest for this field is the analysis of scientific literatures using quantitative citation analysis (Garfield, 1979). Scientific publications typically cite previous related works (Merton, 1968). One may think of the literature as a large connected network, with each published paper as a node, with links to other nodes in the network representing citations to previously published papers. Generally, important review papers in a scientific field will have a higher than average number of citation links to other papers. If one wants to learn about some topic, it is useful to find such a review paper.[1] Any assistant professor worried about getting tenure will also tell you that papers that are heavily cited by other papers are considered important. In terms of the network characterization of the citation structure of science, comprehensive review papers will appear as nodes with many links emanating from them, whereas important

papers will appear as nodes with many inbound links (inlinks) from citing papers. Similar kinds of structures appear when the Web is represented as a network, and these structures may be similarly interpreted to indicate their importance in finding useful information. Here, I use the terms "hubs" (when discussing the outbound link [outlink] structure of nodes) and "authorities" (when discussing the inlink structure of nodes) to refer to these structures on the Web, in keeping with terms used by Kleinberg (1999).

In a networked system, a *hub* refers to a node that connects to one or more other nodes, and *hub size* refers to the number of connections emanating from a hub. A Web page with one or more outlinks may be considered a hub in the Web, and hub size would refer to the number of outlinks. Evolutionary social processes have led to a connection pattern on the Web that resembles the network architecture of many other complex systems such as the cellular metabolic system or networks of social relations, in which a small number of hubs have an extremely large hub size (Barabási, 2002; Barabási & Albert, 1999; Barabási, Albert, & Jeong, 2000; Barabási & Bonabeau, 2003). The architecture of such networks is such that the proportion of nodes having a hub size k decays as $k^{-\gamma}$, $\gamma > 1$, which is known as an inverse *power law distribution*. Specifically, the discrete probability of obtaining a node of size k is

$$P(k) = Ck^{-\gamma}, \qquad (3.1)$$

where C is a constant. This power law distribution for hub sizes on the Web (Barabási et al., 2000) appears linear when plotted in log–log coordinates, as illustrated in figure 3.1a. Power law distributions are characterized as being *scale-free*, because the power-law form appears at all length scales and for any arbitrary subrange of k, quite unlike the more familiar Gaussian distribution. Also unlike the Gaussian, the mean of a power law distribution is not the most typical, and in a typical random sample, most of the instances will be less than the mean.

This scale-free hub pattern on the Web has implications for a forager seeking to navigate the link structure from one page to another. In general, the link distance (or degrees of separation in the graph-theoretic sense) to some target page will be smaller from a randomly selected larger hub than from a random smaller hub. Consequently, a forager concerned

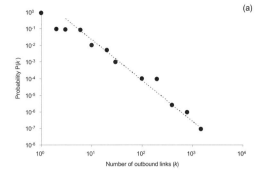

(a)

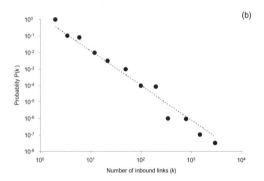

(b)

FIGURE 3.1 (a) The distribution of hub sizes (number of outbound links), k, of pages on the Web is distributed as $P(k) \sim k^{-2.45}$. (b) The distribution of authoritativeness (number of inbound links), k, of pages on the Web is distributed as $P(k) \sim k^{-2.1}$. Based on data presented in Barabási et al. (2000).

with navigation efficiency might adopt the heuristic of seeking larger hubs as a passageway to target content. This seems to be one reason that people often start their Web foraging sessions by going to a large Web portal. Hubs are important because they reduce the cost structure of search. Of course, as one acquires knowledge about the location of Web content relevant to specific tasks, one would use that knowledge to go directly to those locations.

The distribution of inlinks to Web pages (Barabási et al., 2000) also conforms to a scale-free power law (figure 3.1b). A node representing a Web page with one or more inlinks is called an *authority*, and its *authoritativeness* is the number of inlinks from other Web pages. Figure 3.1b presents the proportion of Web pages according to the number of inlinks that connect to those pages. As in figure 3.1a, the distribution in figure 3.1b appears linear when plotted in log–log coordinates, indicating a scale-free power law

distribution. Authoritativeness (number of inlinks) is a good heuristic for judging the relevance of a Web page because inlinks indicate that someone, somewhere, once attended to a particular page and made the judgment that it was worthwhile to create a link for other people to follow. Each link is a kind of implicit recommendation by someone (although the purpose behind that recommendation certainly can range from social benevolence to outright scamming self-interest). The use of authoritativeness as a heuristic for computing the relevance of Web pages is employed in several retrieval algorithms, most notably the PageRank algorithm that underlies the Google search engine (Brin & Page, 1998).

The distribution in figure 3.1b implies that a forager that randomly walks about the link structure of the Web would most frequently end up at Web pages with high authoritativeness. Pages with high authoritativeness would be attractors for foragers operating by blind link choice, but it is also the case that foragers knowingly choose links that seem to be frequently recommended. Authoritativeness and hub size have a weak but significant correlation, which might be the result of socially constructed recommendations for important hubs. Data from a 1997 crawl of the Web by Alexa.com analyzed extensively in Pitkow (1997) and Adamic (2001) show a Spearman correlation of $\rho = 0.23$ (for $N = 259,795$ Web sites) between the rank of a Web site's hub size and its authoritativeness.[2] Evolutionary social processes have tended to create a networked environment that contains attractors (authorities) that tend to draw foragers to socially recommended information and to hubs that are likely to reduce the cost of effort of finding important information.

Topical Patches and Gradients of Relevance

Users often surf the Web seeking content related to some topic of interest, and the Web tends to be organized into topical localities. Davison (2000) analyzed the topical locality of the Web using 200,998 Web pages sampled from approximately 3 million pages crawled in 1999. Davison assessed the topical similarity of pairs of Web pages from this sample that were Linked (had a link between them), Siblings (linked from the same parent page), and Random (selected at random). The similarities were computed by a normalized correlation[3] or cosine measure, r, on the vectors of the word frequencies in a pair of documents (Manning & Schuetze, 1999).[4] The Linked pages showed greater textual similarity ($r = .23$) than did Sibling pages ($r = .20$), but both were substantially more similar than were Random pairs of pages ($r = .02$).

Figure 3.2 is a concrete example of how topical similarity between pages diminishes with the link distance between them. To produce figure 3.2, I used data collected from the Xerox.com Web site in May 1998 (used for another purpose in Pitkow & Pirolli, 1999), and I computed the page-to-page content similarities for all pairs of pages at minimum distances of 1, 2, 3, 4, and 5 degrees of separation (link distance). The similarities were computed by comparing normalized correlations of vectors of the word frequencies in a pair of documents (Manning & Schuetze, 1999). Figure 3.2 shows that the similarity of the content of pages diminishes rapidly as a function of shortest link distance separating them. Figure 3.2 suggests that the Web has topically related information patches.

Of course, what users actually see as "links" on the Web are snippets of text and graphics. Davison (2000) compared elaborated anchor text (the anchor plus additional surrounding text, having a mean of 11.02 terms) to a paired document that was either Linked (the page linked to the anchor) or Random (a random page). The normalized correlation (cosine) similarities were Linked $r = .16$ and Random $r \approx 0$. Davison's analysis of the correlation of proximal cues to distal content confirms our intuition that the cues have ecological validity.

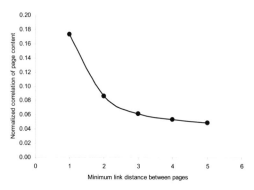

FIGURE 3.2 The similarity (normalized correlation of document content) of pairs of Web pages as a function of the minimum link distances separating the pairs. Data collected from the Xerox.com Web site, May 1998.

Cues associated with links (which are characterized as information scent in chapter 4) are expected to be useful to the information forager in at least two ways. First, link cues provide a way of judging the utility of following alternative paths (i.e., choosing a link from a set of links presented on a Web page). Second, link cues provide a way of detecting that one is moving out of a patch of topical relevance (i.e., by detecting that the utility of information is dwindling as in figure 3.2).

Search Results as Patches with Diminishing Returns

Many large Web portals, such as Google or Yahoo!, provide search engines that retrieve documents from the Web in response to users' queries. The general goal of these search engines to allow users to enter in some representation of their information need (typically as a list of words or phrases) and return a list of easily scanned representations (e.g., link anchor text, or bibliographic citations) of documents that are ranked according to their predicted relevance to the users' needs. Generally, for a forager scanning down a set of search results, there are diminishing returns: The likelihood that a "more relevant" document will be found with more future foraging effort diminishes as a function of how many result items have already been scanned. Generally, a Web forager will be interested in Web search services that frequently give the highest rankings to the "most relevant" items to the user (ideally, the "best" items for any user should always be ranked number one). In economics terms, such search engines provide sharply diminishing marginal returns.

Chapter 1 presents an analysis of a hotel Web site illustrating how one could view search engine results as information patches with diminishing returns for foraging. The hotel Web site example focuses on the relation between price savings and information forging. One may perform a similar analysis of searching for the maximum value (as opposed to minimum price), as might occur in searching for a maximally relevant document or the best product. I believe that a similar related analysis applies to the diminishing returns of foraging for information to understand some particular topic.

Summary

Empirical analyses suggest that the ecology of the information forager on the Web is organized in a hierarchical arrangement of information patches. A number of hypotheses emerge from these observations. The patchy structure of the Web might lead to behavior that is organized around those patches. A forager might be expected to seek out patches of high utility and to leave patches when diminishing returns are detected. The link structure of the Web exhibits scale-free power law distributions of inlinks (authorities) and outlinks (hubs). These regularities might also be exploited by the forager. Information hubs might be expected to be preferred because they are likely to minimize expected costs. Information authorities might be preferred because they are cited by many people (a property exploited in some search engines).

This section has focused on structural regularities in the information environment. The next section turns to discussion of the ecology of task environments in which Web foragers operate.

Representative Web Tasks

Brunswik (1952, 1956) developed the method of *representative design* for ensuring that experimental results would be *ecologically valid*—that results would generalize from the laboratory to important tasks in real world. The basic idea behind this method is to utilize experimental conditions (materials, tasks, etc.) that reflect conditions of the world. Others (notably, Gibson, 1979; Neisser, 1976) have argued strongly that human psychology is exquisitely adapted to its environment and, consequently, is best revealed through the study of tasks and stimuli representatively sampled from the environment.[5] To study how people forage for information on the Web, my colleagues Julie Morrison and Stuart Card and I decided to perform a survey to collect and analyze real-world Web tasks. The purpose of this study (reported in part in Morrison, Pirolli, & Card, 2001) was to develop a taxonomic analysis of the types of Web tasks people view as important along with a catalog of concrete examples. This taxonomy would be the basis for developing laboratory Web tasks.

To collect descriptions of Web tasks, we inserted a survey question into the GVU Tenth WWW User Survey (Kehoe, Pitkow, Sutton, & Aggarwal, 1999) conducted October through December 1998 by the Graphics, Visualization, and Usability Center at the Georgia Institute of Technology (henceforth, the

GVU *Survey*). From 1994 through 1998, the GVU Survey collected information from online surveys on Internet demographics, culture, e-commerce, advertising, user attitudes, and usage patterns. The survey question (henceforth, the *Significance Question*) we used was a variation on those used in the Critical Incident Technique:

> Please try to recall a recent instance in which you found important information on the World Wide Web; information that led to a significant action or decision. Please describe that incident in enough detail so that we can visualize the situation.

The Critical Incident Technique originated in studies of aviation psychology conducted during World War II (Fitts & Jones, 1961), achieved wider recognition with the work of Flanagan (1954), and has evolved many variations in human factors (Shattuck & Woods, 1994), cognitive task analysis (Klein, Calderwood, & Macgregor, 1989), usability (Hartson & Castillo, 1998), and Web use in particular (Choo, Detlor, & Turnbull, 1998). The key idea in this technique is to ask users to report a *critical incident*, which is an event or task that is a significant indicator (either positive or negative) of some factor of interest in the study. The Critical Incident Technique and its variants provide a way to obtain concrete descriptions of events or tasks that are identified as critical (important, significant) by typical people operating in real-world situations. It is aimed at obtaining not a random sample of tasks or events (which is a weak, general method of understanding the world), but rather a sample of tasks or events that are revealing of the domain. As noted by Nielsen (2001), the use of Critical Incident Technique on the Web is also useful in identifying important value-added tasks for Web provider and for gaining insights for innovations on the Web.

Method

Participants in the GVU Survey responded to questionnaires posted on the Web. Participants were solicited through announcements on Internet-related newsgroups, banners randomly rotated on high-exposure Web sites, banners randomly rotated through advertising networks, announcements made to the Web-surveying mailing list maintained by the GVU Survey team, and announcements in the general media. Participants were offered the chance to win a $100 prize for doing the survey. The sampling was not truly random; however, every effort was made to randomly broadcast announcements on highly trafficked areas of the Web.[6] The results of the GVU Survey (Kehoe et al., 1999) include detailed demographic data that can be used to compare the GVU Survey sample to others.

The Significance Question quoted above was part of a subsection of the survey on computer, Web, and Internet use. A total of $N = 2,188$ people responded to the Significance Question, whereas $N = 3,292$ peo-92 people cumulatively responded to questions in the computer, Web, and Internet use section. The highest rate of response was obtained in the demographic section of the survey: $N = 5,022$ respondents.

Results

Demographics

Tables 3.1 and 3.2 provide summary demographic data from the $N = 2,188$ participants who answered the Significance Question, along with comparison data from the Pew Internet and American Life Project's report *Internet Use by Region in the United States* (Spooner, 2003; henceforth the *Pew Survey*). The Pew Survey was based on a daily tracking survey based on telephone interviews conducted by the Princeton Survey Research Associates using a random digit sample of telephone numbers from U.S. telephone exchanges in 2000, 2001, and 2002. Survey results from Internet users ($N = 10,879$) in the Pew Survey

TABLE 3.1 Comparison of age demographics: sample answering the Significance Question in the GVU Survey versus U.S. Internet users in the Pew Survey.

Significance Question (1999)		Pew Survey (2001)	
Age	Percentage	Age	Percentage
16–25	16.1%	18–24	17.2%
26–35	28.5%	25–34	23.2%
36–45	26.2%	35–44	25.8%
46–55	20.0%	45–54	19.8%
56–65	6.8%	55–64	9.6%
66+	2.4%	65+	4.3%

Note: Significance Question percentages are based on $N = 2,148$, which excludes 17 responses in the 11–15 year age group and 23 nonrespondents.

TABLE 3.2 Comparison of sex, race, and income demographics: sample answering the Significance Question in the GVU Survey versus U.S. Internet users in the Pew Survey.

	Significance Question (1999)	Pew Survey (2001)
Sex		
Male	64.8%	49.9%
Female	35.2%	50.1%
Race[1]		
White, non-Hispanic	91.8%	78.0%
Black, non-Hispanic	1.4%	8.2%
Hispanic	1.3%	9.2%
Other	5.5%	4.7%
Income[2]		
Less than $30,000	17.3%	22.7%
$30,000 to $50,000	27.9%	26.8%
$50,000 to $75,000	26.1%	22.5%
More than $75,000	28.7%	28.0%

[1]Excludes 49 nonrespondents for the Significance Question.

[2]Excludes 307 nonrespondents for the Significance Question and 16.5% "Don't know" responses for the Pew Survey.

were based on the 2001 samples and had a margin of sampling error of ±1 percentage point.

Table 3.1 presents a comparison of the ages of the respondents to the Significance Question to the age distribution of U.S. Internet users estimated by the Pew Survey. Note that there are minor differences in the age range defined in the two surveys. Ignoring these minor coding differences, and comparing the surveys by row in table 3.1, the Significance Question of the GVU Survey differs by less than 6 percentage points in all age categories. Table 3.2 presents additional demographic comparisons between the Significance Question and the Pew Survey. Table 3.2 suggests that the Significance Question sample is biased toward white males in comparison to the Pew Survey estimates of the sex and race of the U.S. Internet population.

Tables 3.3 and 3.4 provide comparisons of the frequency of Internet or Web use for the Significance Question and the Pew Survey. It appears that the Significance Question respondents were more frequent users of the Web than the U.S. Internet population as a whole. Table 3.5 provides a comparison of the Internet experience of the Significance Question respondents to the Pew Survey estimates. Table 3.5 suggests that the Significance Question respondents

TABLE 3.3 Frequency of accessing the Web by respondents to the Significance Question.

	Home	Work	School	Public	Other
Daily	79.5%	60.8%	10.7%	0.8%	1.8%
Weekly	13.8%	6.7%	5.3%	2.0%	4.2%
Monthly	1.1%	1.2%	2.0%	4.3%	7.8%
Less than once/month	1.9%	1.8%	3.3%	23.7%	30.6%
Never	3.7%	29.5%	78.7%	69.1%	55.6%

were more experienced than the U.S. Internet population as a whole. The GVU Survey methodology, which focuses solicitations around high-volume Web content, is probably biased toward high-frequency, more experienced users. This actually suits our goal, which was to obtain more expert and experienced assessments of critical Web tasks.

Taxonomic Coding

Two researchers developed the taxonomic coding scheme for responses to the Significance Question, based initially on earlier work (Choo et al., 1998). Over three iterations, the two researchers independently coded the samples of N = 100 responses. After each iteration, the independent codings were compared, discrepancies were discussed, and a revised set of coding definitions were produced for the next round of coding. The resulting coding scheme was organized into three taxonomies: *Purpose taxonomy*, concerning the respondents' reasons for using the Web, *Method taxonomy*, concerning the respondents' methods for achieving their goals, and *Content taxonomy*, concerning the type of information sought or used by the respondents. These coding schemes are illustrated in the appendix. The intercoder reliabilities after the third iteration of developing the

TABLE 3.4 Frequency of accessing Internet in the Pew Survey.

Frequency	Percentage
Several times a day	37.1%
About once a day	25.5%
3–5 days a week	16.2%
1–2 days a week	12.0%
Every few weeks	3.6%
Less often	2.5%
Do not know	3.1%

TABLE 3.5 Time when users started using the Internet.

	Significance Question	Pew Survey
Less than 6 months	3.7%	7.5%
Less than 1 year	7.1%	14.5%
2 or 3 years ago	32.9%	33.9%
More than 3 years ago	56.3%	44.0%

coding scheme were $\alpha = 0.86$ for the Purpose Taxonomy, $\alpha = 0.94$ for the Method Taxonomy, and $\alpha = 0.92$ for the Content Taxonomy.

Response Distributions

Tables 3.6–3.8 show the response distributions coded for the three taxonomies. Table 3.6, which shows the distribution of significant tasks for the Purpose Taxonomy, shows that 25% of the significant tasks involved finding some fact, document, product, or software download, and 75% of significant tasks involved some more complex sense-making task such as making a choice or comparison (51%) or understanding some topic area (24%).

Table 3.7, which presents the response distribution for the Method Taxonomy, shows that critical events were rarely reported to have occurred during Web exploration (2%) or everyday monitoring (2%). To achieve their critical tasks, respondents engaged in directed finding of specific information items (25%) or multiple information items (71%).

Table 3.8 shows the distribution of responses coded in the Content Taxonomy. Foraging for information related to products accounts for 30% of the significant tasks reported by respondents. Foraging for

TABLE 3.6 Distribution of responses to the Significance Question categorized by the purpose for using the Web.

Purpose for Using the Web	Percentage of Respondents
Compare/choose a product or service	51%
Understand some topic	24%
Find a fact	15%
Find a document	6%
Find a product	2%
Find a download	2%

TABLE 3.7 Distribution of responses to the Significance Question categorized by the method used.

Method of Using the Web	Percentage of Respondents
Collect multiple pieces of information	71%
Find particular fact or document	25%
Explore to find what is on the Web	2%
Monitor information	2%

medical information was also a substantial (18%) proportion of the significant tasks. This is plausible given the importance most people attach to their own health and the health of friends and relatives. Another recent report from the Pew Internet and American Life Project (Fox & Fallows, 2003) indicates a growing trend in seeking health-related information among Internet users. Fox and Fallows (2003) report that seeking health information is the third most popular activity on the Internet (80% of adult Internet users have searched for health content), following e-mail (93%) and researching a product or service (83%).

Not surprisingly, the tasks people identify in response to the Significance Question do not reflect what people normally, or typically, do on the Web. Table 3.9 presents comparisons illustrating this divergence. The Web and Internet usage section of the GVU Survey contained the question, "The Web is a versatile tool. Please indicate how often you have used the Web for each of the following categories

TABLE 3.8 Distribution of responses to the Significance Question categorized by the content being sought.

Content Sought	Percentage of Respondents
Medical	18%
Computer	17%
People	13%
Business	7%
Travel	7%
Education	6%
Vehicle	6%
Job	6%
Other products	6%
Finance	4%
Download	1%
News	1%
Miscellaneous	8%

TABLE 3.9 Comparison of Web/Internet activities reported by participants and tasks identified as "significant."

Category	Web and Internet Usage Activities Section	Significance Question
Electronic news	26%	1%
Medical information	13%	18%
Product information/ purchase	37%	30%
Financial information	16%	4%
Job search	8%	6%

during the past 6 months." Table 3.9 presents responses to this question from users who used the Internet on a monthly or more frequent basis alongside comparable categories from the Significance Question. Reading electronic news is a typical task; it rarely is identified as significant.

Summary

Responses to our survey revealed that significant Web tasks are ones in which users are goal driven. Three times as many users reported seeking multiple pieces of information in response to a goal compared to users seeking a single piece of information. The analysis of stated purposes showed the importance of larger scale sense-making activities driving Web foraging, involving the collection of information, understanding it, making comparisons, and making decisions. What is surprising about these results is that the Web is mainly aimed at helping users find specific pieces of information (e.g., through search engines), and this suggests that there is a latent demand for tools to support these broader sense-making activities.

A Laboratory Study of Web Users

Detailed protocol analysis studies have often laid the foundation for the development of models of cognition in complex, semantically rich domains. A study initially reported by Card et al. (2001) was conducted in order to develop a base protocol analysis methodology and to begin to understand behavior and cognition involved in basic information foraging on the Web. These analyses are the basis for developing the SNIF-ACT computational cognitive model presented in chapter 5.

Protocol analysis (Ericsson & Simon, 1984; Newell & Simon, 1972) is a method (or perhaps a family of methods) concerned with identifying cognitive states, their content, and cognitive processes involved in complex tasks such as problem solving. Seminal studies using protocol analysis (e.g., Newell & Simon, 1972) required that participants in experiments think aloud to produce audio recordings while performing a task. Under the right conditions, thinking aloud is assumed to provide data concerning the information that is currently heeded, including goals and the contents of working memory. Classic verbal protocol analysis of problem-solving tasks involves transcribing verbalizations from audio recordings and then coding the verbalizations to identify states of cognitive content. In such studies (e.g., Newell & Simon, 1972), these data are interpreted as reflecting states of search through a problem space and states of knowledge. In our laboratory study of Web behavior, rather than use audio recordings of think-aloud protocols, we used a more elaborate set of instrumentation, including video recordings of participants thinking aloud, logs of Web browser activity, and an eye tracker.

An earlier study of Web users employing verbal protocol analysis techniques was reported by Byrne, John, Wehrle, and Crowe (1999). That study used a day-in-the-life technique whereby all Web interactions were video recorded for one day for a number of individuals who thought aloud while using the Web. The day-in-the-life technique is another method for obtaining and studying real-world tasks. Our goal was to bring realistic Web tasks into the laboratory in order to perform replicable experimental studies in which the same tasks are performed by many people, and the same person performs a variety of tasks.

Method

Participants

A total of $N = 14$ Stanford students participated in the study. Of those students in study, $N = 4$ were subject to detailed analysis.

Materials

Six tasks were developed for the study based on six responses to the Significance Question. The two tasks analyzed in detail, and their original survey sources, are listed in table 3.10.

TABLE 3.10 Tasks analyzed in detail in the laboratory study of Web users.

Task Name	Task	Source Response to Significance Question
City	You are the Chair of Comedic events for Louisiana State University in Baton Rouge. Your computer has just crashed and you have lost several advertisements for upcoming events. You know that the Second City tour is coming to your theater in the spring, but you do not know the precise date. Find the date the comedy troupe is playing on your campus. Also find a photograph of the group to put on the advertisement.	"Searched and found (using Yahoo Canada) for a comedy troupe web site to copy their photo for a poster to be printed and distributed locally for an upcoming community event."
Antz	After installing a state-of-the-art entertainment center in your den and replacing the furniture and carpeting, your redecorating is almost complete. All that remains to be done is to purchase a set of movie posters to hang on the walls. Find a site where you can purchase the set of four "Antz" movie posters depicting the princess, the hero, the best friend, and the general.	"Doing a little research on my boyfriend heritage and the history of the name 'Gatling.' I knew his great-grandfather had invented the Gatling Gun and the name had been passed down over generations. In a search engine, the word 'Gatling' appeared as a movie. I looked up the movie, and went searching to purchase a movie poster from the movie 'The Gatling Gun' It was not a popular movie, therefore the poster was difficult to find. I finally purchased one from a poster company (with a website) located in Boulder, CO. He believes it is the only GG movie poster around."

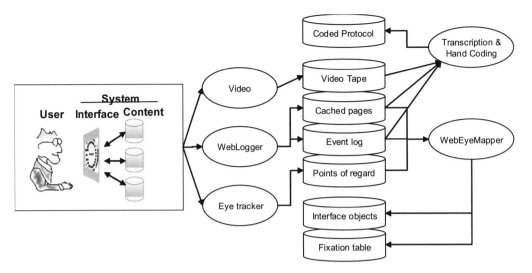

FIGURE 3.3 Instrumentation and analysis methodology in the laboratory study of Web users.

Apparatus

The instrumentation and data analysis system are depicted in figure 3.3. Participants performed their Web tasks using a standard desktop computer running Windows 98 and the Internet Explorer Web browser on a 1024×768 pixel color monitor. As participants worked on Web tasks, a video recorder captured their think-aloud protocols and the computer screen. A program called WebLogger (Reeder, Pirolli, & Card, 2001) collected and time-stamped all user interactions with the Internet Explorer Web browser, including user keystrokes, mouse movements, scrolling, use of browser buttons, and all pages visited. WebLogger also collected and time-stamped all significant browser actions, including the retrieval and rendering of Web content. An ISCAN RK-426PC eye tracker system was used to collect user eye movements. The WebLogger program inserted special event data into the WebLogger data stream and the ISCAN eye tracker data stream that permitted the two sources of data to be synchronized and merged by another program called WebEyeMapper (Reeder et al., 2001).

At *experiment time*, a user worked on a specific task with a Web browser. WebLogger instrumented the Web browser and recorded all significant events and display states in an *event log*. WebLogger events included browser events related to the state of the display. Logged browser events included events that changed the Web page displayed, the portion of the page displayed, or the position or size of the Internet

Explorer window relative to the screen. WebLogger also saved the contents of Web pages. This was done by saving a cache of all pages and associated content that was viewed by the user. Consequently, all the application-level *content elements* of interest as well as their displayed locations at every point in time throughout the user's task were recorded.

At *analysis time*, the eye-tracking data were mapped onto data recorded by WebLogger using WebEyeMapper, as shown in figure 3.3, in order to determine what content was visually focused on by the user at any given time. This has been called the *points-to-elements mapping* problem (Reeder et al., 2001). The eye tracker recorded *points of regard* (PORs) of the eye (the inferred point at which the eye was gazing). In this particular study, the PORs were sampled at 1/60th second intervals. PORs were mapped onto the content elements that were present at the same x-y coordinates at each time slice. First, WebEyeMapper converted PORs from the eye tracker into *fixations* (when the eye remains relatively stable and focused on some location). Then, WebEyeMapper initiated a "playback" of a browsing session based on the WebLogger event log and eye fixation data. WebEyeMapper employed a simulation clock to coordinate the replay of WebLogger events and eye fixations. As the simulation clock advanced, WebEyeMapper directed Internet Explorer to load the same Web pages that the user was viewing at the time indicated by the simulation clock, and directed Internet Explorer to alter its scroll position, window position, and window size as the user did at experiment time. In this manner, WebEyeMapper restored the display state of the browser to the same state, moment by moment, as the user viewed it at experiment time. WebEyeMapper then took eye fixation points, aligned them in time with the simulation clock, aligned them in space with the browser window, and determined what was rendered in the browser at the time of each fixation. For each fixation, WebEye-Mapper wrote to a database the fixation start time and duration; screen, window, and scroll system coordinates; element fixated; and element text fixated.

Procedure

At the beginning of an experiment session, the eye tracker was calibrated by having participants fixate on positions on a 9-point grid that were cued in a random order. Participants were given think-aloud instructions (Ericsson & Simon, 1984) and asked to practice thinking aloud on a mental arithmetic problem and a simple Web task that involved finding the home page for PARC. Throughout the think-aloud procedure, participants were prompted to verbalize if they were silent for more than a few seconds.

Tasks were presented in random order for each participant. Each question was displayed on the computer screen to the left of the Internet Explorer and remained in view throughout the task. If participants did not complete the task within 10 minutes, they were given a hint in the form of a set of search terms that would help them find the target Web page. If participants did not complete the task within 15 minutes, they were given the Web site where they could find the target information. Eye tracker calibration was checked between questions.

Results

Detailed protocol analyses were extremely time-consuming, and consequently, we decided to focus our efforts on protocols collected from four participants working on the Antz and City tasks described in table 3.10. These two tasks were representative of the complete set of tasks in the sense that they were near median in task completion time and near median in task completion time variance. The four participants were chosen because they had the most intact data on these two tasks.

The data collected from participants were merged into a coded Web protocol transcript. Data were drawn from transcriptions of the video recordings of the think-aloud protocol and the WebLogger recording of system and user actions with the browser (including the actual Web pages visited). Several initial passes were made over a subset of the protocols to develop a Web Protocol Coding Guide,[7] which is summarized in the appendix. Sample protocols coded independently by two analysts yielded 91% agreement in the partitioning of the protocol and 93% agreement in the specific codings.

Problem Spaces

Excluding the eye movement data, the participants' protocols suggest that three problem spaces structure the bulk of their Web foraging behavior:[8]

1. A *link* problem space in which the states are information patches (typically Web pages) and the basic operators involve moving from one patch to another by clicking on links or the back button
2. A *keyword* problem space in which the states are alternative legal queries to search engines and the operators involve formulating and editing the search queries
3. A *URL* problem space in which the states are legal URLs to be typed into the address bar of a Web browser and the operators involve formulating and editing the URL strings

The participants' behavior in the Web protocols can be visualized using a Web behavior graph (WBG; Card et al., 2001), which is an elaboration of the problem behavior graphs used in Newell and Simon (1972). Figure 3.4 presents a schematic explanation of the WBG graphical representation.

Figure 3.5 presents the WBGs of the four participants' data on the Antz and City tasks. Since the participants' protocols provide sparse data regarding their evaluations of the pages they visited, we had three independent judges rank the potential utility (information scent) of each page visited in the eight Web protocols. Specifically, the judges were asked to rate the relevance of Web pages to the City and Antz tasks in table 3.10. The judges were presented with every page visited by participants in the Web study and were asked to rate the relevance of the pages (a) after a cursory skimming of the page (initial rating) and (b) after a more thorough examination of the page (final rating). The ratings were done on a

Web Behavior Graph Representation

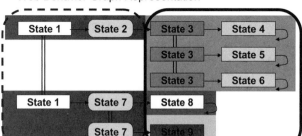

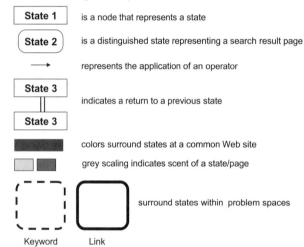

where

Time runs left to right, then top to bottom

| State 1 | is a node that represents a state |

| State 2 | is a distinguished state representing a search result page |

→   represents the application of an operator

| State 3 |
| State 3 | indicates a return to a previous state

▬▬▬   colors surround states at a common Web site

▢ ▮   grey scaling indicates scent of a state/page

┆‾┆ ▢   surround states within problem spaces

Keyword   Link

FIGURE 3.4 Schematic explanation of the components of a Web behavior graph. See color insert.

4-point scale: No Scent (0), Low Scent (1), Medium Scent (2), or High Scent (3). The geometric means of the judges' ratings were taken to reduce the effect of outlying ratings. These final ratings are plotted in the WBGs in figure 3.5 on a scale of white (0), light gray (1), medium gray (2), and dark gray (3).

Following Information Scent

Inspection of figure 3.5 reveals several phenomena. The Antz task is more difficult than the City task. Only one-fourth of participants found a solution to the Antz task, compared with three-quarters of participants who found solutions to the City task. The WBGs for the Antz task show more branches and backtracking than do the WBGs for the City task, which is an indication of less informed search. The participants on the City task moved very directly to the target information, whereas the participants on the Antz task followed unproductive paths.

Antz task participants spent more time visiting search engines and in the keyword problem space. On the Antz task, participants generated about 3.25 separate sets of search results each, whereas on the City task, they generated about 1.25 sets of search results each. One reason for the greater difficulty of the Antz task could be the poverty of information scent of links leading to the desired target information. We asked $N = 10$ judges to rate the information scent of links on the search results pages visited by participants in both the Antz and City tasks. The links were rated on a 4-point scale of Not Relevant (0), Low Relevant (1), Medium Relevant (2), and Highly Relevant (3). The geometric mean rating was computed for each link. The set of all links was split at the median geometric rating score into equal-sized sets of High Rating vs. Low Rating links. The link set was also divided into those that had been Selected vs. Unselected in the eight Web protocols. A two (High vs. Low Rating) by two (Link Selected vs.

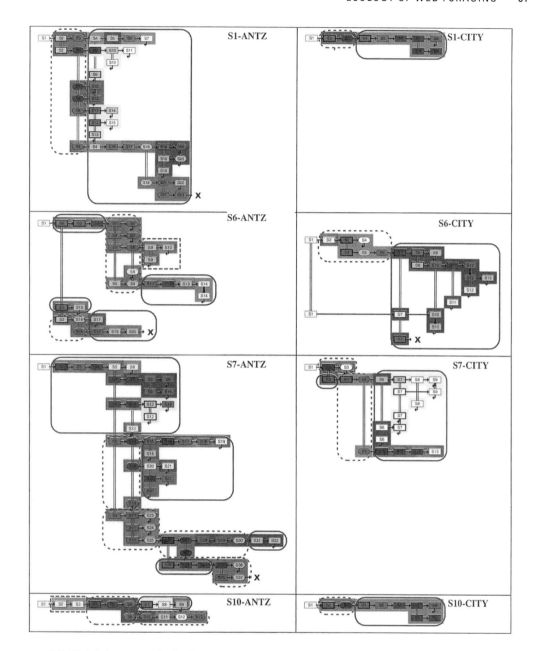

FIGURE 3.5 Web behavior graphs for four participants (rows) working on two tasks (columns). See color insert.

Unselected) contingency table was constructed. A median split analysis on this contingency table showed that higher rated links were more likely to have been the ones selected by the study participant, $\chi^2_{(1)} = 15.46$, $p < .0001$. The links followed by the study participants had a lower information scent average on the Antz task ($M = 1.56$) than on the City task ($M = 2.44$), although the links not followed where about the same for the Antz task ($M = 0.65$) and the City task ($M = 0.62$).

Difficulty of foraging on the Web appears to be related to the quality of information scent cues available to users. Under conditions of strong information scent, users move rather directly to the target information, as is characteristic of the City task WBGs in figure 3.5. When the information scent is weak, there is a more undirected pattern of foraging paths, as characteristic of the Antz WBGs in figure 3.5, and a greater reliance on search engines and Web portals with large hub sizes.

Foraging in Information Patches

Although multiple Web sites were visited by all participants on both tasks, it is apparent that they tended not to flit from one Web site to another. There were more transitions within a Web site than between sites. The ratio of within-site to between-site transitions was $M = 2.1$ for the Antz task and $M = 5.2$ for the City task. Inspection of figure 3.5 suggests that, as the information scent of encountered Web pages declines at a site, there is a tendency for participants to leave the site or return to some previously visited state. From the Web protocols, I identified segments where participants visited three or more pages at a Web site that was not a search engine or Web portal. I found $N = 3$ three-page sequences and $N = 6$ five-page sequences (no other sequences were found). The Web pages in these sequences were divided into the *first page* visited at the site, the *last page* visited at a site, and the pages visited between the first and last page (*middle pages*).

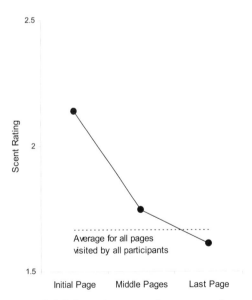

FIGURE 3.6 Information scent of sequences of pages visited at Web sites prior to going to another Web site. Each data point represents the geometric mean of ratings from ten judges. Pages were rates on a 4-point scale of Not relevant (0), Low Relevant (1), Medium Relevant (2), and Highly Relevant (3).

Figure 3.6 presents the scent ratings (initial ratings; see above) of the pages in these sequences. Each point in figure 3.6 is based on the geometric mean of scent ratings of the visited pages produced by the independent panel of raters discussed above. Also plotted in figure 3.6 is the average scent rating of all the Web pages visited by our participants. Figure 3.6 shows that initially the information scent at a site is high, and when that information scent falls below the average information scent, users switch to another site or search engine.

There also appears to be a relation between the amount of information scent first encountered at a Web site and the length of the sequence (the *run*) of page visits at the Web site. I identified $N = 68$ sequences of pages visits (one or more) at Web sites and split these runs two ways: (a) run length ≥ 3 versus run length ≤ 2, and (b) start page information scent $\geq$ median rating versus start page information scent $<$ median. This median split analysis showed that starting with a high information scent was strongly associated with longer runs at a Web site, $\chi^2_{(1)} = 8.69$, $p < .005$.

General Discussion

This chapter provides an initial foray into understanding the behavioral ecology of information foraging on the Web. Significant Web tasks are driven by goals, often set in the context of broader sense-making tasks. Consequently, it is possible to frame the analysis of the task environment and foraging behavior using constructs from the study of human problem solving. Web foraging can be viewed as search in problem spaces. The concept of information scent (proximal cues used to judge the utility of links) emerged as a principal component of the heuristics that drive the problem space search process. Improvements in information scent are related to more efficient Web foraging, and the detection of diminishing information scent is involved in decisions to leave a Web locality. In chapter 4, I present a more detailed rational analysis of the concept of information scent and its relation to foraging efficiency, and a detailed computational model that incorporates information scent into simulations of detailed moment-by-moment problem-solving behavior of Web foragers.

Information on the Web exhibits a patchy structure along several dimensions. The link structure tends to be organized into clusters (generally correlated with Web sites). URLs are named in ways that reflect hierarchical patches. Content tends to be organized into topical localities such that link distances correlate with semantic differences. Search engines dynamically create information patches of links relevant to some query. The patchiness of the Web environment invites analogies to the conventional patch model presented in chapter 2. Figure 3.6 suggests that users choose to leave an information patch when the information scent (a proximal indicator of utility) of encountered Web pages at a site drops below the average information scent of encountered pages. This phenomenon is analogous to the observation that food foragers will tend to leave a patch when the instantaneous rate of gain drops below the rate of gain for the environment. Chapter 4 derives an information patch model based on a patch model of food foraging.

APPENDIX: SUMMARY OF THE SIGNIFICANCE QUESTION CODING CATEGORIES AND WEB PROTOCOL CODING GUIDE

Summary of the Significance Question Coding Categories

Respondents to the Significance Question each provided a detailed account of a significant task they had recently performed on the Web. Samples of the responses to the Significance Question survey were coded along three dimensions: (a) The *purpose* or goal of the task performed, (b) the *method* by which it had been done, and (c) the *content* or topic relevant to the task. A summary of the coding scheme and illustrations are presented in tables 3.A.1–3.A.3.

Summary of the Web Protocol Coding Guide

A Web Protocol Coding Guide was developed to provide coding rules and examples to guide the coding of protocols obtained from participants in Web studies. A summary of these rules is provided below.

Hierarchical Goal Structures

The coding scheme assumes that Web foraging behavior is the result of activity in problem spaces organized around a hierarchical goal structure (Newell, 1990). Each problem space is organized around some goal and a set of state-changing operators. Achieving each subgoal involves the application of operators, such as typing in URLs, clicking on links, and so forth. Goals are assumed to arise through specific cognitive plans that decompose a supergoal into subgoals, impasses that require solution, or environmental triggers.

TABLE 3.A.1 Survey coding categories and examples for the Purpose taxonomy

- *Find*: Use of the Web to download information, find a fact, find a document, and find out about a product
  - *Download information*. Example: "For work, I needed to download a utility for unpacking files, and had to search through a couple of download sites in order to find it."
  - *Get a fact*. Example: "I needed to find out when HANSON was coming out with their new album for my daughter. We went into their website and got the answer. We did this tonight."
  - *Get a document*. Example: "Reference the Java 1.2 API docs—I'm a Java programmer"
  - *Find out about a product*. Example: "Searching for a music CD that was not available in Australia, then purchasing it."
- *Compare/choose*: Use of the Web to evaluate multiple products or pieces of information in order to help the respondent make a decision. Example: "After searching numerous magazines and catalogs for pricing and feature information on the Zip and Zip Plus drives, I was able to determine that an original Zip would be a better decision, and even that the Zip Plus didn't support daisy-chaining. Furthermore, I found that I could get a Zip drive for $30 less if I bought a refurbished unit."
- *Understand*: Use of the Web to help the respondent understand some topic. Category generally includes locating a fact or document prior to sense making. Example: "Last year, did a search on transient ischemic attacks (minor strokes) when my father suffered one to learn about their effects."
- *Uncodable*: (1) Unclear which category the answer fulfills or (2) unable to visualize the situation based on the given description. Example: "Almost daily I find what I consider to be important info. My mind sometimes feels like it is going to explode with the overload."

TABLE 3.A.2 Survey coding categories and examples for the Method taxonomy

- *Explore*: General searching to find what is out there. The search is not triggered by a particular goal. Example: "Stumbled across a Taoist site, got interested, and a bit confused whether or not I already am a Taoist."
- *Monitor*: Sit-and-wait foraging. The search is not triggered by a particular goal; it is a routine behavior. Example: "Discovered a Macintosh news portal www.macsurfer.com. Check it each day to follow the links."
- *Find*: Searching for a particular fact/document/piece of information. Search is triggered by a particular goal. Example: "Trying to find a specific type royalty free photo. Logged on to PhotoDisc, did a search, found the right photo, ordered and downloaded it all online."
- *Collect*: Searching for multiple pieces of information. Searcher is open to any answer, not looking for a particular one. A goal drives the searcher's behavior. Example: "I used WWW search engines to search for sources of technical training. My organization required training on a unique set of skills and I searched for companies that might offer training on those skills. I was able to use the information I found to justify the purchase of training from one of the companies."
- *Uncodable*: (1) Unclear which category the answer fulfills or (2) unable to visualize the situation based on the given description. Examples: (1) "Found an updated driver for a printer that would not work correctly. Was able to get printer working within an hour of being presented with the problem." (2) "As a medical information broker I utilize Web resources on a daily basis to provide information to clients about specific health concerns."

TABLE 3.A.3 Survey coding categories and examples for the Content taxonomy

- *Business*. Example: "I used WWW search engines to search for sources of technical training. My organization required training on a unique set of skills and I searched for companies that might offer training on those skills. I was able to use the information I found to justify the purchase of training from one of the companies."
- *Education*. Example: "Found information about obscure Austrian psychiatrist Otto Weininger for wife's thesis research."
- *Finance*. Example: "I was looking for a home equity loan. I got information about the different routes to take and made several connections with people in that business. I ended up getting a loan with my own bank."
- *Job Search*. Example: "Job searching, checking out a prospective employer's Web site to gather background info. Also to research relocation info on a specific area."
- *Medical*. Example: "Looked up information on a medication to find out the side effects."
- *Miscellaneous*. Codable, but responses do not fit in any other category—Example: "To do my bible studies I always use materials from the World Study Bible (http://ccel.wheaton.edu/wwsb/) and information provided there helps me greatly."
- *News*. Example: "Used it to become familiar with the "Clinton" scandal!"
- *People*. Trying to find [information about] a person or persons. Example: "I found a distant cousin I did not know existed while doing genealogy research. He had his own Web page."
- *Product information and purchase*
  - *Computer products*. Example: "Information on computer motherboards and chipsets (and suppliers of same) led to reconsidering the use of socket-7 based equipment."
  - *Vehicles*. Example: "Went to Edmund's Web page to learn vehicle dealer's costs. Compared to Carmax Web page used vehicle prices to estimate depreciation of new vehicle."
  - *Download*. Example: "Found a freeware utility that I can use on one of my servers."
  - *Other Products*. Example: "Searching for information on digital cameras to make a purchase/not purchase decision."
- *Travel*. Example: "Used the Web to find travel and hotel accommodations, saving myself lots of money and time...."
- *Uncodable*. Example: "I use the net to first identify, then hone, most of my purchase decisions."

Hierarchical Information Structure

The coding assumed that information is arranged into hierarchical patches. The criteria for distinguishing different kinds of information patches include whether participants have names for the different patches (indicating a conceptual distinction) or whether the patches afford different actions (an environmental distinction). The coding specified the following patch types:

- *Web*. The entire Web. At various points, participants specified that the scope of their foraging was the entire Web (e.g., when executing a search on a large search engine portal).
- *Web site*. A Web site often has a *producer* (or author), *content* that is about some topics, and one or more *purposes* that can be achieved by users (e.g., purchases), and it has a *URL*. Some specific subclasses are *portal sites* and *search-engine sites*.
- *Search collection*. In contrast to Web sites, which are relatively static collections that may be fetched by their URL, a search collection is generated by a *query string* submitted to a *search engine* that *indexes* some collection of content. Like Web sites, search collections are about some topically related *content*.
- *Page*. A page can be thought of as containing *link descriptors* (or *links*), *content* (textual or image based), *content elements*, and other elements. Pages may also contain some additional patchy structure, such sidebars and other groupings, or regions. Because pages are the universal structure for accessing content on the Web, they have a wide variety of subtypes, including home pages and product pages.
- *Subpage*. Within pages, there are often distinct visual regions. A subpage is a set of links and/or content grouped together on the page.
- *Content element*. This is the content that is the end point of the foraging. The consumption of content provides the reward for foraging. In theory, we assume that the smallest elements are equivalent to propositions (by definition, the smallest elements of meaning that can be assigned a truth value). In practice, these are small collections of English words and phrases that could be used by a cognitive operator (e.g., in judging the relevance or utility of a link).
- *Link descriptors* (*links*). These give information about another page (URL). *Content links* lead to pages that contain content, and *category links* lead to pages containing other links (index pages).
- *Option*. An option is something that may be specified by the user. These are usually selected via a menu of some sort, a radio button, etc.

Information Needs and Representations

Users represent and reformulate the specification of information that they are seeking. The coding distinguished among the following information needs and representations:

- *Question (task)*. Initially, participants were presented with an external question, aspects of which they would come to internalize and reformulate.
- *Need*. This is an internal goal that characterizes the needed content. Certain aspects of the needed content are "highlighted" or elaborated—the expectation being that these are the concepts that will be used to drive foraging behavior, judge the relevance of items encountered, formulate query strings, and so on.
- *Query*. The actual words (external representation) typed in or selected to be a query to a search engine.
- *URL*. Often, participants specify their information need by formulating (guessing) a URL string that they believe may return the desired content.

Information needs may be operated on by *reading, noting, formulating*, and *reformulating* actions that create, elaborate, or modify their specification.

Information Navigation and Search

Most of the participants' Web behavior involved some form of Web navigation or search. The coding guide specified the following actions that constitute the bulk of protocols:

- *Go-to* ⟨*information-structure-type*⟩ ⟨*specific-structure*⟩, where ⟨information-structure-type⟩ is some type of information patch structure discussed above (e.g., a Web site) and ⟨specific-structure⟩ indicates the particular information patch (e.g., a specific URL such as www.altavista.com); the goal or operator involved in going to some information patch.

- *Search ⟨structure-type⟩ ⟨specific-structure⟩ ⟨specific-query⟩*, where ⟨structure-type⟩ is some type of information patch structure, ⟨specific-structure⟩ is the specific information patch being searched, and ⟨specific-query⟩ is the string of words used in search; the goal or operator involved in using a search engine.
- *Follow ⟨link⟩*, where ⟨link⟩ is a link descriptor; the goal or operator involved in moving from one page to another via a link.
- *Go-forward-in-history, go-back-in-history*, goals and operators for moving through the browser history list.
- *Refresh*, refreshing the page using the browser button.

Evaluations

Participants often evaluated the utility or relevance of Web links, pages, and sites. Evaluations of specific information structures were coded as *High* (the participant indicated that the information seemed useful or promising), *Low* (the participant indicated that the information was somewhat related to a goal), *None* (the participant indicated that the information was unrelated to the goal), and *Null* (the participant did not state the evaluation).

Notes

1. This was one of the heuristics that I consciously used to learn about foraging theory.

2. I thank Lada Adamic and Jim Pitkow for providing me with these data, and Alexa for initially supplying PARC with the data sets.

3. Manning and Schuetze (1999) show a mapping between the normalized correlation and a Bayesian analysis of the log-likelihood odds of a document being relevant given a set of word cues representing the interest of a user.

4. Davison used two additional measures that yielded similar results.

5. See Gigerenzer (2000) for a discussion of psychology's focus on method and inferential statistics that aims to generalize findings to populations of participants, but psychology's underdevelopment of complementary methodology and statistical machinery for generalizing findings to conditions of the world.

6. Further details of the GVU Survey methodology can be found on the Web (*GVU's 10th WWW user survey* [n.d.].)

7. The detailed Web Protocol Coding Guide is available on request.

8. Other problem spaces are evident the protocols, for instance, for navigating through the history list, but are much rarer than the ones discussed here. Other problem spaces could easily be added to the analysis.

References

Adamic, L. (2001). *Network dynamics: The World Wide Web*. Unpublished doctoral dissertation, Stanford University, Palo Alto, CA.

Barabási, A.-L. (2002). *Linked: The new science of networks*. Cambridge, MA: Perseus Publishing.

Barabási, A.-L., & Albert, R. (1999). Emergence of scaling in random networks. *Science, 286*, 509–512.

Barabási, A.-L., Albert, R., & Jeong, H. (2000). Scale-free characteristics of random networks: The topology of the World Wide Web. *Physica A: Statistical and Theoretical Physics, 281*, 66–77.

Barabási, A.-L., & Bonabeau, E. (2003). Scale-free networks. *Scientific American, 288*(5), 60–69.

Brin, S., & Page, L. (1998). The anatomy of a large-scale hypertextual Web search engine. *Computer Networks and ISDN Systems, 30*(1–7), 107–117.

Brunswik, E. (1952). *The conceptual framework of psychology*. Chicago: University of Chicago Press.

Brunswik, E. (1956). *Perception and the representative design of psychological experiments*. Berkeley, CA: University of California Press.

Byrne, M. D., John, B. E., Wehrle, N. S., & Crow, D. S. (1999). The tangled Web we wove: A taskonomy of WWW use. *Proceedings of the SIGCHI Conference on Human Factors in Computing Systems, CHI 1999* (pp. 544–551). Pittsburgh, PA: ACM Press.

Card, S. K., Pirolli, P., Van Der Wege, M., Morrison, J., Reeder, R., Schraedley, P., et al. (2001). Information scent as a driver of Web Behavior Graphs: Results of a protocol analysis method for web usability. *CHI 2001, ACM Conference on Human Factors in Computing Systems, CHI Letters, 3*(1), 498–505.

Choo, C. W., Detlor, B., & Turnbull, D. (1998). A behavioral model of information seeking on the Web: Preliminary results of a study of how managers and IT specialists use the Web. Proceedings of the 61st annual meeting of the American Society for Information Science (pp. 290–302). Medford, NJ: Information Today, Inc.

Cooksey, R. W. (2001). Brunswik's "The conceptual framework of psychology" then and now. In K. R. Hammond & T. R. Stewart (Eds.), *The essential Brunswik* (pp. 225–231). Oxford: Oxford University Press.

Davison, B. (2000). Topical locality in the Web. Proceedings of the 23rd Annual International ACM SIGIR Conference on Research and Development in Information Retrieval (pp. 272–279). Athens, Greece: ACM Press.

Egghe, L., & Rousseau, R. (1990). *Introduction to informetrics: Quantitative methods in library, documentation, and information science*. New York: Elsevier.

Eiron, N., & McCurley, K. S. (2003, May). *Locality, hierarchy, and bidirectionality in the Web*. Paper presented at the Workshop on Algorithms and Models for the Web Graph, Budapest, Hungary.

Ericsson, K. A., & Simon, H. A. (1984). *Protocol Analysis: Verbal reports as data*. Cambridge, MA: MIT Press.

Fitts, P. M., & Jones, R. E. (1961). Psychological aspects of instrument display: Analysis of factors contributing to 460 "pilot error" experiences in operating aircraft controls. In H. W. Sinaiko (Ed.), *Selected papers on human factors in the design and use of control systems* (pp. 332–358). New York: Dover Publications.

Flanagan, J. C. (1954). The critical incident technique. *Psychological Bulletin, 51*, 327–358.

Fox, S., & Fallows, D. (2003, August). *Internet health resources*. Retrieved December 2003 from http://www.pewinternet.org/reports/pdfs/PIP_Health_Report_July_2003.pdf.

Garfield, E. (1979). *Citation indexing: Its theory and application in science, technology, and humanities*. New York: Wiley.

Gibson, J. J. (1979). *The ecological approach to visual perception*. Boston, MA: Houghton Mifflin.

Gigerenzer, G. (2000). *Adaptive thinking: Rationality in the real world*. Oxford: Oxford University Press.

GVU's 10th WWW user survey (n.d.). Retrieved November 4, 2006, from http://www.gvu.gatech.edu/user_surveys/survey-1998–10/#methodology.

Hartson, H. R., & Castillo, J. C. (1998). Remote evaluation for post-deployment usability improvement. *Proceedings of the Working Conference on Advanced Visual Interfaces, AVI '98* (pp. 22–29). L'Aquila, Italy: ACM Press.

Kehoe, C., Pitkow, J., Sutton, K., & Aggarwal, G. (1999, May). *Results of the Tenth World Wide Web User Survey*. Retrieved December 2003 from http://www.gvu.gatech.edu/user_surveys/survey-1998–10/tenth report.html.

Klein, G. A., Calderwood, R., & Macgregor, D. (1989). Critical decision method for eliciting knowledge. *IEEE Transactions on Systems, Man, and Cybernetics, 19*(3), 462–472.

Kleinberg, J. (1999). Hubs, authorities, and communities. *ACM Computing Surveys, 31*, 5.

Manning, C. D., & Schuetze, H. (1999). *Foundations of statistical natural language processing*. Cambridge, MA: MIT Press.

Merton, R. K. (1968). The Matthew effect in science. *Science, 159*(3810), 56–63.

Morrison, J. B., Pirolli, P., & Card, S. K. (2001). A taxonomic analysis of what World Wide Web activities significantly impact people's decisions and actions. *CHI 2001, ACM Conference on Human Factors in Computing Systems, CHI Letters, 3*(1), 163–164.

Neisser, U. (1976). *Cognition and reality*. San Francisco, CA: Freeman.

Newell, A. (1990). *Unified theories of cognition*. Cambridge, MA: Harvard University Press.

Newell, A., & Simon, H. A. (1972). *Human problem solving*. Englewood Cliffs, NJ: Prentice Hall.

Nielsen, J. (2001, April). *The 3Cs of critical Web use: Collect, compare, choose*. Retrieved December 2003 from http://www.useit.com/alertbox/20010415.html.

Pitkow, J. E. (1997). *Characterizing World Wide Web ecologies* (Technical Report No. UIR-R97-02). Palo Alto, CA: Xerox PARC.

Pitkow, J., & Pirolli, P. (1999). Mining longest repeated subsequences to predict World Wide Web surfing. *Proceedings of the Second USENIX Symposium on Internet Technologies and Systems* (pp. 139–150). Boulder, CO: USENIX Association.

Reeder, R. W., Pirolli, P., & Card, S. K. (2001). WebEye Mapper and WebLogger: Tools for analyzing eye tracking data in Web-use studies. *CHI '01 Extended Abstracts on Human Factors in Computing Systems* (pp. 19–20). Seattle, WA: ACM Press.

Resnikoff, H. L. (1989). *The illusion of reality*. New York: Springer-Verlag.

Shattuck, L. W., & Woods, D. D. (1994). The Critical Incident Technique: 40 years later. *Proceedings of the 38th Annual Meeting of the Human Factors and Ergonomics Society* (pp. 1090–1094). Santa Monica, CA: HFES.

Simon, H. A. (1962). The architecture of complexity: Hierarchic systems. *Proceedings of the American Philosophical Society, 106*, 467–482.

Spooner, T. (2003, August). *Internet use by region in the United States*. Retrieved from http://www.pewinternet.org/reports/toc.asp?Report=98.

4

Rational Analyses of Information Scent and Web Foraging

The notion of *information scent* has been introduced in a general way in chapters 1–3. Information scent refers to the detection and use of cues, such as World Wide Web (Web) links or bibliographic citations, that provide users with concise information about content that is not immediately available. Information scent plays an important role in guiding users to the information they seek, and it also plays a role in providing users with an overall sense of the contents of collections. The purpose of this chapter is to provide a rational analysis of Web foraging in which information scent plays a central role.

The concept of information scent has proven to be productive. The SNIF-ACT model of Web foraging described in chapter 5 is driven by an information scent mechanism. In chapter 6, the ACT-IF model of people seeking information in the Scatter/Gather document-clustering browsers uses the same information scent mechanism. More generally, the concept has been useful in understanding user behavior with highly interactive information visualizations

(Pirolli, Card, & Van Der Wege, 2003). In chapter 9, I review how the concept of information scent has influenced design principles and engineering models in human-information interaction. The focus of this chapter is on the underlying rational choice model of information scent. This analysis leads to a Random Utility Model (McFadden, 1974) of navigation choice by users that can be implemented as a spreading activation mechanism (Anderson & Lebiere, 1998; Anderson & Pirolli, 1984). The analysis also leads to a kind of information patch model (chapter 2) that concerns the decision of when to leave a current information patch. Finally, the information patch model, which concerns individual decisions about foraging, can be related to a model of the aggregate behavior of Web foragers called the Law of Surfing (Huberman, Pirolli, Pitkow, & Lukose, 1998) that characterizes the distribution of foraging path lengths taken at a Web site. The Law of Surfing is a way of characterizing how long people stay at a Web site, or what is sometimes called Web site "stickiness."

The Environmental Model

Throughout the foraging literature, it is assumed that organisms base their foraging decisions on predictions about the typology and utility of habitat and the typology and utility of food items (e.g., species of prey or plants). There is considerable evidence that humans show preference for landscape features (aesthetics) that appear to predict high-resource-providing environments (e.g., a savanna), as well as features associated with ease of exploration (Orians & Heerwagen, 1992).[1] Studies in ethnobiology and cross-cultural psychology indicate considerable coherence in the biological categories that have evolved in different cultures and a high correspondence of folk categories to scientific categories of species (Malt, 1995). Entities that are more useful within a culture have much more elaborated categorical structure than do those that are peripherally useful. Humans, like many other organisms, apparently learn to categorize their habitats and biological entities within those habitats, and these categorizations are shaped by utilization. Information Foraging Theory assumes that the information forager also bases decisions on assessments of information habitats and information items and that these assessments are based on learned categorizations and utility judgments. An adaptationist perspective expects evolution to favor cognitive processes that result in categories and judgment processes that reflect the structure of the environment relevant to more adaptive behavior.

In addition to the regularities noted in chapter 3, another regularity is the availability of labeled navigation links from one Web page to another (e.g., figure 4.1), and users appear to prefer following links over other means of Web navigation (Katz & Byrne, 2003). Web page designs have evolved to associate (by human design or automated information systems) small snippets of text and graphics with such links. Those text and graphics cues are intended to represent tersely the content that will be encountered by choosing a particular link on one page and navigating to the linked page. When browsing the Web by following links, users must use these cues presented proximally on the Web pages they are currently viewing in order to make navigation decisions. These link cues are called *information scent*. For the Web user, there is uncertainty about the relationship of the proximal cues to the linked information resources.

The rational analysis of information scent draws on four theories: (1) an extension of Egon Brunswik's (1956) ecological Lens Model that characterizes the judgment problems facing organisms in probabilistically textured environments, (2) Anderson's (1990, 1991) adaptationist theory of categorization that describes how organisms predict unobserved attributes from observed ones, (3) Anderson's (Anderson, 1990; Anderson & Milson, 1989) adaptationist theory of memory that describes how needed information is retrieved in the context of presented information, and (4) a very general and rational theory of choice, based on the Random Utility Model (McFadden, 1974, 1978). The general argument is that information foragers operate in an ecologically rational manner to make choices based on their predictive judgments (under uncertainty) based on information scent.

Examples of Information Scent

Before delving into the analysis, it is worth examining some examples of information scent. Pirolli (1997, p. 3) introduced the notion of information scent as "terse representations of content . . . whose trail leads to information of interest." Figure 4.1 presents some examples of information scent cues. Figure 4.1a is a typical page generated by a Web search engine in response to a user query. The page lists Web pages (search results) that are predicted to be relevant to the query. Each search result is represented by its title (in blue), phrases from the hit containing words from the query, and a URL (Uniform Resource Locator). Figure 4.1b illustrates an alternative form of search result representation (for exactly the same items in figure 4.1a) that is provided by *relevance-enhanced thumbnails* (Woodruff, Rosenholtz, Morrison, Faulring, & Pirolli, 2002), which combine thumbnail images of search results with highlighted text relevant to the user's query. Figure 4.1c is a hyperbolic tree browser[2] (Lamping & Rao, 1994; Lamping, Rao, & Pirolli, 1995). Each label on each node in the hyperbolic tree is the title for a Web page. Finally, figure 4.1d presents the Microsoft Explorer browser with a typical file system view. Each label on a node represents a folder, file, or application.

User interface research is often aimed at investigating the efficacy of alternative forms of information scent cues in aiding navigation. For instance, Woodruff et al. (2002) compared standard presentations of search results (figure 4.1a) with relevance enhanced

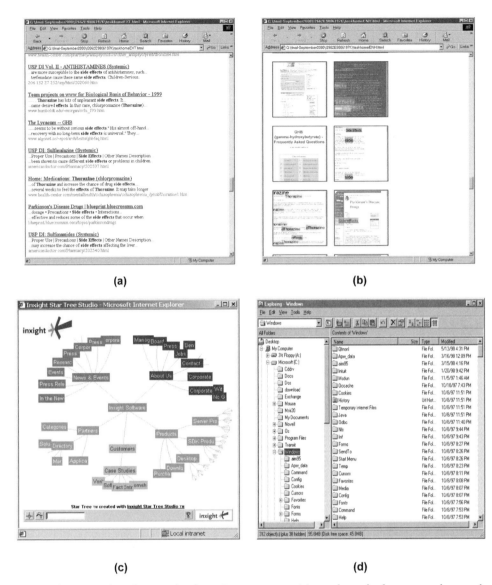

FIGURE 4.1 Examples of proximal information scent cues: (a) search results from a popular search engine, (b) relevance-enhanced thumbnails of the same search results, (c) Star Tree (or hyperbolic tree) presentation of a hierarchy, and (d) Microsoft Explorer presentation of a hierarchy. See color insert.

thumbnails (figure 4.1b), and Pirolli et al. (2003) tested the hyperbolic tree (figure 4.1c) against Microsoft Explorer (figure 4.1d). A general finding is that the superiority of one kind of cue over another is not universal; it depends on the information goal of the user. Another general finding is that for navigation tasks over complex networks of information, very small perturbations in the accuracy of information scent can cause qualitative shifts in the cost of brows-

ing. Consequently, designing user interfaces to have "good" information scent can yield qualitative improvements in usability (chapter 9).

Analogy to Scent in Food Foraging

An analogy between humans following trails of information scent to desirable information and animals following trails of scent to desirable items is shown graphically in figure 4.2. Figure 4.2a shows the path of a male grain beetle in an environment with no directional scent (Bell, 1991). The beetle appears to follow a random path. In figure 4.2b, a wind bearing pheromones has been introduced into the beetle's environment, and the beetle moves fairly directly along the gradient of scent to the sources. Figure 4.2, c and d, shows Web Behavior Graphs (WBGs), from figure 3.5 (57-ANTZ and 57-CITY), repeated here for side-by-side comparison. The WBG in figure 4.2c comes from a user and task in which the Web links had poor information scent (as rated by independent judges), whereas the WBG in figure 4.2d comes from a user and task in which the Web links had better information scent. The search behavior in figure 4.2c is fairly random in the absence of information scent, similar to the beetle's behavior in figure 4.2a, but the

search behavior is fairly direct in figure 4.2d, similar to the beetle's behavior in figure 4.2b.

The Web behavior in figure 4.2, c and d, is at a time scale of many seconds per behavior (e.g., choosing a link on a page takes several seconds). Figure 4.3 presents analyses of eye-tracking data collected in a study (Pirolli et al., 2003) of people using the hyperbolic tree browser or Microsoft Explorer. These eye movements are at a finer time scale than are the WBGs in figure 4.2, c and d. Figure 4.3 presents visualizations of a user's eye movements in the two browsers. Each of the figures is a *disk tree* (Chi et al., 1998).[3] The trees represent the same hierarchical data structure presented in the hyperbolic and Microsoft Explorer browsers (figure 4.1), laid out in a radial manner with the root node at the center. The coloration of the tree links indicates the depth of the tree. The height of the red

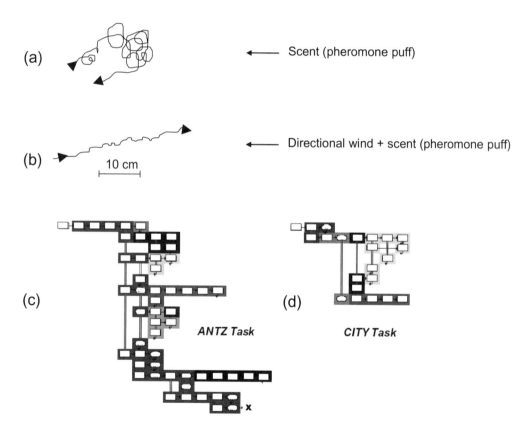

FIGURE 4.2 The foraging paths taken by a male grain beetle (*Trogoderma variabile*) and a Web user: (a) the beetle's search path following a 2 second nondirectional puff of sex pheromone (beetle paths based on Bell, 1991), (b) the beetle's search path in the presence of a constant uniform wind bearing sex pheromone, (c) a web behavior graph (WBG) for a user on a task with poor directional information scent, and (d) a WBG for a user on a task with good information scent. Each WBG box represents a state of the user–system interaction (see figure 3.5 for an explanation of components).

(a) Low scent   (b) High scent

FIGURE 4.3 Eye movements of a single user over tree structures presented in two interactive browsers (data from Pirolli et al., 2003). Circular blue structures represent the underlying data tree structure (only a portion of which would be visible to the user in either browser), green paths represent eye movements in the Microsoft Explorer browser, and yellow paths represent eye movements in the hyperbolic tree browser. The height of the red bars indicates the information scent of nodes. (a) A low-scent task. (b) A high-scent task. See color insert.

bars indicates the information scent of nodes. The overlaid yellow paths represent eye movement data from a hyperbolic user, and the green paths represent eye movements from an Explorer user. For each task in the Pirolli et al. (2003) study, independent raters were used to assess the accuracy of navigation choices based on information scent cues in the top levels of the browser trees. These ratings were used to divide tasks into high-information-scent and low-information-scent tasks. Figure 4.3a shows data from a low-information-scent task. Figure 4.3b shows data from the same user on a high-information-scent task. The eye movements for both the hyperbolic and Explorer browsers are much less dispersed over the tree structure for the high-scent task in figure 4.3b than for the low-scent task in figure 4.3a. Again, high information scent leads to search behavior that moves the user relatively more directly to a goal compared to low information scent.

The Effect of Scent Quality on Navigation Cost

As suggested above, in the complex network organization of the Web, small perturbations in the accuracy of information scent can cause qualitative shifts in the cost of browsing. This can be illustrated by ap-

plication of an analysis of phase transitions in heuristic searches developed by Hogg and Huberman (1987). For a specific arrangement of Web content, interpage links, and information scent on a Web site, it is becoming possible to make model-based predictions about likely time costs of navigation for each specific case. Examples of such models include SNIF-ACT (discussed in chapter 5), Bloodhound (Chi et al., 2003), CWW (Blackmon, Polson, Kitajima, & Lewis, 2002), and MESA (C. S. Miller & Remington, 2004). The approach of Hogg and Huberman (1987), however, provides a way to characterize the general relationship between information scent and navigation costs for the asymptotic case.

Consider an idealized case of browsing for information by surfing along links on the Web. The information structure generally will be a lattice of interlinked Web pages. At each visited page, the browsing will involve choosing a link to pursue from a set of presented links. Assume that the browsing takes the form of a hierarchically arranged search tree in which branches are explored, and if unproductive, the user returns to previously visited pages. To an approximation, this matches the observations described in chapter 3. Although the Web is a lattice, the search process over that lattice tends to follow a treelike form (i.e., a spanning tree is generated by the search process over a more general graph structure of the Web). This somewhat idealized case of hierarchically organized Web search is summarized in figure 4.4. The search tree may be characterized by a branching factor b corresponding to the average number of alternatives available at each decision point. The desired target information may occur at various depths, d, in the search tree (figure 4.4).

An exhaustive tree search process would visit every leaf node. Such a full (exhaustive) search is indicated by the complete set of lines tracing the tree structure in figure 4.4. This exhaustive tree search process would visit b^d nodes. A random tree search that terminated upon encountering a target (goal) node would search about half of the tree on average. Such a random search, indicated by the thin solid lines in figure 4.4, would visit about $b^d/2$ nodes. Information scent could be used as a heuristic to improve this search even further. At each node in the tree (corresponding to a

Web page), some paths could be eliminated by consideration of the information scent associated with links to those paths. Improved information scent would improve the elimination of unproductive paths. If information scent were perfect, then the user would make no incorrect choices. Let us associate a false alarm factor, f, with the probability of failing to eliminate an incorrect link. At the extremes, perfect information scent would correspond to $f=0$ (all wrong paths eliminated) and random guessing would correspond to $f=1$ (no wrong paths eliminated). In figure 4.4, the thick lines illustrate a search involving perfect information scent ($f=0$) and the thin lines illustrate a random search ($f=1$).

According to Hogg and Huberman (1987), the average number of nodes examined in such a hierarchical search process will be

$$N(f,\ b,\ d)=d+\left[\frac{(b-1)f}{2}\right]\sum_{s=1}^{d-1}\frac{1-(bf)}{1-bf}.\qquad(4.1)$$

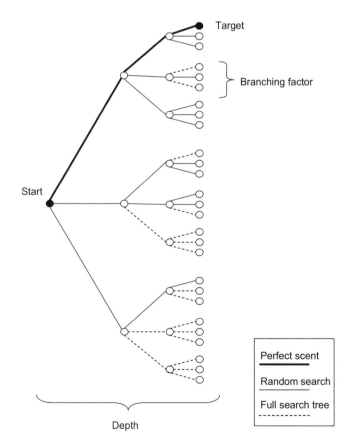

Target

Branching factor

Start

| Perfect scent |
| Random search |
| Full search tree |

Depth

FIGURE 4.4 Idealized search trees for heuristic search under perfect information scent (thick lines) and no information scent (random, thin lines). Dashed lines illustrate additional paths of a full (exhaustive) search tree.

Equation 4.1 captures a three-way interaction of information scent, f, branching factor, b, and depth, d. With perfect information scent ($f=0$), the search cost is just d. In a random search ($f=1$), the search process must visit about half the nodes on average before target information is found.

Figure 4.5 shows the effects of perturbations in false alarm factor more concretely by displaying search cost functions for a hypothetical Web site with branching factor of $b=10$. The search cost is assumed to be largely determined by the number of pages a user must visit before arriving at the desired page. The curves in figure 4.5 represent cost functions for links with false alarm rates of $f=.015, .030, \ldots, .0150$, which is about the range observed empirically in a study of information scent cues (Woodruff et al., 2002). One can see that changes in the search cost accelerate as the false alarm factor increases.

Hogg and Huberman (1987) also present a way of locating the transition between linear and exponen-tial search cost regimes. This threshold can be de-termined as follows. The average number of branches that will be pursued from the average node is

$$\mu(f,\ b,\ d) = \frac{N(f,\ b,\ d)}{d}. \qquad (4.2)$$

Equation 4.2 is plotted in figure 4.6 for a branching factor of $b=10$ and a depth $d=10$. When $fb<1$ and d is very large, equation 4.2 can be stated (Hogg & Huberman, 1987) as,

$$\mu(f,\ b,\ d) = \frac{2-fb-p}{2(1-fb)}. \qquad (4.3)$$

When $fb=1$, the denominator of equation 4.3 be-comes zero and the quantity becomes singular, indi-cating the transition from linear to exponential search (Hogg & Huberman, 1987). Small improvements in the false alarm factor associated with individual links

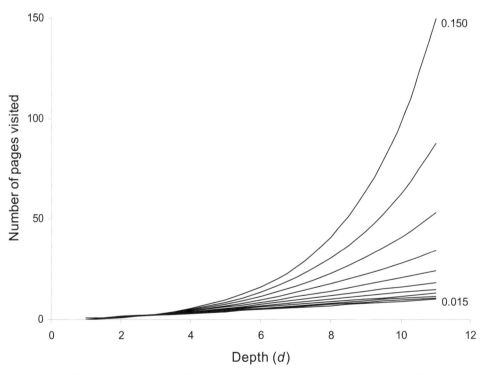

FIGURE 4.5 Effects of perturbations of false alarm rates (f) on number of pages visited $N(f, b, d)$ as a function of the depth of the target information (d) for a hypothetical Web site with an average branching factor of $b=10$. Each curve is computed for a different value of f, ranging from $f=.015$ (bottommost curve) to $f=.150$ (topmost curve) in increments of .015.

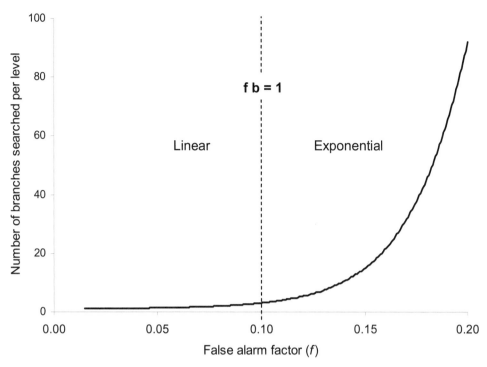

FIGURE 4.6 Number of branches searched per level of search as a function of false alarm factor. There is a transition from linear search costs to exponential search costs at $fb = 1$.

can have dramatic qualitative effects on surfing large hypertext collections. A rational Web user should be motivated to maximize the accuracy of their judgments based on information scent in order to reduce search costs.

Brunswik's Probabilistic Functionalism

In each example in figure 4.1, the *distal* sources of information (e.g., Web pages, articles) are represented by some set of mediating cues (link summaries, relevance-enhanced thumbnails, node labels, bibliographic citations). On the basis of these *proximal* cues, the user must make judgments about what is available and the potential value of going after the distal content. This distinction between proximal cues and distal objects is a well-known aspect of Brunswik's (1956) ecological theory of perception and judgment in a probabilistically textured environment. In Brunswik's Lens Model (figure 4.7), the perception or judgment of a distal object or event is indirect and must be made on the basis of proximal cues. Brunswik (1956) advocated a detailed analysis

of the probabilistic relationships between observer and proximal cues (*cognitive strategy*) and between proximal cues and distal objects or events (*ecological validity*).

Furnas (1997) developed a theory of user interface navigation that uses notion of *residue*, which is very similar to the notion of proximal cues. Furnas (1997) developed a formal theory for the analysis of different kinds of user interaction techniques largely based on discrete mathematics. The theory of information scent presented here adopts a symmetric focus on the user and the user interface and explicitly adopts a probabilistic framework for analysis.

Brunswik's Lens Model in figure 4.7 has to be expanded to deal with Web foraging. The Web user is typically faced with a multiplicity of proximal objects (e.g., Web links) and a complex information need. The task facing the user is to make predictions about unseen distal objects (e.g., unseen Web pages) based on proximal cues and predict whether or not the distal objects have the desired features. The problem facing the information forager can be cast in the following way. In order to make choices, foragers have

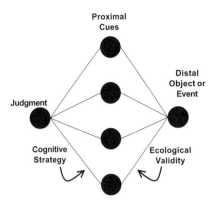

FIGURE 4.7 Brunswik's Lens Model.

a *preference function* for evaluating objects and a *choice rule* for selecting objects based on those evaluations. These evaluations are based on proximal cues. The task of the information forager with an information need is to infer the utility of a distal source of content with respect to that information need. This can be recast as a *categorization* problem in which the information forager must be able to use past experience and the available proximal cues to infer unobserved features of the distal object.

Rational Analysis of the Use of Information Scent to Navigate Web Links

Exemplar Theories of Categorization

It is assumed that mental categories have some form of probabilistic structure. In other words, the psychological categories of humans are not specified by rigid sets of necessary and sufficient conditions, a fact that had posed problems for classical philosophy (Wittgenstein, 1953). Human categories have graded structures (e.g., some things seem more typical of a category than do others), family resemblance structure, and exhibit sensitivity to context (Rosch, 1978). Two kinds of theories about human categorization have emerged, as well as theoretical hybrids that combine the two (Estes, 1997). On the one hand, there are *prototype theories* (e.g., Reed, 1972) that assume that a category is defined by a central abstract summary of its members, a function that predicts similarity between instances and the prototype, and some relation of that similarity function to behavior

(e.g., category judgments and reaction time). On the other hand, there are *exemplar theories* (e.g., Medin & Schaffer, 1978) that assume that a category is defined by a set of instances or examples, a similarity function between presented items and previously experienced items, and a (often memory-based) mechanism that retrieves, and possibly integrates across, stored instances according to that similarity function. In general, it is extremely difficult to distinguish prototype and exemplar theories (Barsalou, 1990), although it is sometimes possible to distinguish specific models (Pitt, Myung, & Zhang, 2002). This chapter develops a utility model that depends on an exemplar-based (or memory-based) category mechanism. Pirolli (2004) discusses a prototype-based theory of categorization for learning the Web environment. Here, I assume that stored past experiences are retrieved, based on proximal features of the current context, and then used to predict the likelihood of desired distal features.

The rational analysis of the use of information scent assumes that the goal of the information forager is to use proximal external information scent cues (e.g., a Web link) to predict the utility of distal sources of content (i.e., the Web page associated with a Web link) and to choose to navigate the links having the maximum expected utility. This rational analysis decomposes into three parts: (1) a Bayesian analysis of the expected relevance of a distal source of content conditional on the available information scent cues, (2) a mapping of this Bayesian model of information scent onto a mathematical formulation of spreading activation, and (3) a model of rational choice that uses spreading activation to evaluate the utility of alternative choices of Web links. This rational analysis yields a spreading activation theory of utility and choice.

Bayesian Analysis of Information Scent

Anderson and Milson (1989) proposed that human memory is designed to solve the problem of predicting what past experiences will be relevant in ongoing current proximal contexts and allocating resources for the storage and retrieval of past experiences based on those predictions. The rational analysis of information scent is framed by a different assumption — that the information forager is making predictions about the expected value of different external actions — but it ends up with a derivation that parallels the rational analysis of human memory.

Figure 4.8 presents an example of a user who has the goal of finding distal information about medical treatments for cancer. The user encounters a hypertext link labeled with text that includes "cell," "patient," "dose," and "beam." The user's cognitive task is to predict the likelihood that a distal source of content contains desired information based on the proximal cues available in the hypertext link labels.

Bayes's Theorem can be applied to the information foraging problem posed by situations such as those in figure 4.8. The analysis begins with a specification of the problem using the odds version of Bayes's Theorem. With some strong simplifying assumptions, this analysis will yield a specification of a simple linear summation that is the basis for a spreading activation mechanism. Spreading activation is similar to other linear summation algorithms found in connectionist (neural) networks. Interestingly, there it has been argued (Glimcher, 2003) that the brain is best viewed as generally performing operations that approximate Bayesian solutions to problems posed by the environment.

The Bayesian analysis developed here (see also Anderson, 1990, chapter 2; Anderson & Milson, 1989) begins with a statement of the problem using the odds version of Bayes's Theorem. This version turns out to be more tractable. The odds that a distal content structure has desired information features, D, given a structure of proximal features, P, can be stated as

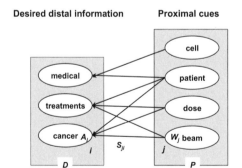

Desired distal information   **Proximal cues**

FIGURE 4.8 A cognitive structure representing some desired goal information (D) and an encounter with some proximal information scent cues (P). The desired information is "medical treatments for cancer," and it is assumed that the proximal cues (e.g., from a Web link) are "cell," "patient," "dose," "beam." Each of the j proximal cues sends activation in proportion to its strength of association S_{ji} to goal elements i, which sum all received activation to A_i.

$$O(D\,|\,P) = O(D) \quad \Lambda(D\,|\,P), \qquad (4.4)$$

where $O(D\,|\,P)$ is the *posterior odds* of distal content D conditional on the occurrence of proximal structure P, $O(D)$ is the *prior odds* of D, and $\Lambda(D\,|\,P)$ is the *likelihood ratio* of D occurring conditional on P. For concreteness, assume that the distal content structure, D, is the information contained on a Web page and that we represent D as a set of concepts corresponding to an information goal. Assume, likewise, that the proximal information scent structure, P, is represented as a set of the concepts corresponding to the words (images, etc.) on a Web link.

Each of the terms in equation 4.4 can be stated in terms of probabilities as follows. The posterior odds are

$$O(D\,|\,P) = \frac{\Pr(D\,|\,P)}{\Pr(\sim D\,|\,P)}, \qquad (4.5)$$

where $\Pr(D\,|\,P)$ is the probability of finding desired information D given the proximal cues P and $\Pr(\sim D\,|\,P)$ is the probability of not findsing D given P. The prior odds can be stated as

$$O(D) = \frac{\Pr(D)}{\Pr(\sim D)}, \qquad (4.6)$$

where $\Pr(D)$ is the probability of D being found and $\Pr(\sim D)$ is the probability of D not being found. One might think of this as being a *history factor* (Anderson, 1990; Anderson & Milson, 1989) that reflects the rate of occurrence of the desired information features in the general environment. The likelihood ratio is

$$\Lambda(D\,|\,P) = \frac{\Pr(P\,|\,D)}{\Pr(P\,|\sim D)}, \qquad (4.7)$$

where $\Pr(P\,|\,D)$ is the probability that proximal cues P would be relevant in the context given the goal D and $\Pr(P\,|\sim D)$ is probability that P would be found in the context if D were not a goal. One might think of this as a *context factor* (Anderson, 1990; Anderson & Milson, 1989) that reflects the relation of the contextual cues to the goal information.

Using the definitions above, equation 4.4 can be stated in terms of probabilities as

$$\frac{\Pr(D\,|\,P)}{\Pr(\sim D\,|\,P)} = \frac{\Pr(D)}{\Pr(\sim D)} \cdot \frac{\Pr(P\,|\,D)}{\Pr(P\,|\sim D)}. \qquad (4.8)$$

The appendix proposes a set of strong simplifying assumptions (that parallel Anderson, 1990, chapter 2) that lead to an odds equation for each individual feature, i, of the desired goal content structure, D, in terms of each individual feature, j, of the proximal information scent structure,

$$\frac{\Pr(i \mid P)}{\Pr(\sim i \mid P)} = \frac{\Pr(i)}{\Pr(\sim i)} \cdot \prod_{j \in P} \frac{\Pr(i \mid j)}{\Pr(i)}, \quad (4.9)$$

where the left side of the equation is the odds of a desired feature i being found given the proximal cues P, $\Pr(i)$ is the probability of desired feature i being found, $\Pr(i)/\Pr(\sim i)$ is the base rate odds of finding i, and $\Pr(i \mid j)$ is the conditional probability of a distal concept or feature i being found given that a proximal cue j is present.

If we use *log odds* instead of just odds, we can cast equation 4.9 into an additive format that will be the basis for the spreading activation mechanism. Taking the logarithms of both sides of equation 4.9 leads to an additive formula,

$$\log\left[\frac{\Pr(i \mid P)}{\Pr(\sim i \mid P)}\right]$$
$$= \log\left[\frac{\Pr(i)}{\Pr(\sim i)}\right] + \sum_{j \in P} \log\left[\frac{\Pr(i \mid j)}{\Pr(i)}\right], \quad (4.10)$$

or

$$A_i = B_i + \sum_j S_{ji}, \quad (4.11)$$

where

$$A_i = \log\left[\frac{\Pr(i \mid P)}{\Pr(\sim i \mid P)}\right],$$
$$B_i = \log\left[\frac{\Pr(i)}{\Pr(\sim i)}\right],$$
$$S_{ji} = \log\left[\frac{\Pr(i \mid j)}{\Pr(i)}\right].$$

S_{ji} corresponds to an information-theoretic measure known as *pointwise mutual information* (PMI) in the information retrieval literature (Manning & Schuetze, 1999, p. 178). As discussed below, PMI has been shown to be a very good predictor of human judgments of the similarity of words i and j.

Mapping the Bayesian Rational Analysis to Spreading Activation

Equation 4.1 provides the rational grounds for a spreading activation theory of information scent. Spreading activation models are neurally inspired models that have been used for decades in simulations of human memory (e.g., Anderson, 1976; Anderson & Lebiere, 1998; Anderson & Pirolli, 1984; e.g., Quillan, 1966). In such models, activation may be interpreted metaphorically as a kind of mental energy that drives cognitive processing. Activation spreads from a set of cognitive structures that are the current focus of attention through *associations* among other cognitive structures in memory. These cognitive structures are called *chunks* (Anderson & Lebiere, 1998).

Figure 4.8 presents a scenario for a spreading activation analysis. The chunks representing proximal cues are presented on the right side of figure 4.8. Figure 4.8 also shows that there are associations between the goal chunks (representing needed distal information) and proximal cues (the link summary chunks). The associations among chunks come from past experience. The strength of associations reflects the degree to which proximal cues predict the occurrence of unobserved features. For instance, the words "medical" and "patient" co-occur quite frequently, and they would have a high strength of association. The stronger the associations (reflecting greater predictive strength), the greater the amount of activation flow. These association strengths are reflections of the log-likelihood odds developed in equation 4.11.

Later chapters present the SNIF-ACT and ACT-IF cognitive simulations that use a spreading activation model derived from the ACT-R theory (Anderson & Lebiere, 1998). The activation of a chunk i is

$$A_i = B_i + \sum_j W_j S_{ji}, \quad (4.12)$$

where B_i is the base-level activation of i, S_{ji} is the association strength between an associated chunk j and chunk i, and W_j is reflects attention (*source activation*) on chunk j. Note that equation 4.12 reflects the log odds equation 4.11 but now includes a weighting factor W that characterizes capacity limitations of human attention. One may interpret equation 4.12 as reflection of a Bayesian prediction of the likelihood of one chunk in the context of other chunks. A_i in equation 4.12 is interpreted as reflecting the log posterior odds that i is likely given P, B_i is the log prior odds of i being likely, and S_{ji} reflects the log-likelihood odds that i is likely given that it occurs in the context of chunk j.

The basic idea is that information scent cues in the world activate cognitive structures. Activation spreads from these cognitive structures to related structures in the spreading activation network. The amount of activation accumulating on the representation of a user's information goal provides an indicator of the likelihood that a distal source of information has desirable features based on the information scent cues immediately available to the user.

Relating the Spread of Activation to the Evaluation of the Utility of Information Foraging Choices

Mapping this spreading activation model of information scent onto a model of rational choice (of navigation actions) involves the use of a Random Utility Model (McFadden, 1974, 1978). Random Utility Model (RUM) theory is grounded in classic microeconomic theory, and it has relations to psychological models of choice developed by Thurstone (1927) and Luce (1959). Its recent developments are associated with the microeconomic work of McFadden (1974, 1978).

For our purposes, an RUM consists of assumptions about (a) the characteristics of the information foragers making decisions, including their goal(s), (b) the choice set of alternatives, (c) the proximal cues of the alternatives, and (d) a choice rule. For current purposes, let us assume a homogeneous set of users with the same goal G with features $i \in G$ (and note that there is much interesting work on RUMs for cases with heterogeneous user goals). Each choice made by a user concerns a set C of alternatives, and each alternative J is an array of displayed proximal cues, $j \in J$, for some distal information content. Each proximal cue j emits a source activation Wj. These source activations spread through associations to features i that are part of the information goal G. The activation received by each goal feature i is A_i, and the summed activation over all goal features is

$$\sum_{i \in G} A_i.$$

The predicted utility $U_{J|G}$ of distal information content based on proximal cues J in the context of goal G is

$$U_{J|G} = V_{J|G} + \varepsilon_{J|G}, \qquad (4.13)$$

where

$$V_{J|G} = \sum_{i \in G} A_i$$

is the summed activation and where $\varepsilon_{J|G}$ is a random variable error term reflecting a stochastic component of utility. Thus, the utility $U_{J|G}$ is composed of a deterministic component $V_{J|G}$ and a random component $\varepsilon_{J|G}$. RUMs assume utility maximization where the information forager with goal G chooses J if and only if the utility of J is greater than all the other alternatives in the choice set:

$$U_{J|G} > U_{K|G} \text{ for all } K \in C.$$

Stated as a choice probability, this gives

$$\Pr(J \mid G, C) = \Pr(U_{J|G} \geq U_{K|G}, \forall K \in C). \qquad (4.14)$$

Because the utilities are stochastic, it is not the case that one alternative will always be chosen over another.

The specific form of the RUM depends on assumptions concerning the nature of the random noise component ε_i associated with each alternative i. It is typical to assume (e.g., Anderson & Lebiere, 1998; McFadden, 1974) that the distributions of the stochastic noise variables ε_i are independent identically distributed Gumbel distributions. The Gumbel distribution (sometimes known as the double exponential distribution) is an extreme value distribution with a cumulative distribution function,

$$F(\varepsilon) = \exp\left(-\exp\left[-\mu(\varepsilon - \eta)\right]\right), \quad \mu < 0, \qquad (4.15)$$

and a probability density function,

$$f(\varepsilon) = \mu \exp\left[-\mu(\varepsilon - \eta)\right] \exp\left(-\exp\left[-\mu(\varepsilon - \eta)\right]\right) \qquad (4.16)$$

where η is a location parameter and μ is a scale parameter. Given this assumption, equation 4.14 takes the form of a multinomial logit,

$$\Pr(J \mid G, C) = \frac{e^{\mu V_{J|G}}}{\sum_{K \in C} e^{\mu V_{K|G}}}, \qquad (4.17)$$

where μ is a scale parameter. If there is only one alternative to choose (e.g., select J or do not select J), then equation 4.14 takes the form of a binomial logit,

$$\Pr(J \mid G, C) = \frac{1}{1 + e^{\mu V_{J|G}}}. \qquad (4.18)$$

For a navigation judgment, we can now specify how the computation of spreading activation yields utilities by substituting equation 4.11 into equation 4.12:

$$
\begin{aligned}
U_{J|G} &= V_{J|G} + \varepsilon_{J|G} \\
&= \sum_{i \in G} A_i + \varepsilon_{J|G} \\
&= \sum_{i \in G} \left(B_i + \sum_{j \in J} W_j S_{ji} \right) + \varepsilon_{J|G}
\end{aligned}
\qquad (4.19)
$$

Equations 4.17–4.19 provide a microeconomic model for the choice of Web links that is grounded in an underlying cognitive model of utility.

It should be emphasized that this theory of information scent is not a part of the standard ACT-R theory. The spreading activation model of information scent is not the same as the ACT-R theory of spreading activation, and the utility model based on information scent is not the same as the ACT-R model of utility. In ACT-R, spreading activation emits from goal chunks and is used to retrieve relevant chunks from memory. In the theory of information scent, cues from the external world are sources of activation, and the activation levels of goal chunks are used to assess utility. In ACT-R, the utility assessments are based on the past successes and failures of actions. In the theory of information scent, the utility assessments are based on spreading activation. One can think of the spreading activation theory of information scent as being a kind of rational analysis of the categorization of cues according to their expected utility. At the beginning of this chapter I presented the general assumption that foragers categorize elements of their environment and predict the utility of those categories. The RUM based on spreading activation provides a mechanistic theory of how that is done in human information foraging.

Estimating Spreading Activation Strengths Using PMI

As discussed in Pirolli and Card (1999), it is possible to automatically construct large spreading activation networks from online text corpora. In other words, it is possible to analyze samples of the linguistic environment to provide the parameters of our cognitive models a priori rather than estimating those parameters a posteriori by fitting the models to behavioral data. The frequency of occurrence of words and the co-occurrence frequency of words near one another can be used to estimate the base strengths, B_i, and interchunk strengths, S_{ji}, in equation 4.12. In the SNIF-ACT model (Pirolli & Fu, 2003) discussed in chapter 5, these strengths are estimated from the Tipster document corpus (Harman, 1993) and from the Web using a program that calls on the AltaVista search engine to provide data. As noted in the appendix, the strength of association, S_{ji}, is the same as PMI. PMI is often presented in an alternative form:

$$\mathrm{PMI}(j, i) = \log\left[\frac{\Pr(ij)}{\Pr(i)\,\Pr(j)}\right], \qquad (4.20)$$

where $\Pr(ij)$ is the probability of two items (e.g., words) occurring together.

Recently, Turney (2001) has shown that PMI scores computed from the Web can provide good fits to human word similarity judgments. Pirolli, Fu, Chi, and Farahat (2005) report on a hybrid system for computing the co-occurrence counts from a corpus needed to generate PMI scores for spreading activation networks. The system is based on the Lucene search engine. Pirolli et al. (2005) used Lucene to index the first 10 million pages of the Stanford WebBase project. The hybrid system used the local crawl to compute the co-occurrence counts and backed off to the Web to collect statistics on very low-frequency items. The Google and AltaVista search engines were used to compute the Web co-occurrence counts. This hybrid PMI approach was tested on the synonym test from Test of English as a Foreign Language (TOEFL) data (Landauer & Dumais, 1997), which is a standard benchmark for Latent Semantic Analysis and other word similarity measurement techniques. The TOEFL set consisted of 80 problem words. For each problem word, four alternative words are presented, and the test asks which of the alternatives is most similar in meaning to the problem word. The hybrid PMI approach scores 66% on the TOEFL, which compares well to students (65%) and Latent Semantic Analysis (64%).

Summary

This section develops the rational basis for a model of navigation choice that is formulated as a Random Utility Model implemented as a spreading activation network. These spreading activation networks can be specified a priori from analysis of linguistic environments that are expected to be representative of the users being modeled. This is consistent with the goal of "parameter-free" cognitive models (Card, Moran, & Newell, 1983). Often, cognitive models in psychology are fit to data by estimating parameters from the data themselves (e.g., through curve fitting). The information foraging models discussed in later chapters have achieved good fits to data using parameters set, a priori, from analysis of the information environment (i.e., using PMI estimates). The entire model of information scent and utility, except the scaling factor, can be determined by statistical analysis of natural language in the environment.

Rational Analysis of Foraging in Information Patches

Chapter 2 presents the conventional patch model from optimal foraging theory (Stephens & Krebs, 1986), which deals with the optimal policy for the amount of time to spend in food patches before leaving. Applications of variations of that model to information foraging are discussed in Pirolli and Card (1999). To deal with Web foraging, here I present another variation that has ties to work investigating stochastic models of food foraging (McNamara, 1982) and studies of the aggregate behavior of large numbers of users browsing on the Web (Huberman et al., 1998).

A Stochastic Model of Patch Foraging

The stochastic model of patch foraging provides an operational definition for a foraging rule that can be stated simply in English as

> forage in an information patch until the expected potential of that patch is less than the mean expected value of going to a new patch.

A version of this rule is implemented in the first version of the SNIF-ACT model of Web foraging discussed in chapter 5.

Assume that the experiential state of the information forager at time i is represented as a state variable $\mathbf{X}_i$, and $\mathbf{X}_i = \mathbf{x}$ is a particular state value. For the present purposes, assume that this state variable includes some representation of the current Web page that has just been revealed and perceived by the information forager. The utility U as a function of the current user state, $U(\mathbf{x})$, of continued (optimal) link browsing in the current information patch can be represented by the expectation

$$U(\mathbf{x}) = E[U \mid \mathbf{X}_i = \mathbf{x}]. \qquad (4.21)$$

In keeping with the discussion above, we might assume that $U(\mathbf{x})$ is determined by choosing links having the maximum expected stochastic utility according to the RUM model. The expected time cost, t, of future (optimal) link browsing can be represented as an expectation,

$$t = E[T \mid \mathbf{X}_i = \mathbf{x}], \qquad (4.22)$$

where T is a random variable representing future time costs. The value $U(\mathbf{x})$ of foraging for time t in the current information patch (e.g., Web site) must be balanced against the opportunity cost $C(t)$ of foraging for that amount of time. This defines what McNamara (1982) called the *potential function*, $h(\mathbf{x})$, for continued foraging in the current patch,

$$h(\mathbf{x}) = U(\mathbf{x}) - C(t), \qquad (4.23)$$

and the optimal forager is one that maximizes this potential function.

McNamara's (1982) model characterizes the opportunity cost $C(t)$ in terms of the overall long-term average rate of gain of foraging, R^*:

$$C(t) = R^* t \qquad (4.24)$$

In the case of information foraging on the Web, we might assume this refers to the overall average long-term rate of gain of foraging on the Web for similar tasks. The intuition behind equations 4.23 and 4.24 is that the utility of foraging in the current patch must be greater than or equal to the average rate of returns for foraging (otherwise, continued foraging is incurring an opportunity cost). In other words, an information forager should continue foraging as long as

$$U(\mathbf{x}) - R^* t > 0. \tag{4.25}$$

The overall average rate of gain, R^*, could be characterized in terms of the mean utility $\bar{U}$ of going to a relevant Web site, the mean time spent setting up to go to the next relevant site (e.g., by using a search engine or guessing and typing URLs), $\bar{t}_s$, and the mean time spent foraging at the next new site, $\bar{t}$:

$$R^* = \frac{\bar{U}}{\bar{t}_s + \bar{t}} \tag{4.26}$$

Assuming equation 4.26, we may rewrite the inequality 4.25 as a rule to continue foraging as long as the rate of gain from the current information patch (e.g., Web site) is greater than the expected rate of gain of going to another relevant information patch:

$$\frac{U(\mathbf{x})}{t} > R^* = \frac{\bar{U}}{\bar{t}_s + \bar{t}} \tag{4.27}$$

This decision to stop foraging in an information patch when the expected rate of gain drops below R^* is a stochastic version of the patch-leaving rule in Charnov's Marginal Value Theorem (Charnov, 1976). Note that the discussion here has implicitly assumed that the information forager has perfect knowledge of the relevant environmental values in equations 4.24–4.27 (i.e., any learning is near asymptote). McNamara (1982) discusses how learning might be incorporated into this patch-leaving rule. In chapter 5, I discuss a specific learning formulation.

Note in equation 4.27 that the average time, t, to go to a Web page that is within the same Web site as the current page being visited may often be approximately the same as the time to go to a Web page at another Web site, $t_s + \bar{t}$. In such cases, the decision rule to continue foraging in equation 4.26 could be reduced to

$$U(\mathbf{x}) > \bar{U},$$

which is the mathematical version of the rule stated in English at the beginning of this subsection: Forage in an information patch until the expected potential of the patch is less than the mean expected value of going to a new patch.

In the SNIF-ACT model discussed in chapter 5, it is assumed that the expected potential of a patch is estimated from the links available on Web pages, relying again on spreading activation from information scent for this assessment. SNIF-ACT also assumes that the average expected value of a new patch is estimated from past experience on the Web.

From Individual Rationality to the Aggregate Behavior of Web Foraging: The Law of Surfing

One interesting consequence of this formulation of foraging in information patches is that it leads to predictions (Huberman et al., 1998) concerning patterns of aggregate behavior on the Web—specifically, what has been called the *Law of Surfing*. Such aggregate distributions are of practical interest because content providers on the Web often want to know how long people will remain at their Web sites (often referred to as the *stickiness* of a Web site). More generally, the ability to relate predictions about the emergent behavior of populations from the rational models of individuals is a way of bridging psychological science and the microeconomics of the Web. The Law of Surfing characterizes the distribution of the length, L, of sequences of page visits by Web users (see also Baldi et al., 2003, pp. 194–199). Figure 4.9 presents a typical empirical distribution of the length of paths taken by visitors to a Web site.

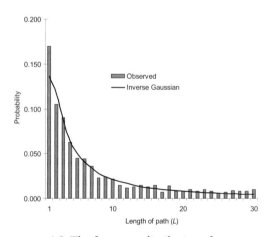

FIGURE 4.9 The frequency distribution of users as a function of depth of surfing. The observed data were collected at the Boston University during late 1994 and early 1995. The fitted inverse Gaussian distribution has a mean of $v = 51.19$ visits and $\lambda = 3.53$.

Note that the distribution is skewed, with the bulk of path lengths being short, and has a long positive tail. The skewness of the distribution and the long positive tail imply that the mean of the distribution will typically be larger than the mode.

The Law of Surfing assumes that a user's path (a sequence of Web page visits) can be modeled as a kind of random walk process. The key insight is that a Web surfer can be viewed as moving around in a kind of space in a way that is analogous to the Brownian motion of a small particle on a liquid surface. In the case of the Web surfer, the movement is in the dimension of expected utility, as depicted in figure 4.10. At any point in time, the Web user is at some page that has some expected utility, and there will be linked pages that define possible moves that can be made by the Web surfer. Some pages may have greater utility, some may have lower utility, and each move will take some amount of time to execute. As noted in chapter 3, linked pages tend to have content that is correlated with the current page, so moves in the space of expected utilities will tend to be small steps away from the current location rather than jumps to arbitrary utility values. Stated more formally, the Law of Surfing assumes that the expected utility from continuing on to the next state, X_t, is stochastically related to the expected utility of the current state, X_{t-1}:

$$U(X_t) = U(X_{t-1}) + \varepsilon_t, \qquad (4.28)$$

where ε_t are independent identically distributed Gaussian distributions with mean μ and variance σ^2.[4] This is known technically as a *Wiener process* (a Brownian motion process) with a random drift parameter μ and noise σ^2.

The next key assumption is that the random walk characterizing the Web forager continues until a threshold expected utility is reached. That is, from an initial starting page in a foraging episode, one expects users to continue browsing (surfing) following the random walk specified in equation 4.28 until some threshold θ is reached. Above, I specified one such hypothetical threshold in equation 4.25. More generally, the Law of Surfing assumes that an individual will continue to surf until the expected cost of continuing is perceived to be larger than the discounted expected value of the information to be found in the future. In the limit, this analysis of Web surfing is the same as the analysis of *first passage times* in Brownian motion. The first passage time problem is depicted

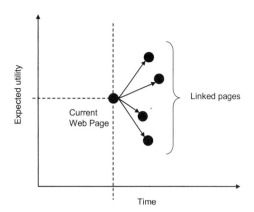

FIGURE 4.10 The Web foraging process of a user can be viewed as a kind of random walk process in which the user can move from a current page to linked pages that have expected utilities that are related to the expected utility of the current page.

graphically in figure 4.11: Given that the random walk process starts at some point (labeled zero in figure 4.11), what is the time taken to first cross a threshold (labeled θ in figure 4.11)? Since the process is stochastic, the solution involves finding the distribution of expected time for a process to move away from the start point to the given threshold.

Rather than length of time to first passage, the Law of Surfing deals with length of path in terms of page visits. As discussed in Lukose and Huberman (1998), it is assumed that this random walk Web surfing process is in the limit the same as Brownian motion. First passage times in Brownian motion are distributed as an Inverse Gaussian distribution (Seshardri, 1993). Applying this result to Web surfing, the probability density function of L, the length of sequences of Web page visits, is distributed as an inverse Gaussian distribution,

$$f(L) = \sqrt{\frac{\lambda}{2\pi}} L^{-3/2} e^{-\frac{\lambda}{2v^2 L}(L-v)^2}, \quad L > 0, \quad (4.29)$$

where the parameter v is the expected value, and λ is related to the expected value and variance as

$$\lambda = \frac{v^3}{\mathrm{Var}[L]}.$$

The parameters of the inverse Gaussian distribution can also be specified directly in terms of the

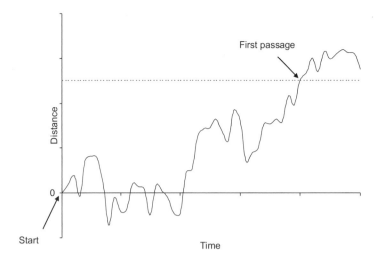

FIGURE 4.11 The first passage time problem concerns the distribution of time taken by random walk processes moving from some start point (located here at zero) to a threshold θ.

underlying random walk (Wiener) process. Given a start state X_0, the parameters are

$$v = \frac{\theta - X_0}{\mu}, \qquad (4.30)$$

and

$$\lambda = \frac{(\theta - X_0)^2}{\sigma^2}, \qquad (4.31)$$

which leads to a slightly different formulation,

$$f(L) = \frac{U - X_0}{\sqrt{2\pi\sigma^2 L^3}} e^{\frac{-(U - X_0 - \mu L)^2}{2\sigma^2 L}}. \qquad (4.32)$$

The inverse Gaussian is a skewed distribution that looks very much like the more familiar lognormal distribution, and it has a number of interesting properties. Web site developers are often interested in the amount of content that users will visit on their Web site (or the amount time they will spend). The Law of Surfing is relevant to characterizing these data of interest.

The Law of Surfing relates the rational analysis of individual Web surfing to aggregate behavior. The law was tested by Huberman et al. (1998) and additionally validated by Lukose and Huberman (1998). Figure 4.9 presents a typical empirical distribution of the length of paths taken by visitors to a Web site, along with a fitted inverse Gaussian distribution

(Huberman et al., 1998). Figure 4.12 plots another distribution of path lengths from another Web site in log–log coordinates. Figure 4.12 has the empirical appearance of a power law distribution with an exponent of approximately $-3/2$. It turns out (Huberman et al., 1998) that this is characteristic of the inverse Gaussian distribution when $\mu < \text{Var}[L]$. In chapter 5, one of the tests of the SNIF-ACT model of individual Web foraging will involve seeing if it will exhibit the Law of Surfing when run as a Monte Carlo simulation.

General Discussion

A theory of information scent has been proposed to address utility assessments, in the context of information foraging. People, as information foragers, face the problem of assessing the prospects of various actions during their search for useful information. Solving this problem requires judgments about the utility of distal information from proximal cues in the perceivable context. The theory presented here builds on Bayesian theories of memory and category formation and the Random Utility Model. The theory of information scent proposes that information foragers have mechanisms that reflect the probabilistic texture of the environment. These mechanisms are used to process local cues to assess the expected value of actions intended to lead to distal information sources.

Web Behavior Graph Representation

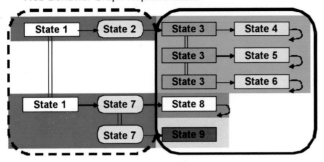

where
Time runs left to right, then top to bottom

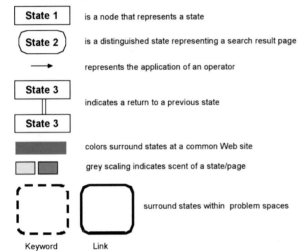

State 1	is a node that represents a state
State 2	is a distinguished state representing a search result page
→	represents the application of an operator
State 3 / State 3	indicates a return to a previous state
	colors surround states at a common Web site
	grey scaling indicates scent of a state/page
Keyword / Link	surround states within problem spaces

FIGURE 3.4 Schematic explanation of the components of a Web behavior graph.

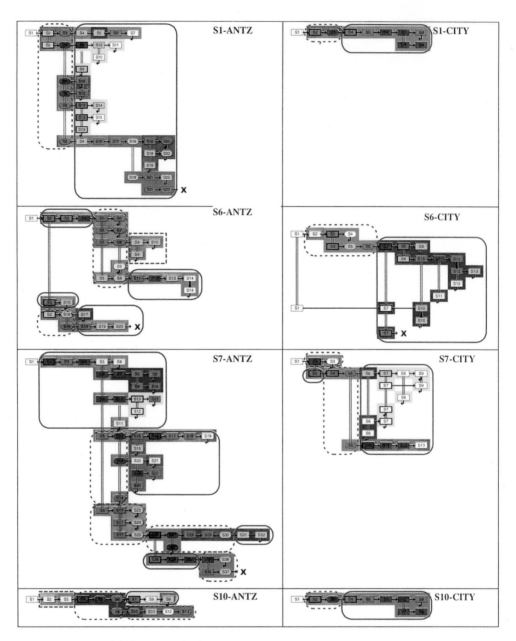

FIGURE 3.5 Web behavior graphs for four participants (rows) working on two tasks (columns).

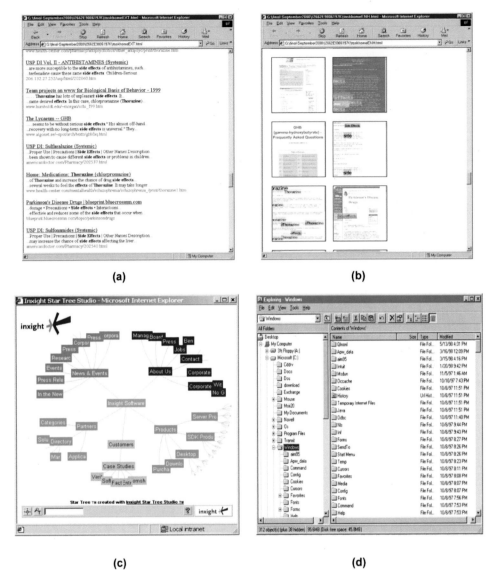

FIGURE 4.1 Examples of proximal information scent cues: (a) search results from a popular search engine, (b) relevance-enhanced thumbnails of the same search results, (c) Star Tree (or hyperbolic tree) presentation of a hierarchy, and (d) Microsoft Explorer presentation of a hierarchy.

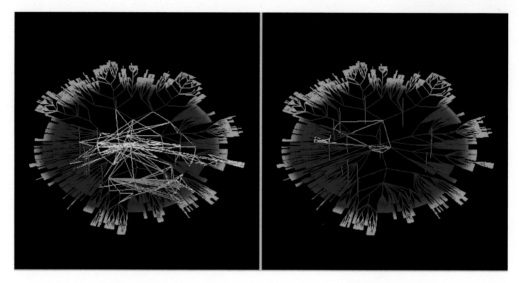

(a) Low scent   (b) High scent

FIGURE 4.3 Eye movements of a single user over tree structures presented in two interactive browsers (data from Pirolli et al., 2003). Circular blue structures represent the underlying data tree structure (only a portion of which would be visible to the user in either browser), green paths represent eye movements in the Microsoft Explorer browser, and yellow paths represent eye movements in the hyperbolic tree browser. The height of the red bars indicates the information scent of nodes. (a) A low-scent task. (b) A high-scent task.

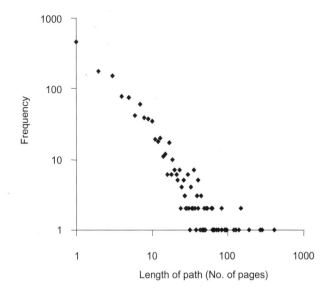

FIGURE 4.12 The frequency distribution of surfing depths on log–log scales. Data collected from the Georgia Institute of Technology, August 1994.

In their classic work on problem solving, Newell and Simon (1972) remarked, "We are not yet ready for a serious ecological study (as proposed say, by Egon Brunswik, 1956)." Given the state of information processing psychology in the early 1970s, it was quite reasonable for Newell and Simon to first establish the efficacy of their novel approach (the analysis of task environments and problem spaces using information processing concepts) and leave "serious ecological study" for a later generation. The research described in this chapter has followed a theoretical and methodological approach that fits an ecological framework for psychology advocated by Brunswik (1952; Cooksey, 2001) that appears to resonate with many recent researchers (e.g., Anderson, 1990; Gigerenzer, 2000; Marr, 1982; Neisser, 1976). As noted in Cooksey's (2001) deft summary, Brunswik's conceptual framework consists of (1) a molar, symmetric focus on the relations between organism and environment, (2) representative design, and (3) an idiographic-statistical scheme of explanation. The theory of information scent was developed with a symmetric focus on the human and the environment, as embodied in an extension of Brunswik's Lens Model. The domain of information scent theory concerns tasks and situations (e.g., Web browsing) that are representative of everyday life. Information scent provides explanations and predictions at the level of individuals (it is idiographic) assuming probabilistic rationality (it is fundamentally statistical).

Advocates of this approach (including me) assume that a greater emphasis on the analysis of ecologically representative problems and on molar, integrative approaches is a powerful heuristic for scientific and practical progress. In the case of information scent theory, careful rational analysis of behavior on ecologically representative tasks and materials has led to an integrated theory that produces models almost entirely by a priori task analysis and parameter estimation from data available in the environment. Chapter 5 presents a computational cognitive model called SNIF-ACT that implements these rational analyses as mechanistic theory.

APPENDIX

Following the lead of Anderson (1990; Anderson & Milson, 1989), a few strong simplifying assumptions are made here. The general scheme is to assume (a) that the probability of a structure (D or P in figure 4.8) is just the product of the probabilities of each of the features of that structure, and (b) that the conditional probability of one element on another is independent of all the other elements. So, it is assumed that the posterior odds in equation 4.4 can be simplified to

$$O(D \mid P) = \frac{\Pr(D \mid P)}{\Pr(\sim D \mid P)} = \prod_{i \in D} \frac{\Pr(i \mid P)}{\Pr(\sim i \mid P)} \qquad (4.A.1)$$

where each i is a feature of the desired information. Equation 4.A.1 states that the odds of finding desired information D given proximal cues P is just the product of finding each feature of D given those cues. The history factor is simplified to

$$O(D) = \frac{\Pr(D)}{\Pr(\sim D)} = \prod_{i \in D} \frac{\Pr(i)}{\Pr(\sim i)}, \quad (4.A.2)$$

which states that the prior odds of finding desired information D is the product of the odds of finding each feature of D. The likelihood ratio is simplified to

$$\Lambda(D \mid P) = \frac{\Pr(P \mid D)}{\Pr(P \mid \sim D)} = \prod_{j \in P} \frac{\Pr(j \mid D)}{\Pr(j \mid \sim D)}, \quad (4.A.3)$$

where each j is a cue element of the proximal structure P. The likelihood ratio is just the product of the likelihood ratios for the desired information D for each fixed cue j.[5]

It is also assumed that the base rate probability of a cue occurring is not meaningfully different than the rate of that cue occurring when the user does not have the specific goal of finding D. So,

$$\Pr(j \mid \sim D) \approx \Pr(j), \quad (4.A.4)$$

and the product in equation 4.A.3 can be rewritten as

$$\frac{\Pr(j \mid D)}{\Pr(j \mid \sim D)} = \frac{\Pr(j \mid D)}{\Pr(j)}. \quad (4.A.5)$$

There are two useful consequences from the reformulation in equation 4.A.5. One is that the following equivalence holds:

$$\frac{\Pr(j \mid D)}{\Pr(j)} = \frac{\Pr(D \mid j)}{\Pr(D)} \quad (4.A.6)$$

Applying assumptions (a) and (b) again, we can decompose this into a simple product:

$$\frac{\Pr(D \mid j)}{\Pr(D)} = \prod_{i \in D} \frac{\Pr(i \mid j)}{\Pr(i)}, \quad (4.A.7)$$

where $\Pr(i \mid j)$ means the probability of finding desired information D containing a feature i given a cue j in the proximal structure P, and $\Pr(i)$ is the base rate probability of finding desired information containing i.

The second useful aspect of this reformulation is that

$$\log \left[\frac{\Pr(i \mid j)}{\Pr(i)} \right]$$

is what is known as pointwise mutual information (PMI), which has been investigated in information retrieval, which has been drawn upon in building these models.

Putting together the assumptions in equations 4.A.1–4.A.7, the specification in equation 4.8 can be rewritten as

$$\prod_{i \in D} \frac{\Pr(i \mid P)}{\Pr(\sim i \mid P)} = \prod_{i \in D} \frac{\Pr(i)}{\Pr(\sim i)} \cdot \prod_{j \in P} \frac{\Pr(j \mid D)}{\Pr(j \mid \sim D)}$$

$$= \prod_{i \in D} \frac{\Pr(i)}{\Pr(\sim i)} \cdot \prod_{j \in P} \prod_{i \in D} \frac{\Pr(i \mid j)}{\Pr(i)}. \quad (4.A.8)$$

This affords the specification of an equation for each feature of the desired information D,

$$\frac{\Pr(i \mid P)}{\Pr(\sim i \mid P)} = \frac{\Pr(i)}{\Pr(\sim i)} \cdot \prod_{j \in P} \frac{\Pr(i \mid j)}{\Pr(i)}, \quad (4.A.9)$$

which is presented as equation 4.9 in the text. The left side of equation 4.A.8 is just the product of equation 4.A.9 for each feature i.

Notes

1. Thanks to Leda Cosmides for suggesting the relevance of landscape aesthetics.
2. Marketed by Inxight Inc. as the Star Tree.
3. Thanks to Ed Chi for computing these disk trees.
4. Note that we are discussing aggregates of different surfers with different stochastic utility functions. The constraint of independent identically distributed Gaussian noise is expected from the Central Limit Theorem.
5. The likelihood of A given B for a fixed value of B is the conditional probability of B given A.

References

Anderson, J. R. (1976). *Language, memory, and thought.* Hillsdale, NJ: Lawrence Erlbaum Associates.
Anderson, J. R. (1990). *The adaptive character of thought.* Hillsdale, NJ: Lawrence Erlbaum Associates.

Anderson, J. R. (1991). The adaptive nature of human categorization. *Psychological Review, 98*, 409–429.

Anderson, J. R., & Lebiere, C. (1998). *The atomic components of thought*. Mahwah, NJ: Lawrence Erlbaum Associates.

Anderson, J. R., & Milson, R. (1989). Human memory: An adaptive perspective. *Psychological Review, 96*, 703–719.

Anderson, J. R., & Pirolli, P. (1984). Spread of activation. *Journal of Experimental Psychology: Learning, Memory, and Cognition, 10*, 791–798.

Baldi, P., Frasconi, P., & Smyth, P. (2003). *Modeling the Internet and the Web*. Chichester, UK: Wiley and Sons.

Barsalou, L. W. (1990). On the indistinguishability of exemplar memory and abstraction in category representation. In T. K. Srull & R. S. Wyer (Eds.), *Advances in social cognition: Vol. 3. Content and process specificity in the effects of prior experiences* (pp. 61–88). Hillsdale, NJ: Lawrence Erlbaum Associates.

Bell, W. J. (1991). *Searching behavior: The behavioral ecology of finding resources*. London: Chapman & Hall.

Blackmon, M. H., Polson, P. G., Kitajima, M., & Lewis, C. (2002). Cognitive Walkthrough for the Web. *CHI 2002, ACM Conference on Human Factors in Computing Systems, CHI Letters, 4*(1), 463–470.

Brunswik, E. (1952). *The conceptual framework of psychology*. Chicago: University of Chicago Press.

Brunswik, E. (1956). *Perception and the representative design of psychological experiments*. Berkeley, CA: University of California Press.

Card, S. K., Moran, T. P., & Newell, A. (1983). *The psychology of human-computer interaction*. Hillsdale, NJ: Lawrence Erlbaum Associates.

Charnov, E. L. (1976). Optimal foraging: The marginal value theorem. *Theoretical Population Biology, 9*, 129–136.

Chi, E., Pitkow, J., Mackinlay, J., Pirolli, P., Gossweiler, R., & Card, S. K. (1998). Visualizing the evolution of Web ecologies. *Proceedings of the Conference on Human Factors in Computing Systems, CHI '98* (pp. 400–407). Los Angeles: Association for Computing Machinery.

Chi, E. H., Rosien, A., Suppattanasiri, G., Williams, A., Royer, C., Chow, C., et al. (2003). The Bloodhound project: Automating discovery of Web usability issues using the InfoScent simulator. *CHI 2003, ACM Conference on Human Factors in Computing Systems, CHI Letters, 5*(1), 505–512.

Cooksey, R. W. (2001). Brunswik's "The conceptual framework of psychology" then and now. In K. R. Hammond & T. R. Stewart (Eds.), *The essential Brunswik* (pp. 225–231). Oxford: Oxford University Press.

Estes, W. K. (1997). *Classification and cognition*. Cambridge: Oxford University Press.

Furnas, G. W. (1997). Effective view navigation. *Proceedings of the Conference on Human Factors in Computing Systems, CHI '97* (pp. 367–374). Atlanta, GA: Association for Computing Machinery.

Gigerenzer, G. (2000). *Adaptive thinking: Rationality in the real world*. Oxford: Oxford University Press.

Glimcher, P. W. (2003). *Decisions, uncertainty, and the brain: The science of neuroeconomics*. Cambridge, MA: MIT Press.

Harman, D. (1993, July). *Overview of the first text retrieval conference*. Paper presented at the 16th annual International ACM/SIGIR Conference, Pittsburgh, PA.

Hogg, T., & Huberman, B. A. (1987). Artificial intelligence and large-scale computation: A physics perspective. *Physics Reports, 156*, 227–310.

Huberman, B. A., Pirolli, P., Pitkow, J., & Lukose, R. J. (1998). Strong regularities in World Wide Web surfing. *Science, 280*, 95–97.

Katz, M. A., & Byrne, M. D. (2003). Effects of scent and breadth on use of site-specific search on e-commerce Web sites. *ACM Transactions on Computer-Human Interaction, 10*(3), 198–220.

Lamping, J., & Rao, R. (1994). Laying out and visualizing large trees using a hyperbolic tree. *Proceedings of the 7th ACM Symposium on User Interface Software and Technology, UIST '94* (pp. 13–14). Marina del Rey, CA: Association for Computing Machinery.

Lamping, J., Rao, R., & Pirolli, P. (1995). A focus + context technique based on hyperbolic geometry for visualizing large hierarchies. In *Proceedings of the Conference on Human Factors in Computing Systems, CHI '95* (pp. 401–408). New York: Association for Computing Machinery.

Landauer, T. K., & Dumais, S. T. (1997). A solution to Plato's problem: The latent semantic analysis theory of acquisition, induction, and representation of knowledge. *Psychological Review, 104*, 211–240.

Luce, R. D. (1959). *Individual choice behavior*. New York: Wiley.

Lukose, R. M., & Huberman, B. A. (1998, October). *Surfing as a real option*. Paper presented at the International Conference on Information and Computation Economies, Charleston, SC.

Malt, B. C. (1995). Category coherence in cross-cultural perspective. *Cognitive Psychology, 29*, 85–148.

Manning, C. D., & Schuetze, H. (1999). *Foundations of statistical natural language processing*. Cambridge, MA: MIT Press.

Marr, D. (1982). *Vision*. San Francisco: W.H. Freedman.

McFadden, D. (1974). Conditional logit analysis of qualitative choice behavior. In P. Zarembka (Ed.), *Frontiers of econometrics*. New York: Academic Press.

McFadden, D. (1978). Modelling the choice of residential location. In A. Karlqvist, L. Lundqvist, F. Snickars, & J. Weibull (Eds.), *Spatial interaction theory and planning models* (pp. 75–96). Cambridge, MA: Harvard University Press.

McNamara, J. (1982). Optimal patch use in a stochastic environment. *Theoretical Population Biology, 21,* 269–288.

Medin, D. L., & Schaffer, M. M. (1978). A context theory of classification learning. *Psychological Review, 85,* 207–238.

Miller, C. S., & Remington, R. W. (2004). Modeling information navigation: Implications for information architecture. *Human-Computer Interaction, 19*(3), 225–271.

Neisser, U. (1976). *Cognition and reality*. San Francisco, CA: Freeman.

Newell, A., & Simon, H. A. (1972). *Human problem solving*. Englewood Cliffs, NJ: Prentice Hall.

Orians, G. H., & Heerwagen, J. H. (1992). Evolved responses to landscapes. In J. H. Barkow, L. Cosmides, & J. Tooby (Eds.), *The adapted mind* (pp. 555–579). New York: Oxford University Press.

Pirolli, P. (1997, March). *Computational models of information scent-following in a very large browsable text collection*. Paper presented at the CHI 1997 Conference on Human Factors in Computing Systems, Atlanta, GA.

Pirolli, P. (2004). The InfoCLASS model: Conceptual richness and inter-person conceptual consensus about information collections. *Cognitive Studies: Bulletin of the Japanese Cognitive Science Society, 11*(3), 197–213.

Pirolli, P., & Card, S. K. (1999). Information foraging. *Psychological Review, 106,* 643–675.

Pirolli, P., Card, S. K., & Van Der Wege, M. M. (2003). The effects of information scent on visual search in the hyperbolic tree browser. *ACM Transactions on Computer-Human Interaction, 10*(1), 20–53.

Pirolli, P., & Fu, W. (2003). SNIF-ACT: A model of information foraging on the World Wide Web. In P. Brusilovsky, A. Corbett, & F. de Rosis (Eds.), *User Modeling 2003, 9th International Conference, UM 2003* (Vol. 2702, pp. 45–54). Johnstown, PA: Springer-Verlag.

Pirolli, P., Fu, W., Chi, E., & Farahat, A. (2005, July). *Information scent and Web navigation: Theory, models, and automated usability evaluation*. Paper presented at the Human-Computer Interaction International Conference, Las Vegas, NV.

Pitt, M. A., Myung, I. J., & Zhang, S. (2002). Toward a method of selecting among computational models of cognition. *Psychological Review, 109,* 472–291.

Quillan, M. R. (1966). *Semantic memory*. Cambridge, MA: Bolt, Bernak, & Newman.

Reed, S. K. (1972). Pattern recognition and categorization. *Cognitive Psychology, 3,* 382–407.

Rosch, E. (1978). Principles of categorization. In E. Rosch & B. B. Lloyd (Eds.), *Cognition and categorization* (pp. 27–48). Hillsdale, NJ: Lawrence Erlbaum.

Seshardri, V. (1993). *The inverse Gaussian distribution*. Oxford: Clarendon Press.

Stephens, D. W., & Krebs, J. R. (1986). *Foraging theory*. Princeton, NJ: Princeton University Press.

Thurstone, L. (1927). A law of comparative judgment. *Psychological Review, 34,* 273–286.

Turney, P. D. (2001, September). *Mining the Web for synonyms: PMI-IR versus LSA on TOEFL*. Paper presented at the Twelfth European Conference on Machine Learning, Freiburg, Germany.

Wittgenstein, L. (1953). *Philosophical investigations*. Oxford: Basil Blackwell.

Woodruff, A., Rosenholtz, R., Morrison, J. B., Faulring, A., & Pirolli, P. (2002). A comparison of the use of text summaries, plain thumbnails, and enhanced thumbnails for Web search tasks. *Journal of the American Society for Information Science and Technology, 53,* 172–185.

5

A Cognitive Model of Information Foraging on the Web

This chapter presents a computational cognitive model that simulates users foraging for information on the Web that was developed over several years of collaboration with my colleague Wai-Tat Fu. This cognitive model is called SNIF-ACT, which stands for Scent-based Navigation and Information Foraging in the ACT architecture. The model, as the name implies, integrates the cognitive theory of information scent and rational analyses presented in chapter 4 with the ACT cognitive architecture (Anderson, 1983, 1990, 1993; Anderson & Lebiere, 2000). The development of SNIF-ACT required the development of a system for validating the model against actual Web user data. We (Pirolli, Fu, Reeder, & Card, 2002) developed a *user-tracing architecture* for testing cognitive models such as SNIF-ACT against data sets that contain *user traces*, which are transcriptions or recordings of user interaction with interfaces to the Web.

Chapter 4 presented observations and rational analyses about the Web. Among the problems facing

the Web forager were (a) the choice of the most cost-effective and useful browsing actions to take based on the relation of a user's information need to the perceived proximal cues (information scent) associated with Web links and (b) the decision of whether to continue at a Web site or leave based on ongoing assessments of the site's potential usefulness and costs. Rational choice models, and specifically approaches borrowed and modified from optimal foraging theory (Stephens & Krebs, 1986) and microeconomics (McFadden, 1974), were used to predict rational behavioral solutions to these problems. It was argued that the cost-benefit assessments involved in the solution to these problems facing the Web user could be grounded in a Rational Utility Model (McFadden, 1974) based on spreading activation between In this chapter, I describe the current status of the SNIF-ACT model and the results from testing the model against two data sets from real-world human participants who worked on unfamiliar information-seeking tasks.

The rational analyses of information foraging on the Web provide characterizations of (a) *what* problems are posed by the task and information environments and (b) *why* particular behavioral solutions (e.g., decisions, actions, policies, and strategies) are optimal. SNIF-ACT describes *how* these rational solutions are implemented in computational cognitive mechanisms. In developing this computational cognitive model, additional constraints coming from the cognitive architecture must be addressed. In particular, SNIF-ACT must employ *satisficing* (Simon, 1955) and learning from experience. These mechanisms arise as solutions to limits on computational resources and amount of available information that are not necessarily considered constraints in rational analyses.

Building on the analyses laid out in chapter 4, SNIF-ACT employs a spreading activation mechanism to determine which actions to take. Spreading activation is assumed to operate on a large associative network that represents the Web user's linguistic knowledge. These spreading activation networks are central to SNIF-ACT, and one would prefer that they be predictive in the sense that they are (a) general over the universe of tasks and (b) not estimated from the behavior of the users being modeled. SNIF-ACT assumes that the spreading activation networks have computational properties that reflect the statistical properties of the linguistic environment. One may construct these networks using statistical estimates obtained from appropriately large and representative samples of the linguistic environment. Consequently, SNIF-ACT predictions for Web users with particular goals can be made using spreading activation networks that are constructed a priori with no free parameters to be estimated from user data.

One reason for developing SNIF-ACT is to further a psychological theory of human information foraging (Pirolli & Card, 1999) in a real-world domain. Real-world problems pose productive challenges for science. New theory often emerges from scientific problems that reflect real phenomena in the world. Such theories are also likely to have implications for real problems that need to be solved. Psychological models such as SNIF-ACT are expected to provide the theoretical foundations for cognitive engineering models and techniques of Web usability such as those presented in chapter 9.

There have been many attempts to understand Web users and to develop Web usability methods.

Empirical studies (Choo, Detlor, & Turnbull, 2000) have reported general patterns of information-seeking behavior but have not provided much in the way of detailed analysis. Web usability methodologists (Brinck, Gergle, & Wood, 2001; Krug, 2000; Nielsen, 2000; Spool, Perfetti, & Brittan, 1999) have drawn on a mix of case studies and empirical research to extract best design practices for use during development as well as evaluation methods for identifying usability problems (Garzotto, Matera, & Paolini, 1998). For instance, principles regarding the ratio of content to navigation structure on Web pages (Nielsen, 2000), the use of information scent to improve Web site navigation (User Interface Engineering, 1999), reduction of cognitive overhead (Krug, 2000), writing style and graphic design (Brinck et al., 2001), and much more can be found in the literature. Unfortunately, these principles are not universally agreed upon and have not been rigorously tested. For instance, there is a debate about the importance of download time as a usability factor (Nielsen, 2000; User Interface Engineering, 1999). Such methods can identify requirements and problems with specific designs and may even lead to some moderately general design practices, but they are not aimed at the sort of deeper scientific understanding that may lead to large improvements in Web interface design.

The development of theory in this area can greatly accelerate progress and meet the demands of changes in the way we interact with the Web (Newell & Card, 1985). Greater theoretical understanding and the ability to predict the effects of alternative designs could bring greater coherence to the usability literature and provide more rapid evolution of better designs. In practical terms, a designer armed with such theory could explore and explain the effects of different design decisions on Web designs before the heavy investment of resources for implementation and testing. Theory and scientific models themselves may not be of direct use to engineers and designers, but they form a solid and fruitful foundation for design models and engineering models (Card, Moran, & Newell, 1983; Paternò, Sabbatino, & Santoro, 2000). Unfortunately, cognitive engineering models that had been developed to deal with the analysis of expert performance on well-defined tasks involving application programs (e.g., Pirolli, 1999) have had limited applicability to understanding foraging through content-rich hypermedia, and consequently, new theories are needed.

Models of Web Navigation

The SNIF-ACT model presented in this chapter is one of several recently developed cognitive models aimed at a better understanding of Web navigation. Web navigation, or browsing, typically involves some mix of scanning and reading Web pages, using search engines, assessing and selecting links on Web pages to go to other Web pages, and using various backtracking mechanisms (e.g., history lists or back buttons on a browser). None of these recently developed cognitive models (including SNIF-ACT) offers a complete account of all of these behaviors that are involved in a typical information foraging task on the Web. The development of SNIF-ACT has been driven by the analysis of the Web environment presented in chapter 3 and the rational analyses presented in chapter 4, and the idea that the development of theory is best achieved through a process of successive refinement of models in a cognitive architecture that is aimed to provide an integrated theory of cognition (Anderson & Lebiere, 1998). SNIF-ACT has focused on modeling how users make navigation choices when browsing over many pages until they either give up or find what they are seeking. These navigation choices involve which links to follow, or when to give up on a particular path and go to a previous page, another Web site, or search engine. SNIF-ACT may be compared to two other recent models of Web navigation, MESA (C. S. Miller & Remington, 2004) and CoLiDeS (Kitajima, Blackmon, & Polson, 2005), which are summarized below.

MESA

MESA (Method for Evaluating Site Architectures; C. S. Miller & Remington, 2004) simulates the flow of users through tree structures of linked Web pages. It is intended to be a cognitive engineering model for calculating the time cost of navigation through alternative Web structures for given tasks. The focus of MESA is on link navigation, which empirical studies (Katz & Byrne, 2003) suggest is the dominant strategy for foraging for information on the Web. MESA was formulated based on several principles: (a) the *rationality principle*, which heuristically assumes that users adopt rational behavior solutions to the problems posed by their environments (within the bounds of their limitations); (b) the *limited capacity principle*, which constrains the model to perform operations that are cognitively and physically feasible for the human

user; and (c) the *simplicity principle*, which favors good approximations when added complexity makes the model less usable with little improvement in fit (see also, Newell & Card, 1985).

MESA scans the links on a Web page in serial order. It navigates with three basic operators that (1) assess the relevance of a link on a Web page, (2) select a link, and (3) backtrack to a previous page. MESA employs a *threshold strategy* for selecting links and an *opportunistic strategy* for temporarily delaying return to a previous page. It scans links on a Web page in serial order. If a link exceeds an internal threshold, MESA selects that link and goes to the linked page. Otherwise, if the link is below threshold, MESA continues scanning and assessing links. If it reaches the end of a Web page without selecting a link, it rescans the page with a lower threshold, unless the threshold has already been lowered or marginally relevant links were encountered on the first scan.

MESA achieves correlations of $r = .79$ with human user navigation times across a variety of tasks, Web structures, and quality of information scent (C. S. Miller & Remington, 2004). It does not, however, directly interact with the Web, which requires the modeler to hand-code the structure of Web that is of concern to the simulation. MESA also does not have an automated way of computing link relevance (the information scent of links), requiring modelers to separately obtain ratings of stated preferences for links. Both of these concerns are addressed by the SNIF-ACT model.

CoLiDeS

CoLiDeS (Comprehension-based Linked model of Deliberative Search; Kitajima et al., 2005) is model of Web navigation that derives from Kintsch's (1998) construction-integration cognitive architecture. The CoLiDeS cognitive model is the basis for a cognitive engineering approach called CWW (Cognitive Walkthrough for the Web; Blackmon, Polson, Kitajima, & Lewis, 2002). Construction-integration is generally a process by which meaningful representations of internal and external entities such as texts, display objects, and object-action connections are constructed and elaborated with material retrieved from memory, and then a spreading activation constraint satisfaction process integrates the relevant information and eliminates the irrelevant. CoLiDeS includes meaningful knowledge for comprehending task instructions, formulating goals, parsing the layout of Web pages, comprehending link labels, and performing navigation actions. In CoLiDeS, these spreading activation networks include representations of goals and subgoals, screen elements, and propositional knowledge, including object-action pairs. These items are represented as nodes in a network interconnected by links weighted by strength values. Activation is spread through the network in proportion to the strength of connections. The connection strengths between representations of a user's goal and screen objects correspond to the notion of information scent. As discussed below, these strengths are partly determined by Latent Semantic Analysis (LSA) measures (Landauer & Dumais, 1997).

Given a task goal, CoLiDeS (Kitajima et al., 2005) forms a *content subgoal*, representing the meaning of the desired content, and a *navigation subgoal*, representing the desired method for finding that content (e.g., "use the Web site navigation bar"). CoLiDeS then proceeds through two construction-integration phases: (1) an *attention phase*, which determines which display items to attend to, and (2) an *action-selection phase*, which results in the next navigation action to select. During the attention phase, a given Web page is parsed into subregions based on knowledge of Web and graphical user interface layouts, knowledge is retrieved to elaborate interpretations of these subregions, and constraint satisfaction selects an action determining the direction of attention to a Web page subregion. During the action-selection phase, representations of the elements of the selected subregion are elaborated by knowledge from long-term memory. The spreading activation constraint satisfaction process then selects a few objects in the subregion as relevant. Another constraint satisfaction process then selects eligible object-action pairs that are associated with the relevant items. This determines the next navigation action to perform.

In both the attention phase and the action-selection phase, spreading activation networks are constructed, activation is spread through the networks, and the most active elements in the network are selected and acted upon. As noted above, LSA is used to determine the relevance (information scent) of display objects to a user's goal.[1] In CoLiDeS, relevance is determined by five factors (Kitajima et al., 2005): (1) semantic similarity as measured as the cosine of LSA term vectors representing a user's goal and words on a Web page; (2) the LSA term vector length of words on a Web page, which is assumed to measure the familiarity of the term; (3) the frequency of occurrence of terms in document collection on which LSA has been computed; (4) the frequency of encounter with Web page terms in a user's session; and (5) literal matches between terms representing the user's goal and the terms on a Web page. These five factors combine to determine the strengths of association among elements representing goal elements and Web page elements, which determine the spread of activation and ultimately the control of attention and action in CoLiDeS.

The primary evaluation of CoLiDeS comes from the CWW Web usability engineering model (Blackmon et al., 2002; Kitajima et al., 2005). CWW is used to find and identify usability problems on given Web pages. This includes prediction of the total number of clicks to accomplish a goal (a measure of task difficulty) and the identification of problems due to lack of familiar wording on Web pages, links that compete for attention, and links that have weak information scent.

Summary

SNIF-ACT, like MESA, is a simulation of how users navigate over a series of Web pages, although SNIF-ACT is not artificially restricted to treelike structures and deals with actual Web content and structures. Similar to MESA, SNIF-ACT is founded on a rational analysis of Web navigation, although the rational analysis of SNIF-ACT derives from Information Foraging Theory (Pirolli, 2005; Pirolli & Card, 1999). This rational analysis guides the implementation of SNIF-ACT as a computational cognitive model. The initial implementations of SNIF-ACT have implicitly assumed a slightly different version of MESA's simplicity principle: SNIF-ACT was developed under the assumption that the complexity of Web navigation behavior could best be addressed by a process of successive approximation. This involves first modeling factors that are assumed to control the more significant aspects of the behavioral phenomena and then proceeding to refine the model to address additional details of user behavior.

As argued in chapter 4, the use of information scent to make navigation choices during link following on the Web is perhaps the most significant factor in determining performance times in seeking information. Small changes in information scent can produce larger—even qualitative—changes to the search costs of navigation. Consequently, the development of SNIF-ACT has focused first on modeling the role of information scent in navigation choice. In this respect, it is much like CoLiDeS (Kitajima et al., 2005). Neither MESA nor CoLiDeS models the decision of information foragers to abandon a particular navigation path and try something else (e.g., a previous page, another Web site, or a search engine). SNIF-ACT incorporates the rational analysis of leaving an information patch outlined in chapter 4.

SNIF-ACT differs in several respects from CoLiDeS. The model of information scent is based on the rational analysis of navigation choice behavior presented in chapter 4. Also unlike CoLiDeS, SNIF-ACT derives from the ACT-R architecture (Anderson & Lebiere, 1998). Although SNIF-ACT does not currently make use of the full set of ACT-R modeling capabilities, one would expect those capabilities to be useful in successive refinements of SNIF-ACT. For instance, SNIF-ACT does not currently make use of ACT-R modules for the prediction of eye movements and other perceptual-motor behavior, which would be crucial to the prediction of how users scan individual Web pages and why users often fail to find information displayed on a Web page. SNIF-ACT also does not make use of ACT-R's capacity for representing information-seeking plans that are characteristic of expert Web users (Bhavnani, 2002). The choice of ACT-R as the basis for the SNIF-ACT model is partly driven by the expectation that other developed aspects of ACT-R can be used for more detailed elaborations of the basic SNIF-ACT model.

Fu and I developed two versions of SNIF-ACT. SNIF-ACT 1.0 was developed and tested against the data set presented in chapter 3 that came from a controlled experiment involving a small number of participants (Card et al., 2001). That detailed set of protocols allowed us to directly test and fine-tune the basic parameters and mechanisms of the SNIF-ACT 1.0 model. SNIF-ACT 2.0 was based on a rational analysis of link selections on a Web page. The rational analysis led to a number of refinements in the model, which was tested against a data set collected by Chi et al. (2003) in a controlled study involving a large number of users working on tasks in realistic settings. The refinements in SNIF-ACT 2.0 included mechanisms in the model that implement a satisficing process that makes link selections, and an adaptive stopping rule that decides when to leave a Web page based on past and current experiences with the Web site.

The focus with SNIF-ACT 1.0 was to fit the behavioral traces of individual users. The focus with SNIF-ACT 2.0 was to fit aggregate user behavior by performing Monte Carlo simulations of the model. Finally, we compared the predictions of SNIF-ACT 2.0 to the Law of Surfing presented in chapter 4 (Huberman, Pirolli, Pitkow, & Lukose, 1998) that was constructed to explain emergent aggregate Web navigation behavior. Although the two models have very different underlying assumptions, we found that the predictions by SNIF-ACT 2.0 are consistent with those made by the random walk model.

SNIF-ACT

SNIF-ACT makes two major predictions concerning (1) link selection and (2) when to stop following a particular path and try another. It extends the ACT-R theory and simulation environment (Anderson et al., 2004). ACT-R is a production system architecture designed to model human psychology and contains three kinds of assumptions about (1) knowledge representation, (2) knowledge deployment (performance), and (3) knowledge acquisition (learning). The basic SNIF-ACT architecture, presented in figure 5.1, includes a *declarative memory* and a *procedural memory*. Declarative memory contains *declarative knowledge*, and procedural memory contains *procedural knowledge*. The distinction between these two kinds of knowledge is close to Ryle's (1949) distinction between *knowing that* and *knowing how*. Declarative knowledge (knowing that) is the kind that can be contemplated or reflected upon, whereas procedural knowledge (know-how) is tacit and directly embodied in physical or cognitive activity.

Declarative Knowledge

Declarative knowledge corresponds to things that we are aware we know and that can be easily described to others, such as the content of Web links or the functionality of browser buttons. Declarative knowledge is represented formally as *chunks* in ACT-R.[2] Figure 5.2 provides a graphical representation of some of the declarative memory chunks involved in a SNIF-ACT simulation of a user performing the Antz task described in chapter 3. The graphical notation in figure 5.2 corresponds to the notation used for network graph representation of human memory in standard textbooks (Anderson, 2000). Each oval represents a chunk.

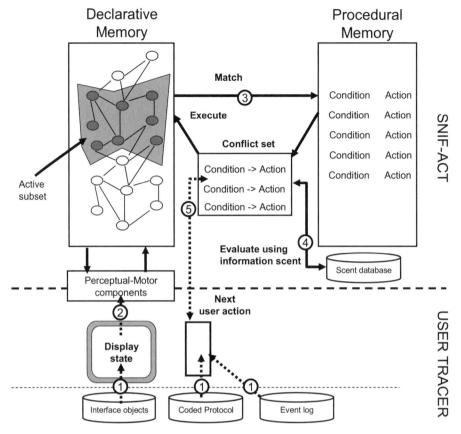

FIGURE 5.1 The SNIF-ACT user modeling architecture (top) builds on the ACT-R theory. The user tracer architecture (bottom) the SNIF-ACT simulation and compares it to user trace data.

Arrows indicate labeled relations among chunks or indicate the type of chunks using the label "is-a." The chunk top goal represents the user's main goal, and it is related (*points*) to the chunk "Antz task," which points to a description of the concepts involved in the task. The top-goal chunk also points to a chunk representing the user's perception of the Internet Explorer (IE) browser, which points to the user's perception of the AltaVista home page that is displayed in the browser and the links that have been perceived on that page. At any point in time, there is a stack of goals that encodes the user's intentions. Goals are also represented as chunks. ACT-R is always trying to achieve the goal that is on top of that stack. At any point in time, it is focused on a single goal.

Since the goal was to not to model how users learned to use the browser, we assumed that the model had all the knowledge necessary to use the browser, such as clicking on a link or clicking on the Back

button to go back to the previous Web page. We also assumed that users had perfect knowledge of the addresses of most popular Web search engines. Declarative knowledge about the browser and the most popular Web sites was simply provided to the model in all the simulations.

Procedural Knowledge

Procedural knowledge is knowledge (skill) that we display in our behavior without conscious awareness, such as knowledge of how to ride a bike or how to point a mouse to a menu item. Procedural knowledge specifies how declarative knowledge is transformed into active behavior and is represented formally as condition-action pairs, or *production rules*. For instance, our SNIF-ACT simulation of a user on the Antz task contains the production rule (or *production*; summarized in English):

Use-Search-Engine:
IF   the goal is Goal*Start-next-patch
      & there is a task description
      & there is a browser
      & the browser is not at a search engine
THEN
      Set a subgoal Goal*Use-search-engine

The production "Use-Search-Engine" applies in situations where the user has a goal to go to a Web site (represented by the tag "Goal * Start-next-patch"), has processed a task description, and is in front of a browser. The production specifies that a subgoal will be set to use a search engine. The condition (IF) side of the production is matched to the current goal and the active chunks in declarative memory, and when a match is found, the action (THEN) side of the production will be executed. Roughly, the idea is that each elemental step of cognition corresponds to a production. At any point in time, a single production is fired. When there is more than one match, the matching rules form a *conflict set*, and a mechanism called *conflict resolution* is used to decide which production to execute. The conflict resolution mechanism is based on a utility function. The expected utility of each matching production is calculated based on this utility function, and the one with the highest expected utility will be picked. In modeling Web users, the utility function is provided by the spreading activation model of information scent presented in chapter 4. This constitutes a major extension of the ACT-R theory.

Utility and Choice: The Role of Information Scent

As users browse the Web, they make judgments about the utility of different courses of action available to them. Typically, they must use local cues, such as link images and text, to make navigation decisions. As discussed in chapter 4, information scent refers to the local cues that users process in making such judgments. The task goal is represented by a set of chunks. The text on the display screen activates a set of chunks, and activation spreads from these chunks to related chunks in a spreading activation network. The amount of activation accumulating on the goal chunks and display chunks is an indicator of their mutual relevance. The amount of activation accumulating on the goal chunks matched by a production is used to evaluate and select productions. The activation of chunks matched by production can be used to determine the utility of selecting those productions.

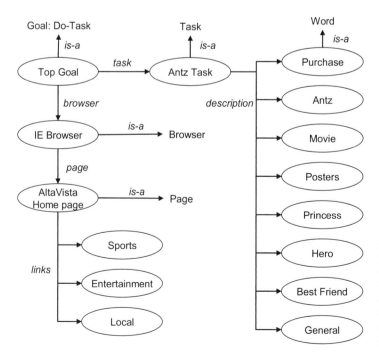

FIGURE 5.2 A subset of the declarative knowledge in the SNIF-ACT simulation of user S1 working on the Antz task first described in chapter 3. Chunks representing the top goal, task description, and browser display are depicted.

For instance, the following Click-Link production matches when a Web link description has been read:

Click-Link:
IF   the goal is Goal*Process-element
      & there is a task description
      & there is a browser
      & there is a link that has been read
      & the link has a link description
THEN
      Click on the link

If selected, the rule will execute the action of clicking on the link. The chunks associated with the task description will have a certain amount of activation. That combined activation will be used to evaluate the rule. If there are two Click-Link productions matching against chunks for two different links, then the production with more highly activated chunks will be selected. As described in chapter 4, the activation level reflects the degree of relevance of the link text to the task description.

Setting the Spreading Activation Networks

We chose to use three sources of text corpora to construct spreading activation networks in SNIF-ACT: (1) the Tipster document corpus (Harman, 1993), (2) Internet data collected by a program that calls on the AltaVista search engine to provide data, and (3) pointwise mutual information (PMI) scores computed from samples of the Web using the hybrid approach described in chapter 4. Specifically, we used corpora 1 and 2 in SNIF-ACT 1.0. We originally started with corpus 1 alone but soon realized that there were many neologisms that were not contained in standard text corpora (e.g., the word "Antz" that was created solely for the title of a movie). We were therefore forced to use corpus 2 to calculate statistics for neologisms that had recently entered the linguistic environment. In SNIF-ACT 2.0, because of the large number of Web pages involved, we chose to use corpus 3 to get a more comprehensive range of word association statistics.

User Tracing

A user-tracing architecture (or user tracer) is a software system that supports a method for developing and testing cognitive models. The particular user-tracing architecture developed in association with SNIF-ACT

is presented in figure 5.1. The top part of figure 5.1 repeats the instrumentation used in the Web study discussed in chapter 3. As indicated in figure 5.1, the output of WebLogger, WebEyeMapper, and protocol analysis is a set of databases that includes the Web Protocol Transcript, WebLogger event log, WebLogger cached pages, and WebEyeMapper element database. These databases constitute the data that provide us with a user trace: a detailed analysis of all the states and events that correspond to a user's performance of a task using the Web. The goal of the modeling effort is to develop a computer program than simulates the user in enough detail to reproduce the same user trace data.

The user-tracing architecture contains the SNIF-ACT user model, and it contains a user comparator subsystem that parses the user's Web traces to maintain a model of the interface states viewed by the user (i.e., the external world of the users). The user tracer runs the SNIF-ACT simulation and compares its behavior to the traces of individual users. It does this by presenting the simulation with the same task that was presented to a user and beginning on the same Web page as the user. The simulation is then run until it decides on some action (e.g., mouse-clicking on a link), and that action is compared to the user's. Then the user trace is used to update the simulated interaction state (e.g., by going to a linked Web page), and this process is repeated until the user's trace is completely compared against the SNIF-ACT simulation.

Figure 5.1 illustrates the sequence of steps taken by the user tracer as it controls the SNIF-ACT simulation model and matches the simulation behavior to the user trace data (each step is indicated by a circle in figure 5.1):

1. Parse the WebLogger event database, coded protocol database, and interface object database to determine the next display state and the next user action that occurs at that display state.
2. If the display state has changed, then indicate this to the SNIF-ACT system. SNIF-ACT contains productions that actively perceive the display state and update declarative memory to contain chunks that represent the perceived portions of the display.
3. Run SNIF-ACT so that it identifies the active portion of declarative memory and matches productions against working memory to select a conflict set of productions.
4. SNIF-ACT evaluates the productions in the conflict set using the information scent com-

putations. At the end of this step, one of the rules in the conflict set will be identified as the production to execute.

5. Compare the production just selected by SNIF-ACT to the next user action and record any statistics (notably, whether or not the production and action matched). If there is a match, then execute the production selected by SNIF-ACT. If there is a mismatch, then select and execute the production that matches the user action.

Steps 1–5 are repeated until there are no more user actions. SNIF-ACT is connected to the user tracer by an interface module that provides the analyst with a simple notation for defining (a) *match patterns*, which define the user action pattern that is associated with a specific production (used to match productions to user actions), and (b) *interface object class to chunk type associations*, which specify how objects on the display are represented by declarative memory chunks (used by productions that perceive the simulated display state).

SNIF-ACT 1.0

SNIF-ACT 1.0 was tested against the detailed protocol data from Card et al. (2001) described in chapter 3. The foremost aim in developing SNIF-ACT 1.0 was to obtain descriptive adequacy of the detailed protocol data, which required fine-tuning of the model. As described in chapter 3, the data set came from $N = 4$ Web users each working on two tasks: (1) the Antz task, which involved finding posters on the Web depicting characters from the movie *Antz*, and (2) the City task, which involved finding an event date for the Second City comedy troupe and a photograph of the group.

Table 5.1 shows the set of productions used in SNIF-ACT 1.0, presented in English-equivalent form. An example trace of the model is shown in table 5.2. The model always started with the goal of going to a particular Web site (usually a search engine) on the Internet. There were two ways the model could go to a Web page: It could type the URL (uniform resource locator) address, or it could use the Bookmark pull-down menu in the browser. Since we are agnostic about which Web sites users preferred and how they reached the Web sites of their choices to start their tasks, we simply forced the model to match users' choices (details of this procedure are discussed further

TABLE 5.1 Productions in SNIF-ACT in their English equivalent forms.

Start-Process-Page:
IF   the goal is Goal*Start-next-patch
     & there is a task description
     & there is a browser
     & the browser is on an unprocessed page
THEN Set & push a subgoal Goal*Process-page to the
     goal stack

Process-Links-on-Page:
IF   the goal is Goal*Process-page
     & there is a task description
     & there is a browser
     & there is an unprocessed link
THEN Set and push a subgoal Goal*Process-link to the
     goal stack

Attend-to-Link:
IF   the goal is Goal*Process-link
     & there is a task description
     & there is a browser
     & there is an unattended link
THEN Choose an unattended link and attend to it

Read-and-Evaluate-Link:
IF   the goal is Goal*Process-link
     & there is a task description
     & there is a browser
     & the current attention is on a link
THEN Read and Evaluate the link

Click-Link:
IF   the goal is Goal*Process-link
     & there is a task description
     & there is a browser
     & there is an evaluated link
     & the link has the highest activation
THEN Click on the link

Leave-Site:
IF   the goal is Goal*Process-link
     & there is a task description
     & there is a browser
     & there is an evaluated link
     & the mean activation on page is low
THEN Leave the site & pop the goal from the goal stack

Backup-a-page:
IF   the goal is Goal*Process-link
     & there is a task description
     & there is a browser
     & there is an evaluated link
     & the mean activation on page is low
THEN Go back to the previous page

below). The major predictions of the model were made when it processed the links on a Web page. There were three major productions that competed against each other when the model was processing

TABLE 5.2 An example trace of the SNIF-ACT model.

Production Fired	Description
Use-Search-Engine	Model started, decided to use a search engine
Go-to-Search-Engine	Retrieved address of search engine from memory
Go-to-Site-by-Typing	Typed address of search engine on browser
Start-Process-Page	Moved attention to new Web page
Search-Site-Using-Search-Box	Typed search terms in search box
Process-Links-on-Page	Prepared to move attention to a link on page
Attend-to-Link	Moved attention to the link
Read-and-Evaluate-Link	Read and evaluated the link
Attend-to-Link	Moved attention to next link
Read-and-Evaluate-Link	Read and evaluated the link
Attend-to-Link	Moved attention to next link
Read-and-Evaluate-Link	Read and evaluated the link
Click-Link	Clicked on the link
...	
Click-Link	Clicked on the link
Finish	Target found

a Web page: Attend-to-Link, Click-Link, and Leave-Site.[3] The utilities of these productions were determined by information scent computations based on the analysis presented in chapter 4.

Using equations 4.12 and 4.13 from chapter 4, we may define the utility of a link L in the context of a goal G as the sum of all the activation received by chunks representing a user's goal from proximal cues associated with a link, plus some stochastic noise ε:

$$U(G,L) = \sum_{i \in G} A_i + \varepsilon$$
$$= \sum_{i \in G} \left(B_i + \sum_{j \in L} W_j S_{ji} \right) + \varepsilon \qquad (5.1)$$

The summation over $i \in G$ indicates the summed activation over the set of chunks associated with the goal G. This includes the base-level activations, B_i, of the goal chunks plus the activation spread from proximal cues associated with the links. The summation over $j \in L$ is the summed activation from proximal cue chunks associated with the link, where W_j is the attentional weight devoted to the proximal cue chunk and S_{ji} is the association strength between proximal link cue j and goal chunk i.

For tasks in which the information goal remains constant throughout the task, we may ignore the base-level activations B_i. This is because the goal chunks i remain the same throughout the task. Consequently, the base-level activations of the goal, B_i, of goal chunks do not change regardless of the link chunks j. Consequently, in the SNIF-ACT models we set B_i to zero.

The model must deal with cases in which a link chunk j is the same as a goal chunk i. In such cases of direct overlap between the information goal of the user and the information scent cues of the link, it is assumed that

$$S_{ji} = B_i. \qquad (5.2)$$

This has the effect of making the activation equation especially sensitive to direct overlaps between information goals and information scent cues.

The model also requires the specification of the attentional weight parameter W_j. We simply assume that the attention paid to an individual information scent cue decays exponentially as the total number of cues increases. Specifically, we set

$$W_i = W e^{-dn}, \qquad (5.3)$$

where n is the number of words in the link and W and d are scaling parameters. Exploration of the parameter space suggested that $W = 0.1$ and $d = 0.2$ provided the best fits throughout the simulations. The exponential decay function is used to ensure that the activation will not increase without bounds with the number of words in a link. In practice, the sum of attentional weights

$$\sum_{i=1}^{n} W_i \qquad (5.4)$$

grows to an asymptote. With the W and d parameters above, we get a growth function for $\sum W_i$ that shows no substantial change (change $< 1\%$) after $n = 20$ words. This fits the observation that increases in the number of words associated with a link appears to benefit the accuracy of judgments up until about 20 words, after which additional increases in word length have no effect (Spool, Perfetti, & Brittan, 2004).

The conflict resolution among productions competing to choose a link follows the discrete choice probability equation presented in chapter 4. The utility of a particular link L is evaluated in the context of a set of available links C. The utility of links is evaluated according to equation 5.1, and the probability of choosing a particular link L from a set of links C in the context of goal G is

$$\Pr(L|C,G) = \frac{e^{\frac{U(G,L)}{\mu}}}{\sum_{k \in C} e^{\frac{U(G,k)}{\mu}}}. \qquad (5.5)$$

In both SNIF-ACT 1.0 and SNIF-ACT 2.0, the scaling parameter μ was set to 1.0.

Several features of equation 5.5 are worth noting. Consistent with traditional theories of choice behavior in psychology (e.g., Luce, 1959; Thurstone, 1927), the choice of a particular action (e.g., link choice) is conditional on the expected utilities of all the actions that are feasible as alternative choices. The probability that a particular link will be chosen does not depend just on the information scent–based utility of that link (which appears in the numerator of equation 5.5), but also on the information scent–based utilities of the competing links (which appear in the denominator of equation 5.5). Also, in general, the size of the set of competing alternatives will tend to affect the choice of a particular action. Finally, note that μ is a scaling parameter that reflects random noise in the Random Utility Model. As μ decreases, the model is more likely to choose the link with the highest information scent–based utility.

SNIF-ACT 1.0 was also used to test the patch-leaving rule derived in chapter 4. The rule was to forage in an information patch until the expected potential of that patch is less than the mean expected value of going to a new patch, or

$$U(\mathbf{x}) > \bar{U}, \qquad (5.6)$$

where $U(\mathbf{x})$ is the utility of the current information patch and $\bar{U}$ is the average utility of going to a new Web site. This rule was observed in the protocol analyses in chapter 3 (see figure 3.6) and is tested more concretely with SNIF-ACT 1.0.

The predictions made by the SNIF-ACT 1.0 model were tested against the log files of all data sets. The model predicts two major kinds of actions: (1) which links on a Web page people will click on, and (2) when people decide to leave a site. These two actions were therefore extracted from the log files and compared to the predictions made by the model. We call the first kind of actions *link-following actions*,

which were logged whenever a participant clicked on a link on a Web page. The second kind of actions was called *site-leaving actions*, which were logged whenever a participant left a Web site (and went to a different search engine or Web site). The two kinds of actions made up 72% (48% for link-following and 24% for site-leaving actions) of all the 189 actions extracted from the log files. The rest of the actions consisted of, for example, typing in URL to go to a particular Web site or going to a predefined bookmark. These actions were excluded because they were more influenced by prior knowledge of the users than by information displayed on the screen.

Link-Following Actions

The SNIF-ACT 1.0 model was matched to the link-following actions extracted from the $N = 8$ (2 tasks × 4 participants) data sets. The user trace comparator was used to compare each action from each participant to the action chosen by the model. Whenever a link-following action was encountered, the SNIF-ACT 1.0 model ranked all links on the Web page according to the information scent of the links. We then compared the links chosen by the participants to the predicted link rankings of the SNIF-ACT model. If there were a purely deterministic relationship between predicted information scent and link choice, then all users would be predicted to choose the highest ranked link. However, it is assumed that the scent-based utilities are stochastic (McFadden, 1974, 1978) and subject to some amount of variability due to users and context. Consequently, the probability of link choice is expected to be highest for the links ranked with the greatest amount of scent-based utility, and link choice probability is expected to decrease for links ranked lower on the basis of their scent-based utility values.

Figure 5.3 shows that link choice is strongly related to scent-based utility values. Links ranked higher on predicted scent-based utilities tend to get chosen by users over links ranked lower. A total of 91 link-following actions are depicted in figure 5.3. The distribution of the predicted link selection was significantly different from random selection, $\chi^2(30) = 18589.45$, $p < .0001$.

Site-Leaving Actions

To test how well information scent is able to predict when people will leave a site, site-leaving actions were extracted from the log files and analyzed. Site-leaving

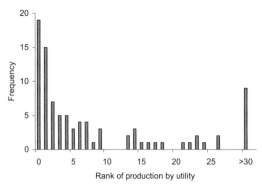

FIGURE 5.3 Frequency that SNIF-ACT productions match link-following actions. The SNIF-ACT production rankings by information scent are computed at each simulation cycle over all links on the same Web page and all productions that match.

actions are defined as actions that lead to a different site (e.g., when the participants use a different search engine or type in a different URL to go to a different Web site). The results are plotted in figure 5.4. Each point is the mean information scent of all the links on the page for site-leaving actions. It shows the four Web pages the participants visited before they left the site (i.e., Last −3, Last − 2, Last − 1, and Last). Figure 5.4 shows that, initially, the mean information scent of the Web page was high, and right before the participants left the site, the mean information scent dropped.

Figure 5.4 also shows the mean information scent of the Web pages encountered right after the participants left the site (the dashed line in figure 5.4),

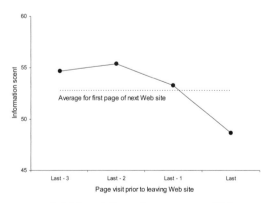

FIGURE 5.4 Mean information scent on a Web page on the last four pages prior to users switching to a new site. The scent scores are in spreading activation units. The dashed line is the average information scent score of the first page at a new Web site.

which tended to be higher than the mean information scent of the page before they left the site. This is consistent with Information Foraging Theory, which states that people may switch to another "information patch" when the expected gain of searching in the current patch is lower than the expected gain of searching for a new information patch. In fact, from the verbal protocols, we often found such utterances as "it seems that I don't have much luck with this site" or "maybe I should try another search engine" right before participants switched to another site. This suggests that the drop in information scent on the Web page could be the factor that triggered participants' decisions to switch to another site.

Summary of Results

The results show that the measure of information scent is able to generate good predictions for user–Web interaction. Most of the links chosen by the participants were ranked high by SNIF-ACT 1.0, suggesting that SNIF-ACT is able to predict which links people will click on a Web page using the measure of information scent. Information scent was also able to predict when people will leave a Web site. It was shown that when participants left a Web site, the average information scent of the site was dropping. The interesting finding was that the information scent of the Web page right before the participants left the site was much lower than that of the Web page that they switched to. It is possible that, from experience, people have built up an expectation of the information scent value of various Web sites. When the information scent value of a particular Web page dropped to a value that is below the expected information scent value of other Web sites, people may decide to abandon the current site and switch to another site.

Figure 5.4, with information scent scores computed automatically, compares to figure 3.6 of chapter 3, where the information scent scores were derived from human ratings. The automatically computed information scent scores appear to predict both the revealed preferences of users choosing Web links and the stated preferences of users rating links.

SNIF-ACT 2.0

SNIF-ACT 1.0 established the viability of the spreading activation model of information scent as a mechanism for predicting navigation behavior. SNIF-ACT

2.0 was developed to be tested against a larger pool of data and to incorporate more detailed mechanisms. The test data for SNIF-ACT 2.0 came from a study by Chi et al. (2003) concerning the validation of the Bloodhound usability testing system. SNIF-ACT 2.0 implements a learning mechanism that, based on experience, dynamically updates the utilities associated with link selection or leaving an information patch.

Tasks and Users

Chi et al. (2003) developed an automated usability testing system called Bloodhound (based on Information Foraging Theory) that is described in chapter 9. In order to test that tool, Chi et al. (2003) collected data from a large number of users working on a variety of tasks at a number of real-world Web sites. A remote testing version of WebLogger (Reeder, Pirolli, & Card, 2001) was developed to collect data from people working on test tasks from their offices or homes. From this study, we selected data from which we could clearly interpret user navigation behavior, which meant we focused on Web sites that tended to avoid the use of dynamically generated Web pages.

This constraint left us with data from 74 participants working at two Web sites on eight tasks per Web site. The Web sites were (1) help.yahoo.com (the help system section of Yahoo!) and (2) parcweb.parc.com (an intranet of company internal information). These are referred to as "Yahoo" and "ParcWeb" below. Yahoo is representative of a Web site that caters to a broad extranet audience. ParcWeb is a Web site that caters to an intranet company audience. Table 5.3 presents information about the Web sites and the tasks. The tasks labeled "a" were considered easy and "b" were considered difficult. Yahoo participants were solicited over the Internet, and ParcWeb participants were solicited at PARC. Each participant was assigned eight tasks, and efforts were made to balance users over tasks and Web sites. Participants could abandon tasks at will. Chi et al. (2003) removed sessions that employed a Web site's search engine (participants had been instructed not to use search).

Wai-Tat Fu and I performed some additional cleanup on the data. We found that a few pages (< 10) tended to attract most of the participants, and some pages were visited infrequently. We eliminated

TABLE 5.3 The tasks given to participants in Chi et al. (2003).

Task	Description
ParcWeb (19227 documents)	
1a	Find the PowerPoint slides for Jan Borchers's June 3, 2002, Asteroid presentation.
1b	Suppose this is your first time using AmberWeb. Find some documentation that will help you figure out how to use it.
2a	Find out where you can download the latest DataGlyph Toolkit.
2b	Find some general information about the DataGlyphs project.
3a	What do the numerical TAP ratings mean?
3b	What patent databases are available for use through PARC?
4a	Find the 2002 holiday schedule.
4b	Where can you download an expense report?
Yahoo (7484 documents)	
1a	What is the Yahoo! Directory?
1b	You want Yahoo! to add your site to the Yahoo! Directory. Find some guidelines for writing a description of your site.
2a	You have a Yahoo! Email account. How do you save a message to your Sent Mail folder after you send it?
2b	You are receiving spam on your Yahoo! Email account. What can you do to make it stop?
3a	When is the playing season for Fantasy Football?
3b	In Fantasy Baseball, what is rotisserie scoring?
4a	You are trying to find your friend's house, and you are pretty sure you typed the right address into Yahoo! Maps, but the little red star still showed up in the wrong place. How could this have happened?
4b	You want to get driving directions to the airport, but you don't know the street address. How else can you get accurate directions there?

the pages with very low frequencies: those with $N < 5$ in the case of Yahoo and those with $N < 3$ in the case of ParcWeb (these represent the 30% of Web pages with the lowest frequency at each site). Instead of matching SNIF-ACT 2.0 against each individual user trace, SNIF-ACT 2.0 was tested in a Monte Carlo fashion. Specifically, SNIF-ACT 2.0 was run as many times as there were users for each task at each Web site, and the aggregate statistics of SNIF-ACT 2.0 were compared to the observed aggregate statistics of users.

Satisficing and Learning

SNIF-ACT 1.0 made the unrealistic assumption that users evaluated all links on a page prior to making a navigation decision. SNIF-ACT 2.0 implements a satisficing process (Simon, 1956) in which links are evaluated in sequence until one is "good enough." To do this, SNIF-ACT 2.0 employs an adaptive learning mechanism that learns the utilities of key alternative productions from experience with Web links and Web pages. The adaptive learning mechanisms are developed within a Bayesian learning framework.

The critical productions in table 5.1 were "Attend-to-Link," "Click-Link," and "Backup-a-Page," which determine which links to follow and when to go back to a previous page (the production "Leave-Site" in table 5.1 was not relevant in SNIF-ACT 2.0 because users were constrained to work within a particular site). For each of these productions, a utility function was developed that calculated the utility of the production at cycle n of the simulation.

For the production "Attend-to-Link," which chooses to attend to and evaluate the next link on a Web page, the utility was defined as

$$U_A(n+1) = \frac{U_A(n) + U(G, L)}{1 + N(n)}, \qquad (5.7)$$

where $U(G, L)$ is defined as in equation 5.1 and $N(n)$ is the number of links attended to on a Web page at cycle n of the simulation. The Bayesian analysis for this adaptive rule is presented in the appendix. Basically, the rule assumes that the user is incrementally improving an estimate that target information will be found, based on sequentially sampling links.

For the production "Click-Link," the utility was defined as

$$U_C(n+1) = \frac{U_C(n) + U(G, L_{MAX})}{1 + k + N(n)}, \qquad (5.8)$$

where k is a scaling parameter, and where L_{MAX} is a link that has been attended to that yields the highest scent-based utility so far encountered and is the link that will be clicked if the production is selected. In the SNIF-ACT 2.0 simulations, we set $k = 5$.

To compute the utility of the production "Backup-a-Page," we defined two average utilities. First, the average scent-based utilities of previously visited pages were represented as $\overline{U}_{Page}$, and then the average of the scent-based utilities of links from 1 to n on the current page was represented as $\overline{U}_L(n)$. Using these averages, the utility of the production "Backup-a-Page" was defined as

$$U_B(n+1) = \overline{U}_{Page} - \overline{U}_L(n) - C_{Back}, \qquad (5.9)$$

where C_{Back} is the cost of going back to a previous page. In the SNIF-ACT 2.0 simulation, the mean scent-based utility of previous Web pages was set to be $\overline{U}_{Page} = 10$ (based on parameters set in the SNIF-ACT 1.0 simulation), and the go-back cost was set to be $C_{Back} = 5$.

An artificial example is presented to illustrate the interaction of utility evaluations for these three critical productions. The scent-based utility $U(G, L)$ of a hypothetical sequence of 15 links was defined using the function in figure 5.5. Then, the utilities of each of the three critical productions were calculated

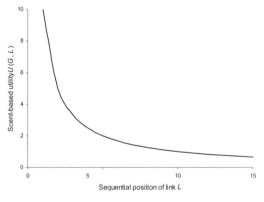

FIGURE 5.5 A hypothetical distribution of scent-based utilities, $U(G,L)$, of links encountered in a sequence on a Web page.

according to equations 5.7–5.9, assuming that the utilities all start at zero. Then, the probability of choice of each production was calculated using the discrete choice probability formulas:

$$\Pr(\text{Attend-to-Link}, n)$$
$$= \frac{\exp[U_A(n)/\mu]}{\exp[U_A(n)/\mu] + \exp[U_C(n)/\mu] + \exp[U_B(n)/\mu]},$$
$$(5.10)$$

$$\Pr(\text{Click-Link}, n)$$
$$= \frac{\exp[U_C(n)/\mu]}{\exp[U_A(n)/\mu] + \exp[U_C(n)/\mu] + \exp[U_B(n)/\mu]},$$
$$(5.11)$$

$$\Pr(\text{Backup-a-Page}, n)$$
$$= \frac{\exp[U_B(n)/\mu]}{\exp[U_A(n)/\mu] + \exp[U_C(n)/\mu] + \exp[U_B(n)/\mu]},$$
$$(5.12)$$

where $\Pr(p, n)$ means the probability that probability that production p will be chosen after n links have been evaluated. The scaling parameter was set to $\mu = 1$.

Given the sequence of scent-based utilities in figure 5.5, the probability of choice of the critical productions is presented in figure 5.6. There is an initial bias to prefer to attend to links because it is useful to learn what links are on the page before taking action (clicking on a link or going back). This bias is implemented by the additional factor k in utility equation 5.8 for Click-Link compared with Attend-Link utility equation 5.7, and because there is a penalty for the cost of going back

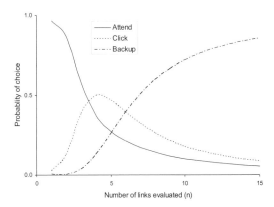

FIGURE 5.6 The probability of choice of the three critical production rules assuming a sequence of links having the scent-based utilities in figure 5.

(C_{Back}) in the Backup-a-Page production (equation 5.9). As more links are evaluated, the number of links $N(n)$ increases and diminishes the relative effect of the penalty k. In addition, the Click-Link production is based on an evaluation of the information scent of the best link so far, and thus its choice probability rises in comparison to Attend-to-Link. After the evaluation of the fourth link, Click-Link is more likely to be selected. The competition between Attend-to-Link and Click-Link implements satisficing, in which links are evaluated until one is good enough to be selected rather than continuing on.

The probability of choice of Backup-a-Page rises continuously in figure 5.6 as the average information scent of links encountered on the current page drops below the average of previously encountered pages. This implements an adaptive stopping rule that is a refinement of the patch-leaving rule used in SNIF-ACT 1.0.

Link-Following Actions

For each task on each of the two Web sites (Yahoo, ParcWeb), SNIF-ACT 2.0 was started at the same Web site pages as did participants in the Chi et al. (2003) study and was run in a Monte Carlo fashion for the same number of times as there were participants recorded for that task, following the user-tracing methodology described above. Figure 5.7 shows a comparison of the frequency of link selections made by the model compared to the frequency of observed selection for the same links. That is, each point in figure 5.7 represents a link. Figure 5.7a shows the scatter plot for the ParcWeb link selection model fit as well as a best-fit linear regression, with $R^2 = .72$. Figure 5.7b shows a similar scatter plot for the Yahoo link selection model fit as well as a best-fit linear regression, with $R^2 = .90$.

The better fit produced for Yahoo over ParcWeb might be due to several factors. First, it should be noted that many of the points in the ParcWeb scatter plot (figure 5.7a) lie near the origin where either the observed or predicted frequencies are low and hence noisier than those lying away from the origin.[4] Second, some effect of previous experience or familiarity may have been involved in the ParcWeb tasks. The users solicited for tasks at ParcWeb were PARC employees, who probably had some experience with the Web site. It is likely that fewer Yahoo participants were as familiar with the Yahoo help system.

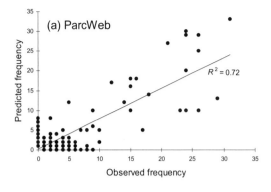

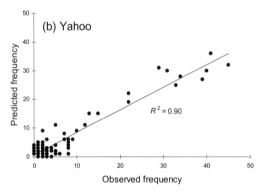

FIGURE 5.7 The scatter plots for the observed frequency of selection of links by the predicted frequency from the SNIF-ACT 2.0 at the ParcWeb site (a) and Yahoo site (b; eight tasks per site).

The fit of the model to the user data in figure 5.7 demonstrates the ability of SNIF-ACT 2.0 to predict the links most likely to be chosen by users across two different Web sites and a wide variety of tasks. These results provide further evidence for the theoretical claim that information scent captures the way people evaluate the relevance of links to users' information goals. From a practical point of view, this ability to predict users' navigation choices turns out to be important in the development of automated usability tools, such as the Bloodhound system presented in chapter 9.

Going Back to Previous Pages

We performed a similar analysis of the fit of the SNIF-ACT 2.0 predictions of users' choice to leave a page and go back to a previous page. We compared the frequency with which the model chose to go back from page A to page B against the frequency of that action by users. Again, these data were drawn from

the same Monte Carlo simulations described above in which SNIF-ACT 2.0 was started at the same pages as those chosen by users, and run on the task for a number of runs equal to the number of participants who performed the task. In this case, the model-fit regression was $R^2 = .73$ for the ParcWeb tasks and $R^2 = .80$ for the Yahoo tasks. The probability that SNIF-ACT 2.0 would choose to return to a previous page increased as the average scent of links on a page diminished in relation to the average information scent of previous pages. The match of SNIF-ACT 2.0 to the data provides additional evidence for this patch-leaving policy identified in chapters 3 and 4.

The Law of Surfing

As discussed in chapter 4, the Law of Surfing characterizes the aggregate behavior of surfers at a Web site. Specifically, the probability density function of L, the length of sequences of Web page visits, is distributed as an inverse Gaussian distribution,

$$f(L) = \sqrt{\frac{\lambda}{2\pi}} L^{-3/2} e^{-\frac{\lambda}{2v^2 L}(L-v)^2}, \quad L > 0. \quad (5.13)$$

Also noted in chapter 4 was the implication of equation 5.13 that data plotted in log–log coordinates will show an approximately straight line with a slope of $-3/2$ for small values of L. Figures 5.8 and 5.9 show log–log plots of the frequency distribution of L for both the SNIF-ACT 2.0 predictions and observed data for ParcWeb and Yahoo, respectively. The slope of these distributions is near $-3/2$ in both figures.

We fit the Law of Surfing to the combined observed data from figures 5.8 and 5.9 (mean $= 2.31$ clicks, variance $= 1.35$). We then compared the cumulative distributions of the fit Law of Surfing, SNIF-ACT 2.0, and the observations (figure 5.10). The fit of the Law of Surfing to the observed data was $R^2 = .98$ and to SNIF-ACT 2.0 was $R^2 = .99$. The observed length of paths of users is well predicted by the Law of Surfing and by SNIF-ACT. Moreover, the behavior of SNIF-ACT is consistent with the Law of Surfing.

General Discussion

This chapter completes a series of three chapters concerning information foraging on the Web. This analysis began with general observations about information foraging on the Web (chapter 3) that revealed

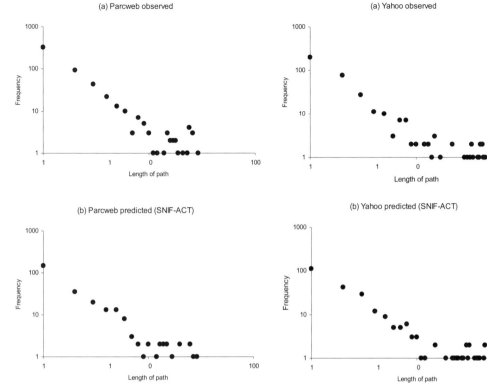

FIGURE 5.8 The frequency distribution of length of path (number of clicks) at the ParcWeb Web site for the observed (a) and SNIF-ACT 2.0 predicted (b) data.

FIGURE 5.9 The frequency distribution of length of path (number of clicks) at the Yahoo Web site for the observed (a) and SNIF-ACT 2.0 predicted (b) data.

the patchy structure of the Web, the important role of information scent in driving navigation, and an apparent patch-leaving policy in which users abandoned surfing at a site when the information scent dropped below the average information scent of new Web sites. This patch-leaving rule was reminiscent of the conventional patch model discussed in chapter 2. Chapter 4 laid out a general rational analysis of *what* problem faced the information forager on the Web and *why* certain solutions were optimal. This led to the development of a spreading activation theory of information scent that provides a Random Utility Model for Web navigation. A rational analysis of when to leave an information patch also led to the Law of Surfing, which describes the number of pages users will visit at a Web site before leaving.

The present chapter completed the series by presenting a mechanistic cognitive model, SNIF-ACT,

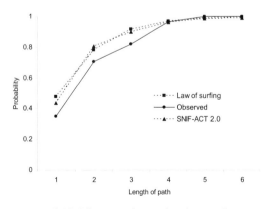

FIGURE 5.10 The cumulative distribution function as a function of length of path (number of clicks) for the observed users on Yahoo and ParcWeb tasks, the fitted Law of Surfing (mean = 2.31 clicks, variance = 1.35), and SNIF-ACT 2.0.

that implements the rational analyses within the constraints of a cognitive architecture. In doing so, we move away from idealizations at the rational analysis level concerning perfect knowledge and unlimited processing. SNIF-ACT incorporates satisficing processes and adaptive Bayesian learning rules to better predict actual Web navigation behavior.

Overall, SNIF-ACT provides excellent fits of individual behavior and aggregate behavior in a variety of tasks by a variety of users. It is remarkable that the core of the model is a simple set of productions (table 5.1) and a spreading activation network parameterized by estimates from online text corpora. However, the structure of the rules and the utility computations from information scent are heavily guided by the earlier rational analyses, which were inspired in many ways by optimal foraging theory.

One advantage of specifying the SNIF-ACT model is that it opens the door to further elaborations. This is because the ACT-R architecture itself (Anderson et al., 2004) provides additional modeling capabilities that are as yet untapped. For instance, ACT-R contains perceptual-motor modules that could be used to provide detailed models of eye movements and the effects of information visualizations and rich media. ACT-R also contains the capability for richer declarative and procedural knowledge representations that might be appropriate in models of expert Web surfers or longer sense-making activities. Given the demands of commerce and public welfare for greater Web usability, and the scarcity of scientific models, there is considerable room for deeper and broader cognitive modeling.

APPENDIX

The analysis below is based on the rational analysis in chapter 5 of Anderson (1990).[5] The analysis aims at providing a rational basis for the utility calculations of the productions in the SNIF-ACT 2.0 model. The goal of the rational analysis is to derive the adaptive mechanism for the action evaluation and selection process as links are sequentially processed. The analysis is based on a Bayesian framework in which the user is gathering data from the sequential evaluation of links on a Web page. The analysis uses the following definitions:

X is the variable that measures the closeness to the target.

S is the binary variable that describes whether the link will lead to the target page.

R is the probability that the target information can be found.

r is the event that the target information exists.

Given these definitions, it immediately follows that

$$\Pr(S=1 \mid r) = R, \qquad (5.A.1)$$

and

$$\Pr(S=0 \mid r) = 1-R; \qquad (5.A.2)$$

we also have the conditional probability

$$\Pr(S,X \mid r) = \Pr(X \mid S,r)\Pr(S \mid r). \qquad (5.A.3)$$

Since the major assumption of the Information Foraging Theory is that information scent (IS) directly measures the closeness to the target, we define

$$P(X \mid S=1,r) = K\sum_{j=0}^{n}\frac{\Gamma(\alpha+j)}{\Gamma(\alpha+n)}IS(j), \qquad (5.A.4)$$

where $IS(j)$ represents the information scent of link j, and K and α are constant parameters of equation 5.A.4. Equation 5.A.4 assumes that the measure of closeness is a hyperbolically discounted sum of the information scents of the links encountered in the past. The use of a hyperbolic discount function has been validated in a number of studies in human preferences (Ainslie & Haslam, 1992; Lowenstein & Prelec, 1991).

We treat this problem as one of sampling the random variables (X, S) from a Bernoulli distribution, with R equivalent to the parameter to the estimated for the distribution. The appropriate Bayesian conjugate distribution convenient for use in updating estimates of R from samples of a Bernoulli random variable is the beta distribution. That is, we assume a prior beta distribution for R, and the user will use the observed information scent of the links on a Web page to update a posterior beta distribution of R. We take R to follow a beta distribution with parameters a and b, after the user has experienced a sequence of links on a Web page, represented as

$$L_n = [(X_1,S_1),(X_2,S_2)\ldots(X_n,S_n)],$$

where each pair (X_i, S_i) describes the closeness to the target and whether the link leads to the target page.

Since the prior distribution of R is a beta distribution, the posterior distribution $\Pr(R|L_n)$ is also a beta, and the new parameters can be shown to be

$$a_{\text{new}} = a + \sum S_i \qquad (5.A.5)$$

and

$$b_{\text{new}} = b + \sum (1 - S_i). \qquad (5.A.6)$$

The posterior predictive distribution for S and X given L_n can be computed as

$$\Pr(S_{n+1}, X_{n+1} | L_n) =$$
$$\int \Pr(S_{n+1}, X_{n+1} | R)\, \Pr(R | L_n)\, dR. \qquad (5.A.7)$$

In our case, our interest lies mainly in the posterior predictive probability that the user can find the target, that is, $\Pr(S_{n+1} = 1, X_{n+1} | Ln)$, which can be computed as

$$\Pr(S_{n+1} = 1, X_{n+1} | L_n)$$
$$= \left(K \sum_{j=0}^{n} \frac{\Gamma(\alpha + j)}{\Gamma(\alpha + n)} \mathrm{IS}(j) \right) \left(\frac{a + \sum S_i}{a + b + n} \right). \qquad (5.A.8)$$

If the user is considering links sequentially on a Web page before the target is found, we have $\sum S_i = 0$. To reduce the number of parameters, we set $\alpha = a$ and $K = 1/a$ and assume that $b = 0$. We now have only one parameter, a, which represents the prior number of successes in finding the target information on the Web. The equation can then be reduced to

$$\Pr(S_{n+1} = 1, X_{n+1} | L_n) = \sum_{j=0}^{n} \frac{\Gamma(a + j)}{\Gamma(a + n + 1)} \mathrm{IS}(j)$$
$$= U(n). \qquad (5.A.9)$$

In the model, the above probability is calculated to approximate the utilities of the productions Attend-to-Link and Click-Link. Putting the above equation in a recursive form, we have

$$U(n) = \frac{U(n-1) + \mathrm{IS}(n)}{a + n}. \qquad (5.A.10)$$

In equation 5.A.10, we set $a = 1$ for the Attend-to-Link production and $a = 1 + k$ for the Click-Link production. By setting the value of a for Click-Link to a higher value, we assume that, in general, following a link is more likely to lead to the target page than attending to the next link on the same Web page. The parameter k is a free parameter that we used to fit the data.

Notes

1. LSA is a technique, similar to factor analysis (principal components analysis), computed over a word × document matrix tabulating the occurrence of terms (words) in documents in a collection of documents. Terms (words) can be represented as vectors in a factor space in which the cosine of the angle between those vectors represents term-to-term similarity (Manning & Schuetze, 1999), and those similarity scores correlate well with such things as judgments of synonymy (Landauer, 1986).

2. The concept of "chunks" can be traced to the work on memory by G. A. Miller (1956).

3. Since participants stayed in the same Web site throughout the whole task in SNIF-ACT 2.0, the Leave-Site production was used only in SNIF-ACT 1.0.

4. Even when low frequencies (<5 selected by user or model) are removed from the analysis, the regression fits remain good with $R^2 = .64$ for ParcWeb and $R^2 = .91$ for Yahoo.

5. Virtually all of this derivation is the work of my colleague Wai-Tat Fu.

References

Ainslie, G., & Haslam, N. (1992). Hyperbolic discounting. In G. Lowenstein & J. Elster (Eds.), *Choice over time* (pp. 57–92). New York: Russell Sage Foundation.

Anderson, J. R. (1983). *The architecture of cognition.* Cambridge, MA: Harvard University Press.

Anderson, J. R. (1990). *The adaptive character of thought.* Hillsdale, NJ: Lawrence Erlbaum Associates.

Anderson, J. R. (1993). *Rules of the mind.* Hillsdale, NJ: Lawrence Erlbaum Associates.

Anderson, J. R. (2000). *Cognitive psychology and its implications* (5th ed.). New York: Worth.

Anderson, J. R., Bothell, D., Byrne, M. D., Douglass, S., Lebiere, C., & Qin, Y. (2004). An integrated theory of mind. *Psychological Review, 11*(4), 1036–1060.

Anderson, J. R., & Lebiere, C. (1998). *The atomic components of thought.* Mahwah, NJ: Lawrence Erlbaum Associates.

Bhavnani, S. K. (2002). Domain-specific search strategies for the effective retrieval of healthcare and shopping information. *CHI 2002 Conference on Human Factors and Computing Systems, Extended Abstracts* (pp. 610–611). Minneapolis, MN: Association for Computing Machinery Press.

Blackmon, M. H., Polson, P. G., Kitajima, M., & Lewis, C. (2002). Cognitive Walkthrough for the Web. *CHI 2002, ACM Conference on Human Factors in Computing Systems, CHI Letters*, 4(1), 463–470.

Brinck, T., Gergle, D., & Wood, S. D. (2001). *Usability for the Web: Designing Web sites that work*. San Francisco: Morgan Kaufman Publishers.

Card, S. K., Moran, T. P., & Newell, A. (1983). *The psychology of human-computer interaction*. Hillsdale, NJ: Lawrence Erlbaum Associates.

Chi, E. H., Rosien, A., Suppattanasiri, G., Williams, A., Royer, C., Chow, C., et al. (2003). The Bloodhound project: Automating discovery of Web usability issues using the InfoScent simulator. *CHI 2003, ACM Conference on Human Factors in Computing Systems, CHI Letters*, 5(1), 505–512.

Choo, C. W., Detlor, B., & Turnbull, D. (2000). *Web work: Information seeking and knowledge work on the World Wide Web*. Dordrecht: Kluwer Academic Publishers.

Garzotto, F., Matera, M., & Paolini, P. (1998). Model-based heuristic evaluation of hypermedia usability. *Proceedings of the Working Conference on Advanced Visual Interfaces, AVI 1998* (pp. 135–145). L'Aquila, Italy: Association for Computing Machinery Press.

Harman, D. (1993, July). *Overview of the first text retrieval conference*. Paper presented at the 16th annual International ACM/SIGIR Conference, Pittsburgh, PA.

Huberman, B. A., Pirolli, P., Pitkow, J., & Lukose, R. J. (1998). Strong regularities in World Wide Web surfing. *Science, 280*, 95–97.

Katz, M. A., & Byrne, M. D. (2003). Effects of scent and breadth on use of site-specific search on e-commerce Web sites. *ACM Transactions on Computer-Human Interaction, 10*(3), 198–220.

Kintsch, W. (1998). *Comprehension: A paradigm for cognition*. Cambridge, UK: Cambridge University Press.

Kitajima, M., Blackmon, M. H., & Polson, P. G. (2005, July). *Cognitive architecture for Website design and usability evaluation: Comprehension and information scent in performing by exploration*. Paper presented at the Human Computer Interaction International, Las Vegas, NV.

Krug, S. (2000). *Don't make me think*. New York: Circle .com.

Landauer, T. K. (1986). How much do people remember? Some estimates of the quantity of learned information in long-term memory. *Cognitive Science, 10*, 477–493.

Landauer, T. K., & Dumais, S. T. (1997). A solution to Plato's problem: The latent semantic analysis theory of acquisition, induction, and representation of knowledge. *Psychological Review, 104*, 211–240.

Lowenstein, G., & Prelec, D. (1991). Negative time preference. *American Economic Review, 81*(2), 347–352.

Luce, R. D. (1959). *Individual choice behavior*. New York: Wiley.

Manning, C. D., & Schuetze, H. (1999). *Foundations of statistical natural language processing*. Cambridge, MA: MIT Press.

McFadden, D. (1974). Conditional logit analysis of qualitative choice behavior. In P. Zarembka (Ed.), *Frontiers of econometrics* (pp. 105–142). New York: Academic Press.

McFadden, D. (1978). Modelling the choice of residential location. In A. Karlqvist, L. Lundqvist, F. Snickars, & J. Weibull (Eds.), *Spatial interaction theory and planning models* (pp. 75–96). Cambridge, MA: Harvard University Press.

Miller, C. S., & Remington, R. W. (2004). Modeling information navigation: Implications for information architecture. *Human-Computer Interaction, 19*(3), 225–271.

Miller, G. A. (1956). The magical number seven plus or minus two: Some limits on our capacity for processing information. *Psychological Review, 63*, 81–97.

Newell, A., & Card, S. K. (1985). The prospects for a psychological science in human-computer interactions. *Human-Computer Interaction, 2*, 251–267.

Nielsen, J. (2000). *Designing Web usability*. Indianapolis, IN: New Riders.

Paternò, F., Sabbatino, V., & Santoro, C. (2000). Using information in task models to support design of interactive safety-critical applications. *Proceedings of the Working Conference on Advanced Visual Interfaces, AVI 2000* (pp. 120–127). Palermo, Italy: Association for Computing Machinery Press.

Pirolli, P. (1999). Cognitive engineering models and cognitive architectures in human-computer interaction. In F. T. Durso, R. S. Nickerson, R. W. Schvaneveldt, S. T. Dumais, D. S. Lindsay, & M. T. H. Chi (Eds.), *Handbook of applied cognition* (pp. 441–477). West Sussex, UK: John Wiley & Sons.

Pirolli, P. (2005). Rational analyses of information foraging on the Web. *Cognitive Science, 29*(3), 343–373.

Pirolli, P., & Card, S. K. (1999). Information foraging. *Psychological Review, 106*, 643–675.

Pirolli, P., Fu, W., Reeder, R., & Card, S. K. (2002). A user-tracing architecture for modeling interaction with the World Wide Web. In M. D. Marsico, S.

Levialdi, & L. Tarantino (Eds.), *Proceedings of the Conference on Advanced Visual Interfaces, AVI 2002* (pp. 75–83). Trento, Italy: ACM Press.

Reeder, R. W., Pirolli, P., & Card, S. K. (2001). Web-Eye Mapper and WebLogger: Tools for analyzing eye tracking data collected in Web-use studies. *CHI 2001 Conference on Human Factors and Computing Systems, Extended Abstract* (pp. 19–20). Seattle, WA: Association for Computing Machinery Press.

Ryle, G. (1949). *The concept of mind*. London: Hutchinson.

Simon, H. A. (1955). A behavioral model of rational choice. *Quarterly Journal of Economics, 69,* 99–118.

Simon, H. A. (1956). Rational choice and the structure of the environment. *Psychological Review, 4,* 181–204.

Spool, J. M., Perfetti, C., & Brittan, D. (2004). *Designing for the scent of information.* Middleton, MA: User Interface Engineering.

Spool, J. M., Scanlon, T., Schroeder, W., Snyder, C., & DeAngelo, T. (1999). *Web site usability.* San Francisco, CA: Morgan Kaufman.

Stephens, D. W., & Krebs, J. R. (1986). *Foraging theory.* Princeton, NJ: Princeton University Press.

Thurstone, L. (1927). A law of comparative judgment. *Psychological Review, 34,* 273–286.

User Interface Engineering. (1999). *Designing information-rich Web sites.* Cambridge, MA: Author.

6

A Rational Analysis and Computational Cognitive Model of the Scatter/Gather Document Cluster Browser

Previous chapters apply the rational analysis method to the information environment of the Web, propose optimization models of information foraging behavior, and describe the SNIF-ACT cognitive model that approximates those optimization models. This chapter extends the rational analysis method to a substantially different kind of information environment and human-information interaction technique called Scatter/Gather (Cutting, Karger, & Pedersen et al., 1993; Cutting, Karger, Pedersen, & Tukey, 1992). Again, the approach involves asking (a) *what* environmental problem is solved, (b) *why* a given behavioral strategy is a good solution to the problem, and (c) *how* that solution is realized by cognitive mechanism. As I show in this chapter, Scatter/Gather interaction poses rational choice problems that are analogous to the problems addressed by the conventional optimal foraging models for diet selection and patch residence time discussed in chapter 2. These conventional foraging models provide a basis for optimization models of Scatter/Gather interaction, and

these optimization models, in turn, are used to shape a production system model called ACT-IF (ACT Information Foraging; Pirolli & Card, 1999). Like the SNIF-ACT model of Web foraging, ACT-IF uses a spreading activation model of information scent.

The Scatter/Gather Task Environment and Information Environment

The Scatter/Gather Browser

The Scatter/Gather system uses the clustering of documents as the basis of a browser suitable for large numbers of documents. Figure 6.1 presents a conceptual overview of how a person interacts with Scatter/Gather. The system uses an automatic clustering algorithm, based on comparing the full text of documents in a collection. Scatter/Gather scatters documents into a set of automatically induced clusters. The first Scatter/Gather window in figure 6.1

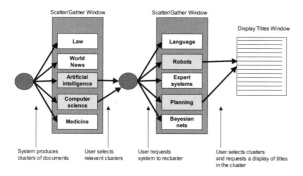

FIGURE 6.1 A schematic view of using Scatter/Gather. The user repeatedly selects (gathers) clusters from the Scatter/Gather window and requests that the system re-cluster (scatter) the selected clusters until the user decides to display and scan titles from the selected clusters.

represents a set of clusters created by Scatter/Gather (only five clusters are presented in this hypothetical interaction, but 10 clusters is a typical number in the real system). Scatter/Gather summarizes the contents of the clusters in a concise way that can be presented to users. Figure 6.1 uses single-word topic labels on the clusters to represent these summaries. The user may gather the documents of interesting clusters into a new subcollection, as shown in figure 6.1, and request that the system repartition the subcollection into a new set of clusters, as in the second Scatter/Gather window of figure 6.1. This process may continue until a small interesting collection of documents is created, and the user decides to read them.

Chapter 2 presents the idea that many information foraging tasks couple operations that *enrich* information patches with operations that *exploit* those patches. In Scatter/Gather, the user engages in a process of repeatedly scattering and selecting clusters to produce an enriched subcollection of documents (i.e., one likely to contain a high proportion of relevant documents) and then exploits that subcollection by displaying the document titles and selecting and opening those of interest for more intensive reading.

Figure 6.2 presents a typical view of the Scatter/Gather interface.[1] The document clusters are represented in separate subwindow areas on the screen. Each cluster subwindow presents a *cluster digest*, which is a small piece of text that Scatter/Gather uses to summarize a topically related set of documents to the user, as shown in figure 6.2. Each such cluster digest begins with a line indicting the cluster label (e.g., cluster 0), the number of documents in the cluster (e.g., 38940), and a set of key words summarizing the central concepts for the cluster of documents (e.g., cell, patient, radiation, dose, beam, disease, treatment). These key words were automati-

cally computed. The next three lines summarize the three most representative documents in the cluster by their source (e.g., "AP"), some words from the title, and a list of words representing the central concepts in the document.

The user may gather those clusters of interest by pointing and selecting buttons above each cluster. On command, the system will pool the subset of documents in these clusters and then automatically scatter that pooled subcollection into another set of clusters. A new screen, like the one shown in figure 6.2, containing the new set of clusters is presented to the user. With each successive iteration of scattering and gathering clusters, the total number of documents in the clusters becomes smaller, eventually bottoming out at the level of individual documents. At some point, the user may choose one or more clusters and request that the system display the titles in those clusters (figure 6.3). That display window contains a list of document titles. By using the mouse to click on document titles, the user may bring up the full text of a document for viewing. Further below, I present models of interaction with Scatter/Gather that draw upon both the patch model and diet model presented in chapter 2.

Internally, the system works by precomputing a *cluster hierarchy*, recombining precomputed components as necessary. The clustering in Scatter/Gather depends on a typical *vector space* model of interdocument similarity (Manning & Schuetze, 1999) in which documents are represented as vectors of equal length, and each component of a vector is some measure of the occurrence of a word in a document. The similarity of two documents may then be computed by a *cosine measure*, which is the cosine of the angle between two vectors, sometimes also known as a *normalized correlation* (Manning & Schuetze, 1999,

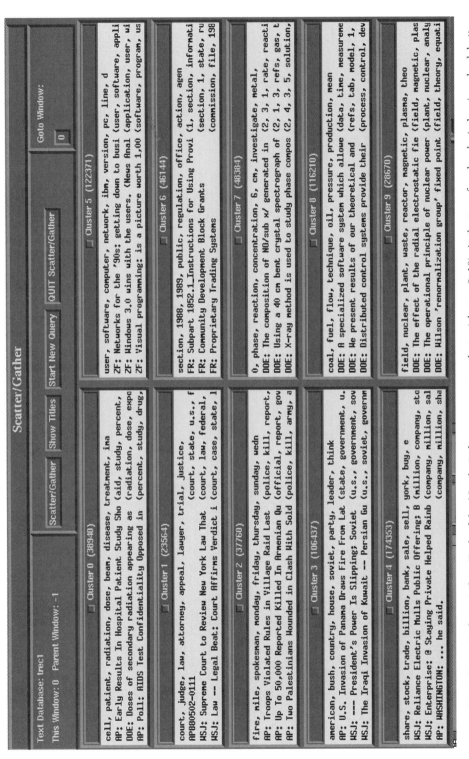

FIGURE 6.2 A Scatter/gather window. Each of the 10 subwindows represents a cluster (clusters 0–10). At the top of each subwindow is a check button, the label for the cluster, and the number of documents contained in the cluster. The text in each subcluster window presents representative words for the cluster (first line) and the titles of the most typical documents in the cluster (lines two through four in each subwindow). The user selects (gathers) clusters by clicking on the check buttons.

```
Contents of cluster 0 from window 2
 0: FR: Railroad Cost of Capital 1987      :  commission, capital, cost, perce
 1: FR: Railroad Revenue Adequacy; 1987    :  commission, revenue, railroad, a
 2: FR: Abandonment of Rail Line; Use of   :  commission, return, rate, cost,
 3: FR: Certain small Aluminum Flashlights :  commission, physical, motion, ex
 4: FR: The New York, Susquehanna and West :  commission, service, 1988, direct
 5: FR: ITEL Rail Corp. and ITEL Corp.;    :  commission, dc, itel, washington
 6: FR: Modifications to the General Purpo :  commission, cost, interstate, co
 7: FR: Certain Minoxidil Powder, Salts an :  commission, investigation, respon
 8: FR: Service Contracts;  Most-favored-s :  contract, commission, federal, s
 9: FR: Survey of Ocean Common carriers    :  survey, ocean, commission, feder
10:FR: Railroad Cost Recovery Procedures   :  commission, railroad, adjustment
11:FR: Capitol Bus Co. Pooling Greyhound   :  pool, greyhaound, washington, har
12:FR: Midsouth Corp.; Continuance in Con  :  commission, interstate, commerce
13:FR: Charge for Shipments Moving on Ord  :  commission, order, notify, freight
14:FR: Santa Fe Southern Pacific Corp. Co  :  1988, commission, southern, pacifi
15:FR: Stone Container Corp. Control Exem  :  commission, stone, interstate, con
```

FIGURE 6.3 The Titles Display window in Scatter/Gather presents the documents of selected clusters as bibliographic citations (left) plus key words extracted from the documents (right). Each line can be clicked to bring up the full text of the document for reading in another window. The tags on the extreme left indicate the collection (all *Federal Register* in this case) source for the document.

pp. 300–303). Specifically, the normalized correlation of two documents is

$$\cos(\vec{x}, \vec{y}) = \frac{\vec{x} \cdot \vec{y}}{\|\vec{x}\| \|\vec{y}\|}$$

$$= \frac{\sum_{i=1}^{n} x_i, y_i}{\sqrt{\sum_{i=1}^{n} x_i^2} \sqrt{\sum_{i=1}^{n} y_i^n}},$$

where $\vec{x}$ and $\vec{y}$ are vectors representing documents, in which the ith element is a frequency count of the number of times word i occurs in that document. The vectors have n elements, which correspond to the significant words in the document collection. The numerator is the *dot product* of the two vectors, and the denominator is the product of *vector norms* (in this case, the Euclidean norm or length of the vectors).

Scatter/Gather browsing and clustering employ methods that take the same amount of time on each iteration, independent of the number of documents clustered (Cutting et al., 1993). Scatter/Gather summarizes document clusters by *meta-documents* containing profiles of topical words central to the cluster and the most typical titles. Topical words are those that occur most frequently in a cluster, and typical titles are those from documents with the highest similarity to a centroid of the cluster. These topical words and typical titles are presented to users to provide them

with a summary of the documents in a cluster. This summary is called a *cluster digest*, and it is the cluster digests that appear in the subwindows of figure 6.2 to represent each cluster.

The user may also choose some set of clusters and display all the titles of those clusters in a Titles Display window (figure 6.3). The user can scroll through the titles, cut and paste the titles into other applications, or double-click on a title to open the associated full-text article.

The TIPSTER Document Collection and TREC Tasks

The empirical studies and the ACT-IF cognitive model described in this chapter deal with a specific version of Scatter/Gather. That version was applied to the TIP-STER text collection, which was created for TREC (Text REtrieval Conference; Harman, 1993). This is a test corpus used to evaluate information retrieval systems. The version we used contained 742,833 full-text documents collected from the *Wall Street Journal*, the Associated Press newswire, Department of Energy technical abstracts, the *Federal Register*, and computer articles published by Ziff-Davis. This corpus has been extensively used by the information retrieval community.

In addition, the studies described here used a sample of tasks (specified as queries) drawn from a set 100 queries developed by the TREC community that

TABLE 6.1 Scatter/Gather tasks selected from the TREC materials.

Easy Tasks

1. Document must discuss end-user computing in general or identify organizations performing end-user computing or showing a capacity for performing end-user computing. To be relevant, a document must discuss end-user computing, or identify organizations either currently engaged in end-user computing or showing a capacity for end-user computing at some time in the future. Indications of the capacity for end-user computing would include any two of the following: (1) previous history of or ongoing decentralization of computing power (moving from mainframes to minicomputers or moving from minicomputers to personal computers or workstations); (2) the purchase of large numbers of personal computers, workstations, and servers; (3) increased computer training of professional and managerial staff; (4) the installation of local area networks (5) investment in 4GL software development tools, desktop publishing, spreadsheets, or database applications.

2. Document will discuss allegations of, or measures being taken against, corrupt public officials of any governmental jurisdiction worldwide. A relevant document will discuss charges or actions being taken against corrupt public officials (be they elected, appointed, or career civil servant) anywhere in the world. The allegations or charges must be specific, e.g., bribes taken from a named group or individual with a given objective, rather than generalized allegations of endemic political corruption, or moves against corporate or private malfeasance (unless linked to an official corruption case).

3. Document will include a prediction about the prime lending rate or will report an actual prime rate move. A relevant document will include a prediction about the prime lending rate (national level or major banks), or will report a prime rate move by major banks, in response to or in anticipation of a federal/national-level action, e.g., a cut in the discount rate.

4. Document mentions a leveraged buyout (LBO) valued at or above 200 million dollars. A relevant document will cite an LBO valued at or above 200 million dollars. The LBO may be at any stage, e.g., considered, proposed, pending, or a fact. The company (being) taken private must be identified. The offer may be expressed in dollars a share.

Medium-Difficulty Tasks

1. Document must identify a crime perpetrated with the aid of a computer. To be relevant, a document must describe an illegal activity that was carried out with the aid of a computer, either used as a planning tool, e.g., in target research, or used in the conduct of the crime, e.g., by illegally gaining access to someone else's computer files. A document is *not* relevant if it merely mentions the illegal spread of a computer virus or worm. However, a document *would* be relevant if the computer virus/worm were used in conjunction with another crime, e.g., extortion.

2. Document describes the principles and mechanisms behind rewritable optical disk technology. To be relevant, a document must describe how rewritable optical disk technology works at length and in significant and comprehensive technical detail.

3. Document will identify trends in global stock markets. To be relevant, a document will identify a trend in at least one of the world's stock markets.

4. Document will report a military coup d'état, either attempted or successful, in any country. A relevant document will identify the country involved, the group responsible for the coup or coup attempt, the target of the coup, and the motivation of the coup plotters. It should *not* be about civilian government shakeups.

Hard Tasks

1. Document will report judicial proceedings and opinions on contracts for surrogate motherhood. A relevant document will report legal opinions, judgments, and decisions regarding surrogate motherhood and the custody of any children that result from surrogate motherhood. To be relevant, a document must identify the case, state the issues that are or were being decided, and report at least one ethical or legal question that arises from the case.

2. Document will report an attempt by the U.S. House of Representatives or a European country to revive the SALT II Treaty ceilings on weapons in order to limit President Reagan's military buildup. A relevant document will describe an attempt to push the U.S. administration to adhere to the limits on weapons proposed in SALT II. To be relevant, the document must identify what group is pushing the policy and what methods they are using to influence the U.S. administration.

3. Document will identify acquisition by the U.S. Army of specified advanced weapons systems. To be relevant, document will provide such specific information as contracts concluded, payments made to contractors, or actual deliveries to the U.S. Army of the following advanced weapons systems: Abrams Tank (M-1), Apache Helicopter (AH-64), Patriot Missile, Blackhawk Helicopter, or Bradley Fighting Vehicle. Congressional discussions of such systems, DoD budget proposals,

(continued)

TABLE 6.1 (continued)

RDT&E activities, overseas sales, component/spare parts/ancillary equipment/services acquisitions, and system modifications are not relevant. In other words, document must report actual or agreed-to deliveries to the U.S. Army of core elements of their most modern weapons systems.

4. Document must describe virtual reality investigations being conducted by entities associated with the military—industrial complex. To be relevant, the document must describe virtual reality applications. In addition, the organization involved in virtual reality applications must be a government agency or an established defense contractor (e.g., TRW, Hughes, Ford Aerospace, etc.).

were associated with the corpus (Harman, 1993). Each TREC query was generated by an expert in some field of interest to the TREC community. Experts also identified lists of relevant documents in the TIPSTER collection that were judged to be relevant to the queries. Examples of these tasks are presented in table 6.1, which were used to develop the rational analyses, empirical studies, and cognitive model described in this chapter. Table 6.2 presents the number of expert-identified relevant documents for the tasks described in table 6.1.

Figure 6.4 presents the basic Scatter/Gather task structure. For each Scatter/Gather window (e.g., figure 6.2), goals were set to process each of the clusters on the screen. Processing clusters entails looking at the

TABLE 6.2 Number of relevant documents and rank for the 12 tasks used in the current studies.

Task	Number of Relevant Documents	Difficulty Rank
Easy		
1	1113	1
2	896	2
3	878	3
4	571	4
Medium		
1	310	48
2	302	49
3	301	50
4	298	51
Hard		
1	55	97
2	52	98
3	40	99
4	38	100

Data are the number of expert-identified relevant documents for the 12 tasks used in the current studies, and rank of the task among the full set of 100 TREC tasks from which the sample was drawn.

clusters and processing the elements (the text summary) for the cluster. After a cluster has been looked at, the cluster can be selected, ignored, or deselected, or the gathered clusters can be reclustered (scattered) or displayed.

Distribution of Relevant Documents Across Scatter/Gather Document Clusters

The Scatter/Gather document clustering algorithm (Cutting et al., 1992, 1993) produces clusters of documents based purely on the documents themselves, without any information about the tasks or queries of users. For a representative set of tasks, one might investigate how documents relevant to the tasks are distributed across the clusters automatically computed by Scatter/Gather. Such data were collected using a computer program by Marti Hearst (personal communication, June 16, 1995) for a sample of $N = 29$ TREC queries from the same test set that included those presented in table 6.1. For each query, a set of 200 documents was retrieved from the TIPSTER corpus using a standard search engine and submitted to the Scatter/Gather cluster algorithm. Clusters containing 50 or more documents were recursively submitted to the clustering algorithm and split into smaller clusters. At each stage, larger clusters were partitioned into a *cluster set* of five subclusters (note that the Scatter/Gather interface in figure 6.1 is based on partitioning clusters into 10 subclusters). This process resulted in a total of $N = 64$ cluster sets over all of the 29 TREC queries. Finally, for each of the cluster sets for each query, the computer program counted the number of expert-identified relevant documents that fell in each cluster.

Figure 6.5 presents the distribution of relevant documents over clusters in these clusters sets as a log-linear plot. The total number of relevant documents,

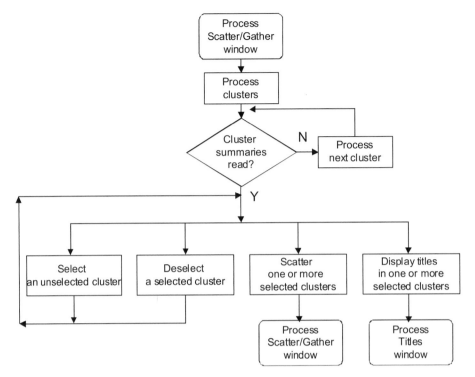

FIGURE 6.4 The basic Scatter/Gather task structure.

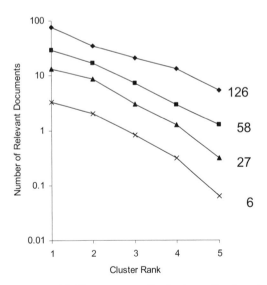

FIGURE 6.5 The average distribution of relevant documents within cluster sets. Cluster sets were ranked by their total number of relevant documents G(X), and each curve was computed as the median of the first, second, third, and fourth quartiles of the ranked sets. Labels next to each curve indicate the median G(X) for the quartile.

G(X), for each cluster set X was calculated. Next, the number of relevant documents in each of the five clusters making up a cluster set was calculated. Then, the clusters within each cluster set were ranked by the number of relevant documents. Table 6.3 presents these descriptive statistics for an arbitrary cluster set. To produce figure 6.5, the $N = 64$ cluster sets were ranked by the total number of relevant documents, G(X). This ranked list of cluster sets was then divided into quartiles, and the curve for each quartile is shown in figure 6.5. The label on each curve is the median G(X) for the quartile.

Note that the curves in figure 6.5 are approximately linear when plotted on a logarithmic scale for the ordinate axis. This suggests that, when clusters are ranked by the relevant documents they contain, the distribution of relevant documents over clusters in a cluster set has an exponentially decreasing form. Note also that the curves in figure 6.5 are approximately parallel. This suggests that the proportion (rather than total number) of relevant documents allocated to each cluster within a cluster set is approximately the same

TABLE 6.3 Distribution of relevant documents in a typical cluster set X.

Cluster Rank	Number of Relevant Documents
1	74
2	37
3	22
4	14
5	2
Total G(X)	148

regardless of the total number of relevant documents contained in the cluster set. Changes in the total number of relevant documents in a cluster set shift only the intercept of the curves in figure 6.5, not the form. Indeed, the empirical distributions in figure 6.5 are well fit by a function of the form

$$g(c, X) = G(X)\, a\, e^{-b(c-1)} \qquad (6.1)$$

where $g(c, X)$ is the number of relevant documents in cluster of rank c in cluster set X. The parameter a scales the curve in the ordinate dimension, and the parameter b $(0 < b < 1)$ is a rate parameter. For the data in figure 6.5, $a = 0.47$ and $b = 0.57$.

The implication of this analysis for the Scatter/Gather presentation of clusters is depicted schematically in figure 6.6. Although Scatter/Gather windows may vary in how many total documents they represent and how many relevant documents they represent, the distribution of relevant documents over clusters (when

cluster are ranked by the proportion of relevant documents they contain) will be the same (on average). It is worth noting again that the Scatter/Gather clustering algorithm has no information about user queries. The regularities shown in figure 6.5 and summarized in figure 6.6 are empirical regularities that emerge from the statistical natural language techniques underlying Scatter/Gather and the statistical nature of tasks in the world.

Rational Analyses

The production rules in the ACT-IF model described below implement the task structure presented in figure 6.4. The flow of control among ACT-IF production rules is determined by a set of evaluation heuristics that are shaped by rational analyses of information foraging in the Scatter/Gather environment. These rational analyses were conducted using a (somewhat idealized) state-space representation of the essential aspects of Scatter/Gather interaction. State-space representations are commonly used to characterize formal processes in computer science (e.g., search in artificial intelligence; S. Russell & Norvig, 2002) and to characterize the range of variable values that can occur in stochastic processes (e.g., Markov models in psychology; Wickens, 1982). State-space representations are also common in optimal foraging theory (e.g., Mangel & Clark, 1988). In this chapter I describe a state-space representation of the possible states of interaction of a user working with Scatter/Gather and the range of variable values characterizing those states.

The rational analyses conducted using this representation focused on two interrelated problems: (a) which clusters to choose from each Scatter/Gather window and which to ignore, and (b) how long to continue the (*enrichment*) process of gathering and reclustering clusters before initiating the (*exploitation*) process of displaying document titles and scanning them for relevant documents. The diet model discussed in chapter 2 informs the rational analysis of the problem of cluster choice. The patch model discussed in chapter 2 informs the rational analysis of the enrichment versus exploitation choice. A third problem requiring rational analysis is dealt with further below, the problem of evaluating the utility of each Scatter/Gather cluster from information scent cues in the cluster digests. This is essentially the same as the information scent problem discussed in chapter 3, and

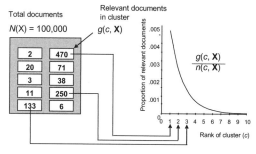

FIGURE 6.6 The number of relevant documents contained in clusters presented in an average Scatter/Gather window will be distributed proportionally according to an exponentially decreasing function of their rank. $N(X)$ is the total number of documents in a cluster, $g(c, X)$ is the number of relevant documents in cluster of rank c, and $n(c, X)$ is the total number of documents in a cluster of rank c.

the spreading activation model of information scent is applied again to Scatter/Gather.

State-Space Representation

The rational analyses were developed using a state-space representation of the idealized interaction of users with the Scatter/Gather system. The analyses were developed using time-cost parameters that were available from a study of Scatter/Gather experts (Pirolli & Card, 1995), which are presented in table 6.4. The analyses assumed an optimizing user who interacted as fast as possible and who chose actions so as to maximize the overall average rate of gain of valuable (relevant) information.

Figure 6.7 presents a portion of a hypothetical state-space representation of Scatter/Gather. Each state corresponds to a system state in which the user confronts a Scatter/Gather window (figure 6.2) or a Display Titles window (figure 6.3). States will be represented as *state vectors*, with components of the vectors representing information about a Scatter/Gather system state, including the time taken so far, the total number of documents associated with a Scatter/Gather window, and the total number of relevant documents associated with the window. A state vector variable will be represented as an uppercase bold $\mathbf{X}$ and a particular state as lowercase bold $\mathbf{x}$. Changes from one state to another are represented by state-change operators, which are depicted as arrows in figure 6.7. Emanating from the starting state on the left side of figure 6.7 are depicted 18 state-change operators that apply to the first Scatter/Gather window encountered by an idealized user. Half of these operators (those labeled δ_{SG} in figure 6.7) represent a user who gathers clusters and requests that Scatter/Gather compute a new set of clusters for presentation in

a new Scatter/Gather window. The other half of the 18 operators (those labeled δ_D in figure 6.7) represent a user who gathers clusters and requests that the system display them in a Display Titles window. The labels $\delta_{SG}(s,\mathbf{x})$ and $\delta_D(s, \mathbf{x})$ indicate that s clusters were gathered (selected) from the Scatter/Gather window in state $\mathbf{x}$. In figure 6.7, there is a path representing a user who gathers two clusters and requests that the system produce a new Scatter/Gather window [$\delta_{SG}(2, \mathbf{x})$], again gathers two clusters and requests a new Scatter/Gather window [$\delta_{SG}(2, \mathbf{x})$], and then gathers two clusters and requests a Titles Display window [$\delta_D(2, \mathbf{x})$]. Other aspects of figure 6.7 are discussed below.

One should note that, in actuality, a user may select any combination of 1–10 clusters. This means that there are $2^{10} - 1 = 1,023$ possible selections of clusters that a user can make from any Scatter/Gather window, and then the user may have those clusters displayed in a new Scatter/Gather window or a new Titles Display window. One might argue that the state-space representation should include $2 \times 1023 = 2046$ state-change operators emanating from every Scatter/Gather window state, as opposed to just the 18 depicted in figure 6.7 emanating from the start state. As will become evident, it is possible to perform the optimization analysis in this section without consideration of full space of possible moves.

Throughout this section, an unrealistic assumption is made, that the user has perfect knowledge about the number of relevant documents contained in each cluster (note that the total number of documents is presented on the Scatter/Gather screen in figure 6.2). This unrealistic assumption is useful for the purposes of coming to an understanding of cost-benefit structure of the Scatter/Gather task. Later, in developing the ACT-IF model, the assumption is that

TABLE 6.4 Estimated time-cost parameters for Scatter/Gather user and system actions.

Parameter	Description	Estimate (Pirolli & Card, 1995)
t_c	Time to scan and judge relevance of all the clusters in the Scatter/Gather window	10 sec
t_s	Time to select a cluster to gather	5 sec
t_{sg}	Time for system to scatter clusters and display new window	23 sec
t_t	Time to scan and judge relevance of a title in the Titles Display window	1 sec
t_g	Time to cut and paste a relevant title from Titles Display window to a bibliography file	5 sec
t_d	Time for system to display a new Titles Display window	20 sec

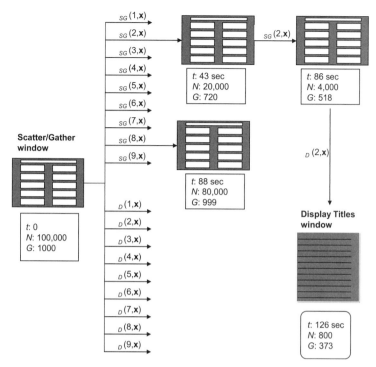

FIGURE 6.7 A portion of a Scatter/Gather state-space representation for a hypothetical task. Associated with states (represented by window icons) are variable values for time (t, in seconds), total number of documents (N), and the total number of relevant documents (G). State-change operators $\delta_{SG}(c, \mathbf{x})$ and $\delta_D(c, \mathbf{x})$ represent possible actions of the user with the system that change the system from one state to another.

the assessment of relevance is carried out by a spreading activation model of information scent.

States

The state of the user's interaction with Scatter/Gather, after some number of steps, k, while working on some query task, is represented by a state variable $\mathbf{X}_k$, which takes on values $\mathbf{X}_k = \mathbf{x}$. $\mathbf{X}_0$ is the initial state. The state variable represents information that allows the definition of the following functions:

$t(\mathbf{x})$ is the time taken so far to reach state $\mathbf{x}$ on a query task.

$N(\mathbf{x})$ is the total number of documents summed over all clusters in the current set of clusters.

$G(\mathbf{x})$ is the number of relevant documents summed over all clusters in the current set of clusters presented on the Scatter/Gather screen.

$n(c, \mathbf{x})$ is the number of total documents in cluster c of state $\mathbf{x}$.

$g(c, \mathbf{x})$ is the number of relevant documents in cluster c of state $\mathbf{x}$.

Following the conventions used in optimal foraging theory (Stephens & Krebs, 1986), the state-space representation assumes that clusters in any Scatter/Gather window state are indexed by c in an order reflecting the proportion of relevant documents they contain,

$$\frac{g(c, \mathbf{x})}{n(c, \mathbf{x})} > \frac{g(c+1, \mathbf{x})}{n(c+1, \mathbf{x})} \quad \text{for } c = 1, 2, \ldots 9. \quad (6.2)$$

This indexing orders clusters by the proportion of relevant documents they contain. Given assumptions made below, this is equivalent to ranking clusters by their *profitability*. This representational assumption about cluster indexing renders the analysis of which optimal number of clusters to select similar to the analysis of optimal diets in the optimal foraging literature. An ancillary effect of this assumption is to reduce the number of state-change operators that

TABLE 6.5 Effects of state-change operators.

Operator Applied to State $\mathbf{X}_k$	New Resulting State X_{k+1}
Gather s clusters and scatter $\delta_{SG}(s, \mathbf{X}_k)$	$N(\mathbf{X}_{k+1}) = \sum_{c=1}^{s} n(c, \mathbf{X}_k)$ $G(\mathbf{X}_{k+1}) = \sum_{c=1}^{s} g(c, \mathbf{X}_k)$ $t(\mathbf{X}_{k+1}) = t(\mathbf{X}_k) + t_c + st_s + t_{sg}$
Gather s clusters and display titles $\delta_D(s, \mathbf{X}_k)$	$N(\mathbf{X}_{k+1}) = \sum_{c=1}^{s} n(c, \mathbf{X}_k)$ $G(\mathbf{X}_{k+1}) = \sum_{c=1}^{s} g(c, \mathbf{X}_k)$ $t(\mathbf{X}_{k+1}) = t(\mathbf{X}_k) + t_c + st_s + t_d$

need to be considered from 2046 to 18 (see above). Figure 6.8 is a schematic representation of the ranking of clusters in a hypothetical Scatter/Gather window according to the profitability of relevant documents they contain.

State-Change Operators

The state space assumes two basic state-change operators: (a) gathering (selecting) the s most profitable clusters and requesting the system to scatter these into a new set of clusters and display these in a new Scatter/Gather cluster window (figure 6.2), and (b) gathering (selecting) the s most profitable clusters and requesting the system to present the documents in a Display Titles window (figure 6.3).

The effects of these operators are summarized in table 6.5. The gathering of the s most profitable clusters from a Scatter/Gather state and the request to scatter those clusters is represented by a state-change operator δ_{SG},

$$\mathbf{X}_{k+1} = \delta_{SG}(s, \mathbf{X}_k). \qquad (6.3)$$

The new state that results from the application of this operator, δ_{SG}, will contain the sum total number of documents that were in those s most profitable clusters that were gathered from the old state,

$$N(\mathbf{X}_{k+1}) = \sum_{c=1}^{s} n(c, \mathbf{X}_k). \qquad (6.4)$$

Similarly, the new state resulting from the operator δ_{SG} will contain the sum total number of relevant documents that were contained in those s most profitable clusters that were gathered from the old state,

$$G(\mathbf{X}_{k+1}) = \sum_{c=1}^{s} g(c, \mathbf{X}_k). \qquad (6.5)$$

The time-cost estimates in table 6.4 can be used to determine the amount of time it takes to perform the gathering and scattering of clusters involved in such a state change. The new state that results from a gathering and scattering of clusters by operator δ_{SG} will occur at time

$$t(\mathbf{X}_{k+1}) = t(\mathbf{X}_k) + t_c + st_s + t_{sg}, \qquad (6.6)$$

which includes the time taken so far, $t(\mathbf{X}_k)$, plus the time taken by the user to scan and judge each of the clusters, t_c, plus the time taken by the user to gather clusters, st_s, plus the time for the system to compute a new Scatter/Gather cluster window, t_{sg}.

Gathering the s most profitable clusters and requesting the system to display document titles in a Display Titles window is represented by the state-change operator

$$\mathbf{X}_{k+1} = \delta_D(s, \mathbf{X}_k). \qquad (6.7)$$

The specification of δ_D is almost identical to that of δ_{SG} above. The number of documents, $N(\mathbf{X}_{k+1})$, in the state resulting from the application of operator δ_D will also be characterized by equation 6.4, and the number of relevant documents $G(\mathbf{X}_{k+1})$ will be characterized by equation 6.5. The time of occurrence for the new state will be

$$t(\mathbf{X}_{k+1}) = t(\mathbf{X}_k) + t_c + st_s + t_d, \qquad (6.8)$$

which includes the time taken so far, $t(\mathbf{X}_k)$, plus the time taken by the user to scan and judge each of the clusters, t_c, plus the time taken by the user to gather s clusters, st_s, plus the time for the system to compute and display a Display Titles window, t_d.

Figure 6.7 illustrates the effects of the application of these state-change operators. Associated with each state in figure 6.7 is a box indicating the total number of documents (N) in the state, the number of relevant documents (G), and the time taken to read the current state (t). Figure 6.7 assumes a hypothetical start state containing 100,000 documents, of which 1000 are relevant. Application of the state-change $\delta_{SG}(2,\mathbf{x})$ produces a new Scatter/Gather window state. Applying equation 6.6, the time of occurrence for the new state would be

$$
\begin{aligned}
t(\mathbf{X}_1) &= t(\mathbf{X}_0) + t_c + st_s + t_{sg} \\
&= 0 + 10 + 2 \cdot 5 + 23 \text{ sec} \qquad (6.9) \\
&= 43 \text{ sec}.
\end{aligned}
$$

Applying equation 6.4, the total number of documents in the new state would be

$$
\begin{aligned}
N(\mathbf{X}_1) &= \sum_{c=1}^{2} n(c, \mathbf{X}_0) \\
&= 2 \cdot \frac{100,000}{10} \qquad (6.10) \\
&= 20,000 \text{ documents}.
\end{aligned}
$$

If we assume that relevant documents are distributed across clusters as found empirically in equation 6.1, then we can apply equation 6.5 to specify the number of relevant documents in the new state,

$$
\begin{aligned}
G(\mathbf{X}_1) &= \sum_{c=1}^{2} g(c, \mathbf{X}_0) \\
&= \sum_{c=1}^{2} G(\mathbf{X}_0) \; 0.47 \; \exp[-0.63 \cdot (c-1)] \\
&= 1,000 \cdot 0.47 + 1,000 \cdot 0.47 \cdot \exp(-0.63) \\
&= 720 \text{ documents} \\
& \hspace{5cm} (6.11)
\end{aligned}
$$

These values for the new state are indicated in figure 6.7. The results of several other state-change operators are also presented in figure 6.7.

Evaluation and Optimal Choice of Information Foraging Actions

The next step in the rational analysis is to develop a characterization of the optimal foraging policy, or the optimal choice of action to make from any given Scatter/Gather state. This involves specification of the evaluation of state-change operators as well as determination of the best choice of operator based on those evaluations. Dynamic programming (Bertsekas, 1995) is one very general optimization algorithm that is, in

principle, applicable to the kind of state-space representation described above. Dynamic programming has been used elsewhere in optimal foraging models (Mangel & Clark, 1988) and should typically be one of the analytic options considered for information foraging analyses.[2]

This algorithm, however, is often computationally intractable in practice when the state space has a large branching structure and it takes many steps to go from a start state to a goal state. Fortunately, the rational analysis of Scatter/Gather can be done using a *greedy algorithm* that relies on *myopic utility evaluation* (Pearl, 1988, pp. 313–337). The evaluation is myopic (or *local*) because it considers only states that are at most one or two moves away from the current state, rather than evaluating all possible future paths to goal states. The algorithm is greedy because it simply chooses the best state-change operator that applies to the current state.

To characterize the elements of the optimal foraging strategy for Scatter/Gather, below I consider a representative problem from table 6.1. Then I consider stages near the end of the process and work backward through the decisions that lead to those end states.

- I use an example initial problem state set to represent the median difficulty task in table 6.1:

  $t(\mathbf{X}_0) = 0$ seconds

  $G(\mathbf{X}_0) = 303$ relevant documents

  $N(\mathbf{X}_0) = 742,833$ total documents

- I assume that the goal is to get to highly profitable *information patches*. The Scatter/Gather Titles Display windows are characterized as information patches whose profitability depends on the proportion of relevant documents that are displayed in those windows.
- The process of gathering clusters and rescattering them is characterized as an *enrichment* process that improves the profitability of information patches. This occurs because the profitability of information patches is dependent on the profitability of the clusters that are selected to be displayed. The selection of clusters to display in a Scatter/Gather Titles Display window is a kind of *information diet* problem whose aim is to choose the best set of clusters to display.
- A trade-off occurs between continuing to gather and scatter clusters and displaying clusters. This

involves a kind of *enrichment-exploitation trade-off* between gathering clusters and rescattering them (enrichment) versus gathering clusters and displaying them (exploitation). As shown below, the process of repeated scattering and gathering at first produces an enrichment of information patches but eventually begins to depress the overall rate of gain of valuable information. The problem is to continue scattering and gathering as long as it enriches the information patches but to stop just before depression occurs.

The Profitability of Information Patches: Titles Display Windows

The display of document titles in a Titles Display window (figure 6.3) is considered an information patch. It is assumed that the information forager scans through the scrollable list of document titles and must spend time processing each document citation, plus some additional amount of time processing each relevant document (i.e., cutting and pasting them into a bibliography file). In the studies described below, the titles were presented in an unordered fashion (random order). Consequently, scanning a list of document titles should produce a linear within-patch gain function such as that shown in figure 2.4. As discussed in chapter 2, the optimal strategy in this situation is to forage until the end of the title list.

The profitability, $\pi(\mathbf{X}_i)$, of information foraging through a Titles Display window in state $\mathbf{X}_i$ is defined as the rate of collecting relevant documents per unit time in that information patch. This rate of gain within the information patch is determined by the number of relevant documents, $G(\mathbf{X}_i)$, that the user has collected, divided by the time cost of processing the items in the Display Titles window. This time cost includes a cost of t_t seconds for each of the $N(\mathbf{X}_i)$ titles that is scanned in a Display Titles window plus a cost of t_g seconds for performing a cut-and-paste operation on each of the $G(\mathbf{X}_i)$ relevant documents. The within-patch rate of gain is

$$\pi(\mathbf{X}_i) = \frac{G(\mathbf{X}_i)}{t_t N(\mathbf{X}_i) + t_g G(\mathbf{X}_i)}. \quad (6.12)$$

Information Diet: Choosing to Display Clusters

The profitability of a Titles Display window is dependent on the clusters that are chosen to be pre-sented. We can define a slightly different profitability function, π_c, that computes the profitability of an information patch that results from the display of titles from a single cluster. If we choose a single particular cluster, c, to present to the user in a Titles Display window, then the resulting profitability of the information patch can be defined as

$$\pi_c(c, \mathbf{X}_k) = \frac{g(c, \mathbf{X}_k)}{t_t\, n(c, \mathbf{X}_k) + t_g\, g(c, \mathbf{X}_k)}. \quad (6.13)$$

Using this definition, we can define the optimal selection of clusters to display. The solution to this optimization problem is analogous to the solution of optimal diet problems in optimal foraging theory.

Suppose an information forager has performed some number of steps, k, is confronted with a Scatter/Gather window (figure 6.2) in state $\mathbf{X}_k$, and chooses some set of clusters to display in a Display Titles window (figure 6.3) in state $\mathbf{X}_{k+1}$. The overall rate of gain, R, for the information patch produced by this choice depends on the relevant documents gained divided by the total time taken to collect those documents:

$$R(\mathbf{X}_{k+1}) = \frac{G(\mathbf{X}_{k+1})}{t(\mathbf{X}_{k+1}) + t_t N(\mathbf{X}_{k+1}) + t_g G(\mathbf{X}_{k+1})} \quad (6.14)$$

The numerator of equation 6.14 is the number of relevant documents, $G(\mathbf{X}_{k+1})$, presented in the Titles Display window in step $k+1$. The denominator is the sum of the time taken from the start of the task, $t(\mathbf{X}_{k+1})$, plus the time it will take to scan all the document titles, $t_t N(\mathbf{X}_{k+1})$, plus the time it will take to process all the relevant documents encountered, $t_g G(\mathbf{X}_{k+1})$. We can now use equations 6.4, 6.5, and 6.8 to specify the rate of gain, R_D, that will be attained by choosing the s most profitable clusters from the Scatter/Gather window in state $\mathbf{X}_k$:

$$R_D(s, \mathbf{X}_k) =$$
$$\frac{\sum_{c=1}^{s} g(c, \mathbf{X}_k)}{t(\mathbf{X}_k) + t_c + st_s + t_d + t_t \sum_{c=1}^{s} n(c, \mathbf{X}_k) + t_g \sum_{c=1}^{s} g(c, \mathbf{X}_k)}$$
$$(6.15)$$

Equation 6.15 specifies a formula for computing the overall rate of gain for different information diets consisting of the s most profitable clusters presented to the user in state $\mathbf{X}_k$.

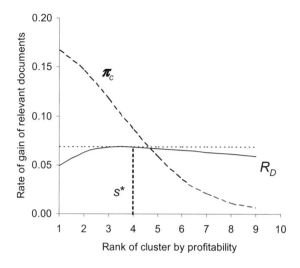

FIGURE 6.8 The optimal diet for Scatter/Gather is to select the most profitable s^* clusters. The diet should include only clusters whose profitability, π_c, is greater than the overall rate of gain, R_D.

To calculate the optimal collection of clusters to display, s^*, we can evaluate R_D for different gatherings of s clusters and choose the gathering that yields the maximum value of R_D:

$$R_D^*(\mathbf{X}_k) = \max_{s=1,2,\ldots9} R_D(s, \mathbf{X}_k)$$

$$= R_D(s^*, \mathbf{X}_k). \qquad (6.16)$$

The user should select the s^* most profitable clusters in a Scatter/Gather window at stage k in order to produce the optimal Titles Display window at stage $k+1$.

Figure 6.8 presents the relationship between the expected profitability of individual clusters (equation 6.13) and the overall rate of gain produced by displaying collections of the s most profitable clusters. Figure 6.8 is intentionally drawn in a way to evoke ties to the graphical version of optimal diet model in figure 2.9. The calculation of the profitabilities, $\pi_c(c, \mathbf{X}_k)$, and the calculation of the overall rates of gain, R_D, assume that relevant documents are distributed according to equation 6.1 and that the total number of documents in state $\mathbf{X}_k$ is distributed evenly over the 10 clusters in the state:

$$n(c, \mathbf{x}) = \frac{N(\mathbf{x})}{10} \qquad (6.17)$$

The evaluations in figure 6.8 are for a state along the optimal solution to a problem that begins with the representative initial state described above. The particular state evaluated occurs at the point at which the

optimal action is to display a selected set of clusters. The calculation of this optimal path by a greedy algorithm is described next.

Enrichment: The Expected Rate of Gain Produced by Gathering and Rescattering Clusters

The optimizing forager invests in gathering and rescattering clusters in order to enrich the Titles Display windows. Each cycle of gathering and rescattering clusters is aimed at improving the proportion of relevant documents under consideration, and it also reduces the total number of documents under consideration. Figure 6.9 shows the effect of this enrichment process. It plots the profitability of information patches, $\pi(\mathbf{X}_k)$, according to equation 6.12 as a function of time invested in gathering and scattering actions by the optimal forager. To produce figure 6.9, the forager was assumed to have always gathered the rate-maximizing set of clusters and reclustered them according to evaluations that are described below. Note that the enrichment process at first produces increasing returns, but eventually the improvements diminish and flatten out.

Figure 6.10 presents the overall rate of gain, $R(\mathbf{X}_k)$, calculated according to equation 6.14 for the same states evaluated in figure 6.9. Figure 6.10 shows that repeated gathering and scattering of clusters at first improves the overall rate of gain up to a maximum, but then the overall rate of gain decreases because the forager is investing increasing time for diminishing or zero improvements in returns.

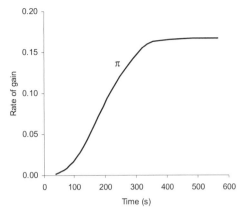

FIGURE 6.9 The enrichment effects of gathering and rescattering clusters on the projected profitability of Title Display states.

Enrichment Versus Patch Exploitation

With a Scatter/Gather window (figure 6.2), the information forager is faced with a decision between the options of (a) continuing to gather and rescatter clusters (enrichment) and (b) displaying clusters and foraging through the display (exploitation). Figure 6.10 suggests that the information forager needs only to decide whether another round of gathering and scattering clusters will yield an improvement or deterioration in the expected rate of gate. If another round yields an improvement, then the forager should gather and scatter clusters; otherwise, the forager should display clusters in a Titles Display window. This suggests a one-step look-ahead evaluation:

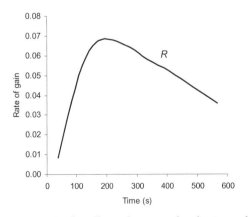

FIGURE 6.10 The effects of continued gathering and rescattering on the overall rate of gain.

1. The evaluation of the gathering and scattering of the s most profitable clusters depends on an evaluation of the new state that results from the state-change operator defined in table 6.5,

$$\mathbf{X}_{k+1} = \delta_{SG}(s, \mathbf{X}_k). \qquad (6.18)$$

2. The evaluation of that resulting state is assessed by the rate of gain that could be achieved by displaying the best set of clusters in that new state,

$$R_D^*(\mathbf{X}_{k+1}). \qquad (6.19)$$

Combining equations 6.18 and 6.19, we can define an evaluation of the expected rate of gain for gathering and scattering the s most profitable clusters,

$$R_{SG}(s, \mathbf{X}_k) = R_D^*[\delta_{SG}(s, \mathbf{X}_k)]. \qquad (6.20)$$

Using equation 6.20, we can define the optimal selection of clusters, s^*, to gather and scatter by

$$R_{SG}^*(\mathbf{X}_k) = \max_{s=1,2,\dots 9} R_{SG}(s, \mathbf{X}_k)$$
$$= R_{SG}(s^*, \mathbf{X}_k). \qquad (6.21)$$

Equation 6.21 states that the user should select the s^* most profitable clusters to gather and rescatter.

The rate of gain specified in equation 6.21 provides an evaluation of continued enrichment, whereas the rate of gain specified in equation 6.16 provides an evaluation of exploitation of the current clusters. Figure 6.11 shows how these evaluations change over time. It was produced by a simulation that explored the states space by varying the amount of time invested in cycles of scattering and gathering clusters and always selecting the rate-maximizing collection of clusters. At each cycle of scattering and gathering, the simulation would determine (a) R_D^*, the maximum rate of gain that could be achieved by foraging through a display of titles, and (b) R_{SG}^*, the maximum rate of gain that could be achieved by one more round of scattering and gathering clusters. Basically, the curve for R_{SG}^* is the same as R_D^* but shifted to the left. Figure 6.11 suggests a greedy hill-climbing regime: If $R_D^* \geq R_{SG}^*$, then the forager should display titles, and if $R_{SG}^* > R_D^*$, the forager should continue scattering and gathering clusters.

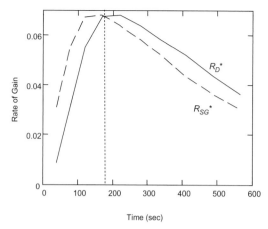

FIGURE 6.11 The average rate of gain yielded by different investments in time spent scattering and gathering clusters, assuming a greedy algorithm based on myopic utility evaluation. To the left of the dotted line, it is more profitable to gather and scatter cluster ($R_{SG}^* > R_D^*$), and to the right of the dotted line, it is more profitable to display clusters ($R_D^* > R_{SG}^*$).

Summary

This section presents a relatively involved rational analysis of the idealized use of the Scatter/Gather system. However, at a general level, the analyses have been guided by hypotheses about analogies between food foraging models and information foraging models of Scatter/Gather. The selection of the optimal set of clusters on every Scatter/Gather screen can be viewed as a kind of optimal diet selection problem, which suggests guidance from the conventional diet model presented in chapter 2. The iterative reclustering of selected clusters has an enrichment effect on the patch of information under consideration. However, at some point continued enrichment is incurring an opportunity cost with respect to simply displaying and exploiting the current cluster set. Because of the nature of moves in the Scatter/Gather state space, it appears possible to use a simple myopic evaluation scheme in which current states, or the results of one-step look-ahead, can be used to hill-climb to an optimum. The next section presents another cognitive model, ACT-IF, that maps this rational analysis into a set of proximal information processing mechanisms to simulate user behavior.

ACT-IF

ACT-IF is a variant of SNIF-ACT, with some tailoring to the Scatter/Gather environment. The declarative memory models the information being attended to and goal information. The production memory contains the production rules in table 6.6 that implement the task structure outlined in figure 6.4. The evaluation functions that select production rules in ACT-IF are based on a spreading activation model of information scent that is very similar to the one developed in the SNIF-ACT model of Web foraging. It is assumed that the cluster summaries on the Scatter/Gather interface spread activation through the declarative memory of the user, and activation simultaneously spreads from the task query. Activation levels are used by ACT-IF evaluation functions to determine which production rules are best to execute. These evaluation functions approximate the rate-optimizing evaluation functions developed in the preceding section.

Production Rules

The Scatter/Gather task structure in figure 6.4 was modeled in ACT-IF with the set of 12 production rules glossed in table 6.6. On the left of the arrows in table 6.6 are mnemonic names for the productions and the conditions for matching declarative memory. To the right of the arrows are the actions of the production rules. Next I discuss how the ACT-IF model evaluates productions in ways that achieve effects similar to those discussed in this analysis of the state-space model.

Utility Assessment by a Spreading Activation Model of Information Scent

Imagine that a user is working on a particular query, Q, such as one of the tasks in table 6.1, and is faced with a Scatter/Gather window (e.g., figure 6.2). The assumption is that the user must judge how the relevant documents in the collection are distributed across the clusters that are presented by Scatter/Gather. For each presented cluster, the user must make a judgment, based on the words available in the cluster digest, about the likelihood of finding relevant documents in that cluster, and then make a decision about whether or not to select (gather) that cluster given the other available clusters. Chapter 4 presents a rational analysis of information scent and describes a spreading activation model of information scent. In this chapter, I assume

TABLE 6.6 Production rules used in the ACT-IF model of the Scatter/Gather task.

Notice-New-Window New window on screen	→	Attend to it & set goal to process it
Attend-to-Window Attend to window	→	Look at window
Unattend-to-Screen Goal is to process a window & different window has appeared	→	Pop the goal
Shift-Attention Another window is present	→	Attend to that window
Process-Clusters Goal is to process Scatter/Gather window	→	Set goal to process clusters
Process-Next-Cluster Goal is to process Scatter/Gather window clusters & one is unprocessed	→	Set goal to process next cluster
Look-at-Next-Cluster Goal is to process next cluster	→	Look at cluster & pop the goal & set goal to process cluster elements
Look-at-Cluster-Elements Goal is to look at cluster elements	→	Look at topics and typical titles & pop the goal

Select-Relevant-Cluster
Goal is to process Scatter/Gather
    window & there is a query
    & there is an unselected cluster
	→	Select the cluster

Deselect-Irrelevant-Cluster
Goal is to process Scatter/Gather
    window & there is a query
    & there is a selected cluster
	→	Deselect the cluster

Do-Scatter/Gather Goal is to process Scatter/Gather window & some clusters have been selected	→	Scatter/Gather the window
Do-Display-Titles *Goal is to process Scatter/Gather* window & some clusters have been selected	→	Display the titles in the window

that users evaluate the Scatter/Gather cluster digests using the same spreading activation mechanisms. The spreading activation networks used to model Scatter/Gather interaction were created from word frequency and word co-occurrence frequency data used in Schuetze (1992), which were computed from the TIPSTER corpus (Harman, 1993). The spreading activation model of information scent for Scatter/Gather employs a model that is similar in form to the Random Utility Model presented in chapter 4. Ideally, the distribution of relevant documents based on the perception of information scent from the Scatter/Gather user interface should be highly correlated with the distribution of relevant documents in the underlying document clusters.

The spreading activation model of information scent for this situation specifies that the utility, $U(c, Q)$, of a particular cluster digest on a Scatter/Gather window is

$$U(c, Q) = V(c, Q) + \varepsilon, \qquad (6.22)$$

where

$$V(c, Q) = \sum_{i \in Q} A_i \qquad (6.23)$$

is the summed spreading activation received by chunks representing the query task from words in the cluster digest, and ε is a Gumbel noise error term. Again, the spreading activation equation for chunk i representing a word in the query is

$$A_i = B_i + \sum_i W_j S_{ji}, \qquad (6.24)$$

where B_i is the base-level activation of i, S_{ji} is the association strength between an associated chunk j and chunk i, and W_j is reflects attention (*source activation*) on chunk j. Based on information scent, the proportion of relevant documents that the user will judge to be in a particular cluster c will be

$$d_P(c, Q) = \frac{e^{\mu V(c, Q)}}{\sum_k e^{\mu V(k, Q)}}, \qquad (6.25)$$

where k indexes each of the clusters on a particular Scatter/Gather window (figure 6.2). Another way of interpreting equation 6.25 is to assume that the user uses information scent to assess the number of relevant documents in a cluster c as the numerator in equation 6.25. This would be analogous to the state-space function $g(c, \mathbf{x})$ defined above. Now we will use spreading activation to provide an indication of the number of relevant documents (and use a subscript "A" to distinguish the new function from the old):

$$
\begin{aligned}
g_A(c, Q) &= \exp[\mu V(c, Q)] \\
&= \exp(\mu \sum_{i \in Q} A_i), \qquad (6.26)
\end{aligned}
$$

and the total number of relevant documents over all clusters on a particular window w will be estimated from spreading activation by

$$
\begin{aligned}
R_A(w, Q) &= \sum_{c \in w} \exp[\mu V(c, Q)] \\
&= \sum_{c \in w} g_A(c, Q), \qquad (6.27)
\end{aligned}
$$

where c indexes each cluster digest on Scatter/Gather window w. This formulation is tested in several ways after fitting the ACT-IF simulation to actual user data.

Evaluation Functions

ACT-IF is a production system that selects a single production rule to execute on each cycle of operation. On each cycle, ACT-IF matches production rule conditions to information in declarative memory, evaluates instantiations of matching rules, and executes the action of the highest evaluated instantiation. The ACT-IF model for Scatter/Gather has evaluation functions of production rules in table 6.6 that are shaped by the rational analysis given in the preceding section. For completeness, however, I redefine several of the functions used in the state-space analysis to conform to the ACT-IF formulation. The assumption in ACT-IF is that each production can be evaluated solely on the information that is matched by the condition side of the rule, plus access to a global time variable. Depending on the specification of the rule in table 6.6, the rule may have access to the following:

Q, the current query (plus its words)

w, the current window

c an individual cluster (plus its words and whether it has been selected)

t, the time taken so far

$n(c)$ the total number of documents in a cluster (available on the window)

s, the set of selected clusters so far on window w

Display of Titles

The Do-Display-Titles production is evaluated on the basis of the rate of gain that would be achieved by displaying and foraging through the set of s clusters that have already been gathered. The evaluation function is a redefinition of R_D in equation 6.15 that now uses spreading activation to estimate the relevant documents in a cluster:

$$R_D(s, Q) = \frac{\sum_{c \in s} g_A(c, Q)}{t + t_t \sum_{c \in s} n(c) + t_g \sum_{c \in s} g_A(c, Q)} \qquad (6.28)$$

The numerator of the evaluation function in equation 6.28 is the total activation-based information scent for the clusters gathered so far. The denominator is an estimate of the total task time it would take to process those clusters.

Scattering Clusters

The Do-Scatter/Gather production is evaluated on the basis of the projected rate of gain that would be produced by one more round of having the system scatter the set of s clusters that have already been gathered.

Rather than do an explicit look-ahead, as done in the state-space analysis above, we used an evaluation function that makes an "approximate guess" about the results of the look-ahead. The evaluation function R_{SG} defined above is replaced by the approximation

$$R_{SG}(s, Q)$$
$$= \frac{g_\Delta \sum_{c \in s} g_A(c, Q)}{(t + t_\Delta) + t_t n_\Delta \sum_{c \in s} n(c) + t_g g_\Delta \sum_{c \in s} g_A(c, Q)}. \quad (6.29)$$

The variable g_Δ is the expected proportional change in relevant documents that would occur with another round of scattering clusters. It was based simply on the assumption that the proportional change on the next step would be about the same as the proportional change on the current step; that is,

$$g_\Delta = \frac{\sum_{c \in s} g_A(c, Q)}{R(w, Q)}, \quad (6.30)$$

where the numerator is an information scent estimate of the relevant documents in the selected clusters and the denominator is the information scent estimate of all of the relevant documents on the current window.

The variable n_Δ is the proportional change in total number of documents that could occur with another round of scattering clusters. Again, this is based on the assumption that the proportional change will be about the same as the change on the current step:

$$n_\Delta = \frac{\sum_{c \in s} n(c)}{\sum_{k \in w} n(k)}, \quad (6.31)$$

where $c \in s$ indexes the selected clusters and $k \in w$ indexes all of the clusters on the window.

Finally, t_Δ is the expected increment in time:

$$t_\Delta = t_c + st_s + t_{sg} + t_d \quad (6.32)$$

This includes an estimated cost for scanning another set of cluster (t_c), selecting another set of clusters (st_s), and performing a Scatter/Gather operation on the current window (t_{sg}) and a Display Titles operation on the next window (t_d).

Selecting and Deselecting Clusters

The Select-Relevant-Cluster production is evaluated on the basis of an activation-based information scent assessment of the profitability $\pi_A(c, Q)$ of the cluster c that it matched on the current Scatter/Gather cluster display window given the current query Q. The ACT-IF model for the Scatter/Gather task assumes that the profitability is evaluated by

$$\pi_A(c, A) = \frac{g_A(c, Q)}{t_g g_A(c, Q) + t_t n(c)}, \quad (6.33)$$

where $g_A(c, Q)$ is the activation-based scent assessment in equation 6.26, and $n(c)$ is the total number of documents in a cluster. The time cost to process all the documents in a cluster is therefore $t_t n(c)$, and the additional costs of processing relevant documents is $t_g g(c, Q)$.

The Deselect-Irrelevant-Cluster production matches an already selected cluster but is evaluated on the basis of the maximum of the current rate of gains estimated by R_{SG} and R_D.

Summary

These evaluations are computed locally, based only on declarative information matched by a production rule plus a time parameter. In concert, however, the evaluations instantiate important aspects of the rational analysis provided by the state-space model:

- The rule evaluations select clusters when their profitability, $\pi_A(c, Q)$, is greater than the current rate of gain for the set of s clusters that have already been gathered. Clusters will continue to be gathered so long as the evaluation of Select-Relevant-Cluster is greater than the evaluation of Do-Scatter/Gather or Do-Display-Titles. This solves the diet selection problem.
- Clusters are deselected when their profitability is less than the expected rate of gain for already gathered clusters.
- The evaluations work to continue gathering clusters and scattering them until the overall rate of gain shows a projected decrease, that is, until $R_{SG} < R_D$. As long as Do-Scatter/Gather has a higher evaluation than Do-Display-Titles, the ACT-IF model will continue to gather and scatter clusters. When the evaluation of these two rules reverses, the model will display titles.

Experiment: Foraging with Scatter/Gather

An evaluation study of Scatter/Gather performed by Pirolli, Schank, Hearst, and Diehl (1996) provided data to test information foraging predictions and the validity of the ACT-IF model. In this study, two groups of participants used Scatter/Gather under slightly different task instructions.

Method

Participants

Eight adults solicited through PARC or the Stanford University graduate program participated in the Scatter/Gather portion of the study as volunteers or were paid $10/hour.

Materials and Procedure

Participants were asked to read the instructions for the experiment and then use the Scatter/Gather system to find articles relevant to given topics in a large and complex collection of text documents. The experiment used the 2.2 gigabyte TIPSTER text collection created for the TREC conference (Harman, 1993), and it used the tasks presented in table 6.1. Four blocks of topics were constructed. Each topic block contained one Easy topic, one Medium topic, and one Hard topic (see table 6.1), in that order. Each participant completed two blocks of topics using Scatter/Gather, and the other two blocks were used for other activities not described here. The presentation order of blocks was counterbalanced over participants, within groups, according to a randomized Latin square.

Scatter/Gather users read a topic query and then proceeded to find as many documents relevant to the query as possible. This required that the participants repeatedly scatter and gather clusters using windows such as figure 6.2 and then choose clusters for display (figure 6.3). The display window would present a list of document titles from the chosen clusters, and the participants would select relevant titles from the list. The titles selected by the participant would then be saved to a file, as the participants' answer to the topic query.

Scatter/Gather participants were randomly assigned to one of two study conditions: Scatter/Gather Speeded ($N = 4$) or Scatter/Gather with Relevance Ratings ($N = 4$). In the Scatter/Gather Speeded condition, participants were given one hour per block to find articles. In the Scatter/Gather Relevance Rating condition, participants were not given a time limit and were asked to complete additional classification and relevance activities: Given worksheets, they were asked to indicate how they would classify each presented cluster (i.e., using words or short phrases) and to estimate what percentage of texts in a cluster seemed relevant to the topic. For most of the analyses described below, I combine the data for the Scatter/Gather groups.

The activities of participants interacting with Scatter/Gather were automatically logged. These log files provide the test data for the ACT-IF simulation. The log files contained time-stamped records of every display presented to the participants and every Scatter/Gather action performed by participants.

Results

A General Analysis of Diet Selection for Scatter/Gather

As a general test of the information diet model, I examined data concerning the selection of clusters for the first step of the interactive Scatter/Gather process. In particular, I was interested in testing the diet model prediction concerning which clusters are selected and how many. This corresponds to the selection of clusters at Level 1 of document clustering in figure 6.1. Later, I present the more detailed ACT-IF model for selecting clusters throughout the Scatter/Gather task. Participants worked on queries at three levels of difficulty, where difficulty corresponded to the number of expert-identified relevant documents in the collection. The number of expert-identified relevant documents across the query tasks was Easy > Medium > Hard (table 6.2). Participants selected more clusters for easier tasks: For Hard queries, they selected $M = 1.38$ clusters; for Medium queries, $M = 1.63$ clusters; for Easy queries, $M = 2.25$ clusters. This is generally consistent with the diet model, which predicts that a forager should select more profitable clusters over less profitable ones: The clusters in the Easy conditions contained more relevant documents than those in the Medium or Hard conditions. As I illustrate below, a coarse application of the diet model predicts the qualitative ordering of the query conditions with respect to the number of clusters selected (Easy > Medium > Hard) and reasonably approximate quantitative predictions.

Table 6.7 presents estimates relevant to the application of an information diet model to Scatter/Gather. To apply the diet selection model, I estimated the subjective assessments of the cluster profitabilities, π_i, for each cluster i at the first Scatter/Gather iteration in all query conditions. The first Scatter/Gather

TABLE 6.7 Optimal information diet analysis for Scatter/Gather (Pirolli et al., 1996).

Task Condition (Rank of Cluster Within Query Condition)	Participants' Estimate of Net Relevant Documents, g_i	Handling Time, t_{Wi} (sec)	Estimated Profitability, π_i (Relevant Documents/Second)
Easy (1)	13,670	957	14.28
Medium (1)	10,400	994	10.46
Hard (1)	11,890	1261	9.43
Easy (2)	5,824	957	6.08
Easy (3)	2,526	957	2.64
Medium (2)	2,607	994	2.62
Hard (2)	1,991	1261	1.58
Easy (4)	1,040	957	1.09
Easy (5)	891	357	0.93
Hard (3)	379	1261	0.30

The optimal diet includes the four highest profitability clusters. This analysis was performed on the 10 clusters encountered on the first Scatter/Gather screen in each Query Condition (30 clusters total).

interaction corresponds to the selection of clusters at the very top level of clustering in figure 6.1. To estimate these subjective profitabilities, I first derived g_i, the subjective estimates of the number of relevant documents in each cluster. These were obtained from the $N = 4$ participants (of the eight total participants) who provided ratings of the percentage of relevant documents in each cluster. I then estimated the time to process each cluster selected at the first Scatter/Gather iteration, t_{Wi}, for the three levels of query difficulty. This was calculated by dividing the total time to complete the query tasks by the number of clusters selected at the first iteration.[3] For clusters selected at the first iteration of Scatter/Gather, the Easy condition required 957 seconds per selected cluster, Medium queries required 994 seconds per selected cluster, and Hard queries required 1261 seconds per selected cluster. Table 6.7 lists the profitability, $\pi_i = g_i/t_{Wi}$, for the top 10 profitability clusters from all three query conditions.

Inspection of table 6.7 reveals that the general qualitative prediction is that the number of clusters selected in query conditions should be such that Easy $\geq$ Medium $\geq$ Hard, which is consistent with observation. To see this, recall that the optimal diet can be constructed by selecting the k most profitable clusters. Since the rows of table 6.7 are in descending rank profitability, drawing an imaginary line across table 6.7 identifies the clusters whose profitabilities lie above the imaginary line. One can verify that drawing imaginary lines for all diets of greater than three clusters will select more Easy than Medium query clusters.

I calculated the overall average rate of finding relevant document citations, using the conventional diet model presented as equation 2.18 in chapter 2, for diets that included the $k = 1, 2, \ldots, 10$ highest profitability clusters in table 6.7. To do this, I assumed that the tasks were performed at a rate of $\lambda = 1/91.9$ min, which is based on the average time taken between query tasks in the same query condition. Figure 6.12 presents the profitability estimates from table 6.7. The leftmost points are labeled with the query conditions in which the clusters occurred. Figure 6.12 also presents the estimates of the overall average rate of finding relevant items R for diets of increasing numbers of clusters, k. The predicted optimal diet is $k^* = 4$ clusters, as calculated by equation 2.18 in chapter 2.

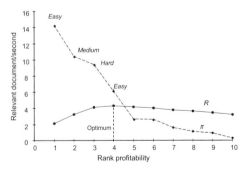

FIGURE 6.12 Analysis of the optimal information diet. The profitability (π) of clusters is ranked and added to the diet in order of decreasing profitability until lower than the rate of gain, R. R is calculated according to equation 2.18 in chapter 2.

According to this application of the diet model, for the Easy tasks, the topmost two clusters should be chosen, and for the Medium and Hard tasks the topmost one cluster should be chosen. These compare favorably to the observed values: Easy, $M = 2.25$ clusters; Medium, $M = 1.63$ clusters; Hard, $M = 1.38$ clusters.

User Tracing

ACT-IF was initialized with a spreading activation network estimated from the TIPSTER corpus, the set of production rules presented in table 6.6, and the evaluation functions described above. For each participant, the simulation was given a series of goals corresponding to the tasks done by the participant and matched through user tracing to the corresponding user logs. The user tracer parsed the participants' actions from Scatter/Gather log files and used this information to maintain a model of the Scatter/Gather screen state. Changes in screen state were "perceived" by the ACT-IF production system, which means that declarative memory elements were created when corresponding objects "appeared" on the screen in the screen state model.

The user tracer ran the ACT-IF production system for one cycle at a time, catching it just as it had evaluated and ranked the productions that matched to the user's current goal and state of working memory. At that point, the ranked list of executable productions (known as the *conflict set*) served as a prediction of the relative likelihood of potential user actions. The user tracer then examined the parsed log to determine the actual user action. The corresponding production in the conflict set was then chosen for execution in ACT-IF, and the user tracer duly updated statistics regarding the match of its predictions against the observed user actions. Following production execution, the user tracer read the next action from the log file and updated the Scatter/Gather screen state model, and ACT-IF updated its declarative memory in accordance with any "perceived" screen changes.

To estimate the scaling parameter μ in equation 6.26, I fit activation-based assessments obtained from Scatter/Gather screen states to estimates of the actual number of relevant documents in clusters. It should be noted that, besides the spreading activation networks, (a) μ is the only parameter estimated for the simulations and (b) this estimation is done based on a priori characterizations of the information environment, not post hoc from user data. The information scent model

in ACT-IF is almost completely specified a priori from the structure of the information environment.

Characterization of Scent in the Scatter/Gather Environment

Equation 6.26 provides a characterization of information scent as prediction of the information forager's assessment of the prospects of finding relevant information. I wanted to understand if the proximal assessment of prospects tracked the actual prospects of finding relevant information in Scatter/Gather. Information scent may fail to track the underlying distribution of relevant documents for either of two reasons: (1) the model is wrong or (2) the Scatter/Gather interface provides a poor reflection of the underlying clustering structure. Good fits, however, should corroborate the validity of the model and the effectiveness of the interface.

For an average Scatter/Gather state s with clusters $c = 1, 2, \ldots, 10$, we may consider two aspects: (1) how the Scatter/Gather clustering algorithm has distributed relevant documents across the clusters and (2) how a person perceives the distribution of relevant documents across clusters, given the proximal cues available. We may then ask how well the two distributions match. The distribution computed by the clustering algorithm is the *distal* distribution of relevant information $d_D(c)$. From the analysis of figure 6.5 and equation 6.1, the proportion of documents falling into cluster of rank c should be

$$d_D(c) = ae^{-b(c-1)}. \tag{6.34}$$

[This is the same as equation 6.1 scaled so that $G(X) = 1$ in order to give a form in terms of proportions.]

The perceived distribution is the *proximal* distribution of relevant information $d_P(c)$. This latter distribution is just information scent equation 6.25 computed for the average state. I computed the summed activation in equation 6.23, $V(c, Q)$, for every cluster on every screen available across all participant log files in the Scatter/Gather study. For every screen, I ranked the clusters $c = 1, 2, \ldots, 10$ in decreasing order of activation value. For a particular cluster rank c, I computed the average activation $\overline{V}(c)$—that is, the average of all clusters at rank c. Using $\overline{V}(c)$, I computed the average information scent of relevant documents as $\overline{g}(c)$, for a cluster of rank c. The distribution of relevant documents across clusters on an average

Scatter/Gather screen was calculated by dividing the activation assessment of a cluster by the total activation assessments of all clusters on the same screen,

$$d_P(c) = \frac{\bar{g}(c)}{\sum_{i=1}^{10} \bar{g}(i)}$$

$$= \frac{\exp[\mu \overline{V}(c)]}{\sum_{i=1}^{10} \exp[\mu \overline{V}(i)]}.$$

(6.35)

Equation 6.35 was fit by numerical methods to equation 6.34 to obtain the curve in figure 6.13 and to estimate the scaling factor μ.

The match of $d_D(c)$ to $d_P(c)$ in figure 6.13 suggests how well the assessment of prospects from proximal cues fits the actual distribution of relevant documents across clusters in an average Scatter/Gather state. One may also examine what happens to these subjective estimates of prospects as a person moves from one Scatter/Gather state to another—as they iteratively gather clusters and then scatter them into a new set of clusters. Optimally, this iterative process should reduce the total number of documents under consideration while increasing the proportion of relevant documents.

First, consider the changes in the underlying clusters as a user works with Scatter/Gather. Assume that there are no backups in the process and that

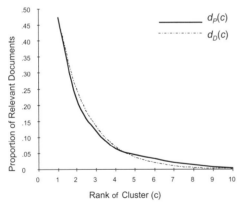

FIGURE 6.13 The underlying distal distribution of relevant documents, d_D, characterizing the clustering algorithm, and the proximal distribution, d_P, characterizing information scent from the Scatter/Gather screen. The distributions characterize the proportion of all the relevant documents (in an average system state) that fall in each cluster. Clusters are ranked in decreasing order of proportion relevant documents.

people iteratively gather and scatter clusters until they finally decide to display the cluster contents. Any task will involve a sequence of Scatter/Gather cluster states, $1, 2, \ldots s, \ldots S$ produced by the iterative gathering and scattering of clusters. The basic observation is that the proportion of relevant documents across all of the clusters in state $s+1$ should equal the proportion of relevant documents (relevant documents divided by total number of documents) in the clusters that were gathered in state previous state s,

$$\frac{\text{relevant}}{\text{total}} \text{ documents in all 10 clusters in } s+1$$

$$= \frac{\text{relevant}}{\text{total}} \text{ documents in all } k \text{ gathered}$$

$$\text{clusters in } s.$$

This is how the proportion of relevant documents changes from one state to the next as one interacts with Scatter/Gather. It is another characterization of the distal structure of relevant information in the environment. It is a characterization of how the distal structure changes over states.

We can ask if the proximal assessment of relevant information tracks the change in distal structure from state to state. Letting $i = 1, 2, \ldots k$ index the k gathered clusters at any state, we can write this relationship as

$$\frac{\sum_{c=1}^{10} g(c, s+1)}{\sum_{c=1}^{10} N(c, s+1)} = \frac{\sum_{i=1}^{k} g(i, s)}{\sum_{i=1}^{k} N(i, s)},$$

(6.36)

where $N(c, s)$ is the total number of documents in a cluster in state s. Each side of equation 6.36 is a proportion where the numerator is the number of relevant documents assessed by activation and the denominator is the total number of documents (this value is presented on the Scatter/Gather screen). Equation 6.36 says that the total proportion of relevant documents in state $s+1$ is equal to the proportion of relevant documents in the k clusters gathered from state s.

Figure 6.14 plots equation 6.36 from data obtained from the user log files. I found all screen states, s, in which a person gathered clusters and then scattered them into a new screen state, $s+1$. I used ACT-IF to compute the information scent provided by each cluster summary in each state using the

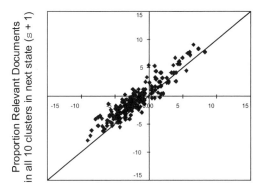

FIGURE 6.14 Expected proportion of relevant documents in a new state $(s+1)$ versus the expected proportion of relevant documents in the gathered clusters from previous state s. The expected values are computed by information scent assessments by model traces of ACT-IF. Logarithmic transformations have been performed on both dimensions.

scaling parameter μ as estimated above. Figure 6.14 plots each one of these s to $(s+1)$ transitions $(N=302)$ as points, where the abscissa plots the model values for the right side of equation 6.36, and the ordinate plots the model values for the left side of equation 6.36 (both scales are logarithmic). If equation 6.36 matched every transition in the log files, then all the points in figure 6.12 would fall on a diagonal line though the origin. There is a good correlation $(R^2=0.76)$,[4] at the predicted slope $=1$, without any new parameters estimated from the data.

Information scent is the proximal means by which a forager judges the value or relevance of distal information sources. ACT-IF computes information scent based on spreading activation from proximal cues on the Scatter/Gather screen. Figures 6.13 and 6.14 show that the ACT-IF model of information scent tracks quite well the underlying (distal) structure of relevant information in the Scatter/Gather clustering system. Information scent matches the underlying distribution of relevant documents across clusters in the average Scatter/Gather state (figure 6.14). Information scent tracks the proportion of relevant information available as one progresses from state to state in Scatter/Gather (figure 6.14). The accuracy of the information scent judgments by ACT-IF corroborate the validity of the scent model

and the effectiveness of the Scatter/Gather interface at communicating the underlying clusters of documents. This is evidence for the ecological validity of the spreading activation model of information scent.

Match to Subjective Ratings

One question is whether or not the spreading activation model of information scent can predict the *stated preferences* of the study participants (in addition to predicting *revealed preferences* in their actions). Half $(N=4)$ of the Scatter/Gather participants provided subjective ratings of the percentage of relevant documents they expected to find in each cluster, that is, ratings of

$$(\text{No. relevant documents/No. total documents})$$
$$\times\ 100\%,$$

in each cluster.

A straightforward hypothesis is that estimates of information scent weighted by the total number of documents in a cluster, $n(c)$ (which is displayed on the Scatter/Gather screen), should map onto these subjective ratings:

$$\frac{g(c,Q)}{n(c)} \qquad (6.37)$$

The ACT-IF simulation provided $g(c,Q)$ and $n(c)$ for productions that matched cluster digests on the Scatter/Gather screen. I extracted these values for each cluster rated by participants. I assumed a simple linear mapping from the simulation estimates onto observed ratings and fit a linear regression to the geometric mean of the participants' ratings:

$$Rating=a+b\left(\frac{g(c,Q)}{n(c)}\right), \qquad (6.38)$$

where a and b are free parameters. Figure 6.15 presents the observed and predicted ratings $(R^2=0.92;\ a=0.32$ and $b=232)$ and illustrates that an information scent analysis, based on an analysis of the proximal cues available in the environment, can provide good predictions of the assessments that users will make of the prospects of finding relevant information.

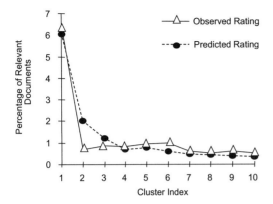

FIGURE 6.15 Observed ratings of the percentage of documents in each cluster that are relevant and the ratings predicted by activation-based assessment of information scent.

Match of ACT-IF to User Traces

The ACT-IF model was matched to the log files from all of the Scatter/Gather participants. On each cycle of each simulation of each participant, the ACT-IF production system ranked productions whose conditions were matched (the conflict set of productions). I investigated how the observed cluster-selecting actions of users compared to the predicted rankings of those actions in the ACT-IF simulation. Ideally, the observed action of the user should have been the highest ranked production in the conflict set of productions on the corresponding simulation cycle.

The histogram in figure 6.16 shows the frequency with which productions at different ranks matched the observed actions. The histogram can be inter-

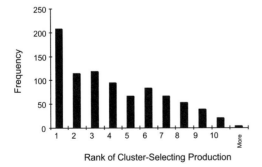

FIGURE 6.16 Frequency that ACT-IF productions match observed cluster-selection actions. The ACT-IF production rankings are computed at each simulation cycle over all productions that match.

preted as reflecting the probability that the actions at a particular rank match the observed actions. Higher ranked productions show better chances of matching user actions. There are a total of $N = 858$ observations in figure 6.17. The χ^2 statistic for comparing the distribution of predicted action selection against random selection was $\chi^2(10) = 400.77$, $p < .0001$.

ACT-IF Test of the Diet Model

A strong test of Information Foraging Theory concerns the selection of Scatter/Gather clusters. Clusters at a state should be selected as long as their profitability, $\pi_A(c, Q)$, is greater than the overall rate of gain for the set of s clusters gathered at that state $R_D(s, Q)$. If we let

$$x = \text{Cluster Profitability} - \text{Expected Rate of Gain}$$
$$= \pi(c, s) - R_D(k, s, t),$$

$$(6.39)$$

then decisions should be to (a) select a cluster when $x > 0$ and (b) not select a cluster when $x < 0$. The threshold, $x = 0$, separating the decision to select versus not select clusters occurs when profitability equals rate of gain.

I used the ACT-IF user-tracing simulation to collect the statistics relevant to these predictions regarding cluster selection. For all clusters seen by Scatter/Gather users, I determined (a) whether or not the clusters were selected by the user and (b) the value $x = $ (cluster profitability − expected rate of gain) as predicted by the ACT-IF simulation. From these observations, I estimated the probability density of selecting a cluster, Select(x), and the probability density of not selecting a cluster, Unselect(x). We should expect that Select(x) > Unselect(x) for positive values of x (cluster profitabilities greater than expected rate of gain) and Unselect(x) > Select(x) for negative values of x (cluster profitabilities less than expected rate of gain).

Figure 6.17 presents these probability density functions. These are based on $N = 2929$ observations. These densities are plotted against $x = \pi_A(c, Q) - R_D(s, Q)$. Figure 6.16 shows that most of the profitabilities for all clusters are close to the value of $R_D(s, Q)$ computed at the time the clusters are presented to users. Despite this, it is clear that there are two distributions whose modes occur on opposite sides of $x = 0$. As predicted, it appears that the threshold $x = 0$ separates the decision to select

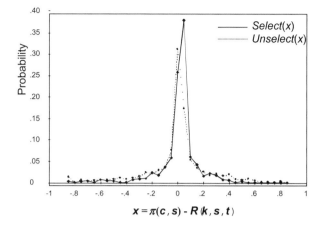

FIGURE 6.17 The probability density distributions for selecting clusters, Select(x), and not selecting clusters, Unselect(x) as a function of the difference between cluster probability and current estimate of rate of gain: $x = \pi(c, s) - R(k, s, t)$.

versus not select clusters. It seems to occur precisely when the cluster profitability equals the expected rate of gain. Figure 6.18 gives a clearer indication of the placement of the threshold. In this figure, I have plotted Select(x)−Unselect(x), and again, $x = \pi(c, Q) - R_D(s, Q)$. The shift in probability of selecting versus not selecting clusters across the threshold, $x = 0$, is significant, $\chi^2(1) = 50.65$, $p < .0001$.

General Discussion

Scatter/Gather is a complex information foraging environment. A cognitive model was developed in ACT-IF by using production rules to implement a task analysis of Scatter/Gather interaction and using spreading activation to compute judgments of information scent. The spreading activation model was determined by the statistics of word frequency and word co-occurrence in the document corpus. The assessment of information scent from spreading activation between external cues and a goal was modeled by a form of interactive cue combinations found in exemplar-based models of categorization. This required a single scaling parameter estimated from an analysis of the concordance of proximal cues on the Scatter/Gather screen to the underlying distribution of relevant documents. Heuristics for selecting productions in ACT-IF were developed from an adaptation (rational) analysis of the Scatter/Gather task, by instantiating the information diet and information patch models. In other, words, the ACT-IF model was determined nearly completely by a priori analysis of the information foraging task and the information environment.

This ACT-IF model yielded good fits to users' ratings of the prevalence of relevant documents in given clusters. The likelihood of cluster selection by users correlated with the ACT-IF rankings of clusters. These correspondences support the basic spreading activation model of information scent.

A general analysis showed that the information diet model could explain the differences in the number of clusters selected for queries of different difficulties. ACT-IF also contains heuristics that implement the information diet model and information patch model. These heuristics determine which clusters will be selected and which will not be selected. The threshold determining the choice of clusters varies with Scatter/

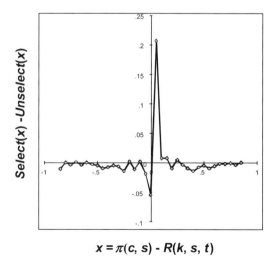

FIGURE 6.18 The difference in density distributions from figure 6.17.

Gather state and task time. Fits of ACT-IF to traces of Scatter/Gather users suggest that this varying threshold has a good correspondence to the varying threshold of Scatter/Gather users.

In chapter 9, I revisit the state-space analysis of Scatter/Gather browser to illustrate the potential for exploring the effects of design trade-offs in different information foraging environments. Although the state-space model makes specific predictions, the effects are consistent generally with the conventional diet model.

Notes

1. This interface was developed by Marti Hearst while at PARC.

2. Dynamic programming rests on the *principle of optimality*: In addition to having a state-space representation similar to the one described in this chapter, dynamic programming assumes that the decision at stage k rests on first solving the subproblems of the optimal decisions at stage $k + 1$ (i.e., working backward from the goal states). In other words, the algorithm depends on (a) being able to evaluate the goal states of a problem, (b) the existence of a recursive relationship between the optimal decision for state k and subsequent states $k + 1$, and (c) independence of the optimal decision for state k from all decisions leading to state k. This solution is often computationally expensive because the general form of the dynamic programming algorithm requires computing and maintaining the evaluations of the optimal decisions for the $k + 1$ states before computing the optimal decision for the kth state.

3. I assumed that participants had gained sufficient knowledge of the Scatter/Gather system for performing these estimates based on warm-up tasks done prior to experimental conditions.

4. Estimated using equation 7 of Kvalseth (1985).

References

Bertsekas, D. P. (1995). *Dynamic programming and optimal control theory*. Belmont, MA: Athena Scientific.

Cutting, D. R., Karger, D. R., & Pedersen, J. O. (1993, July). *Constant interaction-time Scatter/Gather*

browsing of very large document collections. Paper presented at the 16th annual International ACM Conference on Research and Development in Information Retrieval, New York.

Cutting, D. R., Karger, D. R., Pedersen, J. O., & Tukey, J. W. (1992, June). *Scatter/gather: A cluster-based approach to browsing large document collections*. Paper presented at the 15th annual International ACM Conference on Research and Development in Information Retrieval, New York.

Harman, D. (1993, July). *Overview of the first text retrieval conference*. Paper presented at the 16th annual International ACM/SIGIR Conference, Pittsburgh, PA.

Kvalseth, T. O. (1985). Cautionary note about R^2. *American Statistician, 39*, 279–285.

Mangel, M., & Clark, C. W. (1988). *Dynamic modeling in behavioral ecology*. Princeton, NJ: Princeton University Press.

Manning, C. D., & Schuetze, H. (1999). *Foundations of statistical natural language processing*. Cambridge, MA: MIT Press.

Pearl, J. (1988). *Probabilistic reasoning in intelligent systems: Networks of plausible inference*. Los Altos, CA: Morgan Kaufman.

Pirolli, P., & Card, S. K. (1995). *Information foraging in information access environments*. Paper presented at the CHI 1995 Conference on Human Factors in Computing Systems, New York.

Pirolli, P., & Card, S. K. (1999). Information foraging. *Psychological Review, 106*, 643–675.

Pirolli, P., Schank, P., Hearst, M., & Diehl, C. (1996). Scatter/Gather browsing communicates the topic structure of a very large text collection. In *Proceedings of the Conference on Human Factors in Computing Systems, CHI '96* (pp. 213–220). Vancouver, BC: ACM Press.

Russell, S., & Norvig, P. (2002). *Artificial intelligence: A modern approach*. Upper Saddle River, NJ: Prentice Hall.

Schuetze, H. (1992). *Dimensions of meaning*. Paper presented at the Supercomputing '92, Minneapolis, MN.

Stephens, D. W., & Krebs, J. R. (1986). *Foraging theory*. Princeton, NJ: Princeton University Press.

Wickens, T. D. (1982). *Models for behavior: Stochastic processes in psychology*. San Francisco: Freeman.

7

Stochastic Models of Information Foraging by Information Scent

A tradition of cognitive engineering models in human-computer interaction (HCI) focuses on the analysis of individual users, or perhaps a small variety of individual users who might differ in knowledge or strategy. For instance, the GOMS (Goals, Operators, Methods, and Selection rules) analysis of HCI task knowledge (Card, Moran, & Newell, 1983) delivers models of relatively expert, error-free HCI performance. Recently, stochastic models have been developed (Chi, Pirolli, Chen, & Pitkow, 2001; Chi, Pirolli, & Pitkow, 2000; Huberman, Pirolli, Pitkow, & Lukose, 1998; Thimbleby, Cairns, & Jones, 2001) to address empirical regularities that emerge from large aggregates of users navigating through interfaces, ranging from push-button devices to the Web. In this chapter, I present a set of stochastic models of user navigation that make use of the notion of information scent presented in chapter 4 that predicts the navigation of users based on the users' goals and the content cues that are available on the navigation interface. Given a user

task goal and a model of the navigation interface (e.g., a Web site), these models aim to predict the following:

- *User flow*, the pattern of users visiting states throughout the interface
- *Success metrics*, such as the average number of steps to success or the rate at which users will achieve success
- *Stickiness*, the amount of time that users will spend interacting with a navigation interface before leaving it (e.g., the number of page visits at a Web site)

To illustrate the basic approach of these stochastic models, figure 7.1 presents a simple example of the construction of a user flow model. Figure 7.1a is a graph in which the nodes represent interface states and the links among nodes represent transitions from one state to another. This is an example of a *state-space* representation in which the dynamics of system are represented by states and transitions among states.

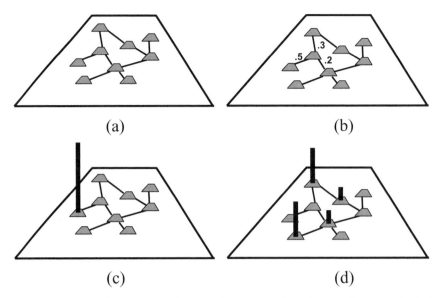

FIGURE 7.1 A user flow example. (a) A graph representation of interaction states (nodes) and transitions among states (links). (b) The assignment of navigation choice probabilities to links emanating from a state. (c) Some number of users (represented by the vertical bar) is assumed to start in one or more states. (d) After some number of moves, the users will have distributed themselves into some set of states (vertical bars).

For concreteness, the nodes in figure 7.1a could represent Web pages at a site and the links in figure 7.1a could represent HTML links among those pages, so the graph in figure 7.1a could represent a Web site.

In figure 7.1b, each of the links emanating from a node is labeled with the probability that users will choose to travel from the current node (state) to the linked node (state). In the case of the Web, this would represent the probability that users will choose to follow a link to an associated page from the page they are currently visiting. Determining these probabilities is key to the correctness of the user flow model. In some discussions (Thimbleby et al., 2001), the designer may make best-case and worst-case assumptions for individual tasks. This chapter explores the use of information scent to compute these *navigation choice probabilities*.

Once the probabilities are assigned, one may assume that a number of users enter the navigation interface at one or more start states. In figure 7.1c, the vertical bar represents some number of users starting at a given state. Users move from current states to linked states according to the navigation choice probabilities. After some number of moves, the users will have flowed through the links and distributed themselves over the states in some pattern such as figure 7.1d (where the number of users at a particular state is again represented by vertical bars). This model of user flow forms the basis of the Bloodhound automated usability testing system discussed in chapter 10.

Markov Models of Usability

Chi et al. (2001, 2000) present a summary of the formal graph-theoretic model and associated algorithm for predicting user flow at a Web site given a user task. This approach made use of information scent. Independent of that work, Thimbleby et al. (2001) proposed a very similar usability analysis approach based on Markov models. That approach did not use the notion of information scent. Because of its simplicity, it is worth reviewing the Markov model approach before presenting information scent and other elaborations that define the stochastic models presented here.

Representing State-to-State Transitions

Figure 7.2 is a graphical representation of the state space for a microwave analyzed by Thimbleby et al.

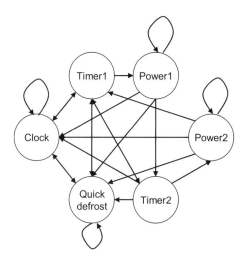

$$\mathbf{L} = \begin{bmatrix} 1 & 1 & 1 & 1 & 1 & 1 \\ 1 & 1 & 1 & 1 & 1 & 1 \\ 1 & 1 & 0 & 1 & 0 & 1 \\ 0 & 0 & 1 & 0 & 1 & 0 \\ 0 & 0 & 1 & 0 & 1 & 0 \\ 0 & 0 & 0 & 1 & 0 & 1 \end{bmatrix} \quad (7.1)$$

FIGURE 7.2 A directed graph representing the state space (states and transitions) for the microwave discussed in Thimbleby et al. (2001).

(2001). Each node represents a potential state of the microwave interface, and device buttons will move the system from one state to another as indicated by the directed arrows. Table 7.1 provides an alternative representation of the graph in figure 7.2. A "1" in a table 7.1 cell indicates that there is a device button that moves the system from state A to state B, and a "0" indicates the lack of a transition. For instance, there is a transition from the Clock state to the Quick Defrost state, but no transition from the Clock state to the Timer2 state.

An even more succinct representation of the information in table 7.1 involves the use of matrix notation. The matrix

represents state-to-state transitions. We assume that the states are indexed $i = j = 1, 2, \ldots 6$:

1 = Clock

2 = Quick Defrost

3 = Timer1

4 = Timer2

5 = Power1

6 = Power2.

$L_{i,j}$ is the element of matrix $\mathbf{L}$ in row i and column j. An entry $L_{i,j} = 1$ represents a transition from state j to state i, and $L_{i,j} = 0$ represents the lack of a transition. The element $L_{4,3} = 1$ indicates that there is a transition from the Timer1 state to the Timer2 state.

As discussed in Thimbleby et al. (2001), Markov models are a widespread mathematical technique for representing stochastic processes. It is based on a representation of the probability of a system transitioning from a current state to another state. The matrix L represents the *potential* state transitions for a microwave. We may instead represent the *probabilities* of a user transitioning from one state to another, where these probabilities might perhaps come from some model predictions, empirical data, or subjective estimates made by an expert. Thimbleby et al. make some assumptions about the probability that a user will press a button in any given microwave state, which results in the *transition probability matrix*,

TABLE 7.1 A state adjacency table representing the microwave state-space graph in figure 7.1.

| To State B | From State A | | | | | |
	Clock	Quick Defrost	Timer1	Timer2	Power1	Power2
Clock	1	1	1	1	1	1
Quick Defrost	1	1	1	1	1	1
Timer1	1	1	0	1	0	1
Timer2	0	0	1	0	1	0
Power1	0	0	1	0	1	0
Power2	0	0	0	1	0	1

1, a device button transitions the system from state A to state B; 0, no transition.

$$\mathbf{P} = \begin{bmatrix} 3/5 & 2/5 & 2/5 & 2/5 & 2/5 & 2/5 \\ 1/5 & 2/5 & 1/5 & 1/5 & 1/5 & 1/5 \\ 1/5 & 1/5 & 0 & 1/5 & 0 & 1/5 \\ 0 & 0 & 1/5 & 0 & 1/5 & 0 \\ 0 & 0 & 1/5 & 0 & 1/5 & 0 \\ 0 & 0 & 0 & 1/5 & 0 & 1/5 \end{bmatrix},$$

where $P_{i,j}$ is the probability that the microwave will transition from state j to state i. For instance, the probability that a user will transition from the Timer1 state to the Clock state is $P_{1,3} = 2/5$. In other words, each element represents a conditional probability,

$P_{i,j} = \text{Pr}(\text{transition to state } i \mid \text{currently at state } j),$

and the sum of all the transition probabilities from a state (e.g., the sum down a column in $\mathbf{P}$) is one:

$$\sum_i P_{i,j} = 1$$

The transition probabilities in $\mathbf{P}$ represent the *quality of heuristic knowledge for navigation*. Often, users navigating through an interface make choices with some degree of uncertainty. That is, their choices are governed by *heuristic knowledge* rather than *perfect knowledge*. If navigation choices were governed by perfect knowledge, then each row in $\mathbf{P}$ would contain a single 1, indicating that a user in any given state always would choose to transit to the same next state (the correct one). The transition probabilities in a Markov model of user interaction capture the uncertainty of users' heuristic knowledge for navigation.

Using a Markov Model to Make Predictions About User-Device Interaction

A basic way of using Markov models is to assume that the system starts in some state, and after some number of state transitions, one predicts the probability that the system will be in certain states. For instance, we might assume that a user interacting with the microwave in figure 7.2 starts in the Clock state (state 1), and we want to determine the probability that a user reaches the Timer2 state (state 4) after two steps. From matrix $\mathbf{P}$, we can see that after one step, the user will transition to state 1 (Clock) with probability 3/5, to state 2 (Quick Defrost) with probability 1/5, and state 3 (Timer1) with probability 1/5. This can also be calculated using matrix algebra (which can be performed with most spreadsheet or mathematical applications). We can represent the initial state as a *state vector*,

$$\mathbf{C} = \begin{bmatrix} 1 \\ 0 \\ 0 \\ 0 \\ 0 \\ 0 \end{bmatrix},$$

where row i represents the probability that the user is in state i. The Markov model can be initialized using vector $\mathbf{C}$, which represents the assumption that the user is in state 1 with probability $= 1$. If we perform matrix multiplication, we get a vector representing the probabilities that the user is in any of the six states:

$$\mathbf{C}_1 = \mathbf{PC} = \begin{bmatrix} 3/5 \\ 1/5 \\ 1/5 \\ 0 \\ 0 \\ 0 \end{bmatrix}$$

If we multiply the vector representing the states reached after one step by the probability transition matrix $\mathbf{P}$ again, we get

$$\mathbf{C}_2 = \mathbf{PC}_1 = \begin{bmatrix} 0.52 \\ 0.24 \\ 0.16 \\ 0.04 \\ 0.04 \\ 0 \end{bmatrix},$$

which indicates the user will be in state 4 (Timer2) with probability 0.04 after two steps after starting in state 1 (Clock). It is also the case that

$$\mathbf{C}_2 = \mathbf{P} \, \mathbf{P} \, \mathbf{C}$$
$$= \mathbf{P}^2 \, \mathbf{C},$$

where $\mathbf{P}^n$ indicates taking the nth power of a matrix (a square matrix multiplied by itself n times). More generally,

$$\mathbf{X} = \mathbf{P}^n \mathbf{C} \qquad (7.2)$$

will result in a state vector $\mathbf{X}$ after n transition steps, where X_i (the ith row of $\mathbf{X}$) is the probability that the system will be in state i, given a starting state vector $\mathbf{C}$, and C_j (the jth row of $\mathbf{C}$) represents the probability that the system starts in state j and a transition probability matrix $\mathbf{P}$.

Of greater interest, however, will be predictions about the rate (number of steps) at which users reach some target information state. For instance, we might be interested in the average number of steps that it takes a user to go from a Web site home page to some specific target Web content at that site. Before I present methods for doing this, it is necessary to first present a theoretically plausible model for the transition probabilities $\mathbf{P}$.

Information Scent

To develop a Markov model of user navigation requires the specification of the navigation choice probabilities (e.g., the transition probabilities that form the matrix **P**). Thimbleby et al. (2001) proposed that one might do this by estimation from empirical data or by exploring mixtures of perfect knowledge with no knowledge (i.e., a user making random choices). The information scent calculation presented in chapter 4 provides a computational approach to make predictions about navigation choice probabilities for tasks and interfaces that involve text content. Chi et al. (2001) discuss additional methods for extending the approach to graphical content.

The case of the Web will use the information scent formulation discussed in chapter 4. Users are assumed to have some goal G that is represented as a set of chunks, $i \in G$. Link navigation choices made by a user are made from a set C of alternative links. Each alternative link J is associated with a structure of displayed proximal cues, $j \in J$, such as text or graphics. Each proximal cue j emits a source activation W_j. These source activations spread through associations to the chunks i that are part of the information goal G. The activation received by each goal feature i is A_i, and the summed activation over all goal features is

$$V_{J|G} = \sum_{i \in G} A_i. \qquad (7.3)$$

The probability of choosing link J conditional on the goal G and the other links available is

$$\Pr(J \mid G, C) = \frac{e^{\mu V_{J|Q}}}{\sum\limits_{K \in C} e^{\mu V_{K|Q}}}, \qquad (7.4)$$

where μ is a scale parameter. The activation of a chunk i is

$$A_i = B_i + \sum_j W_j S_{ij}, \qquad (7.5)$$

where B_i is the base-level activation of i, S_{ij} is the association strength between an associated chunk j and chunk i, and W_j is the source activation from chunk j. As discussed in chapter 4, these values can be computed using pointwise mutual information

(PMI) values obtained from a large corpus such as the Web.

Prediction of User Behavior Based on Markov Models

A Hypothetical Web Site

Figure 7.3 presents a model of interaction with a hypothetical Web site for a specific task. The example in figure 7.3 assumes a simple hypothetical Web site of seven pages that includes medical information for humans and for pets. The user is assumed to have the task of finding "medical treatments for cancer." Page-6 is the hypothetical target page for this task. Each Web page is represented by a node in figure 7.3. Each directed arc is labeled with the text that is used as link labels on the Web pages. For instance, Home-page has two links to adjacent pages that have the link text "human treatment" and "dog treatment."

There are also two numbers labeling each directed arc in figure 7.3. The labels "A = a" represent calculated information scent scores of the text labels in the context of the given task ("medical treatments for cancer"). These were calculated using the spreading activation equation 7.5 with spreading activation networks computed in Pirolli and Card (1999). The labels "p = n" represent the navigation choice probabilities (transition probabilities) computed from the scent scores (the probability that a user having the task of finding "medical treatments for cancer" will choose that Web link and move to the linked page). These were calculated using equation 7.4 with $\mu = 1/100$. For instance, a user with the given task who is at Home-page is predicted to choose the link labeled "human treatment" with probability .62 and move to Page-1.

We can represent the graph in figure 7.3 with a probability transition matrix:

$$\mathbf{P} = \begin{pmatrix} 0 & .33 & .36 & 0 & 1.0 & 1.0 & 1.0 \\ .62 & 0 & 0 & 0 & 0 & 0 & 0 \\ .38 & 0 & 0 & 0 & 0 & 0 & 0 \\ 0 & .38 & 0 & 1.0 & 0 & 0 & 0 \\ 0 & .29 & 0 & 0 & 0 & 0 & 0 \\ 0 & 0 & .32 & 0 & 0 & 0 & 0 \\ 0 & 0 & .32 & 0 & 0 & 0 & 0 \end{pmatrix}, \qquad (7.6)$$

where the first row (or column) corresponds to Home-page, the second row (or column) corresponds to

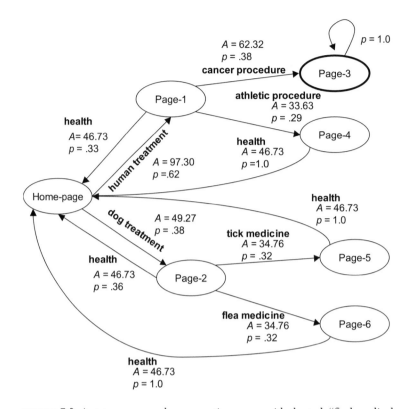

FIGURE 7.3 A state-space graph representing a user with the task "find medical treatments for cancer" interacting with a Web site. Text labels on the arcs represent link text on the Web pages. Labels "$A = a$" on the arcs represent the information scent scores based on link text. Labels "$P = n$" indicate the probability of a user choosing a link as predicted by information scent.

Page-1, the third row (column) to Page-2, and so on. An entry in column i row j means that there is a transition from state i to state j. Note that Page-3 has a $p = 1.0$ transition back to itself as a way of representing the idea that Page-3 is the goal (i.e., users will stay in that goal state rather than move away to a less desirable state). Page-3 is known as an *absorbing state*. Once a system enters an absorbing state, it remains in that state. In contrast, a *transient state* is one for which there is some probability of exiting to another state.

Computing User Flow

Thimbleby et al. (2001) presented a method based on first-passage analysis of Markov models for predicting the expected number of steps to reach a target state. Unfortunately, that method does not apply to Markov models that have absorbing states, such as figure 7.3.

Recall that absorbing states are ones that the system does not leave once it has entered. In the context of simulating Web use, it is often useful to represent a visit to the target content as an absorbing state and leaving a Web site as another absorbing state (this is not represented in figure 7.3).

Predicting the Rate of Arrival at a Target Page

A simple method, conceptually, involves iteratively computing the state vector X (see equation 7.2) representing the probability that a user will be at any state after n steps. That is, we could compute X after one step, two steps, three steps, and so on, and determine the probability that the user reaches the target at each step. To see this more concretely, let us redefine X to be a matrix, where each column t of X represents a vector of state probabilities such that each row i of that column vector represents the probability of being in state i after step t. Let $\mathbf{X}^{\langle t \rangle}$ indicate column t of $\mathbf{X}$. If a hypothetical user starts at the home page (state 0), then

$$\mathbf{X}^{\langle 0 \rangle} = \begin{bmatrix} 1 \\ 0 \\ 0 \\ 0 \\ 0 \\ 0 \\ 0 \end{bmatrix}.$$

We can compute the sequence of system states as

$$\mathbf{X}^{\langle t \rangle} = \mathbf{P}\mathbf{X}^{\langle t-1 \rangle}, \qquad \text{for } t = 1 \ldots n. \qquad (7.7)$$

In our example, for $n = 5$ steps, we would get the matrix

$$\mathbf{X} = \begin{bmatrix} 1 & 0 & .34 & .42 & .12 & .29 \\ 0 & .62 & 0 & .21 & .26 & .07 \\ 0 & .38 & 0 & .13 & .16 & .04 \\ 0 & 0 & .24 & .24 & .32 & .42 \\ 0 & 0 & .18 & 0 & .06 & .08 \\ 0 & 0 & .12 & 0 & .04 & .05 \\ 0 & 0 & .12 & 0 & .04 & .05 \end{bmatrix}.$$

For a particular state, we may plot the probability of being in that state as a function of n. For instance, the first row of $\mathbf{X}$ above contains the probability of visiting Home-page after each step, and the fourth row of $\mathbf{X}$ contains the probability of visiting the target (Page-3)

after each step. Figure 7.4 presents the probability of having found the target (Page-3) and the probability of a return to Home-page over 30 steps.

A second method of calculating $\mathbf{X}$ is based on equation 7.2:

$$\mathbf{X}^{\langle t \rangle} = \mathbf{P}^t \mathbf{X}^{\langle 0 \rangle} \qquad \text{for } t = 1 \ldots n. \qquad (7.8)$$

This will yield the same result as equation 7.7. A third method, based on the analysis of absorbing Markov chains, is presented in the appendix.

Predicting the Number of State Visits

It may often be useful to predict the expected number of visits to states prior to hitting a target. For instance, Web site managers might be interested in the pattern of visit rates to pages other than a target page. Two methods are presented for doing this. A conceptually simple way to do this is to make use of the state × step matrix $\mathbf{X}$ computed by equation 7.7 or 7.8. Note that, for all transient states, summing across a row gives the number of visits to the corresponding state. So, for $n = 30$ steps, the sums would be

Home-page $= 4.226$

Page-1 $= 2.619$

Page-2 $= 1.605$

Page-4 $= 0.759$

Page-5 $= 0.513$

Page-6 $= 0.513$

These reach asymptotic values with increasing n. A precise method derived from the analysis of absorbing Markov chains is presented in the appendix.

Stickiness: Predicting When Users Stop

Web site providers are often interested in both maximizing the rate of user success and maximizing the stickiness of their Web site—that is, the amount of time that users spend at their Web site. One problem with the hypothetical example above is that it assumes that users keep navigating until they find the target content. Users also often give up on their tasks and stop navigating. One simple assumption might be that some proportion, $0 < c < 1$, of users leave on every step or, equivalently, that some proportion, $d = 1 - c$, of users continue to navigate. The method

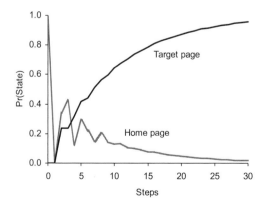

FIGURE 7.4 Probability of visiting the target page versus returning to the home page as a function of steps.

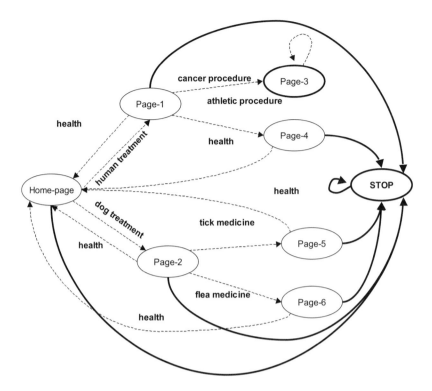

FIGURE 7.5 The state-space graph of figure 7.3 redrawn to include an explicit absorbing stop state that can be reached from any other state.

of computing user flow in equation 7.7 can be modified slightly to "leak" some proportion of users on every step:

$$\mathbf{X}^{\langle t \rangle} = d\, \mathbf{P}\, \mathbf{X}^{\langle t-1 \rangle}, \quad \text{for } t = 1 \dots n \quad (7.9)$$

The effect of inserting d into the equation is that there is an exponentially decreasing number of users that continue to flow as a function of number of steps.

However, as discussed in chapter 4, analyses of Web site usage logs (Huberman et al., 1998) show that the probability that a user will surf through N nonunique pages does not follow a simple exponential model. The Law of Surfing discussed in chapter 4 predicts that the observed distribution of surfing path lengths at a Web site should be an inverse Gaussian distribution (which looks very similar to a lognormal distribution). Recall that the Law of Surfing model assumes that at each step the user evaluates the utility of proceeding to the next page, U_{p+1}, versus a threshold utility of stopping, U_α. If

$$U_\alpha > U_{p+1}$$

(for all next pages), then the user stops.

The Law of Surfing suggests that the stochastic models of navigating by information scent developed above should include a "stop" state in addition to one or more target states, with every other nontarget state connected to the stop state, as in figure 7.5. A fixed information scent score, U_α, is assigned to the links connecting the nontarget states to the stop state. All previously determined scent scores, U_i, for other links among states are reset to zero if $U_i \leq U_\alpha$. This has the effect of capturing the decision to choose to stop rather than follow links that are below the threshold utility for stopping. The resulting modified matrix of scent scores enters into the calculation of the probability of transition matrix $\mathbf{P}$ based on the navigation choice equations described above. In effect, there will now be two kinds of absorbing states: the target state(s) and the stop state.

Figure 7.6 shows the prediction of surfing path lengths for a Web site for children's items.[1] A crawl of

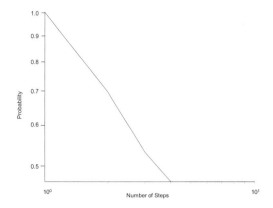

FIGURE 7.6 The probability distribution of surfing depths for a Web site selling children's items as predicted by a stochastic model for the task "find teddy bears."

the Web site was performed, and information scent computations were performed using the task "find teddy bears." A stop state was included in the transition matrix, and a fixed threshold scent score was associated with transitions to the stop state. Figure 7.6 shows the predicted rate at which users will either find the target state or give up. The distribution in figure 7.6 is characteristically linear in log–log coordinates, which fits with the theoretical and empirical analysis of the Law of Surfing.

General Discussion

A single transition probability network can be constructed for an information foraging task that includes the absorbing target states and the absorbing stop state. By simulating the flow of users through a state space such as shown in figure 7.5, one can get the rate of arrival at any of the target states (or any other page) as in figure 7.4, the overall visitation (e.g., page hit) rates, and how many steps users will navigate (stickiness). Web site providers are typically interested in simultaneously maximizing each of these characteristics of their sites. Stochastic models such as the ones presented here provide the basis for making such predictions and for exploring the space of possible designs in search of the best trade-offs of user success, page visits, and Web site stickiness. The Bloodhound system discussed in chapter 9 uses a stochastic model that is very similar to the one presented here.

The purpose of this chapter is not to provide a definitive, fully validated theory, but rather to draw together a coherent well-founded theory that provides opportunities for the development of successful usability techniques and further empirical and theoretical work. There are many questions regarding the underlying assumptions of the models. There are a number of parameters in the models that require research. For instance, the scaling parameters on the choice probabilities in equation 7.4 and the threshold values for stopping need more empirical study over tasks. Furthermore, there is a great deal of research on statistical measurement techniques for studying Random Utility Models that need to be investigated in the context of these stochastic information scent models.

The state spaces used here to illustrate the stochastic modeling approach all involved a very simple strategy that can best be described as hill climbing with no memory. That is, users were assumed to follow the paths of highest utility with no memory of where they have been or any strategic plans or subgoals. This kind of memoryless model may be a good first approximation, as suggested by information-theoretic analyses of user path data (Pirolli & Pitkow, 1999). Expert users do, however, exhibit domain-specific search and navigation plans (Bhavnani, 2002). One way to incorporate alternate foraging strategies into the stochastic models presented here would be to generate and combine multiple state-space models corresponding to multiple strategies. This is similar to techniques used in student models in intelligent tutoring systems (Corbett, Anderson, & O'Brien, 1995). Pirolli and Wilson (1998) presented a measurement approach designed to deal with multiple strategies.

A recent book by Gigerenzer (2000) discusses the interdisciplinary trajectory of stochastic models from astronomy to psychology to statistical mechanics. Adolphe Quetelet (1796–1874) was a Belgian mathematician and astronomer at a time when the normal distribution was used to handle observational errors around the true position of a star. Quetelet had the insight that such reasoning could be applied to human affairs, with an ideal average person (*l'homme moyen*) and actual persons normally distributed about the average. Ludwig Boltzman and James Clerk Maxwell transformed Quetelet's theory of collectives of people into a theory of collectives of gas particles—statistical mechanics. In this chapter, the journey continues by taking models largely developed for statistical mechanics and applying them to the realm of collectives of users foraging for information.

APPENDIX: ALTERNATE METHODS BASED ON THE ANALYSIS OF ABSORBING MARKOV CHAINS

Absorption Rates

The analysis of absorbing chains in Markov models provides another method for computing absorption rates and visit rates. First, one rearranges the transition matrix P into a standard form

$$P = \left(\begin{array}{c|c} A & R \\ \hline 0 & Q \end{array} \right), \qquad (7.A.1)$$

where A, R, and Q are submatrices of P. Matrix A contains all the absorbing state-to-state transitions, R contains transitions from transient states to absorbing states, and Q contains all transient-to-transient state transitions (0 is the submatrix containing no transitions from the absorbing states to other states). Using the matrix P defined in equation 7.11, if we let Page-3 be represented by the first row and column of P and let the Home-page be represented by the fourth row and column (basically swapping the two states), we would get the rearranged version of P:

$$P = \begin{array}{c} \\ \\ \\ \\ \\ \\ \\ \\ \end{array} \begin{array}{cc} A & R \\ \left(\begin{array}{c|ccccccc} 1 & 0.38 & 0 & 0 & 0 & 0 & 0 \\ \hline 0 & 0 & 0 & 0.62 & 0 & 0 & 0 \\ 0 & 0 & 0 & 0.38 & 0 & 0 & 0 \\ 0 & 0.33 & 0.36 & 0 & 1 & 1 & 1 \\ 0 & 0.29 & 0 & 0 & 0 & 0 & 0 \\ 0 & 0 & 0.32 & 0 & 0 & 0 & 0 \\ 0 & 0 & 0.32 & 0 & 0 & 0 & 0 \end{array} \right) \\ \begin{array}{cc} 0 & \quad\quad\quad Q \end{array} \end{array} \quad (7.A.2)$$

The probability of entering an absorbing state is

$$f(t) = R \, Q^{(t-1)}, \qquad (7.A.3)$$

so another method of calculating the rate at which users would reach a target absorbing state would be

$$Y^{(t)} = f(t)' \quad \text{for } t = 0 \ldots n, \qquad (7.A.4)$$

where Y has rows j corresponding to the transient states and each column t contains the probability of

transitioning to the absorbing state on step t after having started in state i. So, the cumulative probability of hitting the absorbing state from state i is

$$p(i, t) = \sum_{u=0}^{t} Y_{i,u}. \qquad (7.A.5)$$

State Visits

Another way of calculating number of visits is based on the analysis of absorbing chains and the representation in equation 7.A.2. The long-term number of transitions spent in transient states (i.e., the delay spent in transient states prior to absorption) is given by the *fundamental matrix*:

$$M = (I - Q)^{-1}, \qquad (7.A.6)$$

where I is the appropriate identity matrix, and the exponent -1 indicates matrix inversion. For our example, this is

$$(I - Q)^{-1}$$
$$= \begin{pmatrix} 2.632 & 2.632 & 2.632 & 2.632 & 2.632 & 2.632 \\ 1 & 2.613 & 1.613 & 1.613 & 1.613 & 1.613 \\ 2.632 & 4.244 & 4.244 & 4.244 & 4.244 & 4.244 \\ 0.763 & 0.763 & 0.763 & 1.763 & 0.763 & 0.763 \\ 0.32 & 0.836 & 0.516 & 0.516 & 1.516 & 0.516 \\ 0.32 & 0.836 & 0.516 & 0.516 & 0.516 & 1.516 \end{pmatrix}.$$

For each column i, each row j contains the number expected number of steps that the state j will be visited if the system starts in state i. So, for our hypothetical example, if a user started on the Home-page, we could read down column 3 and read off the number of visits:

Page-1 = 2.632

Page-2 = 1.613

Home-page = 4.244

Page-4 = 0.763

Page-5 = 0.516

Page-6 = 0.516

The fundamental matrix M provides a way of predicting page hits on the Web. Note that these values are only marginally larger that the ones computed by summation over rows of $\mathbf{X}$ in equations 7.12 and 7.13.

Note

1. Thanks to Ed Chi for providing these data.

References

Bhavnani, S. K. (2002). Domain-specific search strategies for the effective retrieval of healthcare and shopping information. *CHI 2002 Conference on Human Factors and Computing Systems, Extended Abstracts* (pp. 610–611). Minneapolis, MN: Association for Computing Machinery Press.

Card, S. K., Moran, T. P., & Newell, A. (1983). *The psychology of human-computer interaction*. Hillsdale, NJ: Lawrence Erlbaum Associates.

Chi, E. H., Pirolli, P., Chen, K., & Pitkow, J. E. (2001). Using information scent to model user needs and actions on the Web. *CHI 2001, Human Factors in Computing Systems, CHI Letters, 3*(1), 490–497.

Chi, E. H., Pirolli, P., & Pitkow, J. (2000). The scent of a site: A system for analyzing and predicting information scent, usage, and usability of a Web site. *CHI 2000, ACM Conference on Human Factors in Computing Systems, CHI Letters, 2*(1), 161–168.

Corbett, A. T., Anderson, J. R., & O'Brien, A. T. (1995). Student modelling in the ACT Programming Tutor. In P. D. Nichols, S. F. Chipman, & R. L. Brennan (Eds.), *Cognitively diagnostic assessment* (pp. 19–41). Hillsdale, NJ: Lawrence Erlbaum Associates.

Gigerenzer, G. (2000). *Adaptive thinking: Rationality in the real world*. Oxford: Oxford University Press.

Huberman, B. A., Pirolli, P., Pitkow, J., & Lukose, R. J. (1998). Strong regularities in World Wide Web surfing. *Science, 280*, 95–97.

Pirolli, P., & Card, S. K. (1999). Information foraging. *Psychological Review, 106*, 643–675.

Pirolli, P., & Pitkow, J. E. (1999). Distributions of surfers' paths through the World Wide Web: Empirical characterization. *World Wide Web, 2*, 29–45.

Pirolli, P., & Wilson, M. (1998). A theory of the measurement of knowledge content, access, and learning. *Psychological Review, 105*, 58–82.

Thimbleby, H., Cairns, P., & Jones, M. (2001). Usability analysis with Markov models. *ACM Transactions on Computer-Human Interaction, 8*, 99–132.

8

Social Information Foraging

At the end of World War II, the U.S. Director of Scientific Research and Development, Vannevar Bush, published an article titled "As We May Think" in the popular magazine *Atlantic Monthly* (Bush, 1945).[1] The article was both reflective and visionary: The war had been won with the help of the coordinated efforts of scientists, and those resources were available to be applied to the development of new tools to extend the powers of the human mind through more facile command of inherited accumulation of recorded knowledge. "As We May Think" presented seminal ideas about personal computing and hypermedia that inspired computer scientists such as Tim Berners-Lee, Douglas Englebart, Alan Kay, and Ted Nelson to realize aspects of Bush's vision. The problem that inspired Bush was scholarly overspecialization:

> There is a growing mountain of research. But there is increased evidence that we are being bogged down today as specialization extends. The

investigator is staggered by the findings and conclusions of thousands of other workers — conclusions which he cannot find time to grasp, much less to remember, as they appear. Yet specialization becomes increasingly necessary for progress, and the effort to bridge between disciplines is correspondingly superficial. (Bush, 1945, p. 101)

Bush envisioned a device he called the Memex that would allow scholars to forage through personal stores of multimedia documents and to save *traces* of paths through content that could then be shared with other scholars as a way of communicating new findings. The Memex was envisioned as a tool that would increase the capacity of individuals to attend to greater spans of emerging knowledge and would increase the cooperative information sharing that Bush viewed as necessary to improvements in scientific discovery, which he expected to result in increased benefits to society. Bush's vision was not only to improve the foraging ability of the individual user but also to improve communication and collaboration.

So far, this book has focused on information foraging by the solitary user. The discovery of new knowledge, innovations, or inventions, however, is almost universally the result of collective action. This chapter presents a somewhat idiosyncratic review of models and findings in various fields that may provide the basis for the development of theories of foraging by collectives, whether constituted by formal organizational structures or informal networks. I touch upon research from optimal foraging theory, library science, computational ecology, management science, and sociometrics. Across these disciplines, one finds general results concerning the costs and benefits of cooperative foraging, the effects of group diversity, and patterns of social structuring that are correlated with innovative discovery. As in preceding chapters, I present mathematical models that capture the basic elements of these results.

The Problem of Undiscovered Public Knowledge

Specialization is a natural consequence of too much public knowledge for the individual mind to comprehend. Social networks involved in knowledge discovery, such as scientific communities, typically self-organize into a cognitive division of labor, with divisions based on the deliberate exclusion of possibly relevant information (Wilson, 1995). Some knowledge discovery organizations, such as the U.S. intelligence agencies, are formally (and technologically) organized into specialty areas. The worry is that knowledge specialization leads to situations in which all the information required to make an important discovery or decision is in the available record somewhere but is distributed across specialization boundaries with no single set of eyes in a position to see it all and make sense of it.

It is unlikely that we can estimate the number of discoveries that are latent in the published scientific literature because of overspecialization. This unrealized potential, however, has received considerable attention in the information retrieval and library sciences, where it is known as the *undiscovered public knowledge problem* (Swanson, 1986a, 1986b). We may characterize public knowledge (Swanson, 1986b) by making use of the knowledge-level perspective

(Newell, 1982). Public knowledge is that which is directly recorded in publications, plus the implications of that knowledge (i.e., the implicative closure of recorded knowledge). The problem is that some of the implied knowledge may be undiscovered. These implications may include hidden refutations, hidden cumulative strength of individually weak studies, or other hidden links in the logic of discovery.

A concrete example of a hidden hypothesis identified by Swanson (1986a) was the possibility that fish oil might ameliorate the effects of Raynaud's syndrome, which is a blood circulation disorder associated with high blood viscosity, vasoconstriction, and high platelet aggregability. Fish oil has been shown to reduce those factors. Swanson (1986a) presented evidence suggesting that this hypothesis had been implicit in the domain of public knowledge for about 5 ± 3 years but had been unrecognized because the literature on fish oil was independent of the literature on Raynaud's syndrome.

Swanson's (1986a) analysis relied on a simple form of co-citation analysis (Egghe & Rousseau, 1990; Small, 1973). Co-citation analysis involves identifying the frequency that items (e.g., documents, authors) are cited together in the published literature. The assumption is that when a pair of items (e.g., papers or authors) has been cited together in some publication, this reveals an implicit judgment of relatedness or similarity. Swanson identified a cluster of 25 fish oil papers and a cluster of 33 Raynaud's syndrome papers (from a total of 3,000 papers published on the two topics) and argued that these two clusters clearly implied the hypothesis that two topics were related. No documents in either cluster referred to documents in the other cluster. Of the 489 articles that cited papers in these two clusters, there were 362 co-cited paper pairs in the Raynaud's cluster, 173 co-cited paper pairs in the fish oil cluster, and only 7 co-citations that spanned the two clusters. These seven cluster-spanning co-citations were produced by just four broad review papers. Since Swanson's seminal article, there has emerged a substantial literature on techniques aimed at solving the problem of undiscovered public knowledge (e.g., Gordon & Dumais, 1998; Smalheiser & Swanson, 1998; Stegmann & Grohmann, 2003), all aimed at providing the individual with better information retrieval tools. Here, I focus on the issue of how and why information foragers, in their natural environments, use cooperative social means to solve this problem.

Search Parallelization and Failure Risk Reduction Through Cooperation

An overload of public information leads to specialization by people in fields of knowledge discovery. Overspecialization may lead to increases in undiscovered public knowledge—a failure for any one mind to grasp and connect all the dots. Information sharing is usually recognized as a strategy for extending the grasp of the solitary mind across specializations, to reduce the risk of failing to make discoveries implicit in the existing literature.[2] To the extent that individual members of a core specialty can devote some effort to exploring related peripheral specialties, and sharing possible leads with others, one might expect the group to perform more effectively.

Pirolli and Card (1997, 1999) describe a business intelligence agency whose analysts were tasked to write monthly newsletters about core areas such as computer science or materials science. The main purpose of those newsletters was to identify new important science and technology trends. The organization received about 600 magazines, trade publications, and journals each month, and each analyst was responsible for scanning about 50 of these publications (an estimated 500 articles per month). In addition to culling material for their own newsletters, analysts would also notice articles pertinent to the specialties of other analysts and would have such articles copied and routed to the appropriate specialist. An analyst would typically receive about 6–12 relevant articles per month from other analysts, at very little cost. The general belief of the analysts was that such cooperation enhanced the individuals' search capabilities and reduced the risk of missing something relevant to a specialty area that had emerged in a nonspecialty publication. Below, I discuss a more thorough study by Sandstrom (2001) concerning information foraging by an informal network of scientists that exhibits a similar, though more intricate, pattern of information sharing.

Cooperation and the Social Capital of Diversity and Brokerage

Cooperation may yield more benefits than simply making searches more parallel and making them less prone to failure. Membership in a group provides actual or potential resources that can be utilized or mobilized to achieve individual goals. This is known as *social capital* (Bourdieu, 1986; Putnam, 2000), and

much research has focused on determining what aspects of social structure provide such capital. Exposure to a greater diversity of knowledge, hence more novel ideas as a function of the cost of foraging, is another potential benefit of cooperation. From Swanson's co-citation analysis, we may see where innovative discoveries hide. Swanson's analysis reflects a cluster of authors with strong intragroup communication about Raynaud's syndrome and another cluster of authors with strong intragroup communication about fish oil. The important undiscovered knowledge, however, required a bridge between these two social network clusters. Below, I summarize research of the effects of group diversity on cooperative information foraging, as well as the theory that people who provide brokerage of ideas across social clusters are often in positions to make valuable novel discoveries. Since scientists (and many others who do knowledge discovery) are rewarded according to the novelty and value of their discoveries, we might expect individual group members to try to arrange themselves to be in positions that broker knowledge from peripheral fields to the group's core specialty field. One question that arises is why groups do not grow infinitely large (if cooperation and group size produce positive rewards). Another is why network structure is clustered (if every individual seeks to maximize brokerage links). Below I discuss forces that may be involved in producing groups of stable sizes. Issues of cooperative social foraging have been explored in some detail recently by Giraldeau and Caraco (2000). I also discuss a model of information flow that suggests that information flows to groups of limited size.

Information Foraging by Networks of Scholars

Sandstrom (2001) has studied information foraging and scholarly communication among a group of scientists in the field of behavioral ecology. Sandstrom's research combined the bibliometric approach used by Swanson (1986a, 1986b)[3] with structured interviews. Sandstrom (2001) first developed a spatial representation of scholarly publications in behavioral ecology and then had individual researchers in the community identify what they considered to be their core specialty versus peripheral specialties. Additional data were used to distinguish foraging strategies associated with the core versus periphery and to suggest the costs

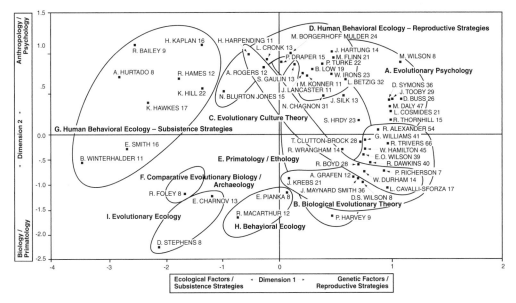

FIGURE 8.1 A map of the field of behavioral ecology produced by a two-dimensional MDS solution of an author co-citation analysis. From "Scholarly communication as a sociological system" by P.E. Sandstrom, 2001, *Scientometrics*, 51, p. 577. Copyright 2001 Akadémeai Kiadó, Budapest.

and benefits of cooperation and the spanning of specialty literatures.

Visual Representation of the Field

It has been demonstrated (McCain, 1986) that author co-citation analysis (ACA) yields representations of intellectual structure of a field that correlate well with the judgments of experts in the field. ACA typically involves (McCain, 1990) the following:

- Selection of authors in a field from existing literature reviews, membership lists for professional societies, conference attendance lists, identification by members in the field, and so on
- Retrieval of co-citation frequencies from bibliographic databases such as the Institute for Scientific Information (ISI) citation indexes
- Compilation of a raw co-citation matrix in which each row *i* and column *j* of the matrix contains the frequency with which author *i* and author *j* were cited in some paper (usually there is some threshold frequency for inclusion in the matrix)
- Conversion to correlation matrix, which contains the pairwise correlations among all authors represented by columns and rows of the matrix, as a way of specifying similarities among authors

- Multivariate analysis of the correlation matrix by methods such as principle component analysis (factor analysis), cluster analysis, or multidimensional scaling to yield a reduced dimensionality representation of the similarities among authors, which can then be visualized in two- or three-dimensional spatial representations

Sandstrom (2001) used ACA to understand the intellectual structure and scholarly communication patterns in behavioral ecology. Figure 8.1 presents the multidimensional scaling (MDS) analysis of $N = 63$ authors selected by Sandstrom (2001) from the literature for 1988–1995. Each point represents an author, and two-dimensional distances represent interauthor similarities (distances projected from multidimensional space down to two dimensions). The clusters, cluster labels, and labels on the two dimensions were identified by consulting domain experts. The upper half of figure 8.1 contains mostly behavioral scientists such as psychologists and anthropologists, and the lower half contains scientists who study nonhuman populations. The left half of figure 8.1 features specialists who study ecological factors and subsistence strategies, whereas the right half features specialists who study genetic factors and reproductive strategies.

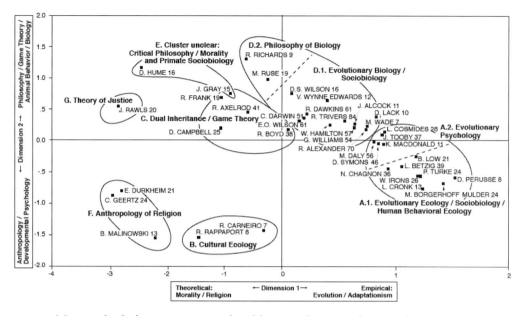

FIGURE 8.2 An individual resource map produced by a two-dimensional MDS solution of an author co-citation analysis of the literature cited by Expert A in Sandstrom (2001). From "Scholarly communication as a sociological system" by P.E. Sandstrom, 2001, *Scientometrics*, 51, p. 587. Copyright 2001 Akadémeai Kiadó, Budapest.

Clusters A–E along the right-center of figure 8.1 are each in the form of a classic horseshoe or convex pattern around a sparsely populated interior, which indicates a coherent multidisciplinary field that has no central authoritative source of theoretical or empirical foundations. There is no small set of "founders" central to the field and cited by authors in all four quadrants of the MDS map. The clusters tend to isolate authors by their disciplinary affiliations due to training or departmental affiliation.

Sandstrom (2001) also conducted a principle components analysis to identify authors who spanned research areas in behavioral ecology. A sizable number (27 of 55) of authors contributed to more than one research area.[4] These authors are likely to be the ones who broker knowledge flow across structural holes in the informal social network of scientists in behavioral ecology.

Individual Resource Maps and Foraging Strategies

In addition to the MDS map of behavioral ecology presented in figure 8.1, Sandstrom (2001) constructed five *individual resource maps* of the literatures used by five individual researchers. This was accomplished by ACA of the individual literature resources used by the five experts, yielding MDS maps similar to figure 8.1 for each individual. The ACA of each expert's personal literature was conducted on the reference lists from two or three papers written by each expert. Each expert was asked to examine the individual resource maps that resulted from MDS and to identify clusters that they considered their *own* core specialty versus *other* related core specialties. There was also a residual cluster of referenced authors that had weak co-citation linkage to the other authors in the individual research maps. These were relegated to an *omitted* peripheral cluster. Figure 8.2 is an example of one of the individual resource maps.

The five experts answered questions about their information foraging strategies for literature in the own, other, and omitted clusters of their individual resource maps (using the information-seeking strategies defined in Ellis, 1989). Socially mediated discovery tended to be the source of core literature (own or other clusters) for the experts, whereas solitary foraging tended to be the source of peripheral literature. Specifically, recommendations from colleagues, papers sent for prepublication reviews, and reprints sent by other authors and editors accounted for 30% of the referenced items. Of these items, 69% were identified as belonging to core clusters (27% to their own clusters, 42% to other clusters). Solitary foraging, involving reading, following references (citation chaining), browsing, monitoring, or deliberate search, accounted for 48% of the referenced items. Of these, 61% were identified as belonging to the peripheral (other) cluster (9% to their own cluster, 29% to other clusters). Communication in the core zone tends to occur through more social means and more toward the prepublication stages, whereas foraging interactions in the peripheral zones tend to involve more solitary or formal mechanisms and occur more toward the postpublication stages. Low-cost handling behaviors are associated with core clusters, and high-cost handling behaviors are associated with peripheral clusters.

Analogy to Hunter-Gatherer Information Foraging

I cannot resist drawing attention to what I find to be a fascinating analogy between scholarly information foraging and a foraging strategy described in the oral history of an Iroquois tribe recounted in Underwood (1993). Much of the oral history of the tribe can be viewed a series of "lessons learned" about strategies for learning about a continually novel environment and continual encounters with new and strange cultures. The oral history reaches back to before the crossing of the Bering Sea by the tribal ancestors, at least 12,000 years ago, and provides a record of their path through Asia, Alaska, the American Pacific Coast, the American Southwest, the Great Plains, and the Great Lakes Region. Along this nomadic voyage, somewhere along the Pacific Coast, a nomadic strategy was learned (from a specific event) in which the tribe as a whole "walked," in the sense of moving one of its encampments (out of two or more) each year, alternating which camp moved from year to year, and this formed an inner "Great Circle" that moved across the land. In addition, young men went on personal journeys around the periphery of this core foraging area to gain information about the surrounding environment. Specifically, the young men traveled "four-circles-around" to the north, south, east, and west for personal learning as well as to return information back to the tribe. The tribe as a whole developed a sophisticated democratic decision-making process about where to go next based on

these inputs. The strategy was summarized in the oral history as follows:

> IT CAME TO BE
>   that the center circle was understood
>   as that which contained
>   the resident learning and Wisdom
>   of the Whole People,
> WHEREAS
>   those four circles dancing at the edges
>   became the personal circles
>   of each of those
>   who together constitute that People
>   (Underwood, 1993, p. 234,
>   capitalization original)

In this quote, the notion of a central core of knowledge with peripheral information foraging outside the core resembles the core-periphery analysis of Sandstrom (2001). The purpose of this strategy—as a way of bringing information from the periphery to the core—also seems to be a feature of the Iroquois strategy:

> *AND IT WAS SEEN AND UNDERSTOOD*
> *THAT THE CENTER CIRCLE*
> *NOURISHED THE WHOLE*
> *PEOPLE . . .*
> *WHEREAS*
> *FOUR-CIRCLES-AROUND*
> *NOURISHED INDIVIDUAL GROWTH*
> *WHICH—RETURNING TO THE*
> *CENTER CIRCLE—*
> *NOURISHED, IN TURN, THE*
> *WHOLE PEOPLE.*
>   (Underwood, 1993, p. 234, capitalization
>   and italics original)

Although this book concentrates on information foraging in modern technical environments, it seems clear that human history is full of examples of cultural strategies for social information foraging that resemble the ones we find in Western society, as well as interesting ones that do not.

Effects of Diversity and the Brokerage of Structural Holes in Social Networks

Homogeneity of opinion, viewpoint, and information resources among a group of information foragers is likely to produce redundancy in what they find and

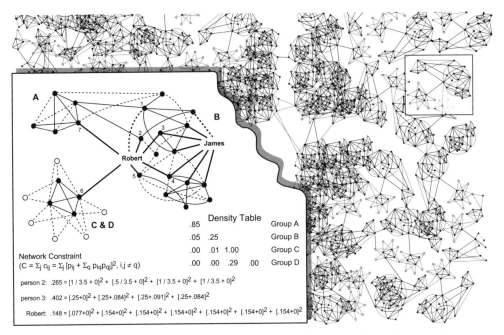

A

B

James

Robert

C & D

Density Table				
.85				Group A
.05	.25			Group B
.00	.01	1.00		Group C
.00	.00	.29	.00	Group D

Network Constraint
$(C = \Sigma_j \, c_{ij} = \Sigma_j \, [p_{ij} + \Sigma_q \, p_{iq}p_{qj}]^2, \, i,j \neq q)$

person 2: $.265 = [1 / 3.5 + 0]^2 + [.5 / 3.5 + 0]^2 + [1 / 3.5 + 0]^2 + [1 / 3.5 + 0]^2$

person 3: $.402 = [.25+0]^2 + [.25+.084]^2 + [.25+.091]^2 + [.25+.084]^2$

Robert: $.148 = [.077+0]^2 + [.154+0]^2 + [.154+0]^2 + [.154+0]^2 + [.154+0]^2 + [.154+0]^2$

FIGURE 8.3 Structural holes and network constraint in social networks. From "Structural holes and good ideas" by R. S. Burt, 2004, *American Journal of Sociology, 110.* Copyright 2004 University of Chicago Press.

how they interpret those findings. In John Stuart Mills's (1848/1987) opinion: "It is hardly possible to overrate the value ... of placing human beings in contact with persons dissimilar to themselves, and with modes of thought and action unlike those with which they are familiar. ... Such communication has always been, and is peculiarly in the present age, one of the primary sources of progress"[5] (Mills, 1898, p. 581). We might expect that groups of cooperative information foragers are more effective if constituted by individuals with some degree of diversity. Individual foragers who are positioned in social networks such that they broker information and ideas across groups might be exposed to a greater diversity of information themselves and be a conduit to greater diversity for their colleagues.

Organization and management studies (Cummings, 2004) suggest that effective work groups are ones that share information and know-how with external members and that effectiveness is improved by *structural diversity* of the group. Structural diversity is variability in features of the group that expose members to different sources of task information,

know-how, and feedback. Such features include geographic locations, functional assignments, number of managers to whom members report, and number of business units associated with the group. Structural diversity contrasts with *demographic diversity* on features such as sex, age, or tenure. Cummings (2004) studied 182 work groups in a Fortune 500 telecommunications firm and found that work group performance (as rated by senior executives) was significantly correlated with an interaction of structural diversity factors with knowledge-sharing factors (no similar interaction was found for interactions of demographic diversity with knowledge sharing).

The findings of Cummings (2004) are consistent with the theory of social structural holes (*structural holes theory*) proposed by Burt (2004). Structural hole theory is grounded in the analysis of social networks as revealed, for instance, by sociograms such as figure 8.3 that capture information flow. The nodes in figure 8.3 represent people or aggregate groups of people, and the links represent information flow. Typically, such social networks of information flow will contain densely connected clusters. The sparse linkages between such clusters constitute *structural holes*. People who bridge such structural holes have an advantage of exposure to greater diversity of information and know-how, and *brokerage* across structural holes becomes a form of *social capital* that translates into the discovery of greater amounts of useful, productive knowledge. Clusters A–C in figure 8.3 are densely connected clusters. Although Robert and James have the same number of social network links (seven), Robert is better positioned to gain from the social capital of brokerage across structural holes. The seven people connected to James are densely connected to one another within cluster B, whereas the seven people connected to Robert are associated with separate groups A, B, and C, and they are not connected to one another. James is positioned to reinforce within-group homogeneity, whereas Robert is positioned to introduce greater diversity into groups. As Burt (2004) summarized:

> Given greater homogeneity within than between groups, people whose networks bridge the structural holes between groups have earlier access to a broader diversity of information and have experience in translating information across groups. This is the social capital of brokerage.... People whose networks bridge the structural holes between groups have an advantage in detecting and developing rewarding opportunities. Information arbitrage is their advantage. They are able to see early, see more broadly, and translate information across groups. Like over-the-horizon radar in an airplane, or an MRI in a medical procedure, brokerage across the structural holes between groups provides a vision of options otherwise unseen. (p. 354)

One of the exciting prospects for the study of social information foraging is improved ability to find and measure social networks using online resources. For instance, it appears that e-mail flow and Web links among personal home pages provide data that can be used to accurately construct social networks (Huberman & Adamic, 2004) and to study information flow.

Network Constraint as a Measure of the Social Capital of Brokerage

The application of structural holes theory involves the measurement of brokerage in social networks using a summary measure called *network constraint*.[6] The network constraint index, $C(i)$, is a summary of the investments (e.g., time, effort, resources) of person i in direct and indirect social relationships:

$$C(i) = \sum_{j \neq i} c_{ij}, \qquad (8.1)$$

where c_{ij} is a squared proportional measure of the indirect and direct relationship between person i and person j:

$$c_{ij} = \left(p_{ij} + \sum_{k \neq i,j} p_{ik}\, p_{kj} \right)^2, \qquad (8.2)$$

where p_{ij} is the proportional strength of i's relationship with j,

$$p_{ij} = \frac{z_{ij}}{\sum_k z_{ik}}, \qquad (8.3)$$

where z_{ij} is a zero to one connection strength measure between person i and j, and where k indexes all of the social network connections to person i.

Network constraint varies with the size, density, and hierarchical structure of the social network around a person. Network constraint is higher if those connected to a person are highly connected to one another (e.g., form a dense cluster in a social network). Network constraint is also higher if those connected to a person communicate information indirectly through a central contact (e.g., form a hierarchical network structure). Higher values of network constraint indicate fewer bridges across structural holes.

A Test of the Relationship of Brokerage to Innovation and Incentives

Two important empirical questions arising from structural holes theory concern (a) whether in fact good ideas arise from the social capital of brokerage and (b) whether individuals have incentive to work their way into brokerage positions. To answer these questions, Burt (2004) studied 673 managers in the supply chain of a large American electronics company. Burt constructed a social network using a standard survey method. From these data, Burt

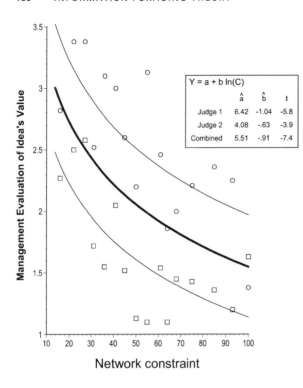

FIGURE 8.4 Idea value decreases as a function of network constraint. Data come from two judges (circles represent Judge 1 ratings; squares represent Judge 2 ratings) on a 5-point scale ranging from 1 = "low value or can't say" to 5 = "value could be high." Thin lines represent separate regressions for each judge, and the thick line represents the regression for combined ratings. From "Structural holes and good ideas" by R.S. Burt, 2004, *American Journal of Sociology*, 110. Copyright 2004 University of Chicago Press.

computed the network constrain measures $C(i)$ according to equation 8.1.

To assess the quality of ideas, Burt conducted a survey in which managers were asked to generate ideas that would improve the company's supply chain management, which resulted in 455 ideas. These ideas were submitted to two senior managers, who were asked to evaluate the value of the generated ideas on a 5-point scale ranging from 1 = "low value or can't say" to 5 = "value could be high." Figure 8.4 presents regressions of idea value ratings on network constraint that show that idea value had a strong negative association with degree of network constraint.

To assess whether managers are rewarded for brokering structural holes, Burt collected background data concerning salary, job evaluations, and promotion measures. Figure 8.5 presents a regression of salary on network constraint. The salaries in figure 8.5 were computed relative to peers by taking into account variables measuring job rank, role, age, education, business unit, and location (which in combination accounted for 78.6% of the variance in salaries). Figure 8.5 shows a strong negative association between salary (relative to peers) and network constraint. Overall, managers who discussed issues with managers in other groups not only were better paid but also were

likely to receive more positive job evaluations and to be promoted.

The results presented in figures 8.4 and 8.5 suggest that brokerage across social network clusters is associated with higher valued ideas and greater rewards (Burt presents many other data analyses that support these conclusions). One may wonder, however, why social networks do not evolve such that the network constraint is uniform throughout, for all people, given that brokerage (low network constraint) appears to be individually rewarding. One possibility is that extragroup cooperation may be substantially more resource intensive and risky than intragroup cooperation, and people vary in their ability to create and maintain extragroup cooperation.

The notion that brokerage across groups is important to success is echoed in many other domains, including jazz (Hatch, 1999), photography (Giuffre, 1999), engineering (Kim, 1998), aerospace research and development (Allen, 1977), and software development (Kraut & Streeter, 1995). Burt (2004) hints that the brokerage of social holes is a social cause of Merton's (1968) serendipity in science, which refers to the experience of observing unanticipated, anomalous, and strategic data that become the occasion for developing a new theory or for extending an existing

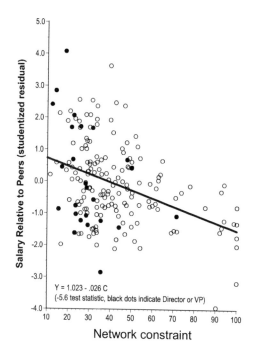

Y = 1.023 - .026 C
(-5.6 test statistic, black dots indicate Director or VP)

Network constraint

FIGURE 8.5 Salary relative to peers decreases as a function of network constraint. (Note: The studentized residual is the raw residual divided by an estimate of the standard error.) From "Structural holes and good ideas" by R.S. Burt, 2004, *American Journal of Sociology*, 110. Copyright 2004 University of Chicago Press.

theory. It seems plausible that the bibliometric arrangement of scientists studied by Sandstrom (2001), in which each scientist spans the core literature of the field in addition to idiosyncratic peripheral areas, might arise from an incentive structure that rewards brokerage of structural holes in the flow of information, know-how, and ideas.

A Basic Model of Social Information Foraging

I have presented evidence that indicates that information foragers, typified by scientists, engage in social exchanges of information and appear to arrange themselves such that they bridge across content areas and informal social networks. Such arrangements may be expected to expose the individual to a greater diversity of hints about where to focus their foraging and sense-making efforts. Research in sociology and management science indicates that the exposure to

diversity that arises from bridging social structural holes is associated with innovation and greater individual rewards. In this section, I draw upon work in optimal foraging theory and computational ecology to develop a very simple basic model of the costs and benefits of cooperative information foraging. Diversity among information foragers is a critical variable in this model. At the end of this section, I discuss the issue of group size.

The basic social information foraging (SIF) model (*basic SIF model*) derives from the quantitative theory of cooperative problem solving developed by Clearwater, Hogg, and Huberman (1992). Many extensions of this model have been developed and tested in computational ecology (e.g., Clearwater, Huberman, & Hogg, 1991; Glance & Huberman, 1994; Huberman & Hogg, 1995), so it is likely that the basic SIF model can be refined to meet many alternative constraints and assumptions. The work of Clearwater et al. (1991) focused mostly on the analysis of the benefits of cooperative search processes. The basic SIF model incorporates some simple general assumptions about the nature of interference costs that arise in cooperation based on the computational ecology studies of group foraging by Seth (2002). Finally, the basic SIF model is cast in the form of the group foraging models developed by Clark and Mangel (1986), which can be used to understand the relation between the size of a group and the individual rewards of cooperation and can also be used to understand why the expected size of groups will tend to be larger than optimal.

Basic Search Assumptions

The basic SIF model assumes a heuristic process of search for useful knowledge in a space of discrete patches of information. It is assumed that a patch of information will yield some amount of utility for one or more foragers. To relate this heuristic search process to time, t, it is assumed that the number of processing steps required to find useful patches of information is large and that the processing steps occur as a Poisson process, with each step occurring at rate λ_s steps per unit of time. The information environment can be characterized by the expected number of steps, T, required to find the next useful patch of information by random search process (i.e., with no heuristic involved and no cooperation). For this unguided, noncooperative search process, the probability, p, of encountering a valuable information patch is

$$p = 1/T, \qquad (8.4)$$

and, because of the Poisson process assumptions, the probability density function for encountering a valuable information patch as a function of time is

$$P_{Find}(t) = \lambda_s \, p e^{-\lambda_s p t}. \qquad (8.5)$$

The expected time to find a patch is

$$t_{Patch} = \int_0^\infty t \, P_{Find}(t) \, dt, \qquad (8.6)$$

which is

$$\begin{aligned} t_{Patch} &= \frac{1}{\lambda_s \, p} \\ &= \frac{T}{\lambda_s}. \end{aligned} \qquad (8.7)$$

Heuristics and Hints

The search heuristic of the individual information forager, i, can be characterized by the proportion, h_i, of remaining search steps that are eliminated (Clearwater et al., 1992; Huberman, 1990). A heuristic of $h_i = 0$ is perfect, and a heuristic of $h_i = 1$ moves the forager no closer or farther from finding a useful information patch. The number of steps required to find a useful information patch is $h_i T$. The average time to find a patch for the heuristically guided, noncooperating information forager is

$$t_{Patch} = \frac{h_i \, T}{\lambda_s}. \qquad (8.8)$$

The basic SIF model assumes that heuristic *hints* are exchanged in cooperative information foraging regarding the likely location of useful information patches (e.g., as was observed to occur among analysts in the business intelligence agency described above). Hints from cooperating information foragers may be characterized by the proportion, h_{ji}, of remaining search steps that are eliminated by the jth distinct hint received by information forager i. Hints may vary in

the validity of the search information conveyed, in how they are interpreted by the information forager who receives them, and in effectiveness depending on when they are exchanged in the search process. For instance, a good hint received late or not utilized will have a smaller effect than the same hint utilized early in search process. Similarly, to the extent that hints may contain redundant (correlated) search information, the effectiveness of hints will depend on what hints have already been processed. The h_{ji} should be interpreted as the *distinct* or *independent* heuristic effectiveness of a given hint given these conditions.

We might also expect that as hints continue to arrive, they eventually repeat earlier information and consequently yield no additional heuristic value in further reducing the search space. This is modeled simply by assuming that there is some maximum number of distinct effective hints, H. The expected number of steps required to find a useful information patch is defined to be

$$k = h_i \prod_{j=1}^{H} h_{ji} T. \qquad (8.9)$$

The average time to find a patch for a heuristically guided cooperating information forager is[7]

$$t_{Patch} = \frac{h_i \prod_{j=1}^{H} h_{ji} T}{\lambda_s}. \qquad (8.10)$$

Huberman (1990) presents a derivation of the law — which I repeat here — that relates the diversity of effective hints to the distribution of the number of steps required to successfully complete a search. Taking the logarithms of the effective values of the hints of a forager, one gets

$$\ln\left(\prod_{j=1}^{H} h_{ji}\right) = \ln(h_{1i}) + \ln(h_{2i}) + \cdots + \ln(h_{Hi}). \qquad (8.11)$$

If the individual distributions of each of terms on the right side of equation 8.11 have finite variance, and the number of hints is large, then the Central Limit Theorem applies, and the logarithms of the hints, $\ln(h_{ji})$, are normally distributed with mean μ and variance σ^2. Therefore, the distribution of the h_{ji}

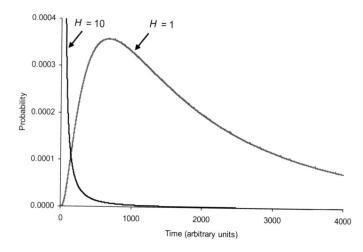

FIGURE 8.6 Probability density function for finding useful information at time t. As diversity increases from $H=1$ to $H=10$, it becomes more likely that useful information will be found sooner.

themselves will follow a lognormal distribution, which has a probability density function

$$\Lambda(\mu, \sigma, x) = \frac{1}{x\sigma\sqrt{2\pi}} e^{\frac{-(\ln x - \mu)^2}{2\sigma^2}} \qquad (8.12)$$

and an expected value

$$E[h_{ji} \mid \mu, \sigma] = e^{\mu + \frac{\sigma^2}{2}} \qquad (8.13)$$

with variance

$$\operatorname{var}[h_{ji} \mid \mu, \sigma] = (e^{\sigma^2} - 1)^2 \, e^{2\mu + \sigma^2}. \qquad (8.14)$$

The properties of the normal distribution imply that a sample of size H of the logarithms of the independent hint values in equation 8.11 will have a mean $H\mu$ and variance $H\sigma^2$.

The probability density function for finding valuable information patch can be characterized as a lognormal distribution,

$$P_{\text{Find}}(t) \approx \Lambda\left(H\mu + \ln\frac{h_i T}{\lambda_s}, \sqrt{H}\sigma, t\right), \qquad (8.15)$$

and the rate of finding valuable information patches can be characterized as a function, $\lambda(H)$, of the diversity of hints,

$$\lambda(H) \approx \frac{1}{E\left(H\mu + \ln\frac{h_i T}{\lambda_s}, \sqrt{H}\sigma\right)}. \qquad (8.16)$$

The average time to find a valuable information patch is

$$t_{\text{Patch}}(H) \approx \frac{1}{\lambda(H)}. \qquad (8.17)$$

Illustration

Figure 8.6 presents the distribution of search times for finding valuable information, $P_{\text{Find}}(t)$, for a non-cooperating process versus a cooperating process with $H=10$ diverse hints. The example assumes the following:

$T = 10000$ is the expected number of search steps with no heuristic or hints.

$\lambda_s = 1$ is the rate of processing steps per unit time.

$h_i = .5$ is the pruning effectiveness of the forager's search heuristic.

$\mu = -1 = \ln(.368)$ is the mean of the logarithms of the hint effectiveness values.

$\sigma = 1$ is the standard deviation of the logarithms of the hint values.

Figure 8.6 shows how the distribution for the probability of finding useful information shifts to shorter times as H increases. The expected time to find a useful patch is

$$t_{\text{Patch}}(1) = 3033 \quad \text{time units,}$$
$$t_{\text{Patch}}(10) = 33.69 \quad \text{time units.}$$

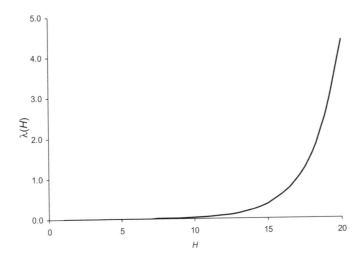

FIGURE 8.7 Increases in the diversity of effective hints, H, improve the rate of finding useful information patches, $\lambda(H)$.

Figure 8.7 shows the improvement in rate of finding useful information as a function of number of diverse hints.

Interference Effects, Optimal Group Size, and Equilibrium Group Size

Many species besides humans forage in groups. Flocks of birds are perhaps the most obvious example of group foraging. One general explanation for the evolutionary advantage of group foraging is that it may lead to improved use of information about food sources in scarce, patchy environments (Clark & Mangel, 1984, 1986).[8] Although there may be positive effects of foraging in a group, foraging groups do not become arbitrarily large, suggesting that there may be some form of interference cost (e.g., intragroup competition) that at some point outweighs the advantages of further increments in the size of groups.

It has been found empirically (Hassell & Varley, 1969) and in computational modeling (Seth, 2002) that there is often a power-law relationship between the number of foragers in a patch and the rate of consumption intake by each forager. To capture this mathematically, one might assume that the individual forager's time to process an information patch in a group of n foragers is

$$\tau(n) = an^c, \tag{8.18}$$

where $0 < c < 1$ is a rate parameter and a is the time to forage for a patch when $n = 1$.

Note that if we assume that an information patch has some finite total amount of value, G, then the expected gain for each of the n agents in the patch (assuming no differences in intake rates) is G/n. The expected time for n agents to find a valuable information patch is $t_{\mathrm{Patch}}(H)/n$ or, equivalently, $1/[n\,\lambda(H)]$. When n agents forage simultaneously, the patch is exhausted in $\tau(n)/n$ time units. We may now cast the basic SIF model as a variation of the conventional foraging models presented in chapter 2 (see also Clark & Mangel, 1986). The rate of gain, for the individual member of the group, is

$$R(n, H) = \frac{\frac{G}{n}}{\frac{\tau(n)}{n} + \frac{1}{n\lambda(H)}}$$

$$= \frac{\lambda(n)G}{1 + \lambda(H) + \tau(n)}. \tag{8.19}$$

Clark and Mangel (1986) discuss the relationship of interference effects to optimal and equilibrium group size. If there were no interference costs associated with group foraging, then we should expect that the rate of gain $R(n, H)$ improves to some asymptote but never diminishes, as in figure 8.8, which assumes that $\tau(n+1) = \tau(n)$ for all $n \geq 1$. The solitary forager should choose to join a group if the expected returns for group foraging are greater than foraging alone; that is,

$$R(n, H) > R(1, 1). \tag{8.20}$$

In the case illustrated in figure 8.8, the solitary forager should always join the group. However, if we introduce an interference cost function of the form in equation 8.19, then we may obtain a peaked rate of gain functions such as the one illustrated in figure 8.9.

Figure 8.9 can also be used to discuss why the equilibrium group size, $\tilde{n}$, may be greater than the optimum group size, n^*. Suppose solitary foragers have joined a group until it has the optimum size n^*. Solitary foragers should continue to join the group as long as the rate of return for group foraging is still above the rate of return for solitary foraging, as stated in equation 8.20. Members of the group may see their individual rates of return diminish from the optimum as new members join the group, but remaining in the group is still better than solo foraging. Consequently, individuals will join the group until the addition of new members makes the individual rate of return less than solitary foraging. Consequently, when $R(n,H)$ peaks, as in figure 8.9, we may expect the equilibrium size to be $\tilde{n} > n^*$.

Summary

Like the conventional foraging models presented in chapter 2, the basic SIF model is surely wrong. However, it serves as a tool to reason generally about several aspects of the power of cooperation and the social capital that is relevant to finding information. The model suggests that as long as the diversity of agents increases with group size, then the size of a group increases the overall power of cooperative discovery. As individual foragers increase the diversity of their cooperating contacts, they will improve in performance. This provides a mathematical rationale for the idea that brokerage positions in social networks provide social capital. The model also provides a rationale for the observed lognormal distribution of innovative discoveries.

A minor dilemma for theories of cooperative problem solving is why groups do not become arbitrarily large. One hypothesis is that there are interference costs that grow with the number of members in a group.[9] These interference costs may reduce the social capital of group foraging down to the level of individual foraging, at which point one would expect an equilibrium group size. In the next section, I review a theory of information flow through social networks that also suggests a limit to group foraging.

Information Flow

The preceding section focused on social foraging from the perspective of the information seeker. One may also consider how specific information flows through a social network of information foragers. One set of models for such flow is based on epidemiological models (Huberman & Adamic, 2004; Wu, Huberman, Adamic, & Tyler, 2004), which is similar to an idea proposed by the evolutionary theorist G. C. Williams (1992, p. 15).

The model of Wu et al. (2004) is based on the application of random graph theory (Bollobas, 1985; Newman, 2002) to the epidemiological models of the spread of diseases. The key idea is that information spreads from person to person in ways analogous to the spread of an infection from person to person. In everyday life, many people receive e-mail from friends

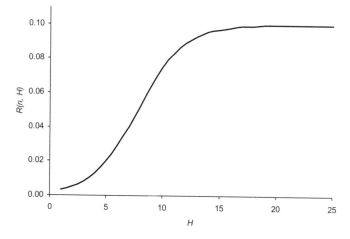

FIGURE 8.8 The individual rate of return, $R(n,H)$, increases to asymptote as a function of n if there are no interference effects. It is assumed that $G = 10$, $\tau(n) = 100$, $n = H$, and $\lambda(H)$ is as defined in figure 8.7.

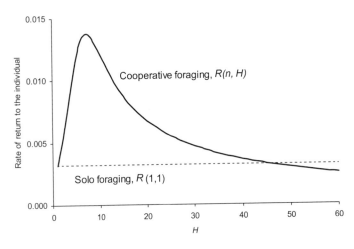

FIGURE 8.9 The individual rate of gain, $R(n, H)$, may have a peaked form when interference costs are included. It is assumed that $G = 10$, $\tau(n) = 100\ n^{0.9}$, $n = H$, and $\lambda(H)$ is as defined in figure 8.7. The dashed horizontal line indicates the rate of return for the solitary forager $R(1, 1)$. The optimum size of the group is $n^* = 7$, whereas the equilibrium size of the group is $\tilde{n} = 45$.

or coworkers containing items (news stories, jokes, observations, etc.) that they thought would be of interest to the recipient. In principle, there is no limit to the spread of information[10] in a fully connected social network, yet in practice it seems that information is passed along for only short distances in social networks. I will forgo the details of the random graph model of epidemiology and provide a conceptual summary of the Wu et al. (2004) model and its explanation for the limited flow of information in social networks.

Wu et al. (2004) assume a social network whose nodes have an outdegree (number of outgoing links) distribution that follows a scale-free power law. That is, the number of links emanating from individuals in the social network has the same form of distribution as the number of outlinks of Web pages charted in figure 3.1. Indeed, this was empirically observed for the networks representing the flow of e-mail discussed in Huberman and Adamic (2004), and it has been observed in the epidemiological domain, as well (e.g., Schneeberger et al., 2004). This means that there are a few members of the social network who have a very large number of social connections, but the typical number of connections is small (and less than the arithmetic mean).

Infectious viruses tend to indiscriminately infect any susceptible individual who comes in contact with a host. Information, on the other hand, tends to be selectively passed on to people that the host believes will find the information useful. Wu et al. (2004) assume that hosts base this selective transmission on characteristics of their social contacts. Individuals tend to form social associations based on the similarity of their characteristics (known as *homophily*), and Wu et al. assume that the similarity of two people diminishes as a function of their distance in a social network (a common observation in sociometrics). If selective transmission is based on individual characteristics, and individual characteristics differ as a function of social network distance, then one is led to infer that transmission probabilities for information should decay as a function of network distance from the host source. Wu et al. (2004) assume a power decay in transmissibility as a function of network distance.

Using random graph theory, it is possible to specify a formula (given the above assumptions) that characterizes the number of individuals that are "infected" by passed-along information at a distance of one link away from the source host, two links away, and so on. As one would expect, the number of nodes increases dramatically as one increases the distances, but this is countered by the decay in transmissibility discussed above. The sum of all the predicted infected individuals across all distances from the host provides a measure of the average total size of an "outbreak" (the number of individuals "infected" by the information). Interestingly, Wu et al. showed that the assumption of a decay in transmissibility with network distance typically leads to outbreaks of finite size. That is, information is typically expected to flow to a subset of finite size of the total social network. Empirical studies of samples of e-mail, numerical simulations using parameters based on observation, and a social network graph based on e-mail patterns suggest that outbreaks in an organization of about 7,000 people are typically limited to fewer than 50 people.

General Discussion

In communities of practice that depend on foraging in overly rich information environments, there appears to be pressure to self-organize into a balance of some division of labor, plus some degree of cooperation. This was evident in the study of social information foraging among scholars. The division of labor is necessary because of the limits of human attention, but some investment in cooperation can lead to increased returns and less risk of missing something important. The power of cooperation is related to the amount of diversity of the information foragers. Greater diversity leads to greater returns for the group and the individual. This is related to the notion that brokerage (diverse social contacts) provides social capital, and there is evidence that brokers in the flow of information are more likely to be sources of innovative discoveries. Although there are benefits to cooperation, those benefits trade against interference effects that ultimately seem to limit the size of groups. In addition, because of the diversity of individuals, and because of the way people associate with like-minded people, information is typically likely to flow to small, finite-sized groups.

A variety of technologies have emerged to exploit or enhance, in some measure, social information foraging. To some extent, the Web, blogs, e-mail, Internet groups, collaborative tagging, and other mundane technologies are all aimed at supporting cooperative information sharing and their success implies their effectiveness.[11] Recommender systems exploit social information to make recommendations (documents, movies, music) to individuals. These include collaborative filtering systems (e.g., Herlocker, Konstan, Terveen, & Riedl, 2004) in which people typically indicate their preference for items in some way (e.g., by rating things such as books), and they receive recommendations based on the preferences of others with similar tastes. Social data mining systems (e.g., Amento, Terveen Hill, Hix, & Schulman, 2003) examine logs of activities of groups of users and automatically create profiles of group or individual preferences that may be the source of novel recommendations. Both kinds of systems have shown success in enhancing the foraging capabilities of the individual.

Given the increased ease with which it is possible to study social networks and information flow in the electronic world, it is likely that there will be more studies of the effects of technologies on social structure and social capital.

Notes

1. This article is available on the Web at http://www.theatlantic.com/doc/194507/bush.

2. As noted in the *9/11 Commission Report* (National Commission on Terrorist Attacks upon the United States, 2004), the biggest impediment to "connecting the dots" in the U.S. intelligence community "is the human and systemic resistance to sharing information" (p. 416).

3. For broad summaries of bibliometric techniques, see Garfield (1979) or Egghe and Rousseau (1990). McCain (1990) provides an introduction to author co-citation analysis.

4. Research areas were identified with factors (eigenvectors) in the principle components analysis.

5. This quote by Mills is used in the opening texts of Swedberg (1990) and Burt (2004).

6. Alternative related measures for *centrality* and *betweenness* (Freeman, 1977) are often use in sociometric analyses of social relations on the Internet.

7. Note that this basic SIF model assumes that the hints are generated at an extremely high rate, following Clearwater et al. (1992).

8. Increased vigilance and protection from predators is another explanation for the advantage of groups (Clark & Mangel, 1986).

9. There is a related idea that increasing group size reduces the ability of groups and their individual members to mobilize collective action (Putnam, 2000).

10. There is no limit in the sense that information can be copied as long as there is a copying resource. There is no conservation of information in the same sense as there is conservation of energy. This has been called the Xerox principle by Dretske (1981).

11. When I asked a colleague for examples of the power of cooperative technologies, her reply was "It's almost too obvious and pervasive these days."

References

Allen, T. (1977). *Managing the flow of technology*. Cambridge, MA: MIT Press.

Amento, B., Terveen, L., Hill, W., Hix, D., & Schulman, R. (2003). Experiments in social data mining: The TopicShop system. *ACM Transactions on Computer-Human Interaction, 10*(1), 54–85.

Bollobas, B. (1985). *Random graphs*. London: Academic Press.

Bourdieu, P. (1986). The forms of capital. In J. G. Richardson (Ed.), *Handbook of theory and research in the sociology of education* (pp. 241–258). New York: Greenwald Press.

Burt, R. S. (2004). Structural holes and good ideas. *American Journal of Sociology, 110*(2), 349–399.

Bush, V. (1945). As we may think. *Atlantic Monthly, 176*, 101–108.

Clark, C. W., & Mangel, M. (1984). Foraging and flocking strategies: Information in an uncertain environment. *American Naturalist, 123*(5), 626–641.

Clark, C. W., & Mangel, M. (1986). The evolutionary advantages of group foraging. *Theoretical Population Biology, 30*(1), 45–75.

Clearwater, S. H., Hogg, T., & Huberman, B. A. (1992). Cooperative problem solving. In B. A. Huberman (Ed.), *Computation: The micro and macro view* (pp. 33–70). Singapore: World Scientific.

Clearwater, S. H., Huberman, B. A., & Hogg, T. (1991). Cooperative solution of constraint satisfaction problems. *Science, 254*, 1181–1181.

Cummings, J. N. (2004). Work groups, structural diversity, and knowledge sharing in a global organization. *Management Science, 50*(3), 352–364.

Dretske, F. (1981). *Knowledge and the flow of information*. Cambridge, MA: MIT Press.

Egghe, L., & Rousseau, R. (1990). *Introduction to informetrics: Quantitative methods in library, documentation, and information science*. New York: Elsevier.

Ellis, D. (1989). A behavioral approach to information retrieval system design. *Journal of Documentation, 45*, 171–212.

Freeman, L. (1977). A set of measures of centrality based on betweenness. *Sociometry, 40*, 35–41.

Garfield, E. (1979). *Citation indexing: Its theory and application in science, technology, and humanities*. New York: Wiley.

Giraldeau, L.-A., & Caraco, T. (2000). *Social foraging theory*. Princeton, NJ: Princeton University Press.

Giuffe, K. A. (1999). Sandpiles of opportunity: Success in the art world. *Social Forces, 77*, 815–832.

Glance, N. S., & Huberman, B. A. (1994, March). Dynamics of social dilemmas. *Scientific American, 270*, 58–63.

Gordon, M. D., & Dumais, S. T. (1998). Using latent semantic indexing for literature-based discovery. *Journal of the American Society for Information Science, 49*(8), 674–685.

Hassell, M., & Varley, G. (1969). New inductive population model for insect parasites and its bearing on biological control. *Nature, 223*, 1133–1136.

Hatch, M. (1999). Exploring the empty spaces of organizing: How improvizational jazz helps redescribe organizational structure. *Organization Studies, 20*, 75–100.

Herlocker, J. L., Konstan, J. A., Terveen, L. G., & Riedl, J. (2004). Evaluating collaborative filtering recommender systems. *ACM Transactions on Information Systems, 22*(1), 5–53.

Huberman, B. A. (1990). The performance of cooperative processes. *Physica D, 42*, 38–47.

Huberman, B. A., & Adamic, L. A. (2004). Information dynamics in a networked world. In E. Ben-Naim, H. Frauenfelder, & Z. Toroczkai (Eds.), *Complex networks* (pp. 371–398). Berlin: Springer-Verlag.

Huberman, B. A., & Hogg, T. (1995). Communities of practice, performance and evolution. *Computational and Mathematical Organizational Theory, 1*, 73–92.

Kim, S.-L. (1998, May). *Measuring the impact of information on work performance of collaborative engineering teams*. Paper presented at the 1998 ASIS Midyear Meeting, Orlando, FL.

Kraut, R. E., & Streeter, L. A. (1995). Coordination in software development. *Communications of the ACM, 38*(3), 69–81.

McCain, K. W. (1986). Cocited author mapping as a valid representation of intellectual structure. *Journal of the American Society for Information Science, 37*(3), 111–122.

McCain, K. W. (1990). Mapping authors in intellectual space: A technical overview. *Journal of the American Society for Information Science, 41*(6), 433–443.

Merton, R. K. (1968). *Social theory and social structure*. New York: Free Press.

Mills, J. S. (1987). *Principles of political economy*. Fairchild, NJ: Augustus M. Kelley. (Originally published 1848)

National Commission on Terrorist Attacks Upon the United States. (2004). *The 9/11 Commission Report*. New York: Norton.

Newell, A. (1982). The knowledge level. *Artificial Intelligence, 18*, 87–127.

Newman, M. E. J. (2002). Spread of epidemic disease on networks. *Physical Review E (Statistical, Nonlinear, and Soft Matter Physics), 66*(1), 016128.

Pirolli, P., & Card, S. (1997). *The evolutionary ecology of information foraging* (Technical Report No. UIR-R97-01). Palo Alto, CA: Xerox PARC.

Pirolli, P., & Card, S. K. (1999). Information foraging. *Psychological Review, 106*, 643–675.

Putnam, R. (2000). *Bowling alone: The collapse and revival of American community*. New York: Simon & Schuster.

Sandstrom, P. E. (2001). Scholarly communication as a socioecological system. *Scientometrics, 51*(3), 573–605.

Schneeberger, A., Mercer, C. H., Gregson, S. A., Ferguson, N. M., Nyamukapa, C. A., Anderson, R. M., et al. (2004). Scale-free networks and sexually transmitted diseases: A description of observed patterns of sexual contacts in Britain and Zimbabwe. *Sexually Transmitted Diseases, 31*(6), 380–387.

Seth, A. K. (2002). Modeling group foraging: Individual suboptimality, interference, and a kind of matching. *Adaptive Behavior, 9*(2), 67–90.

Smalheiser, N. R., & Swanson, D. R. (1998). Using Arrowsmith: A computer-assisted approach to formulating and assessing scientific hypotheses. *Computer Methods and Programs in Biomedicine, 57,* 149–153.

Small, H. (1973). Co-citation in the scientific literature: A new measure of the relationship between two documents. *Journal of the American Society for Information Science, 24,* 265–269.

Stegmann, J., & Grohmann, G. (2003). Hypothesis generation guided by co-word clustering. *Scientometrics, 56*(1), 111.

Swanson, D. R. (1986a). Fish oil, Raynaud's syndrome, and undiscovered public knowledge. *Perspectives in Biology and Medicine, 20*(1), 7–19.

Swanson, D. R. (1986b). Undiscovered public knowledge. *Library Quarterly, 56*(2), 103–118.

Swedberg, R. (1990). *Economics and sociology.* Princeton, NJ: Princeton University Press.

Underwood, P. (1993). *The Walking People: A Native American oral history.* San Anselmo, CA: A Tribe of Two Press.

Williams, G. C. (1992). *Natural selection: Domain, levels, and challenges.* New York: Oxford University Press.

Wilson, P. (1995). Unused relevant information in research and development. *Journal of the American Society for Information Science, 45*(2), 192–203.

Wu, F., Huberman, B. A., Adamic, L. A., & Tyler, J. R. (2004). Information flow in social groups. *Physica A: Statistical and Theoretical Physics, 337*(1–2), 327.

9

Design Heuristics, Engineering Models, and Applications

There is nothing more practical than a good theory.
—*Leonid Ilich Brezhnev*

Nothing drives basic science better than a good applied problem.
—*A. Newell and S. K. Card, "The Prospects for a Psychological Science in Human-Computer Interactions"*

The bulk of this book has presented attempts to scientifically understand and predict human behavior in real information foraging environments. Unlike many experimental paradigms in psychology that deal with esoteric (and enormously fruitful) paradigms and phenomena such as the dual-task paradigm (Heuer, Neumann, & Sanders, 1996), visual search paradigm (Wolfe, 2000), or the Stroop effect (Mayor, Sainz, Gonzalez-Marques, Denis, & Engelkamp, 1988), Information Foraging Theory has evolved through studies of complex task environments and information environments that are representative of those in the real world. This scientific heuristic is based on Allen Newell's maxim[1] that "good science responds to real phenomena or real problems." New theory often emerges from the choice of scientific problems that reflect real phenomena in the world and that have implications for real problems that need to be solved. This chapter assesses Information Foraging Theory in light of another of Allen Newell's maxims, that "good science makes a difference." The

measure of a scientific theory lies in how it solves real problems and how it influences others to solve problems.

Scientific theory provides not only understanding but also prediction and control over the phenomena and problems of interest. In practical terms for those interested in the development of human-information interaction (HII) systems, theory should make the design process, and the products of design, more efficient and effective. This idea is reflected in an observation by Nikola Tesla, the renowned electrical inventor, about how his way of invention contrasted with that of Thomas Edison:

If Edison had a needle to find in a haystack, he would proceed at once with the diligence of the bee to examine straw after straw until he found the object of his search....I was a sorry witness of such doings, knowing that a little theory and calculation would have saved him ninety per cent of his labor. (*New York Times*, October 19, 1931)[2]

In this chapter, I review work—primarily by others—that applies concepts from Information Foraging Theory to solve real-world HII problems. The first set of work comes from the world of design heuristics for Web usability, where information foraging and information scent have had substantial impact (Nielsen, 2003). The second set consists of semiautomated cognitive engineering models for evaluating design choices or inferring user behavior. The third set consists of HII applications that have been developed based on design principles or models motivated by Information Foraging Theory.

Web Usability Design Heuristics

Concepts and metaphors from Information Foraging Theory have been influential in the development of Web usability guidelines. Here, I present summaries of the Web usability advice inspired by Information Foraging Theory from two of the most cited sources of such guidelines. Most of the guidelines address the practical concerns arising from consideration of information scent. Others deal with practical concerns that arise from considerations of information diet and information patch leaving.

Information Scent

Nielsen (2003) presents guidelines by providing the animal foraging metaphors that inspire Information Foraging Theory, abstracting general principles, relating these metaphors and principles to the Web, and pointing out design guidelines implied by these concepts. For instance, the centrality of the rational choice framework of analysis is presented thus:

> Animals make decisions on where, when, and how to eat on the basis of highly optimized formulas. Not that critters run mathematical computations, but rather that suboptimal behaviors result in starvation, and thus fewer offspring that follow those behaviors in subsequent generation.... Humans are under less evolutionary pressure to improve their Web use, but ... people like to get *maximum benefit for minimum effort*. That's what makes information foraging a useful tool for analyzing online media. (Emphasis original)

Nielsen uses the metaphor of animal spoor to present the concept of information scent as cues along a Web path that are related to the user's desired outcome. From the concept of information scent, Nielsen proposes the following guidelines:

- Ensure that links and category labels explicitly describe what users will find at the destination.
- Do not use made-up words that do not have associations to the sought-after items.
- As users drill down on a site, ensure that each page clearly indicates whether they are on the right path.

Spool, Perfetti, and Brittan (2004) use the framework of information foraging and the framing concept of information scent to characterize the scent-following behavior of Web users, characterize things that block information scent, and provide a set of guidelines for Web design. Picking up on the notion in Information Foraging Theory that people "exhibit the same behavior as animals hunting their prey," Spool et al. (2004) noted that "the users we observed seeking content on Web sites displayed just such foraging patterns. Our users would search for a scent trail and, once they had picked one up, would follow it toward their content. As the scent got stronger, they grew more eager. When they lost the scent, they backtracked until they picked it up again" (p. 1).

Using this perspective, Spool et al. (2004) focus on trying to understand Web site design as an efficient match between users' *goals* and the *content* of a site, as opposed to a focus on the structure of a site. This also focuses effort on trying to determine the *trigger words* that will be recognized as information scent by a user with a particular task. As a methodology, Spool et al. (2004) ask users to perform tasks of their own interest at sites, and ask users explicitly to indicate their confidence prior to choosing links, and their assessments of relevance after choosing links, as a method of measuring information scent. Using this focus and approach, Spool et al. (2004) propose that Web design is focused by a set of critical questions that include the following:

- Why are users coming to the site?
- Which page is most important to the user?
- How will users find this page?
- What are the trigger words?
- How are users likely to look for those words?

These questions focus the designer on the relationship of content to user goals and on the construction of paths of high information scent that lead users to desired information.

Investigations by Spool et al. (2004) on the role of information scent on Web usability have uncovered phenomena that ran counter to prevailing usability guidelines. First, rather than the prevailing "shorter is better" principle, it appears that link descriptors containing many trigger words provide better information scent than do shorter descriptors. Second, counter to the prevailing notion that users abhor scrolling, users do not mind scrolling if there are indications that there are high information scent links further down a page. These investigations have also led to the identification of a number of Web site design flaws that block information. These include the following:

- The *iceberg syndrome*, in which users assume that links "above the fold"[3] are representative of unseen content. Because of this assumption, users often fail to scroll to a below-the-fold link because they think all information below the fold is just as irrelevant as the links above the fold.
- *Camouflaged links*, which include cues that many users would mistake as just decorative graphics, which are (not surprisingly) overlooked by users.
- *Banner blindness*, in which information placed above the banner area of Web pages (typically the top 60 pixels) is ignored. This is because people have learned that this is the typical location for banner ads, which most people apparently find to be useless information.
- *Information masking*, which is related to banner blindness and occurs when most of the useful links have been presented in one region (e.g., the center column of a page) but occasionally also in another visually distinct area (e.g., a sidebar column of a page).
- *Links that lie*, which occurs when links appear to lead to something (e.g., "Our complete list of videos") but instead provide something else (e.g., "Our bestselling videos"). This causes users to downgrade the expected utility of the site and the validity of cues that are being presented.
- *Missing words*, which occurs when a link description contains words that are not found on the linked page. Again, this causes a reassessment of the utility of the site and the validity of scent cues provided by the site.
- *Cute link names*, such as marketing names and other clever attempts to invent labels, which often backfire because these words have low strength of association to the concepts that a user is looking for.
- *Misplaced links*, which occurs when links are automatically placed on all pages in a Web site or in a section of a Web site. The link descriptors may mean different things to different users, because those users will be coming to the site for different reasons. For instance, a link labeled "calendar" might suggest one thing to a user reading the sports section of an online newspaper and something else to a user reading the art and leisure section.

Elimination of these design flaws is predicted to improve Web usability.

Table 9.1 presents a sampling of assertions and guidelines derived from empirical studies by Spool et al. (2004). The reader is referred to their work for additional guidelines, facts, and methods.

Information Diet and Information Patches

The information diet and information patch models have also been used by Nielsen (2003) to develop Web usability guidelines. Assuming the principle that users rationalize their choices based on assessments of the amount of good content that will be gained versus the cost of getting that content, Nielsen (2003) proposes that to attract Web users to a site, "the two main strategies are to make your content look like a *nutritious meal* and signal that it is an *easy catch*. These strategies must be used in combination: Users will leave if the content is good but hard to find, or it's easy to find but offers only empty calories" (emphasis original). The implication is that designers need to make their Web sites appear to have high profitability in terms of utility of knowledge gained as a function of cost of interaction.

Nielsen (2003) also notes an implication of the patch model for Web usability. Assuming that each Web site is an information patch, Charnov's Marginal Value Theorem (Charnov, 1976) predicts that, as one reduces the travel time between high-quality sites, the optimal patch residence time should decrease. Travel time between patches is reduced as one enriches the information habitat with a higher prevalence of high-quality information patches. As Nielsen (2003) noted in relation to the prediction of Charnov's Marginal Value Theorem,

TABLE 9.1 A sample of the "Tao of Scent" assertions and guidelines on Web usability from Spool et al. (2004)

- The design communicates scent through links. Each link needs to have strong scent for the content that lies beyond it.
- *Trigger words* are the words or phrases that cause users to click. Scent is strongest when the page presents users with the right trigger words.
- Links work best when they are between 7 and 12 words long; that is, long enough to boost chances of a user's trigger word appearing in a link, and yet short enough to let the user find the word easily.
- Users expect each link to lead to information that is more specific. They do not mind clicking through large numbers of pages if they feel they are getting closer to their goal with each click.
- Users don't mind scrolling. They fail to scroll only when design elements such as horizontal rules suggest that there is nothing more to see.
- Links should accurately describe what the next page contains. Otherwise, users lose confidence in the site.
- When users click on trigger words, they expect to find those words on the next page.
- Trigger words need to be readily understandable. Jargon and cute marketing terms confuse users.

Moving between sites has always been easy but from an information foraging perspective it *used to be best if users stayed put* . . . because the probability that the next site would be any good was extremely low. . . . Google has *reversed this equation by emphasizing quality* in its search results. It is now extremely easy for users to find other good sites. . . . Information foraging predicts that the easier it is to find good patches, the quicker users will leave a patch. Thus, the better search engines get at highlighting quality sites, the *less time users will spend on any one site*. (Emphasis original)

The implications for design are to

- Support short visits
- Encourage users to return using newsletters or other forms of reminder
- Ensure search engine visibility

These guidelines encourage designers to focus their designs on increasing the frequency of visits and to again increase the rate at which users will find useful content upon visitation.

Cognitive Engineering Models

In distinction to the Web usability design heuristics presented above, there are *cognitive engineering models* that have been developed to understand and predict HII behavior based on Information Foraging Theory. The distinguishing features of these cognitive engineering models are that they involve (a) task analysis, (b) calculation, and (c) approximation. For instance, Card, Moran, and Newell's (1983) seminal work on human-computer interaction (HCI) with text editors involved task analysis using GOMS, an approximate model of human information processing mechanisms in the Model Human Processor, and calculation of performance times for various tasks across text editors to yield comparative analysis of HCI performance. In this section, I review cognitive engineering models for predicting design trade-offs in Scatter/Gather (Pirolli, 1998), automated evaluation of Web site navigability (Chi et al., 2003), and automated inference of user tasks (Chi, Rosien, & Heer, 2002).

Design Trade-Offs in Scatter/Gather

Designers of browsers for large and rapidly growing hypermedia repositories will naturally be concerned with alleviating problems associated with rapidly and effectively finding information. Like all complex design problems, however, there will be many interacting constraints and trade-offs in the space of potential designs. These design trade-offs may also vary according to the space of conditions faced by potential users. Furthermore, one may want to predict some of the effects of these designs on user strategies.

For designers of user interfaces, such as browsers, it might be helpful to have techniques that allow one to explore various complex "what-if" design scenarios. For instance, what if system algorithms are made faster as opposed to more accurate? What if presentations are made more informative but slower to read? What if the user has unlimited time as opposed to a hard deadline? What if the user is faced with a repository rich with relevant information versus a poor one? One approach to answering these questions was explored in Pirolli (1998). This involved use of the state-space representation presented in chapter 6.

As illustrated in chapter 6, the state-space approach requires that the analyst find an abstract representation of the different states of interaction, such as the state of a browser display, and the different changes that can be made from state to state, such as the changes that result from user actions. This defines an abstract state space representing the possible paths that HCI may take. One also must have some method for assigning costs and values to different states and moves. In the Scatter/Gather state space presented in chapter 6, the values include the expected number of relevant documents that could be encountered while browsing, and the costs are just the amounts of user time involved.

To explore design trade-offs, one may use different state spaces, with different costs and values, to represent alternative interfaces. In general, one could use optimization techniques such as dynamic programming (Bertsekas, 1995) to perform an evaluation of the different interfaces. However, as noted in chapter 6, the Scatter/Gather state space can be explored using myopic assessments of alternative information foraging actions and a greedy optimization algorithm. Regardless of the appropriate optimization technique, one must be able to find the best-case performance of a proposed user interface design.

For the engineer/designer, such techniques can be tools for the rapid exploration of "what-if" variations in complex designs. For the researcher, it is a technique for exploring and generating hypothesis about the interaction of design trade-offs, task conditions, and user strategies. The use of such state-space optimization techniques should be viewed as a way of making well-informed hypotheses about complex design trade-offs. The validity of the technique will depend on many factors that the designer may wish to check empirically.

Alternative Interaction Spaces

The cognitive engineering analysis presented in Pirolli (1998) compared interaction in the current Scatter/Gather system to proposed design improvements under different kinds of task conditions. The interaction space of the baseline model of the current Scatter/Gather interface was based on empirical data (Pirolli & Card, 1995; Pirolli, Schank, Hearst, & Diehl, 1996) and was essentially the same as the one presented in chapter 6. Variations on this baseline model consid-

ered the simulated effects of, and interactions among, (a) different deadlines, (b) different amounts of available relevant information, (c) possible improvements in interaction time costs, and (d) possible improvements in clustering of relevant information.

Task Conditions

The "what-if" simulations explored two factors affecting task conditions: (1) deadlines and (2) quality of the repository relative to given queries, that is, the number of items in the repository relevant to a given query. The deadline conditions were as follows:

- *Soft deadline*[4] of 720 seconds, which is the mean time taken by Scatter/Gather users studied in Pirolli and Card (1995) who had no time pressure in their task specifications
- *Hard deadline* of 360 seconds

The repository quality conditions were as follows:

- *Sparse repository*, in which there were $R = 303$ relevant documents among the $N = 742,833$ total documents for a given query. This corresponds to the TREC (chapter 6) queries in the medium range of difficulty (Pirolli et al., 1996).
- *Rich repository*, in which there were $R = 865$ relevant documents among the $N = 742,833$ total documents. This corresponds the TREC queries in the easy range of difficulty (Pirolli et al., 1996).

Baseline System Specifications

The baseline model was an early version of the state-space model presented in chapter 6. It used the same time-cost estimates presented in table 6.4 obtained from Pirolli and Card (1995). The baseline model used the state-change operators defined in table 6.5 and characterized the distribution of relevant documents over clusters using the function $g(c, \mathbf{X}_k)$ and estimated parameters defined in equation 6.1 of chapter 6:

$$g(c, \mathbf{X}_k) = G(\mathbf{X}_k)0.47 \exp[-0.63(c-1)], \quad (9.1)$$

where $G(\mathbf{X}_k)$ is the total number of relevant documents in a Scatter/Gather state, and $c = 1, 2, \ldots 10$ indexes clusters in the decreasing order of the proportion of relevant documents they contain.

Alternative Design Specifications

Two system improvements were explored:

- *Faster interaction*, in which the time cost of computing a new Scatter/Gather cluster display was cut by half
- *Improved clustering*, in which the clustering algorithm was improved so that it placed 25% more relevant documents in the best cluster (see figure 9.1), according to the function

$$g(c, \mathbf{X}_k) = G(\mathbf{X}_k)\, 0.60 \exp[-0.92(c-1)], \quad (9.2)$$

where $G(\mathbf{X}_k)$ and c are defined as above

Results

For each variation in task condition and design specification, the optimal information foraging solution was obtained using myopic information foraging evaluations and a greedy algorithm. The results of these calculations provide optimal information foraging solutions that might be considered as predictions of the best-case user performance. The results of these calculations showed that nonintuitive trade-offs emerge regarding the performance of system improvements across task conditions. The simulated best-case

gains of relevant documents for the baseline Scatter/Gather system are presented in table 9.2. Against these baseline data, we can examine the effects of system improvements. Overall, the best-case gains for improved clustering simulations were, on average, 23% better than the baseline system, whereas the faster interaction simulations were, on average, 18% better than baseline. However, improved clustering was not always predicted to be better than faster interaction; there were, in fact, many subtle System × Task interactions.

System × Repository Effects Figure 9.2 shows the results of design alternatives predicted for a faster interaction system and a system with improved clustering, under different repository conditions. With a repository rich with relevant information, the simulations suggested there will be no major difference between the two particular improvements that were examined. However, when the repository is relatively sparse with relevant information, the simulations predict that a system with improved clustering will be superior.

System × Deadline Effects Figure 9.3 shows simulated design changes under different deadline conditions. The simulations suggest that improved clustering will be superior when the deadlines are soft. On the other hand, when there is a hard deadline, with less time available, a system with faster interaction time will have better payoffs.

Effects on Strategy The state-space simulations can also afford some exploration of variations in the optimal information foraging strategies of the user for the different Scatter/Gather system configurations. The optimal information foraging strategies may vary across the different system improvements and task

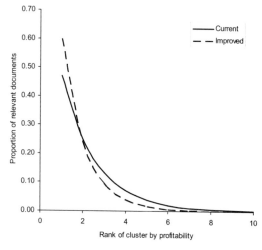

FIGURE 9.1 Proportion of relevant documents distributed across clusters in the current Scatter/Gather system and a hypothetical improved system.

TABLE 9.2 Simulated optimal number of relevant documents gained in the baseline Scatter/Gather system (numbers rounded to integers).

	Deadline		
	Hard	*Soft*	*Mean*
Repository			
Sparse	11	49	30
Rich	16	65	40
Mean	13	57	

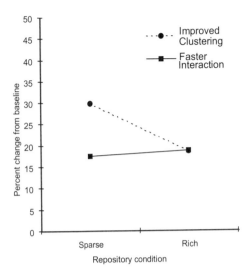

FIGURE 9.2 Simulated percentage improvements in expected number of relevant documents collected by task deadline as a function of repository condition.

conditions. It turns out that the rational analysis shows that strategy shifts across conditions.

Table 9.3 shows the average number of clusters chosen from Scatter/Gather displays in the simulation of an optimal user on the baseline system. The simulations for the faster interaction system and the improved clustering system showed differences only

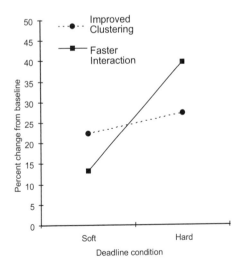

FIGURE 9.3 Simulated percentage improvements in expected number of relevant documents collected by task deadline as a function of deadline condition.

TABLE 9.3 Average number of clusters selected by an optimal user of the baseline system.

	Deadline		
	Hard	Soft	Mean
Repository			
Sparse	1.00	2.17	1.59
Rich	1.00	1.80	1.40
Mean	1.00	1.99	

in the soft deadline conditions. Under soft deadlines, the faster interaction simulations showed the same or more clusters being chosen compared with baseline, whereas the improved clustering simulations showed fewer clusters being chosen. These results are consistent with Information Foraging Theory. The information diet model predicts that fewer clusters should be chosen with improvements in the quality of the environment (in terms of improved rates of return).

Table 9.4 shows the time spent scanning the Display Titles window by an ideal user on the baseline system. Figures 9.4 and 9.5 show the reduction in these scanning times expected for the two system improvements across the task conditions. Under optimal use, a faster interaction system would require the least scanning time in sparse repositories or hard deadline conditions, whereas an improved clustering systems would require least scanning time in rich repositories or under soft deadline conditions.

Again, these results are consistent with the predictions of Information Foraging Theory. The Display Titles windows can be considered information patches. The information patch model predicts that the time spent in information patches should (a) decrease as one goes from sparse to rich repository conditions, (b) decrease from baseline to improved clustering systems,

TABLE 9.4 Time spent scanning the Display Titles window by an optimal user in the baseline condition (sec).

	Deadline		
	Hard	Soft	Mean
Repository			
Sparse	232.0	383.0	307.5
Rich	232.0	310.0	271.0
Mean	232.0	346.5	

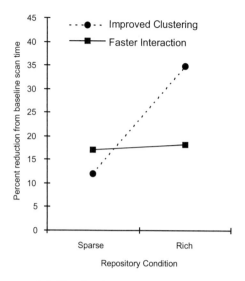

FIGURE 9.4 Simulated percentage improvements in Display Titles window scanning times as a function of repository condition.

and (c) decrease from baseline to faster interaction systems.

Summary

An approximate representation of Scatter/Gather tasks was developed using state-space representations. Optimality analyses were performed to explore some trade-offs in a browser design. Specifically, the analysis explored making the browser system faster (faster

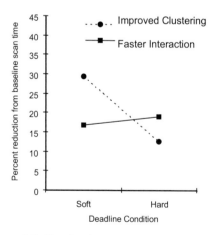

FIGURE 9.5 Simulated percentage improvements in Display Titles window scanning times as a function of deadline condition.

interaction) and making the relevant information easier to find (improved clustering). This kind of cognitive engineering analysis permitted the exploration of "what-if" scenarios testing these hypothetical design improvements against variations in task conditions involving repository quality and deadline conditions. Finally, the optimality analyses permitted the exploration of changes in ideal user strategies across system and task conditions. What was perhaps counterintuitive was the general result that there was no single optimal design alternative that yielded an overall "best" design.

Automated Web Usability Evaluation

The Bloodhound service (Chi et al., 2003) employs a variation of the Web user flow model discussed in chapter 7 to predict Web site usage patterns and identify Web site navigation problems. The service employs a variation on the WUFIS (Web User Flow by Information Scent) algorithm (Chi, Pirolli, Chen, & Pitkow, 2001). This assumes that users come to a Web site with some information goal and forage for information by choosing links based on proximal information scent cues.

Figure 9.6 presents an overview of the process used by the Bloodhound service. A person (the *Web site analyst*) interested in performing a usability analysis of a Web site must indicate the Web site to be analyzed and provide a candidate user information goal representing a task that users are expected to be performing at the site. Bloodhound then must crawl the Web site to develop a representation of the linkage topology (the page-to-page links) and download the Web pages (content). From these data, Bloodhound analyzes the Web pages to determine the proximal information scent cues associated with every link on every page. At this point, Bloodhound essentially has a representation of every page-to-page link and the proximal cues associated with that link. From this, Bloodhound develops a graphical representation in which the nodes are the Web site pages, the vertices are the page-to-page links at the site, and weights on the vertices represent the probability of a user choosing a particular vertex given the user's information goal and the proximal information scent cues associated with the link. This graph is represented as a page-by-page matrix in which the rows represent individual unique pages at the site, the columns also represent Web site pages, and the matrix cells contain

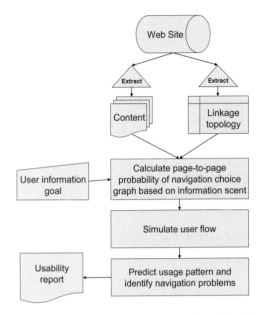

FIGURE 9.6 The conceptual flow chart for the processing done by the Bloodhound Web usability service.

the navigation choice probabilities that predict the probability that a user with the given information goal, at a given page, will choose to go to a linked page. Using matrix computations based on those presented in chapter 7, this matrix is used to simulate user flow at the Web site by assuming that the user starts at some given Web page and iteratively chooses to go to new pages based on the predicted navigation choice probabilities. The user flow simulation yields predictions concerning the pattern of visits to Web pages, and the proportion of users that will arrive at target Web pages containing the information relevant to their tasks.

The Bloodhound service is provided over the Web. Figure 9.7 presents an example of an input screen provided to Web site analysts that allows them to specify user tasks, the Web site URL, and the target pages that contain the information relevant to those tasks. Figure 9.8 shows an example report produced by Bloodhound. In this report, Bloodhound has predicted that 37% of users will be able to find target information relevant to the specified task. The report also shows intermediate navigation pages that are predicted to be highly visited that may be a cause of bottlenecks.

Chi et al. (2003) performed an evaluation of the capability of Bloodhound to predict actual user nav-

igation patterns. Users were solicited to perform Web tasks at their home or office or at a place of their choosing, and their performance was logged using a remote usability testing system. A total of $N = 244$ users participated in the study. Four different types of Web sites were studied with eight tasks of varying difficulty for each site. The comparison of interest was the match between observed and predicted usage patterns for each task and Web site. For each task + Web site, the observed data were the distribution of the frequency of page visits over every Web page. For instance, for a particular task + Web site, the home page might be visited 75 times, another page 25 times, and so on. The comparison was the distribution of page visits for that task and Web site as predicted by Bloodhound. Of the $4 \times 8 = 32$ combinations of Web sites and tasks, there were strong correlations (Pearson $r > 0.8$) of observed and predicted visitation frequencies for 12 cases, moderate correlations ($0.5 \leq r \leq 0.8$) for 17 cases, and weak correlations ($r < 0.5$) for 3 cases. Given that this was the first evaluation of Bloodhound, the results seemed to validate the promise of the approach.

Summary and Related Work

In general, this work has many commonalities with CWW (Cognitive Walkthrough for the Web; Blackmon, Polson, Kitajima, & Lewis, 2002) and MESA (C. S. Miller & Remington, 2004; see chapter 5). In all of these systems, the user is modeled as an agent who searches through a space of decision states, corresponding to Web pages, where the user is faced with a set of alternative actions to choose, and the alternatives are evaluated by some version of information scent. In essence, the user is modeled as performing a kind of heuristic hill-climbing search, where information scent provides the heuristic. These models have been tested against data from users performing tasks that are novel (unfamiliar) where such a heuristic search would be expected. One question for all these models is how well they can be extended to modeling tasks in which the users have considerable background knowledge or expertise.

Automated Analysis of User Goals

Bloodhound infers user *behavior* given a *user goal* and a representation of an *information environment* (a Web site). It is also possible to reverse this process to

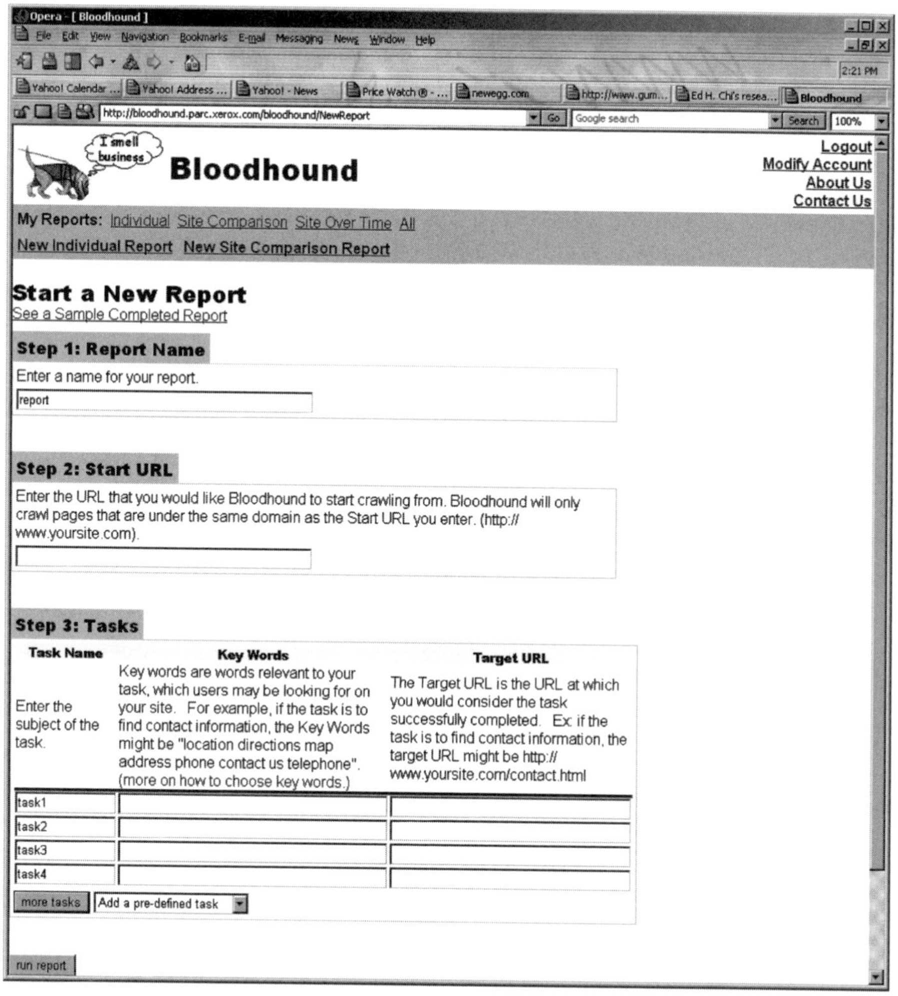

FIGURE 9.7 A Bloodhound page for input from a Web analyst.

infer user goals given traces of user behavior in an information environment. The LumberJack system developed by Chi et al. (2002) is based on one such method of inferring user goals from Web log files, plus techniques for analyzing and presenting results. As suggested above, inference of user goals is crucial to the design of Web sites. Automated goal inference could reduce the resources required for Web site redesign and open the way for on-the-fly personalized Web sites.

The general approach to the problem of inferring user goals from usage logs involves analyzing *navigation behavior* and *Web site features* to construct *user profiles*. Navigation behavior may include the links chosen at each page and the amount of time spent at

each page. Web site features may include the hyperlink structure of the Web site and the content of the Web site pages. The user profiles are some representation, such as a vector of word association strengths, that may be taken to represent users' goals. These profiles, in turn, may be submitted to analysis techniques such as clustering, to group together users with similar information needs.

The LumberJack system (Chi et al., 2002) combines multiple types of data about navigation behavior and Web site features and uses a technique called Multimodel Clustering (MMC) to cluster user profiles (figure 9.9). The Web site is crawled to capture the content of pages (static and dynamically generated). A *document model* is constructed to represent the

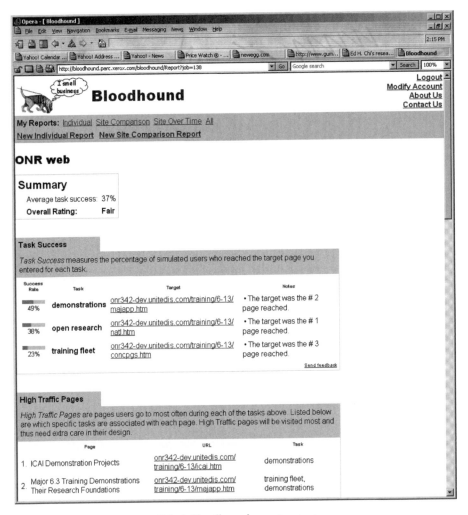

FIGURE 9.8 A Bloodhound report output page.

pages at a Web site. Each document is represent as a vector, where each vector can be divided into four subvectors, each of which represents a separate feature space or modality:

- *Content*, which is a subvector in which each component represents the words that were visible to the user on a page (excluding stop words)
- *URL*, which is a subvector representing each word present in a URL, using "/". "&", and "?" as delimiters
- *Outlinks*, which is a subvector that describes which pages are reachable from the page
- *Inlinks*, which is a subvector that describes the pages that link to the page

These document vectors are normalized through selective application of a TF.IDF[5] weighting scheme.

The LumberJack method (figure 9.9) also processes the Web usage logs to extract a *user session model*. Each user session is represented as a vector that describes information about the pages viewed by the user. Each component of the vector corresponds to a Web page document (i.e., the document model), and cell entries in the vector represent some form of weighting representing some aspect of the user's path through those documents. There are several alternative weighting schemes:

- *Frequency*, in which the weightings representing the number of times Web site pages were visited by the user

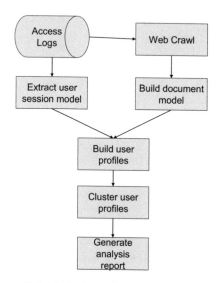

FIGURE 9.9 Method employed by LumberJack to analyze user access logs and produce reports on inferred information needs.

- *TF.IDF*, which normalizes the frequencies
- *Linear order* (or *position*), in which the weights represent the order in which users visited pages
- *View time*, in which the weights represent the time spent on each page
- *Combined*, which is a weighted combination of the other vector weightings

One advantage to this scheme is that, by using various weighting schemes, one may make best use of the available user data or compensate for missing data.

From the document model and user sessions, LumberJack constructs user profiles. The user profile for each user, i, navigating a Web site of N pages involves a combination of the session vector for that user and the document model. Specifically, the user profile, $\mathbf{UP}_i$, is the linear combination

$$\mathbf{UP}_i = \sum_{d=1}^{N} \mathbf{S}_{id}\mathbf{P}_d, \qquad (9.3)$$

where $d = 1, 2, \ldots N$ indexes the pages at a Web site, $\mathbf{S}_{id}$ is the component of the user session vector for user i corresponding to page d, and $\mathbf{P}_d$ is the multimodal document model vector corresponding to page d. To cluster the user profiles using MMC requires definition of the similarity between user profiles. LumberJack uses a cosine measure (normalized correlation) in which each of the m modalities (content,

URL, inlinks, outlinks) involved in representing a document is weighted separately by w_m,

$$\text{Similarity } (\mathbf{UP}_i, \mathbf{UP}_j)$$
$$= \sum_{m \in \text{Modalities}} w_m \cos{(\mathbf{UP}_i^m, \mathbf{UP}_j^m)}, \qquad (9.4)$$

where

$$\sum_m w_m = 1.$$

This is just a variation on the cosine measure discussed in chapter 6.

Chi et al. (2002) evaluated LumberJack using a data set obtained by giving $N = 21$ users 15 tasks for a total of 104 user sessions. A wide variety of weighting schemes were explored in which the goal was to maximize the number of user session profiles that were correctly categorized in a cluster corresponding to the task assigned for that user session by the experimenters. Chi et al. (2002) were able to achieve up to 99% accuracy on some weighting schemes. Chi et al. (2002) found that the content modality of the document model and the viewing time data about the user sessions were the most important factors contributing to high accuracy.

Applications

Relevance-Enhanced Thumbnails

The point was made in chapter 4 that the validity of information scent cues can cause qualitative changes in the cost structure of navigation on the Web. *Relevance-enhanced thumbnails*[6] (Woodruff, Rosenholtz, Morrison, Faulring, & Pirolli, 2002) were developed to improve upon the information scent cues provided by the textual link descriptors in common use today. Relevance-enhanced thumbnails (e.g., figure 9.10) are reduced images of a document that are enhanced by (a) fading the image (desaturation), (b) enlarging certain elements such as the text headers, and (c) creating a semitransparent visual layer of pop-outs that indicate the location of words that the user has indicated are relevant. The highlighting colors and saturation for the pop-outs were determined by the visual search model of Rosenholtz (1999).

Relevance-enhanced thumbnails combine advantages of search through text with search through

FIGURE 9.10 Relevance-enhanced thumbnails resulting from a search for mutual funds.

images. Textual cues can easily convey rich semantic information, whereas images can easily convey pictorial and genre information. This synthesis of advantages in relevance-enhanced thumbnails was demonstrated in an experiment performed by Woodruff et al. (2002). That study presented users with four kinds of tasks: (a) *picture*, which required finding some graphic such as "a giraffe in the wild"; (b) *homepage*, which required genre identification; (c) *e-commerce*, which also required genre identification; and (d) *side-effects*, which required searching for semantic information about drugs. The experiment compared relevance-enhanced thumbnails as representations of links to the standard text representation and just plan image thumbnails. Each task presented users with a task that involved finding some page that satisfied the task and scanning through a give search result page containing 100 links.

Figure 9.11 presents the search times for users performing the four kinds of tasks with the different kinds of link representations. As might be expected,

scanning through plain thumbnail representations of linked documents was better than scanning through text links on the picture tasks, and text links were superior to plain thumbnails when the task required finding the side effects of drugs. Across all four kinds of tasks, however, neither text nor plain thumbnails were superior to relevance-enhanced thumbnails.

The task time differences for the different kinds of information scent cues do not appear to reflect the time required to visual scan the links themselves. Analysis of the user logs in Woodruff et al. (2002) suggested that links were scanned at a rate of about 1/ sec regardless of type of representation or task. However, there was a difference in the rate at which users incorrectly chose to follow a link. Woodruff et al. (2002) calculated a kind of *false alarm* rate that estimated the propensity of users to visit links falsely thinking that they were correct. These results are presented in table 9.5. Comparison of figure 9.11 and table 9.5 indicates that the source of differences in

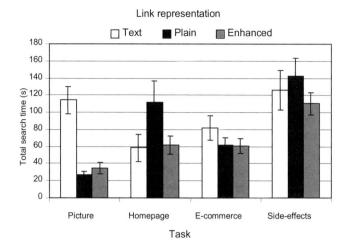

FIGURE 9.11 Total task times for four kinds of tasks requiring search through search results pages each containing 100 links represented by text cues, plain thumbnails, or relevance-enhanced thumbnails. Error bars display standard errors.

task times is related to the false alarm rates for the different kinds of link representations.

The techniques used in relevance-enhanced thumbnails were recently used in the Popout Prism system of Suh, Woodruff, Rosenholtz, and Glass (2002).

ScentTrails

The ScentTrails system (Olston & Chi, 2003) for searching and browsing a Web site is another approach that modifies the rendering of links to enhance information scent cues that are predicted to be particularly useful given users' goals. Figure 9.12 presents an example of a Web site page (not a search result page) that has been modified by ScentTrails as a user browsed at a Web site after having entered the search terms "remote diagnostic technology." In figure 9.12, ScentTrails has made predictions about

TABLE 9.5 False alarm rate estimates for four kinds of tasks requiring search through search result pages each containing 100 links represented by text cues, plain thumbnails, or relevance-enhanced thumbnails.

	Summary type		
	Text	Plain	Enhanced
Task			
Picture	.0565	.0099	.0143
Homepage	.1350	.0267	.0272
E-commerce	.1359	.0524	.0483
Side effects	.0413	.0563	.0426

paths that will lead to relevant pages—perhaps several clicks away—and has highlighted the text cues associated with links that are on the most profitable paths. As described in more detail below, the predicted profitability reflects the degree of relevancy of pages reachable by clicking on a link in relation to the cost (number of clicks) required to reach those pages. Link highlighting is achieved by sizing the text in proportion to the predicted profitability of a link choice.

Conceptually the ScentTrails algorithm works like a variant of the user flow models discussed in chapter 7, or a spreading activation model of memory. In response to a user indicating a particular information goal (e.g., "remote diagnostic technology"), ScentTrails identifies a set of relevant pages at a Web site. Using a graphical representation of the link topology of the Web site, ScentTrails initializes nodes representing those relevant pages with some score corresponding to their relevance (scent). These scent values are then spread through the graph, from the relevant target pages, flowing backward along links (opposite the direction the links would be browsed). At each link, some proportion of scent is lost, so scent diminishes exponentially as a function of degree of link distance. Scent coming from different targets to a node is summed. The net effect of this process is to spread scent back from the target pages through intermediate Web pages at a site in a way that reflects the cumulative scent from paths emanating from a page, and where scent is discounted by link distance. The amount of scent accumulating on nodes is used to scale the highlighting of links to pages representing those nodes.

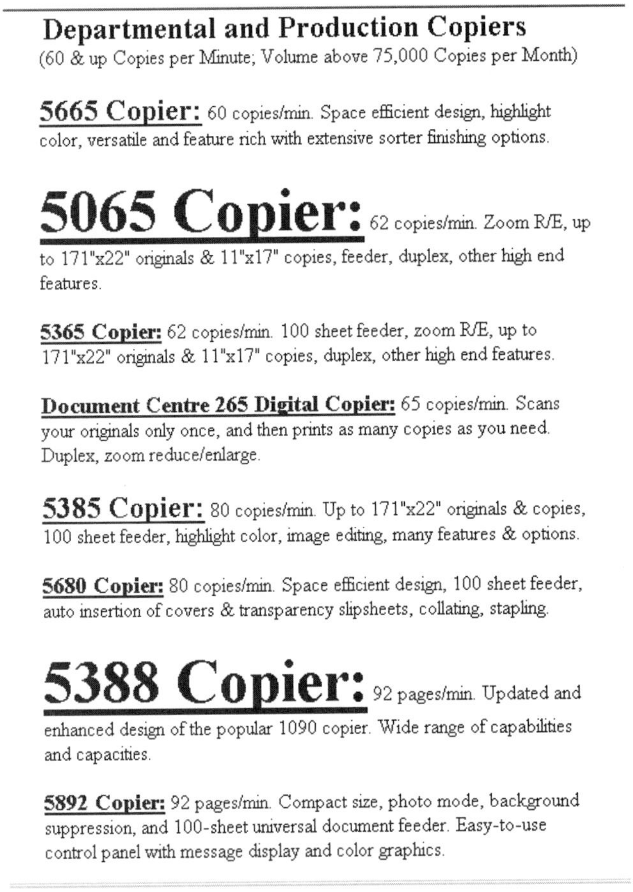

Departmental and Production Copiers
(60 & up Copies per Minute; Volume above 75,000 Copies per Month)

5665 Copier: 60 copies/min. Space efficient design, highlight color, versatile and feature rich with extensive sorter finishing options.

5065 Copier: 62 copies/min. Zoom R/E, up
to 171"x22" originals & 11"x17" copies, feeder, duplex, other high end features.

5365 Copier: 62 copies/min. 100 sheet feeder, zoom R/E, up to 171"x22" originals & 11"x17" copies, duplex, other high end features.

Document Centre 265 Digital Copier: 65 copies/min. Scans your originals only once, and then prints as many copies as you need. Duplex, zoom reduce/enlarge.

5385 Copier: 80 copies/min. Up to 171"x22" originals & copies, 100 sheet feeder, highlight color, image editing, many features & options.

5680 Copier: 80 copies/min. Space efficient design, 100 sheet feeder, auto insertion of covers & transparency slipsheets, collating, stapling.

5388 Copier: 92 pages/min. Updated and
enhanced design of the popular 1090 copier. Wide range of capabilities and capacities.

5892 Copier: 92 pages/min. Compact size, photo mode, background suppression, and 100-sheet universal document feeder. Easy-to-use control panel with message display and color graphics.

FIGURE 9.12 An example of a Web site page rendered in ScentTrails after a user has expressed an interest in "remote diagnostic technology."

An empirical study of ScentTrails was conducted (Olston & Chi, 2003) in which participants worked on a variety tasks on a corporate Web site. The study contrasted (a) a standard *search* interface, (b) a standard browser, (c) ScentTrails, and (d) ShortScent, which was like ScentTrails in all superficial effects but computed scent flow for only one step (i.e., yielding a one-step look-ahead effect on the scent cues). The total task times for the different interfaces are presented in figure 9.13. The scent-based interfaces (ScentTrails and ShortScent) produced significantly faster completion times than did the standard search or browsing interfaces.[7]

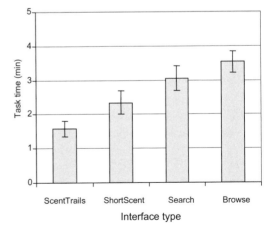

FIGURE 9.13 Task completion times for interfaces modifying link cues in relation to computed scent (ScentTrails, ShortScent) and standard interfaces (search, browsing). From Olston and Chi (2003).

General Discussion

One general test of a theory is its practical utility. The purpose of this chapter is to illustrate applications of the theory to practical matters. The general metaphors and rational principles of Information Foraging Theory have found their way into the community of usability practitioners. The state-space models and stochastic models used for scientific purposes have been repurposed to cognitive engineering models. Design principles, especially concerning information scent, have led to browser design techniques that have shown substantial improvements in information foraging performance.

Notes

1. Allen Newell presented these maxims in an extraordinary talk titled "Desires and Diversions" presented at Carnegie Mellon in December 1991, seven months prior to his death from cancer. The slides from this talk can be found at http://wean1.ulib.org/Lectures/Distinguished%20Lectures/1991/newell/5SLIDES/newell.ppt. A video of the talk can be found at http://wean1.ulib.org/video.asp?target=/Lectures/Distinguished%20Lectures/1991/newell/4VIDEO/output.asf&standalone=true.

2. As Marc Mangel pointed out, this is probably why Edison thought that "Genius is 99 percent perspiration and 1 percent inspiration."

3. The "fold" is an imaginary line on the page above which the content is visible and below which the content requires scrolling to make visible.

4. Soft versus hard refers to the length of time and nothing else about the deadline constraint.

5. TF.IDF stands for term frequency by inverse document frequency (Manning & Schuetze, 1999).

6. Often called simply *enhanced thumbnails*.

7. The apparent difference between the ScentTrails and ShortScent algorithms was not significant with $N = 12$ participants.

References

Bertsekas, D. P. (1995). *Dynamic programming and optimal control theory*. Belmont, MA: Athena Scientific.

Blackmon, M. H., Polson, P. G., Kitajima, M., & Lewis, C. (2002). Cognitive Walkthrough for the Web. *CHI 2002, ACM Conference on Human Factors in Computing Systems, CHI Letters*, 4(1), 463–470.

Card, S. K., Moran, T. P., & Newell, A. (1983). *The psychology of human-computer interaction*. Hillsdale, NJ: Lawrence Erlbaum Associates.

Chi, E. H., Pirolli, P., Chen, K., & Pitkow, J. E. (2001). Using information scent to model user needs and actions on the Web. *CHI 2001, Human Factors in Computing Systems, CHI Letters*, 3(1), 490–497.

Chi, E. H., Rosien, A., & Heer, J. (2002, July). *LumberJack: Intelligent discovery and analysis of Web user traffic composition*. Paper presented at the ACM-SIGKIDD Workshop on Web mining for usage patterns and user profiles, WebKDD 2002, Edmonton, Canada.

Chi, E. H., Rosien, A., Suppattanasiri, G., Williams, A., Royer, C., Chow, C., et al. (2003). The Bloodhound project: Automating discovery of Web usability issues using the InfoScent simulator. *CHI 2003, ACM Conference on Human Factors in Computing Systems, CHI Letters*, 5(1), 505–512.

Heuer, H., Neumann, O., & Sanders, A. F. (1996). Dual-task performance. In O. Neumann and A. F. Sanders (Eds.), *Handbook of perception and action, Vol. 3: Attention* (p. 113). San Diego, CA: Academic Press.

Manning, C. D., & Schuetze, H. (1999). *Foundations of statistical natural language processing*. Cambridge, MA: MIT Press.

Mayor, J., Sainz, J., Gonzalez-Marques, J., Denis, M., & Engelkamp, J. (1988). Stroop and priming effects in naming and categorizing tasks using words and pictures. In M. Dennis, J. T. Richardson, & J. Engelkamp (Eds.), *Cognitive and neuropsychological approaches to mental imagery* (p. 69). Dordrecht, Netherlands: Martinus Nijhoff Publishing.

Miller, C. S., & Remington, R. W. (2004). Modeling information navigation: Implications for information architecture. *Human-Computer Interaction*, 19(3), 225–271.

Nielsen, J. (2003, June). *Information foraging: Why Google makes people leave your site faster*. Retrieved February 2004 from http://www.useit.com/alertbox/20030630.html.

Olston, C., & Chi, E. H. (2003). ScentTrails: Integrating browsing and searching on the Web. *ACM Transactions on Computer-Human Interaction*, 10(3), 177–197.

Pirolli, P. (1998, April). *Exploring browser design tradeoffs using a dynamical model of optimal information foraging*. Paper presented at the CHI 1998 Conference on Human Factors in Computing Systems, Los Angeles, CA.

Pirolli, P., & Card, S. K. (1995). Information foraging in information access environments, *Proceedings of the Conference on Human Factors in Computing Systems, CHI '95* (pp. 51–58). New York: Association for Computing Machinery.

Rosenholtz, R. (1999). A simple saliency model predicts a number of motion popout phenomena. *Vision Research*, 39, 3157–3163.

Spool, J. M., Perfetti, C., & Brittan, D. (2004). *Designing for the scent of information*. Middleton, MA: User Interface Engineering.

Suh, B., Woodruff, A., Rosenholtz, R., & Glass, A. (2002). Popout Prism: Adding perceptual principles to overview+detail document interfaces. *CHI 2002, ACM Conference on Human Factors in Computing Systems, CHI Letters*, 4(1), 251–258.

Wolfe, J. (2000). Visual search. *Encyclopedia of Psychology*, 8 (p. 207). New York: Oxford University Press.

Woodruff, A., Rosenholtz, R., Morrison, J. B., Faulring, A., & Pirolli, P. (2002). A comparison of the use of text summaries, plain thumbnails, and enhanced thumbnails for Web search tasks. *Journal of the American Society for Information Science and Technology*, 53, 172–185.

10

Future Directions

Upward, Downward, Inward, and Outward

This last chapter is an opportunity to discuss some ways in which Information Foraging Theory can extend to include a broader range of scientific phenomena and a broader range of information technologies. Of course, there is an endless pace of innovation in technology and media that could provide an endless set of questions for Information Foraging Theory. The profusion of handheld devices, voice systems, rich content, and so forth, already presents great challenges. Here, I limit myself to consideration of the psychological and social domains that seem fruitful for theoretical exploration.

To organize discussion I will arrange possible paths as upward, downward, inward, and outward.[1] Roughly, these moves are in the space of Newell's time scales of analysis presented in chapter 1 (table 1.4). Upward paths would take the theory more deeply into the realm of social information foraging (chapter 8). Downward would move into the fine-grained details of cognition, perception, and attention (e.g., eye movements). Inward would delve into elaborations of ex-

pertise, learning, and individual differences that would expand our understanding of the cognition involved in information foraging. Outward would expand the theory to a more inclusive set of tasks related to information foraging.

Upward

The Web was designed to support cooperative information foraging (Berners-Lee, 1989). One of the interesting recent trends is the rapid rise of a variety of technologies that directly support cooperative foraging on the Web through such mechanisms as collaborative tagging and wikis.[2] These systems include shared bookmarking systems such as Web sites where people collectively categorize and label Web pages.[3] Collaborative tagging has emerged as grass-roots strategy for parallelizing the collective search process of a community and for reducing the risk of failing to uncover a pattern that might be missed by an individual. Typically, collaborative tags provide labels for topics (e.g., who or what something is about), media type (blog, Web page, citation, etc.), categories and category refinements, qualities, tasks, users (the person doing the tagging), and the links to the actual content. Some systems (e.g., Connotea) provide some automatically extracted tags from content that they store (e.g., author and keyword tags extracted from bibliographic citations).

Traditionally, document repositories have been organized by central authorities. Similarly, knowledge representations in many application systems have relied on ontologies constructed by knowledge engineers. One approach to providing a semantic organization to the Web is to have one designed by authority. This has been the approach to designing the Semantic Web (Daconta, Orbst, & Smith, 2003). On the other hand, collaborative tagging systems support a decentralized method that allows individual users to organize content for their own purposes, share those organizations with others, and reap the benefits of collective sense making (Golder & Huberman, 2006). Unlike hierarchical topic organizations or ontologies, tagging systems tend to be nonhierarchical, with items tagged in many different ways. Although users may come from a variety of backgrounds with a variety of interests, with no centralized editors or guidance on rules for tagging, empirical research (Golder & Huberman, 2006) shows that stable consensus content organization patterns emerge. It appears that most, if not all, entry of tags is done for personal use, apparently at low cost to the individual and with low interference costs for cooperation. The apparent benefit to the individual user is that tags produced by others in the community provide filtering, search, and navigation capabilities that would have required considerable individual effort. In the terms of the basic social information foraging model (basic SIF model) presented in chapter 8, participation in the community involves the production and communication of improved information scent ("hints" in the basic SIF model).

Weblogs (blogs) are another form of social information foraging that has exploded in recent years. Unlike traditional Web pages, blogs support the rapid posting and exchange of articles, comments on those articles, links to resources, trackbacks (links to other sites that refer to the posting), and a variety of metadata tags. Networks of blogs rapidly form in which information (or opinions about information) flows from one author to the next. Blogs are used to support a variety of functions, including analogs to journals about topical materials ranging from political analysis and opinion to product reviews, business marketing, and organizational awareness.

There is already a body of work that suggests that blogs have many of the same characteristics as the Web discussed in chapter 3.[4] Interestingly, blogs are often discussed using ecological terms, and the notion of a "blogosphere" is widespread (e.g., Adamic & Glance, 2005). Much of the work on the topic of computer-supported cooperative work has focused on workgroups and organizations. The rise of distributed social information technologies provides an opportunity to explore the development of models such as the basic SIF model presented in chapter 8 or the epidemiological model of Wu, Huberman, Adamic, and Tyler (2004). It is likely that there will be continuing efforts in economics (e.g., Benkler, 2005) to develop models of community-based peer production that improve content development and information foraging systems. The marriage of such economic models with anthropological and psychological approaches could be extremely fruitful, just as the marriage of approaches has been for the core Information Foraging Theory presented in this book. Just as online bibliographic databases provided rich data for the analysis of scientific communities (e.g., Egghe & Rousseau, 1990; Garfield, 1979; Small, 1973), the online data available about social foraging patterns provide an opening for detailed quantitative predictive models of economic and social patterns of information production and exchange.

Downward

Although I have been involved in eye-tracking research on users working with complex information visualizations (Pirolli, Card, & Van Der Wege, 2003), a detailed model has not yet been developed that addresses information foraging down to the level of visual attention and perception. What seems clear is that information scent plays a dominant role in controlling the flow of interaction, and it appears that visual layout has much less effect. This can be illustrated using the Pirolli et al. (2003) study of the hyperbolic tree.

The hyperbolic tree was introduced in chapter 4 (see especially figures 4.1c and 4.3). The hyperbolic tree browser is an example of a focus + context technique. Focus + context visualizations (Card, Mackinlay, & Schneiderman, 1999) are one class of information visualization that attempts to maximize the use of display resources for presentation of information. The theme of such visualizations is to provide an overview of all the data (or at least a large part of the data) while a user simultaneously processes some specific subset. The hyperbolic tree is used to display large hierarchical tree structures. As can be seen in figure 4.1c, more display space is assigned to one part of the hierarchy (focus) than to others (context). Lamping and Rao (1994) discuss how this is achieved by laying out the hierarchy in a uniform way on an imaginary non-Euclidian hyperbolic plane and then mapping this plane to the Euclidian space of a circular display region. Initially, the hyperbolic tree browser presents a tree with the root at the center. New parts of tree hierarchy can be brought into view, in smooth animation, by using the mouse.

Pirolli et al. (2003) performed an experiment, using an eye tracker, that required users to find information in tree structures in the hyperbolic tree browser and a more conventional browser (the Microsoft File Explorer). The conventional browser used a two-dimensional tree layout that required users to scroll to expose parts of the tree or to click on nodes to expand them. Of interest were the data for simple retrieval tasks such as "Find the Banana node," which required that users navigate through the hierarchy until they found a node labeled "Banana." In the Microsoft File Explorer, this could be done by clicking on folders to open them, until a target file was found. For instance, the "Banana" task could be done by opening a folder labeled "Things," then a subfolder labeled "Natural," then a subfolder labeled "Vegetable," then "Fruits," then "Tropical," then "Banana." In the hyperbolic tree browser, the user could navigate through same labeled nodes (e.g., by clicking on nodes to bring them to the center of the display, which would reveal additional subtrees in the hierarchy).

Pirolli, Card, and Van Der Wege (2000) developed a measure of information scent, called *accuracy of scent* (AOS), based on an independent survey in which participants rated, for each experimental task, the node labels at the top levels of the tree structure used for all of the tasks. High-scent tasks were ones in which many users correctly identified the tree node labels along the path to the target. The "Banana" task discussed above was an example of a high-scent task in which the labels were judged by users to be sensible. Low-scent tasks were ones in which few users correctly identified the tree node labels along the path to the target. For instance, one low-scent task required users to find the node labeled "Library of Congress," and the labels on the path through the hierarchy were "People" → "Specific People" → "Organizations" → "Governmental" → "United States" → "Legislative Branch" → "Library of Congress."

The Pirolli et al. (2003) eye-tracking studies found that the hyperbolic tree users searched more tree nodes and were 38% faster than users of the more standard Microsoft File Explorer. However, the performance of the hyperbolic tree users was found to be highly modulated by information scent. Figure 10.1 shows the effect of information scent (measured by AOS) on performance times and learning (improvement in time across two sessions) with the hyperbolic tree and Explorer. The effects of information scent (high vs. low) are greater than the effects produced by changes to the layout (hyperbolic vs. Explorer), and there is an interaction of information scent with the type of browser (the hyperbolic browser shows greater superiority in performance time at low information scent, especially when coupled with practice over sessions).

There is also evidence that when users detected a weak information scent or no scent, they were less efficient in visually searching the areas of the hyperbolic display that have a higher density of visual items (the context area toward the periphery of the hyperbolic tree). On low-scent tasks, where the tree labels provided low amounts of information scent, users of the hyperbolic tree dispersed their visual search over more nodes in the tree structure than did users of the Explorer. On high-scent tasks, where the tree labels provided high amounts of information scent (leading rather directly to the target node), users of both the hyperbolic tree browser and the Explorer browser dispersed their visual attention over narrower regions of the tree. Figure 10.2 shows that users visited more nodes in the tree with the hyperbolic browser. Low-scent tasks caused them to increase the number of nodes visited much more than was the case for the Explorer browser. Users of the hyperbolic browser appeared to be more adversely affected by low-scent tasks than were users of Explorer. In low-scent tasks, the hyperbolic users engaged in more costly visual search.

The effect of information scent on the use of the hyperbolic tree leads to a reexamination of some of

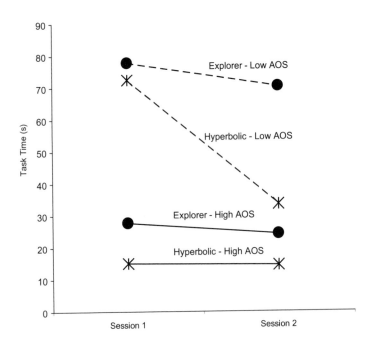

FIGURE 10.1 Performance times in on the hyperbolic browser and Microsoft File Explorer browser as a function of information scent (AOS) and practice session. Data from Pirolli et al. (2003), experiment 2.

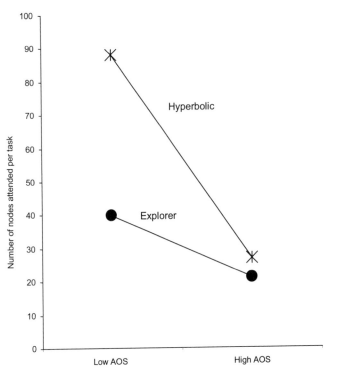

FIGURE 10.2 Number of fixations per task on the hyperbolic browser and Explorer browser as a function of information scent. Data from Pirolli et al. (2003), experiment 2.

its underlying design assumptions. The hyperbolic tree, like many other information visualizations, seems to assume that "squeezing" more information into the display "squeezes" more information into the mind. The Pirolli et al. studies suggest that this simple assumption is probably wrong. Visual attention and visual search interact in complex ways with the density of information on the display as well as task-specific factors such as information scent or "pop-out" of information from the display (Wolfe, 2000). There appear to be two countervailing processes affecting visual attention in focus + context displays: (1) strong information scent improves visual search, whereas (2) crowding of targets in the compressed region of the focus + context degrades visual search. Further empirical studies of information visualizations, informed by basic research on visual search and visual attention, may provide more complex information foraging models on which new design principles may emerge (e.g., Hornof & Halverson, 2003).

Inward

In chapter 5, I outlined a general strategy for the development of SNIF-ACT that favored the early development of approximate models followed by later refinements to such models. There are many ways in which models such as SNIF-ACT could be refined by addressing such issues as learning and individual differences in expertise.

SNIF-ACT is a model of Web use that addresses users dealing with unfamiliar information tasks requiring access of unfamiliar Web sites. Bhavnani (2002) performed a classic expert-novice study of Web users. Health care experts and online shopping experts were each given some health care tasks and some online shopping tasks. That is, each group of experts worked on some tasks within their domain of expertise and some tasks outside their domain of expertise. Outside their domains of expertise, the participants behaved as the SNIF-ACT model would predict. However, within their domain of expertise, experts gave evidence of having strategic plans that guided their information foraging efforts. For instance, a health care expert might set subgoals to first find a reliable government collection, and then access reliable publications and verify the information by visiting other specific sites. A typical shopping expert had a plan that included subgoals for finding product review sites and then product

comparison sites. People become experts in finding information in particular topic domains, and one aspect of that expertise is strategic plans that shape information foraging behavior.

The direct development of models of expert information foraging could involve standard knowledge elicitation techniques (e.g., Chipman, Schraagen, & Shalin, 2000) aimed at uncovering domain-specific declarative knowledge and strategic planning knowledge. One aspect that would need to be addressed is differences in the spreading activation networks used to predict information scent judgments. Recall the assumption made in chapter 4 that the spreading activation networks reflected an individual's history in the environment, so different spreading activation networks would need to be formulated for experts versus novices. This problem has been addressed in a limited way by Marilyn Blackmon and her colleagues (Blackmon, Kitajima, & Polson, 2005; Blackmon, Polson, Kitajima, & Lewis, 2002), who use different document collections to represent different "semantic spaces" for different kinds of users. The semantic spaces are computed by Latent Semantic Analysis over different collections that represent different languages (e.g., French), as well as different levels of reading (e.g., first grade through college) and specific content areas (e.g., psychology and biology). The general issue, however, is developing a systematic method for producing a collection that one confidently believes represents a particular group (or individual), so that the collection could be used to generate the needed spreading activation networks.

Pirolli (2004) presented a possible approach to modeling how people learn domain-specific spreading activation networks for information scent judgments. The model, called InfoCLASS, applies a theory of human category formation (Anderson, 1990, 1991) to data collected in the Scatter/Gather study reported in chapter 6 in which users browse information with different user interfaces on different tasks. Not reported in chapter 6 were data from an ancillary task: After performing the tasks with Scatter/Gather or a standard search engine, users were asked to draw diagrams representing their conception of what types of documents were available in the information system. Users can be compared on the richness of their reports. The similarity of users' conceptions can be determined by comparing the diagrams they report (e.g., by comparing the specific categorical structures observed in reports A and B). The InfoCLASS category model is used to make qualitative predictions regarding (a) the *richness* of mental categories about the external information formed by users and (b) the *conceptual consensus*, or degree of similarity of mental category structure, among a group of users.

The basic idea in InfoCLASS is that users elaborate their memory structure with induced categories as in figure 10.3, where it is assumed that the user has the goal of searching for new medical treatments for cancer. The user encounters a Web link that activates the cognitive chunks representing the words "cell," "patient," "dose," and "beam." There are associations between the words and a category chunk that represents the "health" genre of documents. From that "health" chunk, there may be associations to the chunks that comprise the user's goal. The category associations in figure 10.3 coexist with the memory-based associations discussed in chapter 4. In figure 10.3, activation spreads from the chunks associated with the information scent cues on the right, through the "health" chunk, to the goal chunks on the left. The strengths of the associations again reflect a Bayesian log odds computation: (1) the log odds that some array of information scent cues will lead to a particular category of information (reflected in the associations from the information scent cues to the category), and then (2) the log odds that that category of documents contains information that the user is seeking (reflected in the associations between the category and the goal information).

In InfoCLASS, the strengths in figure 10.3 are learned by a Bayesian learning scheme proposed by Anderson (1991). This scheme specifies the learning of (a) the conditional probability that members of a category will have given features (represented as chunks) and (b) the conditional probability that an item with certain features is a member of a category. The InfoCLASS learning algorithm relies on a *coupling parameter* that determines the overall likelihood that any two items belong to the same category (which is used to determine if an item is novel enough to form a new category). In this algorithm, every set of information scent cues that is perceived as a coherent object, such as a graphic or link text, is referred to generically as an *item*. As users encounter items, the items are categorized by the following process:

- If there are no existing categories (e.g., this is the first time a user has visited a Web site), then create a new category and assign the item as a member of the category; otherwise,
- Determine the probability that the item comes from a new category, and compare that to the maximum of the set of probabilities of the item belonging to an existing category,
- Assign the item to a new category if that is more probable; otherwise,
- Assign the item to the highest probability existing category.

An InfoCLASS category learning model was developed that was exposed to the exact same interface interactions users in study of Scatter/Gather reported in chapter 6. The model captures the basic superiority of Scatter/Gather over standard search engines

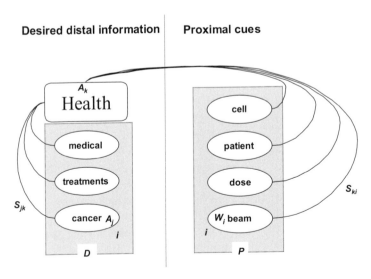

Desired distal information   **Proximal cues**

FIGURE 10.3 The cognitive representation of the goal "information on new medical treatments for cancer" and a set of proximal cues. The "Health" node represents a learned category.

in promoting more coherent category structures across users. More generally, the model is one approach to capturing the development of one aspect of information foraging expertise. The discussion in the preceding section suggested that social processes are involved in altering the external landscape of information scent cues, through the use of mechanisms such as collaborative tagging. Categorization models such as InfoCLASS might address the changing internal mental structure that interprets those cues.

Outward

In chapter 1, I presented the notion that information foraging activities often arise as part of a search for knowledge required to solve ill-structured problems. Together with my colleagues in the User Interface Research Area at PARC, we have been studying a broad class of tasks we call sense making (D. M. Russell, Stefik, Pirolli, & Card, 1993). Such tasks involve finding and collecting information from large information collections, organizing and understanding that information, and producing some product, such as a briefing or actionable decision. Examples of such tasks include understanding a health problem in order to make a medical decision, forecasting the weather, or deciding which laptop to buy. In general, these tasks include subtasks that involve information foraging, but they also involve structuring content into a form that can be used effectively and efficiently in some task.

One way to understand the structure of task environments and principles of psychological adaptation is to study extreme expert performance. One way to understand sense-making tasks would be to find and study sense-making experts. Toward those ends, we have been studying experts (as well as novices) in intelligence analysis. We expect that these studies will provide a scientific basis for design insights for new sense-making technologies. In addition, this psychological research should yield task scenarios and benchmark tasks that can be used in controlled experimental studies and evaluation of emerging sense-making technologies.

The initial phase of this psychological research involves cognitive task analysis (CTA) of subject matter experts in intelligence analysis. The CTA involves knowledge elicitation techniques derived from applied psychology that yield information about the knowledge, thought process, and goal structures that underlie observable task behavior (Chipman et al., 2000). One purpose of a CTA is to yield "broad brushstroke" models of analyst knowledge and reasoning at a large grain size of behavioral analysis.

Figure 10.4 represents our notional understanding of the analyst's process derived from our CTA.[5] The rectangular boxes represent an approximate data flow we have seen across several analysts. The arrows represent the process flow. The processes and data are arranged by degree of effort and degree of structure. This is a process with lots of back loops that seems to have one set of activities that cycle around finding information and another that cycles around making sense of the information, with plenty of interaction between these. This process diagram summarizes how it is that an analyst comes up with novel information.

The overall process is organized into two major loops of activities: (1) a *foraging loop* that involves processes aimed at seeking information, searching and filtering it, and reading and extracting information (Pirolli & Card, 1999), and (2) a *sense-making loop* (Russell et al., 1993) that involves iterative development of a mental model (a conceptualization) that best fits the evidence. Information processing can be driven by *bottom-up* processes (from data to theory) or *top-down* (from theory to data). Our CTA suggested that top-down and bottom-up processes are invoked in an opportunistic mix.

The foraging loop is essentially a trade-off among three kinds of processes touched upon throughout this book: exploration, enrichment, and exploitation (e.g., reading). Patterson, Roth, and Woods (2001) observed that analysts tended to begin with a broad

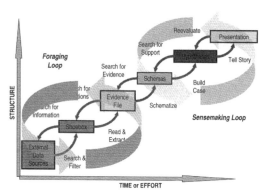

FIGURE 10.4 A notional model intelligence analysis based on a cognitive task analysis of experts.

set of documents, for instance, one that was retrieved by a high-recall/low-precision query, and then proceeded to narrow that set down into successively smaller, higher precision sets of data, before reading and analyzing the documents. More generally, we may consider these as three processes that trade off against one another under deadline or data overload constraints. Typically, analysts cannot explore all of the space and must forgo coverage in order to actually enrich and exploit the information.

The sense-making loop involves substantial problem structuring (the generation, exploration, and management of hypotheses), evidentiary reasoning (marshaling evidence to support or disconfirm hypotheses), and decision making (choosing a prediction or course of action from the set of alternatives). These processes are affected by many well-known cognitive limitations and biases, which in turn can affect information foraging activities:

- *Span of attention for evidence and hypotheses.* Human working memory has inherent capacity limits and transient storage properties that limit the number of hypotheses, the amount of evidence, and the number of evidentiary relations that can be simultaneously heeded. Reasoning about evidence and hypotheses has an exponential cost structure. The verbal protocols of analysts revealed how rapidly the number of relations (patterns) among data can grow, such as the social networks of foreign scientists or the calling networks among suspected terrorists.
- *Generation of alternative hypotheses.* Human perception is biased toward interpretation of information into existing schemas and existing expectations. Human reasoning is subject to a variety of well-documented heuristics and biases (Tversky & Kahneman, 1974) that deviate from normative rationality. In problem structuring and decision analysis, people typically fail to generate hypotheses. Time pressures and data overload work against the individual analyst's ability to rigorously follow effective methods for generating, managing, and evaluating hypotheses.
- *Confirmation bias.* People typically fail to consider the diagnosticity of evidence and fail to focus on the disconfirmation of hypotheses. Evidence is fit to existing schemas of thought.

In addition to foraging through the vast space of external information, the sense-making loop can be viewed as search through a problem space of interpretations of the data. Indeed, it appears that the entire foraging + sense-making process can be viewed as a variation of *dual-space search* (Klahr, 2000; Klahr & Dunbar, 1988) observed in scientific reasoning. In dual-space search, there is a problem-space search process aimed at collecting evidence that will be relevant to testing a hypothesis, and another problem-space search process around the generation of hypotheses.

Adaptive Value of Information Foraging

Two general issues remain central to the assumptions laid out at the beginning of this book. Following the lead of G. A. Miller (1983), it was assumed that humans have evolved to become extreme informavores. One set of questions concerns the ultimate causes of the selection of information foraging behaviors by evolution. A second concerns the specific historical or proximal events that have shaped human information foraging behavior.

Related to these issues, one question that has received some formal analysis concerns the adaptive value of information seeking and gathering. On the one hand, information about greater spans of the environment (e.g., time and space) could provide greater control over it ("knowledge is power"), if such control is feasible. But, some organisms (and, more specifically, their genetic information) can replicate over vast ranges of the earth with very little of their phenotype devoted to information collection. For instance, *Cyanophycea* (blue-green algae) have constituted a significant portion of the earth's biomass for a considerable span of time and do not seem to be under threat from information-gathering competitors in their niche.

A recent survey article (Johnstone & Dall, 2002) on information and adaptive behavior reports that information acquisition has become an increasingly important topic in evolutionary-ecological approaches to behavior. As discussed in chapter 1, to the extent that the environment is uncertain, and to the degree that reducing that uncertainty would lead to better choice of actions (in terms ultimately of fitness), and the cost of gathering information is outweighed by the improvements gained, then it is generally rational to be an information seeker. A body of research (Dall & Johnstone, 2002; Mangel, 1990; Stephens, 1987, 1989) has developed models that address this problem by proposing that it is solved by information gathering from (tracking) the environment. Formal analysis of tracking an uncertain environment suggests that information gathering should be sensitive to the ratio of costs of missing productive opportunities by not gathering information to the costs of gathering data when it may not truly provide information of value (e.g., because the world has not changed in a way that affects the forager's options). However, tracking even an uncertain environment is not always the optimal policy (for a good discussion, see Stephens & Krebs, 1986). Social information foraging (Giraldeau & Caraco, 2000) in which information can be exchanged efficiently can mitigate the costs of gathering information and appears to be one of the core adaptations of social insects (Adler & Gordon, 1992). It seems that understanding the conditions under which information foraging is of value, and how much of it is optimal, remains to be explored in human information foraging.

To generalize, information gathering and collection appears to be a general solution to the problem of organisms dealing with uncertainties in the environment. And, there is a good deal of discussion that suggests that the "Great Leap Forward" of approximately 40,000–60,000 years ago, when *Homo sapiens* migrated out of Africa and underwent enormous cultural change, was in part the result of an adaptation that fostered the development of cultural variation to deal with uncertain (novel) environments. It is notoriously difficult to formulate testable theories about the proximal historical factors that drove the evolution of cognition, so I restrain from developing just-so stories about the evolution of hominid information foraging cognition.

Focusing on the present, however, there is a great opportunity to study the adaptiveness of various organizational and cultural strategies for information foraging and the impact of those strategies more generally on success. In anthropology, it seems clear that cultures vary in the degree to which they value and develop information gathering strategies. For instance, the Iroquois oral history documented by Underwood (1993) and discussed briefly in chapter 8 is a kind of cultural manual for collecting, verifying, storing, and using information to deal with centuries-long exploration of new territories. Diamond (2005) suggests that New Guinea highlanders have avoided environmental tragedy, despite heavy agriculture and substantial population densities, through continual curiosity

and experimentation about plants, techniques, and so on, that is culturally instilled. Perhaps comparative study and formal analysis of emerging new informavore cultures for information exchange in the pervasive electronic media could help us understand the taxonomy of strategies that are out there for acquiring and sharing information, and the circumstances in which they are adaptive.

Notes

1. The title of this chapter is an allusion to a reflective article about optimal foraging theory by Stephens (1990).

2. A wiki is a specific kind of Web page that facilitates easy addition and modification of content. The Wikipedia project (www.wikipedia.org) is an encyclopedia developed primarily through grassroots contribution of content using wiki software.

3. Examples of the tagging Web sites include del.icio.us and Connotea.

4. For instance, see the discussion of the scale-free distribution of inbound and outbound blog links at see http://www.kottke.org/03/02/weblogs-and-power-laws.

5. I acknowledge the contributions of John Bodnar, Stu Card, Danny Bobrow, Ron Kaplan, and Mark Stefik to the development of the two-dimensional (Effort × Structure) representation.

References

Adamic, L. A., & Glance, N. (2005). The political blogosphere and the 2004 U.S. election: Divided they blog. In *2nd annual workshop on the weblogging ecosystem: Aggregation, analysis and dynamics.* Retrieved October 1, 2005, from http://www.blogpulse.com/papers/2005/AdamicGlanceBlogWWW.pdf.

Adler, F. R., & Gordon, D. M. (1992). Information collection and spread by networks of patrolling ants. *American Naturalist, 140,* 373–400.

Anderson, J. R. (1990). *The adaptive character of thought.* Hillsdale, NJ: Lawrence Erlbaum Associates.

Anderson, J. R. (1991). The adaptive nature of human categorization. *Psychological Review, 98,* 409–429.

Benkler, Y. (2005). *The wealth of networks: How social production transforms markets and freedom.* New Haven, CT: Yale University Press.

Berners-Lee, T. (1989). *Information management: A proposal.* Geneva, Switzerland: CERN.

Bhavnani, S. K. (2002). Domain-specific search strategies for the effective retrieval of healthcare and shopping information. *CHI 2002 Conference on Human Factors and Computing Systems, Extended Abstracts* (pp. 610–611). Minneapolis, MN: Association for Computing Machinery Press.

Blackmon, M. H., Kitajima, M., & Polson, P. G. (2005). Web interactions: Tool for accurately predicting Website navigation problems, non-problems, problem severity, and effectiveness of repairs. *CHI 2005, ACM Conference on Human Factors in Computing Systems, CHI Letters, 7*(1), 31–40.

Card, S. K., Mackinlay, J. D., & Schneiderman, B. (1999). *Information visualization: Using vision to think.* San Francisco: Morgan-Kaufmann.

Chipman, S. F., Schraagen, J. M., & Shalin, V. L. (2000). Introduction to cognitive task analysis. In J. M. Schraagen, S. F. Chipman, & V. L. Shalin (Eds.), *Cognitive task analysis* (pp. 3–23). Mahwah, NJ: Lawrence Erlbaum Associates.

Daconta, M. C., Orbst, L. J., & Smith, K. T. (2003). *The Semantic Web: A guide to the future of XML, Web services, and knowledge management.* West Sussex, UK: John Wiley & Sons.

Dall, S. R. X., & Johnstone, R. A. (2002). Managing uncertainty: Information and insurance under risk of starvation. *Philosophical Transactions of the Royal Society of London, Series B, 357,* 1519–1526.

Diamond, J. (2005). *Collapse: How societies choose to fail or succeed.* New York: Viking Penguin.

Egghe, L., & Rousseau, R. (1990). *Introduction to informetrics: Quantitative methods in library, documentation, and information science.* New York: Elsevier.

Garfield, E. (1979). *Citation indexing: Its theory and application in science, technology, and humanities.* New York: Wiley.

Giraldeau, L.-A., & Caraco, T. (2000). *Social foraging theory.* Princeton, NJ: Princeton University Press.

Golder, S. A., & Huberman, B. A. (2006). The structure of collaborative tagging systems. *Journal of Information Science 32*(2), 198–208.

Hornof, A. J., & Halverson, T. (2003). Cognitive strategies and eye movements for searching hierarchical computer displays. *CHI 2003, ACM Conference on Human Factors in Computing Systems, CHI Letters, 5*(1), 249–256.

Johnstone, R. A., & Dall, S. R. X. (2002). Information and adaptive behaviour. *Philosophical Transactions of the Royal Society of London, Series B, 357,* 1515–1518.

Klahr, D. (2000). *Exporing science: The cognition and development of discovery processes.* Cambridge, MA: Bradford Books.

Klahr, D., & Dunbar, K. (1988). Dual space search during scientific reasoning. *Cognitive Science, 12*(1), 1–48.

Lamping, J., & Rao, R. (1994). Laying out and visualizing large trees using a hyperbolic tree. *Proceedings of the 7th ACM Symposium on User Interface Software and Technology, UIST '94* (pp. 13–14). Marina del Rey, CA: Association for Computing Machinery.

Mangel, M. (1990). Dynamic information in uncertain and changing worlds. *Journal of Theoretical Biology, 146,* 317–332.

Miller, G. A. (1983). Informavores. In F. Machlup & U. Mansfield (Eds.), *The study of information: Interdisciplinary messages* (pp. 111–113). New York: Wiley.

Patterson, E. S., Roth, E. M., & Woods, D. D. (2001). Predicting vulnerabilities in computer-supported inferential analysis under data overload. *Cognition Technology and Work, 3,* 224–237.

Pirolli, P., & Card, S. K. (1999). Information foraging. *Psychological Review, 106,* 643–675.

Pirolli, P., Card, S. K., & Van Der Wege, M. M. (2000). The effect of information scent on searching information visualizations of large tree structures. In V. d. Gesù, S. Levialdi, & L. Tarantino (Eds.), *Proceedings of the Conference on Advanced Visual Interfaces, AVI 2000* (pp. 161–172). Palermo, Italy: Association for Computing Machinery.

Pirolli, P., Card, S. K., & Van Der Wege, M. M. (2003). The effects of information scent on visual search in the hyperbolic tree browser. *ACM Transactions on Computer-Human Interaction, 10*(1), 20–53.

Russell, D. M., Stefik, M. J., Pirolli, P., & Card, S. K. (1993, April). *The cost structure of sensemaking.* Paper presented at the INTERCHI '93 Conference on Human Factors in Computing Systems, Amsterdam.

Small, H. (1973). Co-citation in the scientific literature: A new measure of the relationship between two documents. *Journal of the American Society for Information Science, 24,* 265–269.

Stephens, D. W. (1987). On economically tracking a variable environment. *Theoretical Population Biology, 32,* 15–25.

Stephens, D. W. (1989). Variance and the value of information. *American Naturalist, 134,* 128–140.

Stephens, D. W. (1990). Foraging theory: Up, down, and sideways. *Studies in Avian Biology, 13,* 444–454.

Stephens, D. W., & Krebs, J. R. (1986). *Foraging theory.* Princeton, NJ: Princeton University Press.

Tversky, A., & Kahneman, D. (1974). Judgment under uncertainty: Heuristics and biases. *Science, 185,* 1124–1131.

Underwood, P. (1993). *The Walking People: A Native American oral history.* San Anselmo, CA: A Tribe of Two Press.

Wolfe, J. (2000). Visual search. *Encyclopedia of Psychology, 8,* 207.

Wu, F., Huberman, B. A., Adamic, L. A., & Tyler, J. R. (2004). Information flow in social groups. *Physica A: Statistical and Theoretical Physics, 337*(1–2), 327.

Name Index

Adamic, Lada, ix, 51, 66n2, 155, 161, 162, 184
Adler, F. R., 191
Aggarwal, G., 53
Ainslie, G., 106
Albert, R., 50
Allen, T., 156
Amento, B., 163
Anderson, John R., viii, ixn1, 9, 15, 17, 18, 19, 23, 24, 27n3, 68, 69, 76, 77, 78, 79, 85, 89, 91, 93, 106, 145, 187, 188
Aristotle, 13

Bacon, Francis, 3, 14
Baldi, P., 39, 82
Barabási, A.-L., 50, 51
Barow, J. H., 17
Barsalou, L. W., 76
Bechtel, W., 17
Belkin, N. J., 15
Bell, W. J., 31, 71

Benkler, Y., 184
Berners-Lee, Tim, 16, 148, 183
Bertsekas, D. P., 121, 170
Bhavnani, Suresh, 12, 27n5, 93, 145, 187
Blackmon, Marilyn, 72, 91, 92, 174, 187
Bobrow, Danny, 191n5
Bodnar, John, 191n5
Bollobas, B., 161
Boltzman, Ludwig, 145
Bonabeau, E., 50
Borchers, Jan, 101
Borgman, C. L., 15
Bourdieu, P., 150
Brentano, F., 21
Brezhnev, Leonid Ilich, 166
Brin, S., 51
Brinck, T., 90
Brittan, D., 99, 167
Brunswik, Egon, 20, 23, 48, 53, 69, 75, 85
Budiu, Raluca, ix

Burt, R. S., 154, 155, 156, 157, 163n5
Bush, Vannevar, 16, 148
Byrne, M. D., 57, 69, 91

Cairns, P., 137
Calderwood, R., 53
Caraco, T., 150, 191
Card, Stuart, vii, viii, ix, 4, 6, 17, 18, 19, 23, 24, 46n2, 53, 56, 58, 59, 68, 80, 81, 89, 90, 91, 92, 101, 110, 118, 137, 141, 150, 166, 169, 170, 184, 185, 189, 191n5
Case, D. O., 14
Cashdan, E., 31
Castillo, J. C., 53
Charnov, E. L., 7, 31, 35, 44, 45, 82
Chater, N., 17
Chen, K., 137, 173
Chi, Ed, ix, 71, 72, 80, 86n3, 93, 100, 101, 103, 137, 138, 141, 147n1, 169, 173, 174, 175, 177, 179, 180

Subject Index